To George —
all best
from

Emmett Watson
&

Tiger

1993

My Life
in Print

Other books by Emmett Watson:

Digressions of a Native Son, 1982
Once Upon a Time in Seattle, 1992

My Life in Print

by
Emmett Watson

Lesser Seattle Publishing

Published by Lesser Seattle Publishing
Printed in the United States of America

Copyright material has been reprinted with permission of:

The Saturday Evening Post
Seattle Post-Intelligencer
Seattle Times
Sport Magazine
Sports Illustrated

Design by Laura Lewis

Library of Congress Catalog Card Number: 93-85145

ISBN 0-9634102-2-9 (cloth)
ISBN 0-9634102-3-7 (paper)

Once again with love:
Betty, Nancy and Lea.

Table of Contents

Editor's Explanation

Emmett and I were in Copenhagen on some sort of boondoggle about 15 years ago. Given a sunny Sunday afternoon, we opted to take a ferry to Malmö, Sweden, for lunch. As the passengers boarded, a sizable number of sturdy Nordic men brushed past a young woman with a large case at her feet and her arms full of bundles. Having acquired his manners in a different era, Emmett offered to help. The case was heavy. He stowed it in the stern. By the time we entered the passenger cabin, only two of the airplane-style seats were empty. Emmett ended up next to the young woman. I sat some distance away. Early in the trip across the slender strip of Baltic Sea separating Denmark from Sweden, I glanced across the cabin and saw Emmett pulling out his notebook and beginning to take notes on a conversation he was having with her.

"Did you get a column?" I asked when we reached the other shore.

"No," Emmett replied glumly.

"What happened?"

"Well," he said, "while I was interviewing her, she fell asleep."

No conclusions about Emmett's charm should be drawn from this anecdote. Rather it illustrates two essential elements of the columnist's trade: It's a constant burden, and it's never easy.

At the time, the incident afforded me a chuckle at Emmett's expense. Later, recounting the story won me extra helpings at more than one dinner table. Still later, I gained the essential insight. That came when I was given a column of my own. Mine was once a week. Piece of cake.

Wrong.

Sisyphus's rock was a metaphor for a column. Roll out one and the obligation for the next immediately smacks the columnist in the chest. Every moment of a columnist's day-to-day life must be weighed and measured against one standard: Can this experience, thought, person, animal, vegetable or mineral be cut and sewn into 800 stylish words? No? Okay, how about 800 lumpy words? The pressure is unrelenting. I found myself dreaming columns, dreaming the actual writing of them, with the words flowing like champagne. In the mornings I only remembered the dream, never the words. In the mornings it was always a struggle.

I grew to admire my friend Emmett Watson from a different angle. As a reader, as an aficionado of columnists and as a newspaper editor, I had long appreciated how good Emmett was at his trade. Now I understood how damn difficult his job was, how artfully he achieved artlessness. And, in those days, he was writing six columns a week! Not for all the tea in China, I thought.

I gained two other insights into Emmett's character. Once I had thought him to be the messiest person extant. Actually, I still think that. Install a word processor and a chair in a half-filled Dumpster, plunk Emmett on the chair and his office would be recreated exactly. Down to the tiniest disorderly detail. (Oh, Tiger would have to be installed, too.) But a proper reading of this picture is that Emmett has simply got his priorities in order. One through ten is the column, always the column. Housekeeping is well down the list, and no columnist ever gets that far.

The second insight has to do with procrastination. Emmett is a willful, determined procrastinator. That characteristic, I've come to understand, is a reaction to the relentlessness of deadlines. The next column cannot be put off. So everything else is, and, as a result, Emmett is as sane today as when he began pushing that rock up the hill five decades ago.

To assemble this book, I took a fifty-year journey backwards, into the brittle, yellowed pages of the old Seattle Star. I found a Seattle and an America that were less polished, more innocent and not nearly as self-conscious. I found a young man with normal-length eyebrows wearing a big suit and nursing a modest ambition, namely to hold onto a job by working harder than everyone else around him. Fortunately, for him and for us, Emmett Watson lucked into the thing he could do best. He had a talent for writing, a talent that quickly propelled him into the forefront of Seattle's newspaper scene. He's held that ranking ever since, a remarkable achievement that this volume will amply demonstrate.

Reading, and rereading, Emmett's entire body of work was a treat for this fan. However, it did not make my task easy. Hemingway once said that good writing consists of knowing what to leave out. As an editing standard, I found that too difficult. Instead, I finally decided to include what I most enjoyed personally. Then I cut the pile in half rather arbitrarily. This technique will please few of his other fans. I've heard many of you refer to specific columns that Emmett wrote—some of them decades ago—that were among your favorites. You will not find all of those here. For that I apologize. Please remember that Emmett has been doing what he does for half a century. Reprinting all the good stuff would consume what remains of our precious old-growth forest. In recompense for leaving out certain writings that you hoped to find, I'm sure I've included gems that you had not previously laid eyes on or had forgotten. Furthermore, I prevailed upon Emmett to comment on his own writings. In doing so, he has enriched this volume with fresh work that demonstrates he's still at the top of his game.

So sit back, relax and enjoy. Ahead of you are fifty years of good road, crafted by the master.

Fred Brack
July 1993

Prologue

Who He?

Digressions of a Native Son, 1982

IT IS ALWAYS ADVISABLE TO WEAR A WINDBREAKER and perhaps a stocking cap when reading the first few paragraphs of any story about Seattle. Too often the prose becomes high-flown and gusty, beginning with lyrical descriptions of scenery in and around the city, followed by extravagant claims for its cultural substance, continuing with much rhapsody about water, quaint ferries, trees and shorelines. As a native, I have no objection to such beginnings. Except in extreme cases, when the writing comes perilously close to being bad poetry, little harm is done.

One reason such stuff gets written about Seattle is that a lot of us—particularly natives—actually do become impossibly lyrical in trying to describe the city. July is a productive month for this kind of writing about Seattle and the Northwest. In July, you see, the average precipitation is only .71 inches; so we tend to forget that in January the eternal, maddening grayness produces 5.79 inches of moisture—the peak month of a winter full of clouds, rain, wind and malignant sloppiness.

But give Seattle a few spring days of sunshine and nobody ever heard of winter. Many years ago the historian Stewart Holbrook wrote the set piece of Northwest narcissism: "Like many a native, I am privately of the opinion that this entire region should be set aside as one great park before it is wholly overrun by foreign immigrants like me."

Seattle is full of people with an almost orgiastic compulsion toward the outdoors, but I am not one of them. I have never caught a salmon in Puget Sound. I have never climbed Queen Anne Hill, let alone Mount Rainier. I have never walked a nature trail in the Arboretum. My first childhood impression of the outdoors was having wet feet. I still claim the elementary school record, established at Lafayette grade school, in West Seattle, for coming down with consecutive colds in one winter.

Without getting flowery about it, I guess Seattle is all they say it is—a lovely place to live. "The scenery is great but the cast is lousy," happens to be a much-quoted line about Seattle. It is alleged to have been uttered by Joe Frisco, the late great comedian, but Mr. Frisco notwithstanding, it seems to me that the people who make Seattle a city have never been given enough credit.

In a lifetime spent in Seattle, I have come to know an astonishing variety of people. In certain circles I am regarded as an "authority" on Seattle—a notion you are sure to dismiss if you continue to forage through these pages. For twenty-six years my job was writing about Seattle. Five and six days a week, nine hundred words a day. That adds up to 216,000 words a year, and in January 1982 I decided that was too damned much.

Nobody is sure who was responsible for this overkill. The editors who first hired me have long since retired, or died, so blame is hard to fix. Probably the person most to blame for my being a newspaper columnist was a man named Arthur Cummings. His work, begun in the 1880s, had the most to do with getting me into the newspaper business.

In my youth and early twenties I had a vaulting, if unrealistic, ambition to become a professional baseball player. I grew up on the streets and playfields of Seattle, never bothering much about our wondrous scenery; the mosaic of my dreams was the inside of a baseball park. My goal was to get out of Seattle—to Detroit, St. Louis or New York, where I would play major league baseball.

But Arthur Cummings prevented this. It was Mr. Cummings who, in the late nineteenth century, developed the idea that, by cracking one's wrist at the precise moment of throwing a ball, you could deliver it with a downward spin. He is the man who invented the curveball. This innovation, refined by many pitchers since, precluded my ever playing baseball for money.

But for a brief time I actually did draw paychecks from a professional baseball team. I operated from the safety of the bullpen for the old Seattle Rainiers, of the now-changed Pacific Coast League. A man named Bill Skiff, the team's cerebral leader, inherited me as his second-string catcher. Since I was what the sportswriters call "a local product," Mr. Skiff was once interviewed by sportswriters on my qualifications. He had a kindly way of putting things.

"This Watson," one of the sportswriters asked, "does he throw well enough to play this league?" "Well, he is adequate," said Mr. Skiff, cautiously, "I would say adequate is a good way to describe it."

"Does he have enough experience?"

Mr. Skiff said he doubted it. "After all, he's just out of the University of Washington, where I hear he took some classes in literature or English, or something. So he's a little short on experience."

"Does he hit well enough?"

"That's hard to say," hedged Mr. Skiff, who knew it wasn't hard to say at all. Mr. Skiff may not have heard of Arthur Cummings, but he knew I couldn't hit a curveball. He fielded a few other queries, at which point he felt compelled to speak positively.

"I will tell you about this kid, Watson," he said, taking a deep breath. "He does one thing as well as any catcher I've ever seen. I have watched a few catchers in my time—Cochrane, Dickey, Hartnett and Harry the Horse Danning. I will tell you this. None of them could squat better than Watson."

The ability to squat soon was transferred from a catcher's normal position to sitting before a typewriter. The editor of the old Seattle Star, a well-known figure named Cliff Harrison, formed the opinion that it would be nice to have a former Rainier writing about his former team. His opinion was concurred in by the sports editor, Chick Garrett, the guy who helped me get started in the newspaper business. Both were probably wrong. But at least I was out from under the cursed legacy of Arthur Cummings.

Since this book is not about baseball, but about the Seattle I know and some people in it, you have a right to scan my other credentials. I was born at latitude 48°30' north, longitude 122°18' west, about two miles north northwest of what is now Runway 31R at Boeing Field. Nobody ever heard of Boeing in those days. My cribhood was spent in a house on a bluff overlooking the Duwamish tide flats. The Indian word *Duwamish* means "running water," which is more than we had in our house at that time. By going up in the Space Needle you can easily see the bluff on which I lived, but don't do it on my account. It's not worth the two dollars they charge for the elevator ride.

At the age of fourteen months, following the death of my mother, I was taken out of one family and adopted (more or less) into another. My father, the "adopted" one, dug basements for a living. He was a fine man, and my "adopted" mother was the queen of my young life. I loved them both very much, and I was lucky to have had such parents, who may have been "adopted" but were my "real" mother and father. My father dug basements all over Seattle. Going along with him, with his wagon and horses, was my first introduction to many of the neighborhoods that make up the city. It took a lot of rain to stop my father from digging basements, so as a result I got on intimate terms with Seattle's superior quality of mud.

To this day I cannot drive through West Seattle without seeing a house for which my father dug the basement. I also can't read a local tourist pamphlet which tells you that Pittsburgh or New Orleans gets more total rain than Seattle without thinking of all that mud.

During those early years I learned to play a fair game of straight pool after the usual apprenticeship of rotation. (In rotation the balls are sunk numerically, one-to-fifteen, a note I toss in for the benefit of those with a deprived childhood.) I learned to play pool at the corner of California and College because my father kept his own private bottle of bootleg whiskey in the back room of the pool hall. He went there quite often, so I got in a lot of practice.

As a result of my father's profession and playing baseball all over town, I got around somewhat. I learned that black kids went to Garfield High (and no place else), that the "rich" kids went to Roosevelt or Lincoln, that Ballard had a lot of Swedes and that Franklin High, in Rainier Valley, drew a lot of Italians and Japanese. At West Seattle, where I finally started high school, the scholars were mostly white middle class; at Franklin, where I went later, I first chewed raw garlic with a kid named Ralph Yorio.

It was entirely possible then to grow up in Seattle without any significant awareness of such things as ethnic or racial prejudice. Though I liked the Japanese at Franklin, it never occurred to me to resent their being called "skivvies." One of my early sports heroes was a football player named Homer Harris. He was a big, rangy end who played under a remarkable coach named Leon Brigham at Garfield High. Being terribly naive, I couldn't figure out why Homer Harris didn't play for the Washington Huskies. It was only later that I learned that "niggers didn't go to Washington." Instead, Homer Harris went to Iowa, where he became the first black athlete ever to be elected captain of a Big Ten team.

It was inevitable that I would seek him out and that we would become friends. One day I asked Homer why he didn't go to Washington. After all, he was so good, so gifted, that he could have broken the barrier right there.

"Ice cream cones," he said, with a faint, bitter smile. "They offered me ice cream cones." Then he went on to explain. Homer Harris was, indeed, so talented that Washington, which didn't take "niggers," simply had to make some kind of a recruiting effort to get him. "I remember the coach came around to my house," he said. "He didn't seem very happy about being there. And when he told me, 'You'll have to live at home if you play for Washington, but we'll give you books, tuition and all the ice cream cones you can eat,' I knew I'd go someplace else."

One small advantage to being raised in a virtually all-white community, I suspect, is that you live in a kind of vacuum. I don't remember West Seattle as being anti-anything, although its racism probably was deep-seated, just as it was everywhere else in those days. It may just have been that because we were somewhat insulated, it was possible for a young mind to be blank of prejudice. At any rate—and I am grateful—my parents never drummed any hate and fear into my dear little ear. So it developed that names on prominent Seattle stores, names like Druxman, Weisfield, Lerner, Schoenfeld and Bergman, rang no significant bells in my consciousness. I used to haunt Hiawatha Playfield to watch a tall, ambling man named Sam Ginsberg play baseball, attaching no religious connotation to his name. Sam hit long, towering home runs and he was funny and friendly and liked to have kids around. Later, when I was having a tough winter in college, Sam helped me get a job at Frederick & Nelson, where I "swamped" packages on a truck he drove.

I once dated a girl named Shirley. She lived in one of the "WASP" neighborhoods near Franklin High School, one of the "rich" districts, and the thing I liked about her was the big sofa in her living room and the active social life of her parents. They went out a lot. One evening after a session on this sofa, which didn't add up to anything that would interest a juvenile court, she asked me a strange question. "Are you a Jew?" she said.

Innocence wasn't a pose I had to feign in those days. "What's a Jew?" I asked. She looked at me as though trying to make up her mind. "Are you just playing dumb or don't you really know?" I must have blushed, because she said, "No, I guess you aren't one of them. But if you were, you wouldn't be here. My father would never allow a Jew in this house."

Things like that can happen anyplace, I suppose, but it happened to me; it was part of the Seattle I knew as a kid. I don't know what ever happened to Shirley's father, the hater of Jews, but I know that Sam Ginsberg won a shirt-selling contest at Frederick & Nelson because he had so many friends.

The Seattle I knew wasn't at all like the place you read about today. We took its beauty for granted and didn't try to hustle tourists with it. This was before they knocked out those wonderful cable cars on Yesler, James and Madison. Mountains, water, beaches, trees and views were something you had, like mud and wet feet, and you didn't brag about one and apologize for the other. My first hint of Seattle's remote insularity came when I heard Jim Phelan, the hard-bitten old Washington football coach, proclaim that "Seattle is the last stop on the line—when the train stops here, it backs up."

Only later did I realize that Jim was just sticking the deep needle into a service-club mentality that looked upon Seattle as the center of the universe. I suppose there is no real harm in calling Seattle "the most beautiful city in America," or nicknaming it "the Emerald City," and kicking pebbles when we get picked as "America's most livable city." It's hard to determine how we truly rank in these matters; I suppose we're in the first division and might even make the playoffs.

Another claim I've heard all my life is that Seattle is "the boating capital of the nation." That one is another booster statement, hard to verify, but again it does us no harm. There are frightening numbers of boats around, but being what might be termed a seagoing claustrophobic, I never had much fun on boats. The only boats that ever gave me much pleasure in Seattle were the big battleships and cruisers that used to anchor in Elliott Bay during "Fleet Week." When the Navy came, that was a signal for us to rush down to First Ave. and watch the gobs at work during shore leave. About three good fights a night was average.

The way you got to First Ave. from West Seattle was by thumb or street car, those rattly old orange things. They clanked and swayed over an incredible old wooden trestle, high above Spokane St., weaving and shaking until you had to close your eyes to keep from getting a headache. They came off the trestle and went up First Ave., and you got off at Pike St., which was the real heart of the city. From anyplace on downtown First Ave. you were within easy walking distance of the waterfront (Railroad Ave. then) and the Skid Road.

The old waterfront was for real. It wasn't a place for tourists (a tourist stood a fair chance of getting rolled), or boutiques and import shops; it was crowded, smelly, tough and altogether splendid. During World War II, I worked as a longshoreman on those docks, usually down in the ship's hold, stacking cement, lumber, booze and toilet paper, the kind of stuff it took to Preserve Our Way of Life in the South Pacific. As one of Harry Bridges' more reluctant permit workers, I didn't see much that was quaint on the old waterfront. I do know that when the wind whipped off Elliott Bay in January, it was wise to cover the private parts of a brass monkey. Before that I used to hustle the London Evening Standard and the London Daily Mirror aboard the English ships which came in. There were certain fanatics among the crew who chipped in to pay the outrageous sum of fifty cents a copy to get the "football" scores, and it was only later I learned they were talking about soccer.

It is difficult sometimes to remember that whole generations have grown up with the belief that Pioneer Square is a neighborhood of boutiques, kite shops, imported furniture stores, fancy bars, fashion stores and flower shops. No, kiddies, it wasn't always like that. The Pioneer Square (we never called it that) I once knew was a gamy and sometimes dangerous place to be. Tough gangs from Ballard and West Seattle would roam the old Skid Road "hunting gooks," which meant there was some sort of atavistic satisfaction in beating up Filipinos.

This was long before the Volvo invasion; Skid Road then was a haven for loggers, dockworkers, tree toppers and a heavy flow of transients. The metamorphosis of Pioneer Square, whose early, lively atmosphere waned throughout the 1950s, began in the mid-1960s. An architect named Ralph Anderson and a remarkable fellow named Dick White, an ex-waiter at Rosellini's Four-10, began buying up and restoring old buildings. Dick White developed a Midas touch rather late in life, and he probably is the only millionaire I ever really rooted for. It was Anderson and White who touched off the wave of sandblasting and renovation to revive an important part of Seattle not yet smothered by glass and aluminum.

Another guy who did a lot to dramatize Pioneer Square is Bill Speidel, whose books on early Seattle history still sell briskly. Speidel, who publishes Seattle Guide, a local dope sheet for tourists, still keeps an office in the Skid Road. He runs the underground tours in Pioneer Square and owns a tavern called Doc Maynard's, named after the amiable pioneer, much given to booze and collecting wives. Ever since I was a kid I've heard about the celebrated "Seattle Spirit." "The Seattle Spirit," Speidel once told me, "consists of a handful of people in Seattle who know what's going on. The rest we just keep around for bulk."

So now in Pioneer Square, the old skid road, you can buy imported Irish sweaters, expensive French Camembert, tailored leather clothes, decorator lamps and carpets—trophies and trinkets for the invading armies of MasterCharge. But in the 1930s, you could get a bowl of soup for a nickel, in a place run by a suspicious old son of a bitch who made you put the nickel on the counter before you got the soup.

Henry Broderick used to say, tongue in cheek, "We had a better class of bums in the old days." The late Mr. Broderick, who was a semi-pioneer himself, had his office at Second and Cherry, at the edge of the skid road. Outside of Henry's office was a garbage can where the down-and-outers used to forage. On one occasion, when Henry saw a bum rooting around in the garbage can, he left a meeting in his office and went outside. With a crumpled dollar bill in his hand, Henry joined the bum by putting his head down in the garbage can. Then he pulled up the dollar bill. "Look what I found!" he exclaimed. "Here, you were here first, you take the dollar." The bum smoothed the bill out between his fingers. "Thanks," he said. "I guess some rich bastard threw it away."

Of all the characters around the Skid Road, few topped Henry himself. During his early years, he buddied around with Bill Boeing when the founder of the airplane company had only seven employees in a barn on Lake Union, yet Henry himself never flew in an airplane—not until he boarded a 707 on his ninetieth birthday. Henry never owned a car. He spent between $2,000 and $2,500 a year on taxicabs and figured he wasn't too far behind the game. At one point in his life, when Henry was seriously ill in Providence Hospital, a call went out for blood donors. No fewer than twenty-seven cab drivers arrived at the hospital to volunteer.

I was never a licensed delinquent, but I ranked fairly high in the truancy department. An afternoon in a burlesque house was always more fun than a class in mechanical drawing at James Madison Junior High. And there were six Chinese lotteries on Main Street alone. In later, less innocent years, I always suspected that a lot of down payments on houses in Laurelhurst and Mount Baker were made with what it took to keep those lotteries open. The cops seemed to be well greased.

Playing the Chinese lottery was kind of ceremonial, the thing you did when you first hit the skid road. You might hit it lucky on the "short draw." Outside each Chinese lottery was a street shill, usually caucasian, who'd whisper "Short draw, buddy," or "Chuck-a-luck inside." Lord knows why he whispered.

The inside of a Chinese lottery was usually spare and uninspiring, except for the rattle of dice in the chuck-a-luck cage. This was for high rollers, meaning guys who had jobs. For a dime you could play "short draw," winners announced every hour, or "long draw," winners announced once a day. To give you an idea of post-Hoover prosperity, guys used to get up a "pool," by chipping in a penny or two cents apiece, sending a messenger over from the waterfront to play the short draw.

My buddies and I always played the short draw. It took less than an hour to find out if you hit it big for six or seven dollars. In the back room at a long counter you got a green slip for a dime with the numbers and Chinese writing on it. There were Chinese ink pots full of gummy, thick ink and you painted out the numbers with a little brush on a bamboo handle. There was one lottery at Second and Washington; right outside was a police call-in box. The owner of the Chinese lottery called up headquarters and complained: "That call box is ruining my business.

Your boys stop to call in and it scares the customers away." The next day the call-in box was moved around the corner.

The Skid Road was where I had my first drink of whiskey in a speakeasy. It was also where I first fell in love, or thought I did. Her name was Babe. She worked in a house on Maynard Ave. near where the Seattle Lighting Fixture Company store is today. She couldn't have been more than nineteen. She had natural, genuine blonde hair, which she wore long, and she had a fine, smooth complexion, about the color of vanilla ice cream, and she was no makeup junkie.

If you came early in the evening, around eight, before the fashionable hour, she wasn't too busy and had time to talk. Babe's boss, the madam, was a congenial old crone who took a liking to me. When I told her I planned to go to college if I could scrape up the money, she affirmed her belief in higher education. She gave me what she called a "student rate," a dollar instead of the usual two.

When she wasn't keeping regular office hours, Babe lived up near Volunteer Park. As most Seattle people know, Volunteer Park is a city showcase, partly because of the Seattle Art Museum, and because of its beautiful rolling acreage, which gets a big play in picture books and tourist guides. Until his death six years ago, the art museum was presided over by Dr. Richard E. Fuller, a saintly fellow, whose mother, Margaret Elizabeth MacTavish Fuller, donated the museum to the city and stocked it with a lot of jade and oriental art. Dr. Fuller's gifts, good taste and donations made it one of the better museums in the country.

The point here is that the first time I visited Volunteer Park was not to view stuff in the museum. It was to see Babe. It was the only time she let me see her outside of office hours. We went to the museum, which was free, thanks to Dr. Fuller, and then we walked around the reservoir in Volunteer Park. Babe didn't say much but she looked great, even out of her natural habitat, not losing any of her glamour the way Austrian ski instructors do when they dress up in street clothes and take an honest job.

I told Babe that I'd made up my mind to enter the University of Washington if I could borrow the first quarter's tuition. I told her maybe I could even get some financial help by playing baseball for the Huskies. To impress her, I even hinted that I might pick up a few thousand dollars playing professional ball. This was long before I met some of the more skilled users of Arthur Cummings' invention.

Babe wanted to know how many people went to the university. "The enrollment is about ten thousand," I told her. "A lot of them are women. You ought to go there yourself. Even if you work nights, you can take day classes." "How many guys go to the university?" she wanted to know. I guess her mind worked along special lines.

"About six thousand," I said. "Jesus!" Babe exclaimed. "Don't tell them about the student rate."

That was the last time I saw Babe except for a couple of times in her professional capacity. So I was forced into a grim period of celibacy while trying to get into the university with a 1.45 grade point average. A history teacher I knew at West Seattle was a big help. Ed Liston not only was a history teacher, he was a good semi-pro pitcher, and often I would catch him in a game on Sunday and sit in his class on Monday. Ed sent me out to see the dean of men at the university, a fine old gentleman named Herbert Thomas Condon, who handled special admission cases. When Dean Condon got a look at my high school transcript, it was one of the few times I ever saw blood drain from a man's face. But he let me in on probation.

Growing up as I did, hanging around the Skid Road, First Ave., the waterfront and dreaming mostly about baseball, it wasn't hard at all to get a 1.45 grade point. But I did get into the university, and Tubby Graves, the baseball coach, got me jobs punching out mutuel tickets at Longacres and later he got me a job at Boeing's Plant One down on the Duwamish. I'm glad I worked for Boeing once, because this kind of puts the "Made in Seattle" stamp on me.

My Boeing interlude was in 1939, when Boeing was building thirty-eight B-17C's for the RAF and our own Army Air Force. Along with these, they were building ten Boeing Stratoliners, model 307, the first four-engine commercial transports. They built five of these for Trans World Airlines, three for Pan Am and one for Howard Hughes. Because of school, I worked the swing shift. It would be nice to relate that I was part of a team that produced the goods that won World War II. The truth is, I never saw anything that even looked like an airplane.

When I first arrived at Boeing, they gave me a file. From four o'clock to midnight all I did was file. Pieces of aluminum—hundreds of them, all shapes—were cut from a template by a band saw. The saw left the aluminum with a "burr" which was jagged and sharp. My job was to file off the burr. Eight hours a night. Four hundred and eighty minutes. It was dreadful, mind-numbing work. A few times I deliberately cut a finger on this burr. The idea was that you could get a half-hour break to visit the infirmary. That's how awful it was. But I'm glad I did it for a while, because I met Manny, a fellow filer. Manny lived on a houseboat on Lake Union and he was a Marxist.

He was my introduction to the way thousands of Seattle people lived on houseboats. There were maybe twelve hundred houseboats then, most on Lake Union, but some of them on the Duwamish River. You'd really be stretching a point to call them quaint, although some of them probably were. I remember that the Duwamish houseboats were called "the Broadmoor of Hooverville," the real Hooverville being a shacktown which sprang up on the downtown waterfront after Mr. Hoover laid his egg. Houseboats in Seattle now number only a few hundred, and some of these look like condos in good neighborhoods.

Anyway, Manny's houseboat was down on Lake Union, not far from where Ivar Haglund's Salmon House is today. As I said, Manny was a Marxist, which indicates what can happen to a man when he has to file burrs off metal for a living. But he was a good influence on me. He read voraciously. He loved to argue and liked to question everything I thought I was learning up on the campus. Manny was really the first editor I ever had.

He would read and dissect stuff I had written, quarreling loudly with viewpoints, syntax and punctuation. One day he said, "You have a way with words, but you must have diarrhea of the typewriter. Read Westbrook Pegler," he advised, referring to one of Mr. Hearst's curmudgeon columnists. "Pegler is a reactionary bastard but he knows how to put words together so they don't run off the page. Maybe someday you can make a living writing for a newspaper. You won't get rich, but it beats hell out of filing aluminum."

Manny was right on all counts. Six years later the old Seattle Star hired me. There followed a four-year interlude at The Seattle Times. This was altogether a pleasant stop, since I worked with, and sometimes for, one of the best city editors in the country, Henry MacLeod. I also worked with a young guy who used to be around in the early mornings about the time I was finishing up after ball games. He was a fellow I got to be friends with, a fellow named Jim King, who is now identified on The Times' masthead as executive editor. We still have an occasional lunch and tell fibs to each other.

The last man to hire me was a man named Lee Ettelson, a tall, impeccably dressed, urbane product of San Francisco and New York, who came here and stayed a spell, making it as brief as he could. Lee was one of those designated hitters the late William Randolph Hearst used to send around to stir up his then-formidable chain of papers. Because of Ettelson, along with the managing editor, a fine man named Ed Stone, I settled into a pleasant sort of aviary known as The Post-Intelligencer.

Lee Ettelson, whom I privately called "the Spanish Duke" because of his regal bearing and high shirt collars, made no secret of his belief that Seattle was only a generation removed from the Indian ladies who used to rub urine in their hair. He knew all about the egos of alleged writers, and once, when he detected a swelling of my own ego, delivered a pronunciamento which is hard to forget: "A columnist is just a clerk who got lucky. I've always contended that if you give anybody two-column play in a newspaper and let him prattle on every day, he'll develop a following. No matter how bad he is."

The shift from sports to writing about a whole city was somewhat gradual; some say it roughly paralleled the increase in smog above Seattle. But for some twenty-six years, from once a week to three times a week, to five, then six, that is what happened. A crazy way to make a living but a lot of fun. Some nine hundred words a day, pounding the phone, walking the streets, poking around, scribbling notes, and occasionally getting sandbagged by some anecdote that had appeared in the Reader's Digest three months before. I got sued for libel twice and lost both times. During those years the Pulitzer people were strangely silent about my work. But once, when I interviewed George Lincoln Rockwell, the American Nazi, he told me I would be high on his hit list when he came to power. I must have done something right.

Early on, I thought of Seattle as small, provincial and much too circumscribed for my undoubted genius. I begged Lee Ettelson to get me transferred to Los Angeles. Lee may have had his own opinions about Seattle, but he sensed I belonged here. He knew that, in a figurative sense, I was born with webbed feet. He knew that I probably would never be happy living anywhere else. But he said he would do what he could about getting me out of here. Then he added: "I can't imagine why anybody lucky enough to be raised in Seattle would want to live in Los Angeles. But I guess," he sighed, "somebody always marries the fat girl."

Nothing came of this early attempt to bolt. Since those days, I've traveled extensively. Each return home has been better than the last. I've returned to Seattle hundreds of times by air, and always have considered it a lucky flight if the plane arrives a little before dusk on a decent day.

This is the perfect way and the perfect hour to come home. Seattle at its best: the plane begins its long descent south of Olympia, coming down over the islands and beaches of Puget Sound, up along Vashon Island for the wide, sweeping approach to the south. At this precisely right time of arrival, you get the full sweep of it—the mountains we boast about, the lakes and trees and curving shorelines and, because it is dusk, the thousands of cool vapor street lights cutting and crossing and weaving over the hills of the city. Turning inbound to Runway 16L at Sea-Tac Airport, the plane crosses the "outer marker" of the Instrument Landing System precisely over the parking lot of the Boeing plant, at exactly 1,700 feet from the ground. There, on your left, is Lake Washington, the two floating bridges, and to the west, on Elliott Bay, are the ships and the docks and the cranes and the mouth of the Duwamish River, above which I was born.

Not to sentimentalize, but at times like this I'm glad I didn't marry the fat girl.

Fifteen years ago I made a pilgrimage to Basel, Switzerland, to look up an old Seattle citizen I knew about. I found him in a compound of sixteenth and seventeenth century buildings grouped along the St. Albanvorstadt. Inside was a courtyard, and off the second-floor living room was a large room with a grand piano. In a smaller room beyond was a large painter's easel which held a bright, uncompleted abstract. The window shutters opened on the courtyard, and when he composed music and played, birds would actually fly in and perch on his music stand. He had just returned from a show of his paintings in London and another in Paris, where he had received the Order of Arts and Letters from the Louvre—which is the equivalent of the French Legion of Honor for artists and writers. He was formidable looking, a handsome figure of a man, gray-white hair and beard; his speech was trenchant, sometimes angry, often eloquent, a speech of soft rhythm laced with American slang, colloquialisms and an occasional curse. Mark Tobey was seventy-seven when I found him.

Although Mark Tobey was twenty-two when he moved here, he became a confirmed, devoted citizen of Seattle. Much of his work is a priceless record of the Pike Place Market I first knew. This was long before it fell into disrepair and its enticing location became so attractive to developers. It was before architect Victor Steinbrueck and a body of determined citizens rallied the voters to save the Market from the wrecker's ball. Tobey had agreed to see me because he knew I had fought to save the Market he knew and cared for.

The Rhine flows through Basel, and Tobey insisted we walk along the promenade. He seemed to take pleasure in pointing out the great old houses and a large ancient church which began at the Rhine's edge and towered upward. But it soon became clear that he wanted to talk about Seattle.

"It is a rare thing when an artist becomes involved in the city where he works, and I became involved with Seattle long ago. I have always tried to say the right things about it. I have always tried to do what I could." Of course I knew that Tobey had donated some of his work to raise money to save the Market. He walked briskly, arms clasped behind him, talking as he walked, remembering Seattle and the Market, remembering "the old men who used to lean against the buildings."

Then abruptly he asked, "Do you know why I became involved in Seattle? It was because of the beautiful nights and the clouds and the salt air. But mostly it was because of the people. The people are what make up a city. It isn't always the place, you know. Tell me," he asked, a touch of indignant sadness in his voice, "are they going to ruin it? Is Seattle going to become another sprawl?"

I said yes, the sprawl was already malignant. But I told him that Seattle was still, for all of its towering, obscene buildings, ugly parking lots and freeways and vulgar signs, a pretty good place to live. I told him that the Market still was much in danger. He nodded, then said: "I worked hard in Seattle, I love Seattle. That is where I made my name. But tell me, what of First Avenue? If they destroy that street, they destroy another part of our city. What of the old people, the poor people there? They have a right to live! Where will they go?"

I didn't answer, but I remembered a shop on First Ave. where I once hocked a homemade ukulele for fifty cents, and how I used to crash the First Ave. theatre by climbing the fire escape on Post Alley and going in an open window through the boiler room. I wanted to tell him that Turko, the news vendor, was still alive and that the Army-Navy surplus stores still thrived, but I could not tell him what would happen to the old people, the poor people.

"I have a lot of fame," he said, "but not much money. There is a great pull to go back to Seattle, but it has lost so much. They try to save it, but not the right way. Always the big, big effect and they end by destroying it. The government takes their money and then gives it back so they can build those silly buildings. Gosh damn them all!"

We walked for a while, then returned to climb many steps in order to cross the foot bridge which spans the Rhine, moving toward the old part of Basel where Tobey lived. He stopped for a long time at the top of the steps to catch his breath. "I will come back some day when my health fails. What I like best about Seattle are the people I know."

He never returned. Tobey died six years ago in Basel at the age of eighty-five. Seattle had changed too much for him—the Seattle of glass, aluminum, asphalt, and tall impersonal buildings; the march of "progress" wasn't for him, the growing vulgarity that does not alloy well with the beauty we boast about. Probably he would not care that what he was saying is what this book is about: "The people are what make up a city, it isn't always the place, you know."

Emmett Watson's Newspaper Career

The Seattle Star

June 10, 1944	First byline appears.
March 26, 1945	First column appears. Called "The Bullpen Barber." Runs irregularly.
May 10, 1945	Column name changed to "Behind the Boxscore."
February 2, 1946	Column name changed to "From the Pressbox."
April 27, 1946	Last byline appears in The Star.

The Seattle Times

April 28, 1946	First byline appears in The Times.
October 22, 1946	First column appears. Called "The Press Box." Runs irregularly.
February 25, 1948	Column name changed to "Dr. Watson's Needle."

Emmett Watson

This, Our City

The Seattle Post-Intelligencer

February 2, 1950   First column appears. Called "Quick Watson —
                          The Needle." Later becomes "Watson's Needle."

August 14, 1956   First non-sports column appears. Called "This,
                          Our Town." Runs once a week, while
                          "Watson's Needle" continues in sports section.

May 18, 1959   Non-sports column, now called "This, Our
                          City," begins running three times a week.
                          "Watson's Needle" cut back to twice weekly.

November 19, 1962   "This, Our City" goes to five days a week.
                          "Watson's Needle" discontinued.

September 22, 1969   "This, Our City" title is dropped. Column
                          becomes simply "Emmett Watson."

The Seattle Times

October 30, 1983   Return to The Times after 33 years at The Post-
                          Intelligencer.

Caricatures by Bob McCausland

Most people are dead at my age,
and you can look it up.

—Casey Stengel

Part 1
In the Beginnings

Back at Franklin High School, circa 1936 and 1937, I let it be known to my old baseball coach, Ralph (Pop) Reed, that I would like to be the next Paul O'Neil. O'Neil was a reporter and feature writer for The Seattle Times, then for The Seattle P-I. (He would go on to Time and Life magazines.) He had a dense yet smooth style; he became a star in Seattle. I remember Pop Reed asking, "Can you type?"

I said no. So he said, "Well, you'd better sign up for typing classes. You couldn't take your hat off in a newspaper if you can't type." So after two semesters I became a fair typist, and this was a great asset doing theme papers at the University of Washington. I never took journalism in college. Because of a slipshod life in high school, I lacked the required math and foreign language requirements to get into journalism school. But there was a more discouraging barrier. These were the times of the Great Depression, and one's hopes of getting a job—any job—on a newspaper seemed so remote I gave it no serious thought.

But I did take a lot of courses required of journalism majors—literature, history, anthropology, psychology, sociology—the liberal arts mix. I didn't know what I wanted to "be"—maybe an anthropologist or perhaps a teacher. By 1942, when I got out of school, World War II was very much on, so I did what any sensible kid did in those days; I got a job paying one dollar an hour at Todd Shipyards. I was classified 4-F in the military draft because both ears had been operated on for what they then called "radical mastoids." It happened just before sulfa drugs began to be used to cure ear infections in a matter of days. I was deaf, or at least hard of hearing. Hearing aids in those days came about as big as a car battery, so working in shipyards and longshoring suited my talents. I had everything except a respectable work ethic. In those days, too, I picked up ten or fifteen bucks a game playing semipro baseball. I even did this without using an assumed name while playing amateur baseball at the UW. I never got caught at it.

So it was wartime work. You were in "defense" work, so you couldn't hop from job to job, unless it was within a defense industry. I worked at Todd Shipyards, played some baseball, worked at Seattle-Tacoma Shipyards on Harbor Island, and later became one of Harry Bridges's finest, a "permit man" working on the Seattle docks. (We permit workers were not allowed to join the union because the ILWU had jobs to protect for union members overseas who would return in peacetime.) If you've never done any of these things, don't feel deprived. You didn't miss a thing. It was miserable, long-houred, cold and demeaning work. All muscle, no brains.

By the summer of 1944, it became apparent that the good guys were finally going to win. Germany, Japan and their teammates began to reel. During these war years, I edited and wrote for a paper called The Umpire. It was published by an organization of bush-league players; we called ourselves The 3-and-O Club. The Umpire was a newsletter sent overseas to Northwest baseball players, pros and bushers, who were serving in England, France, Italy and the South Pacific. It carried news and gossip and often reports of baseball friends who had been killed in action. But the war was rapidly coming to an end; as Norman Corwin once described it, it was "a time when the samurai warrior laid down his sword in front of a grocery clerk from Baltimore." Or Seattle, or any other American city you can name.

It was also a time, in a figurative sense, when you kicked the women and children aside to reach the lifeboats. I was scared to death I wouldn't get a job in so-called "private industry" when the war ended. I had a friend at the UW, a marvelous athlete and person named Bill MacDonald, who later became dean of men at Western Washington University in Bellingham. Because I knew that Bill's father was an ILWU official, I went to Bill with my problem. Bill said, "Go see my dad," which I did. Using whatever power he had as an ILWU official, Bill's father got me off the waterfront and free to take a non-defense job.

My first try came when Ben Evans, head of the Parks Department, gave me a job as recreational director at Broadway Playfield. As it happened, I succeeded Dick Gyselman, the great Seattle Rainiers third baseman. Broadway Playfield didn't last long because one day Chick Garrett, sports editor of the old Seattle Star, came up to the playfield to see me. The Umpire, that little paper that I mostly edited and wrote, paid off. Chick had seen my stuff in it, and he offered me a job covering baseball for The Star. For once, I played it cagey. I said, "Sure, I'd like to cover baseball, but I want to do everything else, too." It worked, and I got my first newspaper job on space rates. Because of the wartime "manpower freeze," The Star paid me with vouchers, redeemable for cash at the front counter, thus avoiding putting me on the books officially and breaking the manpower-freeze law. Cliff Harrison, the managing editor, would vary the weekly vouchers—sometimes $28, sometimes $32, but mostly $28.

It was glorious. Now, remember, I was just a couple of months off loading boxcars on cold, windy, Elliott Bay mornings. I was terrified that I might lose this sinecure. This fear has stayed with me all through journalism, the fear that someday I would have to return to honest work. At the time I knew nothing about journalism. It was only later that I learned what a talented bunch of people were teaching me. I even took another job. When baseball didn't need covering, I worked full-time as a fill-in for United Press, whose offices were right in The Star city room. I worked all day at The Star editing copy, writing fea-

tures and columns and making up the sports page in the back shop. At 5 p.m. I moved into the United Press office, rewriting news stories, creating my own features, trying to stay ahead of those damned teletype machines. I got off at 1 a.m. and was back at The Star's sports desk by 7 a.m.

Presumably because they liked me, the veteran Star hands took me down to the nearby Press Club at 7th and Union. It was here that I learned to like whiskey sours. But I also learned much about newspapering and the politics thereof, and formed the abiding conviction that there is no such word as "irregardless."

The Star had long been a part of my life because we took it at home. My father thought it represented the views of the working man better than either The Times or The P-I. He may have been right. As a kid I used to relish a column called "Home Brew," a bow to the illegal booze-making common in those days. The column was written by Art Shannon. "Home Brew" was mostly homespun humor whose little jokes even a kid could understand. When I joined The Star, "Home Brew" was long gone, having been replaced by a short, equally folksy, front-page column called "Squawk McGuff," written by the inimitable Jim Egan.

Cliff Harrison, the former sports editor and outdoors writer, was the managing editor who signed my vouchers. The saintly, soft-spoken Chick Garrett was the lone sports staffer, so he taught me everything from headline writing to making up the sports page in the back shop. Chick once went out and floated a $200 personal loan to send me on a trip to cover a UW football game in Los Angeles. The Star was like that, and so was Chick. Another outgoing, pleasant man was Loe Pardee, an all-purpose newsman who worked as city editor, on the copy desk and later as news editor.

The Star was by no means a clown paper, only a paper perennially on the shorts. It had some great people on it. It was Ed Guthman's first paper; when I arrived, Ed was away fighting the war in Italy. He would later go over to The Times and win a Pulitzer Prize. Dave Belknap was the assistant city editor. He later held two bureau-chief jobs for United Press before he became South American correspondent for the Los Angeles Times. Gradually, I began to realize how good these people really were. One remembers John Randolph, a jovial, all-purpose news reporter who went on to become a top foreign correspondent for Associated Press.

Every paper today has an "action" or a "hot line" kind of troubleshooting column. There is nothing new under the sun, or at least that part of it shining on Seattle. The Star had a column called "Mr. Fixit," written by a number of staffers in their spare time, most notably by Buzz Busselle. Ann Landers is big these days, but back then so was "Cynthia Grey," under whose by-line staffers (both men and women) dispensed advice to the lovelorn.

The Star's last city editor was Eddie Hill, who, along with Cliff Harrison, Phil Taylor and some others, went to The P-I after The Star folded in 1947. On the last day of publication, Eddie called a staff meeting and urged them all, out of journalistic pride, to make the final issue a good one. As the troops returned to their desks, Eddie quietly picked up the phone and applied for a job at The P-I.

Whatever else it accomplished, The Star was an aggressive "third paper" in a three-newspaper town. In part, it was responsible for making a regional radio celebrity out of baseball broadcaster Leo Lassen. To this day, people talk about Lassen, even ranking him above the redoubtable Dave Niehaus of the Seattle Mariners. I was on the baseball beat only a short time when Leo befriended me. When we were in our cups, Leo would relate wild, wonderful stories about his days as The Star's sports editor and later managing editor. The Star was then owned by the Scripps chain, and Leo remembered bitterly, "One day the Scripps people came in and fired everybody making more than $35 a week. That's how I got canned."

Lassen caught on as a press agent for the old Seattle Indians baseball team and later took over as the team's broadcaster. He was an instant and lasting success.

My days at The Star and United Press rewarded me with dozens of friends and counselors: photographer Vic Condiotti, Phil Taylor, Vic Westphal, Willard Coghlan, Jack Pyle, Ruth Howell. Pyle went on to a fine newspaper career in Tacoma. Much later, after her family was reared, Ruth Howell came out of newspaper retirement and for several years headed The P-I's editorial pages.

During the time when I doubled up by working at United Press, I met a very talented lady, one who helped me immensely in the business of writing. Her name was Aline Mosby, and she worked in the UP bureau when I did. She was lithe and beautiful and had wonderful strawberry-blonde hair. That was the surface part that pleased the eye. But underneath was a professional, exacting toughness. She went on from Seattle to become the United Press correspondent in Hollywood. She worked in a number of places, and she also made a name for herself working for United Press out of the Moscow bureau and wrote a book about these difficult years. Later, she headquartered in Paris, where she now lives in retirement.

Defining The Star, my first newspaper job, brings to mind Fred Carter, a photographer on that paper. He was another counselor. "Kid, stay here for a while, but move on," he said. "Just figure you are working in a great school of journalism."

The Star was my first beginning. There would be others.

My first byline in The Star read "Emmitt," an inaccuracy scarcely noted by anyone, except perhaps the ghost of Robert Emmet, the starry-eyed Irish revolutionary after whom I was christened. My subject was Johnny Nenezich, the umpire, who at last had made the Pacific Coast League after a bush-league apprenticeship that sometimes paid him a dollar a game. In his 80s, Nenezich's good spirits, wit and vast anecdotal reserves landed him a host position at the Metropolitan Grill in downtown Seattle, which is where I last saw him.

Evidence that I was raw and untutored is readily apparent in this story; punctuation is shaky, syntax lame. Copyediting and typesetting were weak, too—was the Spokane outfielder named McCormick or McCormack? I don't remember. I only remember how fiercely I wanted to succeed, to hold on to a job that would keep me away from the awful labor of longshoring.

My eager, but unrequited, love affair with newspapering almost came to an abrupt end a mere two weeks after it began. I was still catching semipro ball on the side, getting 15 bucks a game. Two games a week and I equaled or exceeded my weekly vouchers on The Star. But in one horrific game, I almost blew it all.

I was catching for Gibson Carpets. We were playing the local Coast Guard team, which was loaded with in-service professional players. Not the least of these was Ray Orteig, a fine hitter who later caught for Yakima, San Francisco and Seattle. Orteig hacked at a high, floating knuckleball, and the foul tip broke and dislocated the little finger on my right hand. It took three doctors to set the finger, and I ended up with a huge cast and some kind of metal suspension system to keep the dislocated finger in place. Until I made some painful, inventive adjustments, I was virtually useless around a typewriter. But luck held, the thing healed and I stayed on. It was the last baseball game I ever played; I didn't want to risk this newspaper job I had, this lucky opportunity, on another baseball injury. I didn't have a baseball future, I knew, but I might have a newspaper future.

One minor footnote: That same summer I wrote a long, painfully typed feature story on Al Libke, a professional star with the Rainiers who would eventually go to the major leagues. The burly, loose-jointed Libke was not only a fine hitter, he was an outstanding pitcher in the wartime Shipyard League. I wrote this story about Al that said, in part, that he hurled "a no-hitter against the Everett Tyees." I was too timid on the "I" key in those days, so I never mentioned that I caught Al Libke's no-hitter.

John Nenezich

Seattle Star, June 10, 1944

BUSH BALL PLAYERS ARE BEATING A PATH TO THE DOOR of Sicks' Seattle stadium this week where the Oaks and Rainiers are locking horns in deadly combat.

One of their gang finally is getting a break. Yessir, teamed with the veteran Jack Powell is none other than John Nenezich, crown prince of the bush-league umpires.

Many a Sunday they've cussed him for calling them out on a third strike, and more than a few of them can thank John Nenezich for an early shower when they argued too long and too loud. But this is different. Johnny is one of them, and they're all pulling for him.

Invariably, the question goes: "How's Johnny doing? Has he missed any yet?"

"He called a close one in the clutch," someone will reply. "But the guy didn't beef, so it must have been right."

Then the session starts, the bushers begin reminiscing back over the 13 years that John has been calling 'em around Seattle.

They remember the time in Yakima, in 1935, when George Burns, the ex-Seattle manager, had charge of the Yakima Indians in the Northwest League. He had a very troublesome catcher named Callegari, who was giving every umpire in the league a bad time. And he was giving John a bad time, too—for a while. Finally John gave him the iron thumb, throwing him out of the contest.

"You bum!" screamed Burns. "You can't throw him out, he's the only catcher I've got. What'll I do?"

"Catch yourself, you're big and strong," shot back John. "Play ball!"

And they tell of the time last year in the Shipyard League when Alan Strange was managing the Sea-Tacs. Strange, never speechless in front of an umpire, began to dress John down on a close decision. John took it patiently. When Strange turned to go back to his position, he called back over his shoulder: "Miss another one, and I'm coming back!"

"Come back once more," John replied, "and you'll keep on walking—right into that dressing room." And that was the end of the beginning of that.

Johnny's favorite story on himself concerns Levi McCormack, the Indian outfielder, playing for Spokane one year. John was working the plate, and behind him were several thousand wild-eyed Spokane fans. McCormack, hitting in the clutch, took a third strike right down the middle.

"Strike three!" called John. McCormick turned, knowing he was out, but hating to admit it in front of all those people. Suddenly, a bright idea struck him. He held up his hands, about two feet apart, in a measuring gesture.

"John," he said. "I went fishing yesterday and I caught a fish, just that long."

Spokane fans, to this day, think Johnny called out McCormick on a pitch that was "just that wide."

They remember the time he tossed three of the four Nokes brothers out of a game in Rainier Valley, causing them to lose the ball game and the league lead. Or the verbal tiffs he used to have with Freddie Hutchinson, when Freddie was winning games for Franklin High School. And the time Edo Vanni sat on the mound in Renton, in a one-man sit-down strike against one of Nenezich's decisions.

They had a nickname for him in those days, too—"The Little Caesar," inspired by his similarity to Edward G. Robinson in both looks and demeanor.

But they're all at the ballpark this week, those who can make it, pulling for John to "cut the mustard." The bush-league enemies are his best friends, because he's a good guy and they like him.

"Nice call, John!" they yell. "Nice goin', you blind man." And the fans look about them in wonder. Something is wrong here—half the crowd is pulling for the umpire. That's because they don't know ballplayers, and because they don't know Johnny Nenezich.

No major sporting event to my knowledge was ever held in Mt. Shasta, California. The reason one of my early Husky football stories was so datelined was because, on the long train ride through Oregon, northern California and the Bay Area, Mt. Shasta was the site of a Western Union office. During the short stop in Mt. Shasta, you had to race to Western Union, drop off the copy and race back to catch the train. Trains in those days were jammed with wartime passengers, and it was impossible to work from a seat. One had to show ingenuity. In this case, I made sure the ladies' room was empty. Then I darted in, locked the door and set up my portable typewriter on the washbasin. The story was written in a rocking train amidst the din of outraged and desperate women pounding on the door.

Dough was tough to come by in those days. The next football season, 1945, was still more or less a war year; players came and went with the Huskies, according to the needs of the military. To make some extra money, the UW athletic director at that time, Al Ulbrickson, offered me the job as press agent for the Husky football team, even though I would continue to work for The Star. This was a blatant conflict of interest, but Cliff Harrison and Chick Garrett at The Star okayed the deal, mostly because they were paying me a pittance. So I dutifully went around to Royal Brougham, sports editor of The P-I, and Sandy McDonald, who was Royal's counterpart on The Times. Both agreed to this double-dipping as long as I didn't give The Star

inside stuff. It was fun for a while, but then one day Washington played Washington State.

It was a scoreless tie with three minutes left to play. Then a freshman halfback for Washington, Gordon Hungar, sprinted 38 yards to win the game for the Huskies. Everybody descended on me, the poor flack. Hell, I had never even heard of Gordon Hungar. On Sunday, Brougham began his story like this:

"His picture wasn't in the program nor his name in the newspapers, but a fuzzy-cheeked freshman halfback named Gordon Hungar got up from among the third-string substitutes on the far end of the bench just in time to give Washington a thrilling 6-0 win over Washington State yesterday."

That was my one venture into flackery. I was a total flop.

UW Prepares for USC

Seattle Star, October 21, 1944

MT. SHASTA, CAL. — En Route With the Washington Huskies—This may not be the most unorthodox football season in Husky grid history, but it's doubtful if any Washington club ever prepared for the big game of the season under more trying circumstances.

After practicing all week, with one-half of the squad taking final exams and the other half worrying about them, Coach Ralph Welch ran into the payoff last night when two of his key men missed the train at Portland.

Sometime during the two-hour layover in the Rose City, Dick Hultgren, reserve Halfback, and Quarterback Dick Ottele lost their way between the dining room of the Multnomah Hotel and the Union Station.

Whether or not the two will arrive in Los Angeles in time for the Huskies' night workout in the Coliseum is questionable; but if they don't, Welch's starting lineup—especially in the case of Ottele—may be materially changed.

It's no secret that the Husky coach is counting on that pre-game practice under the lights. The last real scrimmage session enjoyed by the Huskies was a 71–0 romp a week ago over a hapless Whitman Missionary team, which could hardly be called a tough two hours.

For the first time in one solid week, the didactic Husky mentor hoped to gather his squad together in one unit and polish up offensive and defensive assignments.

But with a first-string quarterback and reserve halfback taking in the scenery somewhere between Portland and San Francisco, Welch can't exactly see the humor in the situation.

How about the remaining 26 members of the traveling squad? For the first time in a week they've had a chance to really concentrate on football, and midweek confidence is beginning to fade just a bit.

Perhaps they've had time to think about guys like Jim Hardy, Don Hardy, Marshall Romer, John Ferraro and George Callahan—men who have been through the football mill and don't scare in front of a capacity crowd.

Perhaps they remember newsreel pictures of the Trojans scoring four touchdowns last year in the Rose Bowl, with that same Jim Hardy firing touchdown passes to fleet and elusive receivers.

Maybe Ends Hank Melusky, Dick and Les Hagen are thinking about how they'll have to spend some 60 minutes charging Hardy like General Patton on a rampage.

Perhaps Tackles Bill McGovern, Harry Rice and Jim Sanderson are wondering how they'll stand up under the incessant pounding they will surely receive from the powerful Trojan running backs.

And maybe Center Gordy Berlin and Fullback Keith DeCourcey are wondering if they can hold a reputably weak Husky pass defense together when the chips are down.

But also, perhaps, the whole squad is thinking that Monday night they can turn in the biggest upset on the Coast by smacking down the vaunted men of Troy. At any rate, they are going to try.

B ecause I was the only hand in the sports department, sports editor Chick Garrett more or less told me to set up my own column. This is the first one, my columnar headwaters, called "The Bullpen Barber." Since, as a catcher with the Rainiers, I had been assigned the job of warming up pitchers, the "bullpen" part was fitting. "Barber" was baseball slang for a talkative person, as some barbers were, and are. Reflecting the tenuous toehold I had in the newspaper industry, my columns ran irregularly, and name changes occurred frequently: "Watson Says," "Behind the Boxscore," "From the Pressbox."

"The Bullpen Barber" Debuts

Seattle Star, March 26, 1945

SAN FERNANDO, CAL. — The Rainiers are showing a spirit of hustle and drive that makes you think of those three pennants hanging from the masthead at Sicks' Stadium. Every once in a while you reflect now nice it would be to have another one—the first since 1941.

There isn't much said around camp, but you can tell the players are thinking about it, even at this early date.

It shows up in the way burly Ted Norbert is driving himself to get in condition; in the smiles of satisfaction when Charley Aleno busts one against the left-field wall; in the way veteran hurlers like Carl Fischer, Byron Speece and Sylvester Johnson take that extra lap around the park when they're dog-tired after a day's workout.

Only a club with confidence in itself works like that, and the feeling prevails from the lowest rookie to Skipper Bill Skiff himself.

There are so many encouraging signs this spring, like the way George McDonald adds a prewar professional polish to the infield at first base.

The spark Joe Dobbins has picked up (four hits Saturday and two yesterday is enough to give anyone a spark) after his listless play last year is another highlight of the camp.

Small talk, heard in the dressing room, adds to the optimism. Little signs of encouragement: Palica looks good today . . . Lyman is throwing better . . . Matheson and Kats may report . . . Aleno is a real hustler.

It's too early yet to make any sound predictions, but one thing is certain: This club will be heard from.

One of the most popular youngsters in camp is Kenny Benham, the tall, silent right-hander.

Kenny is handicapped by a bad leg, the victim of infantile paralysis. He can't run fast enough to beat out any kind of an infield hit, but he's overcome one of the toughest plays a pitcher has to make—covering bunts on either side of the mound.

And so far Kenny has kept the opposition at bay quite handily in the few times he's worked. His control is developed to the point where he keeps his fastball where hitters have a tough time getting a solid cut at it, and he knows how to change the pace exceedingly well for a young pitcher.

But mostly, the players like the way he tackles his work. In spite of his handicap, he's one of the first ones out and the last one to leave the field when workouts are over.

Right now, with the pitching staff the way it is, Kenny has a swell chance to break into the lineup on the first Rainier road trip. And you can bet your last cigarette that every one of the eight guys behind him will be playing their heads off to see that the courageous kid comes out on top when he gets his chance.

Baseball could use more guys like Kenny Benham.

Ballplayers Return from War

Seattle Star, February 1, 1946

IT IS NICE TO SEE THE PROFESSIONALS COMING BACK.

Millions of words have been bandied over the question of just how lousy the quality of wartime baseball was. It was pretty lousy, really.

Yet a number of folks, in and out of baseball, have pointed out that the element that makes any game a success is competition—not the closeness to perfection attained.

People will support two bad teams as well as two good ones, providing they're evenly matched.

Coast Conference football was very ordinary in quality last fall and several falls previous. Yet the colleges packed 'em in. Coast League and major league baseball made the managers blush, but not the guy at the ticket window.

People put it on the line and got their money's worth. They'd do it again this year, too.

But fortunately the pros are coming home by the dozens and

hundreds, and this year the Coast League will present as fast a circuit as ever. (It's still double-A ball—don't let that extra "A" fool you.)

But it will be fun again to watch the game played by the truly good ones.

Dick Barrett will be back with the hated Beavers, and we'll have that great curveball to see again . . . And man, how he can throw it! He makes it crack off in sections . . . And it's something to watch helpless hitters trying to get a solid piece of it. It was always his best clutch pitch, and they say some of 'em couldn't hit it even when they knew it was coming. His fastball was nothing fearful, but baby, he could make that deuce snarl and whine.

And of course Torgie will be here . . . the Earl of Snohomish . . . certainly one of the finest prospects to hit this league since Williams and DiMaggio . . . It's fun to watch a young guy, with all that strength, leveling on a misguided fastball with nothing but raw power . . .

The quality of shortstopping will jump with the return of Linsay Brown to Portland and Joe Hoover at San Francisco. Neither can hit the ground with a bat, but leave that to the sluggers . . . Those two were born with a glove on . . .

There are dozens of others—it would take a column to name 'em— some young and coming fast, some with a few good years left.

There'll be a few heartaches when some of the older ones find they can never come back and when some of those who were here all the time watch helplessly as the pace quickens and they can't keep up.

Just three more weeks now until the camps open and baseball starts another year.

Dutch Reuther Talks

Seattle Star, April 4, 1946

KLAMATH FALLS, ORE. — Even a lonely stretch of Highway 99 yields its story.

A few miles south of Weed, Cal., a battered sign—RISBERG'S—stands out with an arrow pointing down a narrow road to the left. Below the big letters are the words "cocktails—dancing."

Risberg . . . Risberg . . . Chicago . . . 1919 . . . Black Sox.

Swede Risberg was the shortstop of the infamous Chicago Black Sox, who sold out the World Series that year to gamblers. The same guy . . . Highway 99—RISBERG'S.

And driving the car, right alongside of you, is the hero of that series, a left-handed pitcher named Dutch Reuther, who toiled for the winning Cincinnati Reds. Whispering Dutch, one-time manager of the Seattle ball club, now scouting for the National League Cubs.

"It's the same guy," he said, in a low, hoarse voice. "He was one of the guys that sold it out."

Then for 50 miles along Highway 99 Dutch talked . . .

How he hurled one victory for the Reds, blasted out two triples and a single and drew a base on balls and split the winner's share, only to find out a year later the Series had been fixed; how he looked up and said to his wife, when scandal broke: "Well, honey, I thought I beat the greatest team in the world—and now I find out they weren't even trying."

Then he told of the way Happy Felch, a good fielder, misjudged a fly ball and complained of the glare in the outfield. It was a cloudy day.

And how Lefty Williams, a pitcher with great control who hadn't walked 30 men all year, suddenly walked seven Reds in one game. The way Eddie Cicotte, the outstanding right-hander of his time with hairline control, hit the first Cincinnati man who faced him right in the small of the back.

And Dutch told of Risberg, a picture shortstop, picking up a cinch double-play ball, missing the bag at second and firing high into the stands.

And Shoeless Joe Jackson—the greatest of them all—hitting like mad all during the Series, just as though he didn't know the outcome had been written in the script.

But he couldn't have read a script; he couldn't read or write anything. He just remembered to throw a World Series.

How long ago? There were Jackson, Cicotte, Weaver, Felch, Risberg and three others . . . They sold it out cheaply in a sordid deal that helped only the gamblers and nearly wrecked baseball . . . There was a year of silence . . . then the explosion and the trial . . . 26 years ago.

Reuther, who helped win the Series, was subpoenaed as a witness and told what he could.

"At the time," he said, "everything seemed all right. But now, looking back, I can see where the fix was on. I can't forget the way Risberg handled that double-play ball—it was awful."

Soon the trial was over, and eight men walked out of the courtroom, convicted and guilty.

And the small boy, looking tearfully up at his hero, the great Jackson, and pleading: "Say it ain't so, Joe."

Then came Landis, in 1921, ruling with an iron hand.

And he barred them all . . . Shoeless Joe Jackson, Cicotte, Risberg and the rest. Banished them forever from baseball, out of the game and into the dark chamber of oblivion.

"The Press Box" survived and went with me when I joined The Seattle Times in the spring of 1946. I had worked with and against Alex Shults, The Times' baseball writer, and when he was made sports editor, he said, "Come on over." There was no hesitation. The Times was big-time. After the freewheeling journalism school at The Star, the stately Times was like entering a lint-free news laboratory. Though Shults was the sports editor, my real boss was a tall, thin man, Russell McGrath, who wore tweed suits and an eyeshade. He was roughly comparable to Lee Kwan Yew, today's authoritarian leader of Singapore. McGrath ruled with an iron hand, doing so through short memos that came out of his office like shrapnel. An example of McGrath's deadly memos concerned a story I did that referred to a "verbal agreement." His scathing, but effective memo said, "Watson: All agreements are verbal—they are either written or oral." He was a fine editor, and he treated me with consideration. "The Press Box" column about Fred Provo, a UW halfback returned from the war, was my first groping in a stylistic experiment; McGrath liked it, and he gave it a plug on the front page.

On Sportswriting

Seattle Times, October 22, 1946

MOST GUYS WHO TALK ABOUT THEIR BUSINESS are strictly squares and frightful bores, so, if you don't want to be bored for the next five minutes, go fix the furnace or something.

Because we are going to talk about sportswriters for a while.

You think the athletes you read about are glamorous characters? . . . Fascinating people? . . . Full of wit and sparkling conversation? Nuts.

There is more fun in one screwballish sportswriter than a whole roomful of muscle-headed guards, left-handed pitchers and canvasback fighters. The guys who glamorize the goons are the elite guard of the sports racket to my mind, and we should have a Hall of Fame for them, like at Cooperstown, or some place where the beverage laws are liberal.

There are giants in the press box, just as there are on the playing field—men like Grantland Rice, Paul Gallico, Ring Lardner, Heywood Broun, Damon Runyon, John Lardner and dozens of others. Past and present, they've made athletes famous and sometimes rich, yet most of the public have no idea just how they work or what their problems are.

The first problem of any guy who sits down at a typewriter to dazzle his readers is to think up a good "lead." The "lead" is the first few words of a story. It is supposed to catch the reader's interest and start things off with a bang.

The classic lead of all, I think, was the one written by Grantland Rice, when he christened the Notre Dame backfield the Four Horsemen. It was written October 19, 1924, just after Knute Rockne's great team had beaten a strong Army eleven.

> *Outlined against a blue-gray October sky, the Four Horsemen rode again. In dramatic lore they are known as Famine, Pestilence, Destruction and Death. These are only aliases. Their real names are Stuhldreher, Miller, Crowley and Layden . . .*

Then there is the one written by the late Heywood Broun about Babe Ruth. The details of this one are lost, but it is remembered that Ruth had been stopped cold by some enemy pitcher, only to blast one out of the park in the late innings to win for the Yankees. As the game ended the younger sportswriters crowded around Broun to see what the great man would use for a lead. Broun, a big man, hunched over his typewriter and began to peck away slowly: *"Ruth, crushed to earth, shall rise again . . . "*

Broun had done nothing more than substitute "Ruth" for "Truth" and use an old saying for his lead. He did this another time when the Babe, almost single-handed, slaughtered John McGraw's Giants in a 1923 World Series game with two home runs and a pair of walks.

Broun started this one out: *"The Ruth is mighty and shall prevail. He did yesterday . . . "*

Another good one was John P. Carmichael's (Chicago Daily News) opening description of the first Louis-Conn fight, when Billy threw caution to the breeze in the 12th round and tried to slug with the champ.

"It's an old, old story," Carmichael wrote. *"The gun wasn't loaded as Billy (The Kid) Conn toyed with it. But suddenly it went off!*
"The Brown Bomber was just a dud, after all. The fuss had burned itself out and nothing had happened. So Billy The Kid went over to pick it up. Then it exploded!"

Oh, yes, we said there were screwballs in the sportswriting business, didn't we? Well, there's always the one about the big northern paper which sent its ace down to cover a gigantic Rose Bowl game some years back.

It was a whale of a ball game, and the whole news staff crowded around the Associated Press–Western Union printer to catch the first words of their traveling clarion's account of the game. But something must have gone wrong. Apparently the writer had overmatched himself with a good blend. Here were the only words that came out of the reporter's long trip to Pasadena: *"All is confusion. Pick up A. P."*

Another one was used in a recent national magazine story which described the perils and pitfalls of a road trip with the Brooklyn Dodgers. This particular incident told of a rookie sportswriter making his first trip around the National League circuit. The Dodgers were playing St. Louis.

In order to give his readers more color, the youngster was describing each ballpark in detail. He was working away in the press box, when he suddenly paused to ask a question of one of the veteran scribes.

"Pardon me, is that west?" he asked, pointing directly at the sun, settling down beyond the left-field fence.

The veteran regarded the youngster a moment, then answered slowly: "Well, young man, if it isn't, you've got a hell of a story."

Fred Provo Returns

Seattle Times, October 29, 1946

YOU COME BACK OLDER, HEAVIER, SMARTER, and with a decent respect for being alive. You return with scars on your back, and a jagged one across your chest, to a game they said you'd never play again.

It's a nice day. You come out of the tunnel in front of 40,000 people, and the sunlight hits the gold "33" on your jersey, a nicer number than a G. I. dog tag.

The program says you're Fred Provo, a left halfback.

The student section, bigger than it's ever been before, is yelling like every other section of its kind, and most of the rooters don't remember when Freddy Provo was a third-string halfback in 1942.

The Husky left halfback, who runs like there was a law against being tackled, is back to play a safer game. He had a large piece of the Second World War laid right in his lap as a 21-year-old sophomore.

So thank you, please, not anymore. Let's toss a coin, or argue the next one out. Wars are dangerous.

The kid from Vancouver, Wash., was helping the 82nd Airborne Division push up the lower belly of the Belgian Bulge. A long way from the Beta Theta Phi House, where the meals are good and the biggest hazard is a touch by one of the brothers.

Freddy Provo got hit; a piece of a German mortar clipped him across the chest, high up on the right side. Not so bad, walk a thousand yards to the aid station and they'll fix you up. But one doesn't walk in the middle of a war. He crawls and zigs and zags.

After 500 yards there is a weakness which comes from loss of blood.

"To hell with this," said Freddy Provo. "We'll walk a while."

For 500 yards more you walk on borrowed time and thank your stars the German boys with rifles are afflicted with temporary astigmatism.

The aid station is friendly. They've got you on a table and everything is set for the Army medicos to go in and get that piece of metal.

But suddenly there isn't any aid station. There is a loud noise from a German 88-millimeter job arriving uninvited. Some of the others are on the floor, and when the debris clears, you are worse off than ever.

Three pieces of the German shell have been added to the one you had before. Tech. Sergt. Provo has become a nonvoting stockholder in Krupp Munitions, Ltd.

The Husky stadium looks good these days, some two years later, and even UCLA and USC are friendly in their off moments. It's nice to be back, but the stand at the goal line in a hospital in France . . . Well, it's nice to be back.

There was a friendly Army doctor who took a great deal of pride in his work. He went into Tech. Sergt. Provo's chest and shoulder, removing the bits of metal. Very close.

"Everything's going to be all right," the doctor said. "No matter what they tell you later, you'll play football again. None of the nerves are damaged. The muscles will heal. Just hang in there . . . Take it easy."

The other doctors shook their heads. Not so good. Football? Not a chance.

For six months, you lay in the hospital, often thinking of home. Or frosh football at Washington in 1941. Of varsity ball in 1942, enough to make a letter.

And the high school league at Vancouver, under Dutch Shields. The Southwest Conference prep battles, when you were a star, on the first team. Those were the days you'd run wild against Aberdeen, wrecking Phil Sorboe's defense.

"That Provo," he'd say, "he beat me again."

A nice guy, Sorboe. Coaching now at Washington State. Maybe you'll get a crack at the Cougars when you get back to Washington. If you ever play again.

But Tech. Sergt. Provo kept on remembering what the other doctor had said: "You'll play again, no matter what they tell you."

In the hospital a big fullback from Cornell, himself a casualty, helped Tech. Sergt. Provo exercise the arm he used to throw passes with. A lot of work, every day.

"Keep trying, kid," the fullback said. "You won't be a third-stringer when you go back to Washington. You're putting on weight."

You walk down East 47th Street from the Beta House, older than the others, heavier than when you left, and, like the Cornell fullback said, no longer on the third team.

It was quite a war, but next time let's have the diplomats fight it out with adjectives at 30 paces.

Football? We've won two and lost three. But there was that satisfying battle against Washington State at Pullman three weeks ago. Just like old times.

"That Provo," Sorboe said, after the game. "He beat me again."

Even three years after acquiring a byline in the newspaper business, those cold loading docks I had escaped remained lodged in my memory, and fear persisted that my wonderful life would end abruptly with a dismissal slip. In the fall of 1947, The Times sent me back to cover the World Series between the New York Yankees and the Brooklyn Dodgers. For a Seattle newspaper, this was unheard of, a singular financial extravagance. I arrived at my New York hotel. I had nothing to write, nothing to justify the Times' considerable investment, but I set to work anyway. What came out was a piece about a twilight visit to Yankee Stadium, "the house that Ruth built." The feature earned telephonic backslaps from home. They brought me no comfort, for the story was a total fabrication.

I never went near Yankee Stadium until the World Series started. The entire story was a fraud. But I think now it's safe to confess. McGrath is gone from this green footstool, and the statute of limitations has run out.

Yankee Stadium "Beheld"

Seattle Times, September 29, 1947

NEW YORK — There we stood, the guy and I, in the twilight in Yankee Stadium, a few hours before the opening of the 44th World Series. A yawning, lonely, darkened, triple-decked Yankee Stadium . . . the biggest ball park in all the world.

The men are still at work, getting it ready for the 13th fall Series since it was built in 1923, getting it ready for the 70,000 baseball fans who will jam it tomorrow, when the Yanks and Dodgers start fighting it out for the blue chips.

"The joint's empty," the man was saying. "Look, why don't you come back tomorrow? There's nothing to see now."

He was wearing coveralls and he had let me in. He might have been anybody, even MacPhail, except for the clothes. He thought I was nuts, and maybe he was right.

He wanted to know where I was from, and when I told him, he said: "Seattle? Where's that?" (I think he really meant it.)

But anyway, there it was—Yankee Stadium—three decks high, towering into what was left of a Sunday twilight in New York. Empty and dark, but curiously alive.

You knew you were looking at part of the hopes and dreams of every kid with a ball glove in the sandlots of America. You were seeing it the way they would see it, the way you had read about it . . .

It really wasn't Sunday night—it was any year and any day you wanted to make it. The seats were not empty any more, because the Yankees were playing, and the seats were never empty when the Yankees played.

You could see Lefty Gomez, who never lost a game in 12 Series starts, hurling against the Giants in 1936. Standing there like a little boy, watching an airplane overhead, while the whole country hung on every pitch.

"Old 'Poosh-'em-Up' " Tony Lazzeri is at bat with the bases loaded against the Cardinals in 1926. And out of the Card bullpen shuffles Grover Cleveland Alexander, with a hangover that would stop a horse. And he strikes Tony out.

You see Lazzeri almost erase the memory of that one ten years later by hitting a home run against the Giants with the bases loaded, the second grand-slammer in Series records.

Frankie Crosettie is there at shortstop, and you hear him barking encouragement to Red Ruffing. The tall, indolent slugger from San Francisco is just beginning to establish himself as one of the great players of modern times. DiMaggio is there, too.

And Dickey, master mechanic of the catchers; patient little Miller Huggins; slender Herb Pannock; bullet-armed Bob Meusel; the tragic shadow of Lou Gehrig; fleet Earl Cooms; "Twinkletoes" George Selkirk; Marse Joe McCarthy; and Artie Fletcher, the greatest sign-burglar of them all.

Murderers' Row . . . the Bronx Bombers (four straight pennants and four straight world titles) . . . fabulously generous in dividing the spoils of victory.

There is another figure, too, bigger than all the rest. He's standing on match-stick legs, barrel torso crowding the plate, big bat waving before the explosion.

The roar of the crowd swells as he connects, and Babe Ruth is trotting slowly around the bases; there is never any hurry when Ruth connects.

And suddenly you know you are looking at Babe's home here in the twilight—the House That Ruth Built—and you have a little better answer to why Yankee Stadium is more than just an empty ballpark to a stranger.

But the man in the coveralls wouldn't understand. "There's nothing to see now," he had said.

There is, if you know how to look.

Doggerel, or versifying, was common on sports pages of those days. I think the practice was started by the great Grantland Rice, whose verses were a step up from doggerel. My efforts never attained Rice's heights, and I'm thankful this sort of thing went out of fashion.

Song of the Bleacherite

Seattle Times, April 14, 1947

You can talk about your hockey with its danger and its spills; you can write
in glowing tribute about football with its thrills.

To some the rapid cagers have their glories and their fame; and to some
the sport of boxing is the only thrilling game.

There are those who like their swimming, and it has a certain touch; there
are some who like their checkers (but at thinking, I'm not much).

If you've ever met a horseman who loves the Sport of Kings, he'll tell you
from the shoulder that the Gee-Gees are the things.

Ask a duffer in the clubhouse, and he'll tell you as a rule, that there's
nothing in the country that can beat "cow-pasture pool."

Let a fencer once get started on the virtues of the foil, and he'll keep you
there till midnight, giving out the gushing oil.

As for rowing, yes, we like it (the admission's always free); but let those
who want it have it—it looks like work to me!

The endurance tests of track and field are strictly on the square; and yet
you get a thrill just thinking of the vaulters in the air.

And even bowling has its fun, when the fat men toe the line; and snooker,
pool and billiards, they tell me all are fine.

The skiing crowd will thrill you, with their adjectives and raves about the
courage of a jumper on a pair of barrel-staves.

Every game is loved by some who cannot see the rest; and each will tell
you long and loud his pastime is the best.

To every man I give his taste, with some I will agree—but when spring is
in the ozone, there's only one for me.

Take your halfbacks and your jumpers and your goalies and your nags;
take your swimmers and your skiers and your human punching-bags.

Wrap 'em all up in a package, and I wouldn't trade you fair, for the thrill
of knowing spring is here—with baseball in the air!

The pennant race has started, and it's time to close up shop, for the annual
day they open, when the lid is off the top.

(Boss, I'm leaving early; in fact, I'm on my way; duty calls me home this
afternoon—Grandma's funeral is today.)

So you sit up in the bleachers, and the sun is shining down; rooting for
your favorites, and the glory of your town.

You razz the opposition, and you boo the lowly ump; and you second-
guess the players (and the manager's a chump!).

You munch upon a hot dog, and you wash it down with beer, while the
game slips through the innings, with the climax drawing near.
The score is close, the game is tight, and every movement counts; when
victory sweet, or dark defeat, depends on every bounce.
And here it is, the ninth is here, the home team's down a run; if we can
only make that tally . . . it's all we need—just one.
There's a bobble in the infield, and the bleachers stamp with joy, as our
slugger walks up to the plate—the hometown's fair-haired boy . . .
With the patrons yelling madly for a hit to tie the score, the slugger waves
his bludgeon and you hear the grandstand roar.
Now the pitcher toes the rubber, and the coaches bark their cry; the
fielders, tense, are waiting for a welcome outfield fly.
Then the crack of ball on wood, the runner digging in . . . a streak of white
across the sky . . . the pitcher's dark chagrin;
On and on it travels . . . up and on some more . . . growing smaller in the
distance . . . where only birds can soar;
The fielders back up to the wall, in helpless gesture there; and sadly, oh,
so sadly! they look up in the air;
And then you know it's over, and you know the game is won; a mighty
homer did it, and the slugger's work is done.
So I've only tried to tell you of the game I love the best; let me keep on
watching baseball, and you can have the rest.
Bowling, boxing, hunting, fishing—football, basketball and track; I've
seen 'em all come through the years, and to you I'll give 'em back.
Just let me sit up in the bleachers; say, boy, that's the thrill for me! When
the home team's on the rampage, and their bats are swinging free!

"Dr. Watson's Needle" made its debut on February 25, 1948, in The Times. Its origin lay in Sir Arthur Conan Doyle's stories about Sherlock Holmes and his bumbling, well-meaning colleague, Dr. Watson. I seemed to fit the role.

"Dr. Watson's Needle" Debuts

Seattle Times, February 25, 1948

THE CAUSE OF CLEAN SPORT WAS DONE NO SERVICE by that episode in Tacoma the other day—the one where the pinball-machine player tossed a bartender through a plate-glass window. Dispatches relate how the player was winning too consistently to suit the barkeep, who had been studying his technique and decided that use of a metal wire to run up scores was a flagrant violation of the rules.

The upshot of the thing found the pinball player throwing the bartender through a window, although he was later brought to heel by the police (Tacoma's finest). In the athlete's possessions were an 18-inch steel wire, a small hand drill and $8.50 in nickels.

This sort of thing hurts the game. I deplore it as a convert to the Cause of Clean Sport.

Whither are we drifting? Baseball was years getting over the Black Sox scandal; pro football suffered immensely from the Hapes-Filchock case; boxing may never recover from the Graziano affair. Has commercialism foundered the sport of pinballing?

It's true that pinballing is a game for a tiny few professional practitioners these days. The majority of players are in over their heads. But beating pinball games still is a live art, and the true champions should be respected.

Aside from whatever pleasures this Tacoma player might get from lofting bartenders through windows, he should have thought of the sport. Drills and steel wires!

It has been many years since your correspondent felt the clean thrill of snapping the plunger to send a skillfully hit ball into the 1,000-hole.

I recall (with a tear) the soda refectory in West Seattle, operated by a kindly merchant, name of Rothschild. Those were the days of simple pinball games, when a man's skill counted for something. The payoffs were in trade—double-dip marshmallow sundaes, chocolate shakes, hard ice-cream and tutti-frutti.

We were true amateurs. We predated the coming of the complicated, multicolored, automatic, blinker-lighted, streamlined nickel-grabbers of today. Our battles against The Machine were duels of mutual trust—they had no "tilt" gadgets then.

The rewards were never high in The House of Rothschild, but the scores were within easy reach, and you got a good run for your nickel. I always took tutti-frutti.

Eventually the modern "skill" games got us. The mechanized boards with their involved patterns and trappings . . . They aren't skill games at all, but contests of blind chance against prohibitive odds. But we left our mark for a few surviving experts to follow.

We developed the all-important "body-English"; we improved the art of kibitzing (give only well-meant advice; don't destroy the player's concentration; don't lean on the board; always root against the machine).

We pioneered the "snap-shot" and the "slip-shot" and the lost art of the "let-go" shot. We devised delicate shades of "slapping" and "pounding" and "jiggling" to steer an errant marble into the high-score holes and out of the "gutter."

Maybe I understand that man in Tacoma a little better than the cops. Perhaps he wouldn't surrender, as we did, to The Machine. I'm not defending him, for his act did a great disservice to the Cause of Clean Sport.

We amateurs quit gracefully. We didn't resort to hand drills or steel wires to beat the modern contraptions.

Well, maybe once in a while, before those suspicious "tilt" gadgets came along, we sort of jiggled the board beyond the accepted rules of conduct, and it's been on my conscience ever since.

If Mr. Rothschild is reading this, I hope he understands.

The gang that hung around that drugstore has broken up now, Mr. Rothschild. Some of us went to school; some went to work; some became sportswriters, and others made money.

And we miss those days of the simple boards and easy scores, and tell me, Mr. Rothschild, do you still have tutti-frutti?

▼

I had been a featurist, a columnist and a baseball writer at The Times for four years. I became a full-time columnist, Dr. Watson, three or four a week, because I contracted polio. I was in the isolation ward at Harborview Hospital for three weeks and could easily have croaked or been irreparably maimed. When I got out, I remembered Hemingway's famous line in *To Have and Have Not*, in which Harry, the smuggler, said, "God takes care of rummies." I wasn't a rummy, but God, or his designated hitter, took mercy. Because the disease was so debilitating, I didn't have the strength to move about much, so they told me, "Work in the office and use the phone; just do columns by calling up people."

Then out of the blue, in the winter of 1950, came this sharp-witted man named Lee Ettelson. Lee was a wunderkind for the Hearst newspaper chain, and he set about hiring me to work for

The Post Intelligencer. It was an agonizing decision because I liked The Times and the people who ran it, plus there was always that apprehension that the Hearstian hierarchy (maybe the Old Man himself) might decide that my talents were more suited to one of the empire's Mexican tin mines.

But I went. The P-I, under Ettelson, featured me on its front pages for days—pictures of me, or my family; an autobiographical article; altogether a grotesque Barnumesque build-up. But somehow it all worked, and I stayed for 33 years.

A Reluctant Autobiography

Seattle Post-Intelligencer, January 30, 1950

RE THE REQUEST FOR A SYNOPSIS OF MY LIFE, up to and including this morning, the following is offered as a short summary, with almost no regrets:

As a small child, I was born hard by the Duwamish mud flats on November 22, 1918, and immediately struggled through a phase of diaperism into a stage known, roughly, as adolescence. My family has been of no help in compiling details of this latter stage, possibly because they want to forget the whole thing.

My school years were marked by a trail of broken and defeated English teachers and one high school principal who developed a nervous "tic" as the result of our association. The last I heard he was under the care of a psychiatrist. Prognosis: doubtful.

About 1934 I began an assault on professional baseball which fell somewhat short of beating Mickey Cochrane out of a job. My failure in baseball can be traced to two deep mysteries of the game—the fastball and the curveball.

I stayed with the Seattle Rainiers long enough to learn the bunt sign and drink two cups of coffee. Bill Skiff, the manager, released me in 1943.

"Kid," he said, "you have a great future. Offhand, I cannot imagine where it might be, but I'm sure you have a great future. Drop back and see us sometime."

In the realm of higher education, I attended the University of Washington, taking such subjects as literature, psychology, history, anthropology, economics, sociology, philosophy and Bulgarian folk dancing. I flunked every physical education course I ever took.

I got into the newspaper business because of its lavish salaries. After a brief apprenticeship at the old Seattle Star, I was raised to a cool $28 a week. That kind of money doesn't grow on bushes.

But enough of all this. The "I" key on this typewriter is getting overworked.

Shake hands with a guy who is happy to be here.

It was Groundhog Day when I first poked my head above ground at The P-I. All the hoopla was over. It was time to go to work. The boys in the legal department, in a bow to the Times' copyright, decreed a change. The column title was altered from The Times' "Dr. Watson's Needle" to "Quick Watson, The Needle," a reference to Sherlock Holmes' addiction to cocaine shots. We were more innocent, or ignorant, then.

"Quick Watson, The Needle" Debuts
Seattle Post-Intelligencer, February 2, 1950

IT DEVELOPS THAT THE SEATTLE POST-INTELLIGENCER has plowed a lot of new ground in the field of photography lately, recording the social, professional and mating habits of one (1) sportswriter, namely me.

There was Watson reading a paper; there was Watson looking thoughtful (a rare triumph of graphic art); there was Watson taking a stroll; and there was Watson surrounded by his three beautiful income-tax deductions.

"There is one picture missing," observed a nearby cynic. "When do we get a look at Watson doing some work around here?"

In addition to the pictorial introduction, considerable prose got written about your correspondent. In sum total it informed P-I readers that Watson's stuff would put them in the aisles . . . possibly in a stampede for the door to obtain fresh air.

I do not recall exactly how I got here. It had to do with a classified ad, trying to sell my stuffed duckbill platypus (native of Tasmania). Never mind how I got the duckbill platypus. A man's personal life is his own.

"Look," said the girl at the classified counter, "why don't you just unload this what-is-it on the sports department? Nothing looks out of place up there."

That sounded reasonable. In fact, a sports personality came as close as anybody to buying my pet platypus. His name was Casey Stengel (native of California), and we had a deal cooked up where Stengel got the platypus and I got Phil Rizzuto, but negotiations broke down at closing hour.

The P-I Building holds many strange and beautiful creatures. The first fellow I bumped into said his name was Durling, an old standby of the organization.

"Do you know," stated Mr. Durling, "that there are more green-eyed honey-blondes with six children in Amarillo, Tex., then there are in Toledo, O.? I will check our Horses and Women Department on this. Who invented the dropkick?"

"Abraham Lincoln."

"Right. Have a stogie."

I stumbled over the next fellow, who also is an old P-I standby. He was writhing angrily on the floor, a copy of *My Day* clutched in his fingers, frantically chewing on the fat of a table leg. Said his name was Pegler, whoever that is.

A man came charging down the hall with a marketbasket under one arm and a Rhode Island Red under the other.

"Know how many eggs I collected today?" he demanded. "Six!"

Another old P-I standby was standing by in the hallway, leaning on a broom. He was the janitor.

"Where is the sports department?" inquired your correspondent.

"Sports department?" he replied, puzzled. "Didn't know we had one."

Well, what with one thing and another, I arrived at the sports department to be greeted by a man named Brougham (native of Seattle) who, as I understand it, is running a sort of guest column until the regular sports editor returns from vacation.

"Who were the Four Horsemen?" he demanded, looking up from his typewriter.

"Layden, Nagurski, Stuhldreher and Jim Thorpe," I replied, quick as a flash.

"Well, whattya know!" said Mr. Brougham, happily. "Now then. Who was the greatest ballplayer—Babe Ruth or Red Grange?"

"Well," I replied cautiously, "personally, I give the duke to Ruth, but that's only one man's opinion."

"Perhaps you are right," agreed Mr. Brougham, thoughtfully. "One thing more—how many gymnasiums in Seattle?"

"Not enough," replied your correspondent.

"That does it!" cried Mr. Brougham, springing to his feet. "Welcome to the P-I sports staff. Your future is assured. You can start right now by changing all the typewriter ribbons. Good luck."

By the way—would anybody like to buy a stuffed duckbill platypus?

By now I had begun to accumulate stories that could be fashioned into columns. You do this by staying up late, not drinking too much and scribbling notes later.

Babe Ruth

Seattle Post-Intelligencer, February 7, 1950

WITH ALL BUT A FEW SCATTERED PRECINCTS reporting, they elected the Babe as baseball's outstanding player of the half-century. Well, that figured. His plurality left enough spare votes to win him a seat in Congress, which is all right, too—if he were alive to take it—because the Babe was never one to pass up a few laughs or a warm debate.

Ty Cobb was second in the sportswriters' voting. He always has been second, a fact which he admitted, in a grudging special sort of way when he managed Detroit. His pitchers were said to have orders never to "knock down" Ruth, no matter how much devastation the Ruth bat was causing the Tigers.

"Leave him alone," Cobb would growl. "Don't let nothin' happen to him. He's the guy that's making money for the rest of us."

And he was, too. Every time Ruth jacked a raise out of Colonel Ruppert, lesser wages went up in proportion.

Ballplayers, many of whom worship money only short of holding services at the U. S. Mint, have a kindly regard for Ruth, and they, as much as anybody, have contributed to the Ruth legend. Wherever ballplayers gather to talk baseball (and what else do they talk about?), his name inevitably gets into the conversation. I have never seen this to fail.

There is a slight risk in tossing a few Ruth stories out and saying they have never been printed before. That is another factor of the Ruth legend, but a minor one. But I have never seen the one Dutch Reuther tells, which is as good as most Ruth stories, and more printable.

Reuther, the old Seattle manager, now a scout for the Giants, was one of the few men who matched Ruth's appetites, solid and liquid. Naturally, they became fast friends.

It was one of those spring exhibition tours, involving Cincinnati and the Yankees. Reuther, then with Cincinnati, and Ruth were seeing a lot of each other. One night, over a bottle of 7-Up, or something, they cooked up a deal.

"Look," said Mr. Reuther. "In tomorrow's game, I'll be pitching against you. If the score isn't close, or . . . by the way, how far can you hit a baseball?"

"I'll be blank-blank if I know," answered Ruth.

"Let's find out," suggested Reuther. "When you see me tip my cap, you get set. Because I am going to groove one for you. I'll throw my best shot right down the gut. You see how far you can hit it."

Everything went fine until cap-tipping time. Mr. Reuther tipped his fedora. Mr. Ruth got ready. The ball arrived as advertised—right down the middle. The only hitch that developed came when Ruth drove it back through the pitcher's box like the bullet out of a .30-.30, hitting Mr. Reuther on the thigh.

Dutch couldn't walk for three weeks.

Ruth was playing against the Giants in an exhibition series in 1933, and a young man named Paul Richards was doing the catching against him. Pitching to Richards was a Giant recruit whose name somehow gets lost for the moment. It was a 1–1 ball game into the ninth, and, in the classic manner, Ruth sent everybody home on schedule by hitting one just over the Connecticut border.

The two teams came off the field. Ruth walked slightly ahead of Richards, who was close beside the angry young pitcher.

"That is the last one that big clown will ever hit off me," muttered the youngster.

Ruth turned and grinned. "Why? . . . Where you going, son?" he said, pleasantly.

The Ruth legend includes poignant stories—all of them pretty well documented by photographers—of the Babe arriving through snow-storms to take his place at hospital bedsides. By choice or not, Ruth seldom made his sick calls unaccompanied by cameramen.

It is a fair country cab ride from New York's Commodore Hotel to Yankee Stadium. Jo Jo White, the young Detroit outfielder, was hailed by the Babe. "Come on, kid," he said, "ride with me and save yourself a couple of bucks."

The two got out of the cab at Yankee Stadium. It was long before game-time, which may have explained the early arrival of a fellow in a wheelchair, a tragic spastic paralysis case, who perhaps wanted to avoid being jostled by the crowds.

As though this were a common occurrence, Ruth got behind the wheelchair and guided it through the players' entrance, on down the ramp to the Yankee dressing room. Jo Jo went about his business.

"Then I got curious," relates White. "I went back over by the Yankee clubhouse. The door was open. I looked in. There was just the Babe and this crippled fellow, having a real nice talk. The Babe had given him a brand new autographed glove and one of his hats. That's all there is to it, but it's the best Ruth story I know."

There were no photographers present.

Baseball was never enough, was it? Emil Sick, the owner of the Rainiers, had taken his team to Palm Springs for spring training, and, within days, I had an entire town of enraged merchants on my neck for suggesting that their oasis was a tad pricey. To avoid the desert equivalent of tar-and-feathers—probably involving a cactus—I wrote a half-apology and lived to indulge myself in many more spring-training expeditions.

Pricey Palm Springs

Seattle Post-Intelligencer, February 27, 1950

PALM SPRINGS — There are more Cadillacs and swimming pools per capita in Palm Springs than in any city in the United States. Is there a better way to size up a town's fiscal standing?

You have heard of "floating populations" . . . Well, the population of Palm Springs jumps from 7,300 in August to over 22,000 in January. Who are the floaters? They are people with Cadillacs who come here from Seattle and other arctic wastelands to swim in the swimming pools.

Take a short walk down the town's main street, Palm Canyon Drive, and you will see license plates from virtually every state in the union. From October 1 to May 15 is a period called "the season" by local residents.

I do not mean to imply that Palm Springs natives consider this period open season on tourists, but then, I have never heard of a bag limit, either. A restaurant will serve you some pretty good lamb chops in this town for around $4.75 a pair, and if you drop in for a haircut, the damage is only $2.25.

If you are a light sleeper, you might wake up with the horrible realization of what you are paying for your bed. Six to 12 bucks is a fair stipend for a night's lodging, $15 to $25 for a studio apartment; $25 per slumber is not an unusual figure, but then, of course, you can always stay at the Racquet Club for a $40 to $75 tab every 24 hours.

Permanent Palm Springs residents do not like to have these figures kicked around in public, on the theory that they may scare away a millionaire or two, so keep this under your hat. Let the millionaires look out for themselves.

A long time ago, when Cecil B. deMille was making *The Ten Commandments*, he took a company of 1,300 extras up north of Los Angeles on location. On one side of the road were the women, on the other side the men. At 5:30 a.m., they were roused from their slumbers by a bugle. The bugle was blown by the current mayor of Palm Springs, Charles Farrell.

Mr. Farrell later became a movie actor himself, reaching the pinnacle of public adulation in a thing called *Seventh Heaven*, with Janet Gaynor. Later on, talking pictures came in, and Charley Farrell went out. He had a high-pitched, almost squeaky, voice.

Farrell is no "honorary" mayor. He takes an active part in community affairs, attends all council meetings, kisses the right number of infants and runs his town like La Guardia ran New York. He was one of the moving spirits which got a million-dollar bond issue floated, part of which built a ballpark for the Seattle Rainiers.

Palm Springs nestles at the base of Mount San Jacinto, a 10,800-foot hill that shades some parts of the city in the late afternoons. There are times when this town needs shade—summer temperatures hit 118 degrees. This is the time of year when millionaires flee for cooler weather and the natives batten down the hatches.

The town's resort hotels, motels and villas are closed tight. Wrapping paper is taped over the windows and buckets of water are placed in rooms to create moisture, so the extreme heat won't crack the walls. Lawns are left to burn out.

When September comes, lawns are replanted. In three days the grass comes up; in 10 days you have to mow it.

We mentioned Mount San Jacinto. The latest plan is to construct a tramway (huge cable, with basket attached) from Palm Springs to the top of the mountain. During the winter months, you can change from your bathing suit into your ski clothes, board the tramway, and in 15 minutes you will be skiing in a winter paradise.

You want to live here? You can buy a lot for anywhere from $1,300 (near the ballpark) to $15,000, near the mountain. No house on the lot. If you want a house, the grunt comes to about $25,000—if you want a swimming pool.

Earl Sheely, house dick of the Rainier bankroll, estimates that this little training journey will set the club back $20,000, about a third more than usual.

But in return for the expense, a visitor to Palm Springs is treated to the finest winter weather on the face of the earth. This piece is being written at 8 o'clock in the evening of Feb. 25, and a garden party is being held outside my cabin door.

Which reminds me, it is growing rather late and I haven't dipped a toe in the pool yet today.

▼

Palm Springs Strikes Back

Seattle Post-Intelligencer, March 9, 1950

PALM SPRINGS — The seven members of the city council met the other day to discuss the disposal of garbage, which turned out to be your correspondent. Seven methods were suggested, all of which brought a happy gleam to the eyes of Palm Springs merchants.

"This Watson, this . . . this creature . . . " suggested one councilman, "why don't we run over him with a Cadillac?"

"Let's drown him in the Racquet Club pool," said another.

"Hang him."

"He said we had $4.75 lamb chops," was a fourth solution. "He should have some—garnished with cyanide."

"I'm for shooting," said a fifth.

"He said we had $2.25 haircuts," said still another councilman (a barber). "Let me give him one—with a saw."

"I have a better solution," said the seventh member of the council, a noted sadist. "Make him read his own column. That would kill anybody."

It is easy to see that your correspondent is considered a worse calamity than rain in Palm Springs. I do not know who has been taking potshots at Mickey Cohen, the state's No. 1 clay pigeon, but I'll bet Cohen said something about the town's high prices.

Since an economic report on Palm Springs appeared in this space last week, I have been informed of the following facts: Haircuts do not cost $2.25; they cost $1.25. Rooms at the Racquet Club do not sell for $40 to $75 per night; the damage is only $12 to $18. Charles Farrell, the mayor, did not leave the movies when talkies came in; he made 40 talking pictures. Lamb chops do not go for $4.75 a pair (even with cyanide).

You can buy a lot here for less than $1,300 and almost never for

$15,000. A pretty good house can be had for $10,950, a house with very low mileage. And you don't have to pay $25 a night for a place to sleep—but you can do it in a pinch.

That is a powerful lot of corrections I have set down here. Do they atone for my crimes? Well, partly.

Mr. Farrell, the mayor, a peace-loving man who doesn't care to have a lynching on his hands, drew your agent aside for a fatherly talk.

"Take my advice, kid," said Mr. Farrell, "stay out of the barbershops in this town. Those boys use razors."

It is time for another correction. Mr. Farrell does not have a high-pitched, squeaky voice. He has a moderately tuned set of vocal chords, guaranteed not to rasp or go flat, a voice which crooned sweet nothings into the ear of Janet Gaynor in *Seventh Heaven* and *Sunny Side Up*, and enough smash hits to make him the Van Johnson of his day.

How long ago was his day? Caution is the keynote here. Farrell is the youngest former actor of his age in history.

Mr. Farrell and I drove out to the Racquet Club for a look around, and it is amazing how low the prices really are. The refreshments didn't cost a cent, possibly because he owns the place.

"Look," said Mr. Farrell, "why don't you walk around town and write a piece about the things which don't cost much? All the radio guys used to make jokes about our town—how expensive it was. We finally showed them the error of their ways. Take a look around."

Friend, it was a revelation. Prices here compare favorably with any place in the country. You can buy a Cosmopolitan Magazine for 35 cents, parking meters are a nickel, milk shakes come to 20 cents, a shoe shine is a quarter, and stamps can be had for three cents. There is no charge whatever for air, water and advice, and where else can you get bargains like that?

The Palm Springs Chambers of Commerce, junior and senior, threw a dinner (no charge) for the Seattle Rainiers. Your correspondent was presented with a large syringe, complete with needle, and a suggestive label on the outside. It said: "Facts."

"Please return the needle," said Mr. Farrell, "we have to give it back to the veterinary."

Is the veterinary expensive in Palm Springs? Good Heavens, NO! You can get a horse inoculated for practically nothing.

asey Stengel was prob- ably the most intelligent man I ever met while covering baseball. Forget the double-talk and all such Stengel-isms. He was as educational as he was funny. When Casey was managing the Oakland club in the Pacific Coast League, I would hang around after games at Sicks' Stadium and drive him back to his hotel just so I could enjoy his talk, which was straight-forward in those days. Later, after he was manag- ing the Yankees, on two occa- sions I found myself as his audience of one while he went into his striding, gesticulating monologues. The first time was in 1948, after the Yankees had won the World Series; I encoun- tered him in the lobby of the Biltmore Hotel in Los Angeles. Then, in the 1950s, he came to Seattle for a banquet, and I ended up in his hotel room listening until nearly dawn. By then, as a way of being coopera- tive with the press but avoiding saying anything the sportswriters could understand that would get him in trouble, he had mastered his celebrated double-talk. That night, deep into some story about how the Yankees had treated him at contract time, he suddenly broke off the double- talk and asked me, "You don't know what I'm talking about, do you?" I said something like, "Well, I guess I do." He grinned and resumed his act, while I remained entranced, well aware that I was in the presence of genius, and history. All you had to do to set Casey off was say, "Hello, Casey." I wrote dozens of pieces about him. I'm still grateful.

Casey Stengel

Seattle Post-Intelligencer, May 8, 1952

THERE IS A SPECIAL, POIGNANT SCENE which takes place in almost any ball game, no matter who wins. I refer to a dramatic point of interest when the manager, his patience used up, comes out to relieve a staggering pitcher of his duties.

You know how it goes. The manager comes out, palms up, to receive the ball. The pitcher (with reluctance) forks it over. Infielders, trapped in the shooting gallery, wave reassurance to their loved ones as the reliever, his connecting rod heated up, comes in to stop the carnage.

The pitcher then trudges to the showers, where his only hazard is a stray piece of soap on the floor.

Rogers Hornsby, a strong-minded manager, brought a variation to this scene by playing a stationary role. He refused to leave the dugout. Hornsby is an ambidextrous derricker. With his left, or bullpen arm, he waves the new man in; with his right, or his "that's all" arm, he hooks the incumbent to safety. Mr. Hornsby's method precludes tender pats on the back, or differences of opinion between himself and the pitcher. Or does it?

"What if the pitcher won't come out?" asked Mr. Casey Stengel, when the question was put to him. "What does Hornsby do then, hey?"

Man and boy, Mr. Stengel has relieved a lot of pitchers in his time, when he was managing such defenseless doormats as the Boston Braves and the Brooklyn Dodgers of 15–20 years ago.

Lately, of course, as a dignified mastermind of world champions, Casey has become associated with people like Raschi, Reynolds and Lopat, who stick around for nine innings. But when he was managing Brooklyn, Mr. Stengel made reference to Walter (Boom-Boom) Beck, a first cousin to almost all enemy batters. Mr. Beck pitched, briefly, on a Dodger club that also included the reasonably immortal Hack Wilson, when the barrel-type slugger was finishing his career.

"Boom-Boom had a 4–0 lead, by what combination of miracles I will never know," related Mr. Stengel. "Wilson is playing left field for me. It is a hot day, and Wilson is sweating off a load of beer he took on the night before."

To hear Mr. Stengel tell it, Boom-Boom's lead ranked second only to sitting on an active volcano for sheer uncertainty. Infielders brought down line drives that threatened to drag them to death; outfielders scaled new heights in the legalized robbery of making catches. Not for nothing did they call Mr. Beck "Boom-Boom." The average fan could duck out for a short beer while his fastball was traveling to the plate.

By the seventh inning, those line drives were going through. With his 4–0 lead disappearing to no lead at all, Mr. Stengel trudged to the mound to officiate at the coronation of a new pitcher.

"Gimme the ball," said Casey.

"No," said Mr. Beck, firmly.

"Look," said Casey. "You done well up to now, but that 4–0 lead you had—it's gone. Now just gimme the ball and we will bring anoth—"

"No," said Mr. Beck, with dignity. "I'll just pitch to a couple more hitters and you'll see I still got my stuff."

"Stuff?" said Mr. Stengel, bitterly. "Listen, you gimme the ball right now, or I will separate you from it with a bat."

Naturally, this seminar took a little time, and Mr. Hack Wilson, glad of a chance to catch his breath, kneeled down in left field to brood over his misspent evening at the beer tap. He rested his head on his arms and waited for the conference to end.

"I said," repeated Mr. Stengel, "give me the ball before the company cancels its policy on my infielders."

"All right," replied Mr. Beck, the picture of outraged dignity, "here's the ball."

Instead of handing it to his manager, Boom-Boom wheeled and threw it against the left-field fence before stalking off the diamond. The ball landed against a tin sign in left field with a clatter that could be heard in the Bronx. Mr. Wilson, hearing this familiar sound, awakened suddenly from his slumber, turned around in time to see the ball bounding off the fence. He retrieved it rapidly, whirled and made a perfect throw to third, where previous experience with Brooklyn pitching told him the runner would arrive. It was an extremely interesting sight—even for Flatbush.

Back in the dugout, Boom-Boom was kicking a water bucket in high dudgeon.

"Stop kicking that bucket," ordered Mr. Stengel.

"Why?" sneered Boom-Boom. "You afraid I'll break it?"

"No," said Mr. Stengel. "I'm afraid you'll break your foot, and then I can't sell you."

In other days, the early 1950s, when I pursued notoriety and solvency with a used typewriter and an unused brain, there was always a fear of failing. I had this recurring notion that someone—an authority figure—would come up to me and say, "Watson, you just haven't got it. The way it was with you in baseball—good field, no hit. The charade is over. You just can't make a living by putting words on paper." Failure would mean going back to working on the docks, to those awful, bone-chilling mornings, 7 a.m., on Pier 54, loading or unloading ships, the damp, cruel wind coming from the southwest—how I had dreaded those mornings.

So I worked very hard at newspapering, getting every cliché, every sports bromide exactly right, no matter how numbing the repetition. Thinking there might be wealth in this racket someday, I enrolled in a class at the UW on how to write fiction. In those days, there was a "formula" for writing commercial short stories. They actually taught it at the university. The formula said, in effect, that you had to have a likable, believable hero and preferably a romance, too, and your hero had to overcome a problem, or an obstacle, that was lousing up his life. There was more to it than that, of course, but that was the substance of those formula stories—pluck, perseverance, love conquers all, et cetera and et cetera.

Because I worked nights at The P-I, I showed up at 9 a.m. at Bob Mansfield's class on the UW campus. I don't remember whether Mansfield was a full professor, but he was a full human being and all that implies. His lovely wife, Norma, was herself a star fiction writer in the high-paying "slick" magazines of the time. The "formula," it was said, was first examined, broken down and refined by a remarkable UW English professor named George Savage, who finished his distinguished academic career at UCLA. Savage passed on his course to other UW teachers, particularly Mansfield and Bill Worden, himself a great writing star at

The Saturday Evening Post. Mansfield and Worden taught both fiction and nonfiction. I wanted fiction—that's where the money was, the glory and the dream.

How can I describe the old, for-real, Saturday Evening Post? It has been called "the gospel of American-style living," and indeed it was. It was aimed at the heart of Middle America. The Norman Rockwell covers alone put the term "Americana" in our language. The old Post extolled American values the way no other magazine, Reader's Digest possibly excepted, ever did.

For one thing, it was founded by that splendid gentleman, Ben Franklin himself, in 1728. It was published in Independence Square, Philadelphia, and at its zenith more than six million sound, solid, patriotic Americans read it.

Each weekly issue averaged four to six short stories, at least seven full-length articles, one "novelette" and two serials. Here you found Clarence Budington Kelland and his legendary "Scattergood Baines" character. The Post featured C. S. Forester's "Horatio Hornblower" and Doug Welch's famous "Mr. Digby" stories. It was Welch who urged me on in fiction writing, and it was Welch, my colleague at The P-I, who persuaded his own agent, Carl Brandt, to take me on.

In the old Saturday Evening Post, you also found the byline of Norman Reilly Raines, the creator of "Tugboat Annie," a character based on Thea Foss, founder of the Foss Tugboat Company on Puget Sound. As noted, Seattle's Bill Worden was one of the Post's stars—and I remember thinking that his short story, "Speak to Me of the Black Glass Mountain," was one of the greatest I'd ever read. And Pete Martin wrote his famous profiles of celebrities ("I Call on Lucy and Desi," among others). The great single cartoon panel, "Hazel," the sardonic domestic, even rated a spot in the table of contents. The Post paid big prices for memoirs (Gen. Eisenhower, Whittaker Chambers, Bing Crosby, et al.) and no less of a giant than Somerset Maugham wrote for The Post, because the dough was there.

This is the league I would break into. This was the league that would remove all bad dreams of the longshoring art, freeing me of that tiny touch of fear when I was called into some editor's office. If others can do it, why not me?

So I turned in my first short story for Bob Mansfield's class in the winter of 1954. Bob used a "class critique" method; every-body had to read everybody else's story. Then the stories were discussed, chewed over, evaluated. When my turn came, nobody said anything. It was tentatively titled, "Ride The Big Horse," and one of my classmates thought it sounded like a popular movie of that time, *Ride the Pink Horse.* Mansfield shook his head. "Never mind the title," he said. "Editors itch to change titles." And then he said: "I think you'd better get this off to Carl Brandt right away."

A few days later, I arrived in New York to cover the old Pacific Coast League winter meetings. I was staying in the Biltmore Hotel. The phone in my room rang. "This is Carl Brandt," the voice said, "I just sold your story to The Saturday Evening Post for $800. That's for a first-time writer. You'll get more later."

And then Brandt said: "I want you to get on a train tomorrow and go to Philadelphia. I want you to meet Bob Fuoss. He's the managing editor. Then I want you to meet Ben Hibbs, he's the big man down there."

One short story, one sale. Eight hundred dollars! How long had this been going on? And tomorrow I was entering the Temple of Heaven! I had struck it rich in the Klondike itself.

I was $800 rich; I had New York's top literary agent; I had

more ideas for stories. It was on this euphoric tide that I discovered Brooks Brothers, and I also discovered a half-dozen bars with my sportswriting buddies, with whom I celebrated my new-found source of wealth. Everything's on me, boys, I'm a regular in The Saturday Evening Post. They know me down there.

I met Ben Hibbs, a strong, almost god-like presence. I walked through the sacred portals of The Saturday Evening Post, Independence Square, Philadelphia. Here I found those huge, almost intimidating Norman Rockwell originals—these originals today must be worth millions. In Ben Hibbs's office, other editors and plenipotentiaries came to shake my hand—the whiz kid from Seattle, who wastes his time dictating baseball stories from Sicks' Stadium. I was overcome by the majesty of it all; at any moment, I expected Ben Franklin himself to emerge from the men's room.

That was the high point.

Try as I might—try as I did—that was it. The only short story I ever sold. At first, the rejection letters were lengthy and kind. Carl Brandt kept me among his stable of famous craftsmen, but all the nice letters added up to one sentence: "Nice try, anyway." Later, the rejection letters became shorter, even somewhat curt. It didn't take a building to fall on me, just a few of those rejection bricks smashing into my ego: my fiction-writing career was over a moment after it began; I was a one-day wonder.

As for my only published piece of fiction, Bob Mansfield had been right: the editors had changed the title. It was now called, "The Quarterback Who Couldn't Take It." My hero was a nice guy—the formula, remember—named Joe Mitchell. He was actually a composite of several guys I had known in college: a kid who was a bit cocky but not quite sure of himself, a kid who needed to do some growing up, a kid of good instincts but a bad tendency to evade reality. The coach in the story, Risberg, was really a combination of two people I knew well: Jimmy Phelan, the great Husky coach, and Johnny Cherberg, who himself coached the Huskies and who would later become the state's lieutenant governor. The girl Joe loved was also a composite, but I think she came closest to being the one I married.

The Quarterback Who Couldn't Take It
Saturday Evening Post, September 25, 1954

HE WATCHED THE PLAY DEVELOP INTO A PASS PATTERN. The two State ends raced deep and hooked, while the halfbacks went down and out, flaring toward opposite sidelines to spread the Tech defenders. Tech linemen poured through, clawing and grabbing, trying to get at Russell Palmer, the State passer, who danced uneasily behind his protective cup of blockers. Palmer set himself to pass and got it off—wide and too low for Yeager, the State end. Yeager dived and missed. He grabbed a handful of grass as he got up, tossing it away in a full-blown gesture of disgust.

Joe Mitchell smiled—that one had turned out bad. Sitting high in the stadium, Joe Mitchell pulled his coat tighter against the sharp October air and wished that he could be in the huddle to hear what Yeager was saying.

He's crabbing Palmer, Joe thought. *Like he did me. But I'm not there any more. How do you like it, Yeager!*

Enjoying himself, Joe Mitchell almost forgot the girl next to him. He turned and grinned. The collar of her coat was high against her cheeks. She wore a State corsage which Joe had bought; Kathy Miller was a sight to see, even when she frowned. She was frowning now.

"Stop worrying," he said. "They'll win."

She held up two crossed fingers. " 'They,' Joe?"

He laughed easily. "That's what I said." He watched a substitute get off the State bench and trot into the game. "See? Risberg knows. He sent the word along to tell Palmer to stay on the ground. State can run against this club."

Palmer followed orders well. He sent State's backs, young men of excellent training and solid conformation, stomping through the Tech line, which bent and cracked. State scored in seven plays and Brewster, the halfback, converted to make it 7-0. A Tech fumble late in the game opened the door again, through which Brewster slammed for a second touchdown. Watching Yeager trudge off the field at the end, Joe Mitchell thought, *He wishes he had me back, the jerk. Well, he can have anything else he wants, but he can't have me.*

They sat in the waffle shop on the avenue near the campus, in the back booth. The place was full of State students, some with gold-and-blue rooters' caps; the atmosphere was crowded with football talk and a warm, Saturday-night feeling. Joe broke a straw and make the letter K in front of the girl.

"K is for Kathy," he said. "When we're married I'll buy you a pearl-handled grocery cart. In fact, I'll—Hey, what's wrong?"

Nothing," she said. "Let's take a walk."

They crowded past the students, three-deep before the counter, and one of them turned to Joe and said, "Mitchell, how did you like Palmer today?" Joe knew it was a dig, but he refused to be irritated.

"Great," Joe Mitchell said. "Simply great. The game was great. The team was great. Even Yeager was—" Joe Mitchell suddenly saw Chris Yeager coming in the door, big and block-shouldered, looking at him intently, but with no expression. Joe finished the sentence, "Great." He took Kathy Miller by the arm and they went out, walking down the avenue.

"A pearl-handled grocery cart," he was saying brightly, "with direction indicator and back-up lights."

"Joe?"

"Present."

"Why did you quit the team? What are you trying to prove?"

"I'm trying to prove that football is a game that little boys can play," he said. "I am a middle-aged senior, going on twenty-four. A time for serious thinking. They say the outside world is full of pitfalls for the ignorant. Let's—"

"Stop it." The anger was soft in her voice.

They moved along in silence. Joe felt her withdraw and wondered to himself, *How much does she know?* He didn't care about the rest—about Risberg, or Brewster, or what people might be saying. But he cared about Kathy, who saw through his glibness, and saw, perhaps, the fester of his bitterness. Suddenly he was angry too.

This was something Kathy couldn't understand—a private thing, and full of hate. How long ago? Two years, when they were sophomores on a practice field, when Yeager torpedoed in on Palmer's blind side. Joe remembered watching Palmer, set to pass, and the large, hurtling figure of the end who used his elbows carelessly and free. Yeager came up hard across Palmer's face and the kid flipped over sideways, falling on his elbow. Joe remembered feeling sick as he bent over the rolling figure on the ground.

"It's a tough game." There was nothing, no sign of regret in Yeager's voice. Joe looked up at the broad, rather flat face, and saw the faint, thin line of a smile. Joe didn't like his eyes. Joe didn't like any of him.

"This kid's hurt," he said. "You didn't have to—"

"He's hurt," Yeager agreed. "Nobody sent for him. Watch yourself, Mitchell; you might be next."

That was the start of it, Joe remembered. He felt a chill, a flicker of anger and contempt for one possessed of senseless cruelty. Joe visited Palmer in the hospital, where they tried to joke about the strange contraption that held a separated shoulder in the proper place for healing. Palmer's arm was never quite the same. Joe remembered, when Russ came back a year later, that the smooth overhand motion was gone; he threw his passes sidearm.

"If I ever get in a game," Palmer had said to Joe, "do me a favor, will you? Gimme the loan of your arm."

Joe's dislike for Yeager turned into a contest of hatred. He tortured the big man with tiny digs and gentle barbs, never moving quite beyond the line that led to blows. Yeager, as subtle as a sack of cement, tried to hit back; then cultivated a deep and sullen silence. They made a strange alliance on Saturdays. Joe's undoubted skill in passing blended well with Yeager's gift for shaking loose in a broken field. Then, in the Southern game this year, it happened.

Joe poked his head into the huddle, just like any other time, and called the deep pass to Yeager. Joe faked the handoff to Brewster and danced back, sighting Yeager, wild and loose in the secondary, breaking for the south sideline. Joe set himself to throw. He caught a flash of red jersey, the Southern tackle, coming hard on his blind side, just as he got the pass away.

The sky was near, yet far away, then dark and light, then full of stars. He felt nauseated. He recognized Tony Pelletoni, the trainer, with a bottle in his hand. The rest of the day was a jagged pattern of confusion. Three times Joe hurried passes to avoid getting hit again; two were intercepted before Risberg, not without mercy, pulled him out. Southern rejoiced in a 14–7 upset.

Joe dressed alone, a figure of remorse, wishing the codeine would take away the throb in his head.

". . . I tell you," a voice was saying, Yeager's voice, full of anger, "the guy choked up. After that guy hit him, he froze."

The two others with Yeager looked guilty as Joe said, "I did what?"

Yeager turned slowly and Joe remembered the tiny smile from before—the day he was bending over Palmer. "You might be next," Yeager had said. This time he said, "You froze. You choked up."

Joe aimed his punch at Yeager's broad face, but the big man, moving quickly, grabbed him in a bear hug and backed him hard against the locker.

Joe remembered the heavy mockery in Yeager's voice, "No, sonny boy; no rough stuff. I might forget I need you. Nothing's going to happen to pal Joey—not as long as you can still throw me that ball."

How long? Two years ago, on a practice field, the dislike turning into hatred, the cool alliance on Saturdays, then the final, ludicrous humiliation in the locker room. One bad day. "I need you," Yeager had said, unconsciously revealing his big weakness. More than anything, Joe knew, Yeager liked the attention, the thought of being known as "Chris Yeager, All-American." You couldn't tell Kathy this, Joe thought. Instead, you walked out, you quit, leaving Yeager and his vaulting, shallow ambitions behind. You hit him where it hurt, because without someone to throw those passes, Yeager was just another meatball.

These were the things that Kathy didn't have to know, he thought, as they walked together down the avenue, warm with lights and far from hate.

"Joe?"

"H'm'm?"

"I'm sorry I was angry. I guess you know I don't care whether you play football or not. It's just that you act glib, kind of evasive when I ask."

"Ah, I wasn't much," he said. "Except for passing, Palmer's just as good, maybe better. I guess it got too serious, no fun. You know?"

She nodded.

The days were shorter and it was colder now, and Joe Mitchell spent his afternoons in the library until it was dark; then walked home through the few lights that glowed from the building on the campus. Joe Mitchell sometimes saw the men he once played with, along the avenue or in the halls. They all spoke, but none stopped.

State went on winning. Risberg had the stuff to grind out victories, although they were narrower, especially the last two. Palmer's passing, unspectacular and often risky, was something they used infrequently, like a pitcher's change of pace. It wasn't Palmer's fault, Joe thought. The guy was good enough, but his throwing arm was limp and lacking snap. Yeager's moments of attention, Joe noted with satisfaction, were not what a man with All-American fever needs. Joe was at the cigar counter in the Union Building when the freshmen came along.

One of them said to another, loud enough to be heard, "That's Joe Mitchell. He does not choose to play."

Joe turned. "Something wrong with that?"

"Oh, nothing wrong," the young man said. "Not a thing. Oh, heavens, no!"

Joe saw the pin on the boy's sweater and noticed quickly that this was one of Yeager's frat brothers.

"Sure," the kid said, for the enjoyment of the others, "the big boy's in our house. He ain't no Red Skelton, but he didn't quit the squad."

Joe's jaw tightened, but he put the impulse down. He turned instead and walked away. Once, heading for his advanced-math class, Joe Mitchell passed Dean Risberg on the campus. The State coach, a sometimes friendly man, stopped him.

"How're things, Mitchell?"

"Fine, coach," Joe said; then added: "The team looks good."

"Good spirit," Risberg said, "We let the other team know we're in the game. Nice to have seen you, Mitchell. Ah—if you ever want to see me, my door is always open."

He needs a scriptwriter, Joe thought. *How does he come up with lines like that?*

"Well, that's fine, coach. Luck."

Joe knew the "spirit" crack was meant for him. He wondered how Yeager enjoyed the funny papers on Sundays, now that Brewster and Westfall, the fullback, were getting all the raves. *Mr. Yeager, bless his little heart, Mr. Yeager reads Orphan Annie, now that I'm not around to lay that ball in his puffed-up chest.*

He walked with Kathy in the evenings, and Joe wondered if she noticed how they stayed away from places where people hepped on football might be found. He met Yeager only once. Coming home one night, Joe saw the big man was waiting in the lobby. Yeager was anything but hostile, and Joe knew, with a touch of satisfaction, that this was worth everything. Yeager had to work at what he wanted to say. "Uh—Mitchell"—Yeager took a deep breath—"we had some differences. I mean—well, the team—I mean, they're jamming up our running game, and we haven't got anybody—" Yeager's voice hung in embarrassment.

"You need a writer, too," Joe said.

"What?"

"Sorry, Yeager," Joe grinned. "I'm packing a tough load. Seventeen hours this quarter, you know? All tied up, like—" Joe paused, then added softly, "As tight as Palmer's arm."

State played away from home that Saturday, in Western's home park, and Joe listened to the radio. Western scored twice in the first quarter, and Palmer, forced to take chances, went to the air. He hit two, then got one intercepted, and State had to make a stand inside its own twenty before the half ended. In the second half it was Brewster and Westfall and Van Doren, the State backs, chugging every play—three yards, five yards, two yards, six yards. The hard way. Palmer laced in two passes, which helped, and State managed to get off the hook, 14-13. Brewster kicked the big point.

The phone was ringing when he came into the dorm that night. He picked up, and Kathy said, "Joe Mitchell, please."

"It's me," said Joe. "If you can't take me out to dinner, can I have the money instead?"

"Idiot. Pick me up in half an hour."

They found a place off the avenue which was not too crowded, and nice for holding hands.

Suddenly she said, "I know all about it, Joe."

"So?"

"I heard two girls talking in the library today. One of them was the Goodwin girl—the one who goes with Brewster. They were talking about you."

"It's my blue eyes," he said, sliding into glibness again. "My clean-cut, boyish look, my nose like Gregory Peck's. Ah"—he sighed—"if I only had his money!"

"The girl—the Goodwin girl—was telling the other one why you quit. They said you got hurt in the game with Southern. You were afraid to come back."

"Women talk," he said brightly. "Goes on all the time. Haven't you heard?"

"I did hear," she said, "and that's what I heard."

"I tripped over the fifty-yard line," he said. "I stumbled on a chalk mark and sprained my toe. Let's go see *Death of a Salesman*. A few laughs—"

"Let's go home." Her voice was cold, and this time, he knew, she wouldn't say, "I'm sorry, Joe."

Even if he could put the rancor he felt toward Yeager into words, Kathy wouldn't understand. She wasn't a person who could understand hatred; she was warm and serene and kind, so you gave her the quick wisecrack, the small talk to cover the questions in her eyes.

"I guess maybe we better had," he said.

She was a stranger at the door. A cool and lovely stranger who had looked him over and made up her mind, and what she decided wasn't favorable.

"My father had a horse, once," she was saying at the door, softly, as to a child. "A big horse. One day, in the barn, I climbed—"

"A horse," he sighed. "Listen, what's a—"

"—I climbed up and frightened him, and then I fell. How I got out of there, I don't remember, but I was afraid to tell my father."

"Kathy, get off it, please," he said. "It's only a game—a silly game. I—"

"Later I told everybody I didn't like the big black horse. My father had a way of knowing things. Finally, one day, he took me by the hand and led me out to the barn and lifted me up on the big horse. He was there and I was there, and then I saw it wasn't the horse at all. It was me."

"Look, if it's just going back—"

"No, Joe, it's more than that. Something is making you hide from me, from everything. I don't know what it is, but—well, you've got a big horse to ride somewhere. Don't call me anymore, Joe."

He went back to his room and opened up a book, but the pages were all about nothing. He turned on the radio, where a disk jockey tried to sound like Edward R. Murrow. He switched it off and lay back on the pillow, but his thoughts were full of Kathy and the soft, sad finality in her voice. He thought of Yeager. *You win a little, you lose a little,* he said to himself. *Make it, win a little, lose a lot,* he thought. Suddenly he wanted to talk to somebody, anybody, a guy with understanding in his soul, a guy who—

Joe looked at the clock, which said eleven. He found a dime and went down to the lobby and the phone.

"This is Russ Palmer," the voice answered. "Who? . . . Oh, Joe. . . . Yeah, not a bad flight back. What's up? . . . Where?"

They met at Vito's Bar and Grill, a place off-campus where the food was plentiful, if not exactly superb. *If I ever need a psychiatrist,* Joe thought, *I'll meet him in saloons and restaurants. This is my day for restaurants; personal problems à la carte.*

Russ Palmer said about the game, "Risberg chewed up four cigars that second half. That Brewster! What a game he played! They ought to have him stuffed and mounted! Van Doren too."

They ate in silence for a while.

"Russ?" Joe pushed the sentence around in his mind. It wouldn't push. "What did you think—I mean, when I quit the squad?"

Palmer looked down at his hands. "I kind of liked it," he said finally. "There's a little larceny in all of us, I guess, and when you didn't come back, that gave me a chance to move in." He flipped a fork. "I wish I had your arm to throw."

The waitress came with coffee. Joe watched Palmer undress two lumps of sugar and stir them, slowly; then take the spoon out and examine it carefully before laying it in the saucer. Palmer laughed.

"It's a real personal thing, isn't it?" Palmer said, at last. "When something happens that you don't even admit—Oh, hell! The time I got hit, two years ago, you know?"

Joe said he knew.

"I never told anybody this, but I was scared. I wasn't much. It seemed too easy to just not come around anymore. My passing?" Palmer shook his head. "Not much ahead but scrimmage and a seat on a hard bench. But I did—I came back."

"You came back," Joe nodded. He started to say something, then stopped, but had to go ahead when he saw that Palmer was watching him intently. "Russ," he said, "did you hate him?"

"Yeager?" Palmer said. "That's not hard, is it? Sure, I did. The big meathead. Bully-boy with All-American ants in his pants. Yeah, I hated him"—Palmer laughed—"because he made me afraid. I hated him almost as much—"

"As yourself?"

"Come on in, Joe," Palmer said. "The water's fine."

Joe remembered now—the Southern tackle, four feet wide and nine feet tall, coming at him, the taped hands swinging eagerly; then the quick, panicky feeling as he tried to hold his ground and sight receivers down the field. *I was groggy. The hell I was. What did I think when Yeager crippled Palmer that time? What was it he said to me—"you might be the next." Something about the way they come at you, game after game, year after year, it gets you. There's a little of it in all of us, and it comes out sometimes. A way you feel. Something you ate.*

Palmer was looking at him.

"Sorry, Russ," he said. "Let's go."

He left Palmer and walked around. It was two o'clock on Sunday morning when Joe Mitchell crawled into bed, tired enough to sleep.

On Monday morning he heard Risberg saying, "I've seen it happen before, what happened to you." Risberg sighed. "Ballplayers," he said to the world at large. "I get fifteen grand for knowing what goes on out there, and young punks think they can fool me. You think I don't know about you and Yeager?"

Risberg stopped talking and Joe thought this might be the end. He couldn't blame Risberg if he showed him the door.

"My quarterbacks," the coach went on, "can play this game in a tuxedo. They look nice and cute, faking and passing and handing off. Parlor magicians. But there's one time my quarterback has got to be tough—that's on a pass. He's got to stand his ground and look down the barrel of the gun, and he can't flinch and he can't hide."

Joe nodded.

"All right," Risberg said finally. "You can come back. I don't promise anything. You know the time. Be ready."

There were times in the next few days when Joe Mitchell thought that surely he could never rise again. Muscles, unused for weeks, ached in protest. His former teammates gave him the benefit of no doubts. Once, in scrimmage, a third-string halfback said, "Nice pitching, Mitchell." *A lad of sensitivity,* Joe thought.

Third seat from the end, wrapped in a blanket, Joe Mitchell saw the game with Polly. Joe sat on the bench and watched State wrap it up as Brewster, Westfall and Van Doren strained for precious yards, helped only by an occasional, cautious pass that Palmer threw to keep the defense honest. *Not today or any day,* Joe thought. Well, one more game and that was that. State got through, 14-6.

The next week was not like any other he had ever known. Risberg lashed his squad with lip and tongue, for the final game, the Aggie game, three days away. A team with no defeats, the Aggies, a team with backs who stomped and stormed, a team well buttressed with a group of heavy intellectuals up front. This was one, Joe doubted, in which the legs of Brewster or any of the others would be enough to win. Once Joe thought that Risberg's anger centered on him alone, as though the coach, seeing in him the cause of State's frustration, gained satisfaction from watching him get slammed.

"Frisk him! Hit him!" Risberg screamed, each time that Joe faded to pass against the varsity. And then it happened. Dancing back, Joe saw his receivers covered, felt the tiny poison of fear in his stomach, the danger point of panic. He let the ball go wildly, much too soon, as a wave of linemen sent him crashing to the ground. They weighed a ton.

"You threw too quick," Risberg said. The disappointment in his voice was not a pretty thing to hear.

Joe knew that Risberg would never use him now; the old pro saw what Joe had felt—a little spot of fear, like a dark shadow in a dream, always there, the thing that split apart the seams of self-control. His touch was gone. Like a pilot who had crashed, he had waited too long to fly again.

"Those scrubs," Palmer said to him, "they don't protect much, do they?"

Joe slumped against a locker. "Don't make it easy, Russ. You saw what happened. I'm washed out, like a faded jersey."

They sold the saucer out, television notwithstanding. Another audience of millions-plus, invited free, sat in on what the networks like to call the "Game of the Week." *For me it's just the last,* Joe said to himself, watching the Aggie boys, all dressed in white, come trotting on the field. Pennants waved and people yelled and cheering shook the sod. State won the toss—perhaps the only thing they'd win all day.

Aggie boys, schooled to jam in tight, jarred Brewster and Westfall as Palmer sent them on hopeless missions to the line. Forced to throw, Palmer gambled three times; he lost once. The Aggies intercepted and brought it deep. They went over in seven plays. Again, before the half, they made a second score and living-room tacticians across the land saw the handwriting on their screens. State was bottled at the half, 14-0.

The second half began and Joe wondered if Kathy was here or if she cared that he had tried. *A guy should get maybe a B for effort,* he thought. *That's worth something.* He saw Yeager loafing twice and wondered if the big man would sulk away his one slim chance for All-American. *I beat him,* Joe thought. *Now we're both licked. A double knockout.* Sorrow rumbled from the stands, and Joe saw Westfall limping to the bench, clobbered hard by a giant Aggie tackle.

The kid next to Joe was brooding over State's disgrace. "Some horse," he said, pointing to the Aggie tackle.

"Some stable," Joe replied, in envy of the Aggies as a group.

Joe Mitchell heard a cymbal sound from somewhere in the distance far away—what was that? What Kathy said, the night she said good-by, in a voice to be remembered, soft and sad and final, at the door: "You've got a big horse to ride." He threw the blanket off and was standing next to Risberg, a man who wallowed in distress. *A lousy little chance,* Joe thought, *a chance to get it back.* He had a hold on Risberg's arm.

"What have you got to lose?"

Risberg turned and looked at Joe. He looked at the scoreboard, which said: 14-to-0; then he looked at the timer's clock, which told that time would soon be something beyond recall.

"The mouths of babes," Risberg sighed. "What have I got to lose? Go ahead."

Joe leaned into the huddle and saw the eyes were full of doubt. A running play? Joe called the pass—the buttonhook he knew Van Doren liked. He placed his hand gently on the center's rear, turned and wheeled, and faded back to throw. He set himself, saw Yeager cutting down and out, drawing the secondary to the sideline, then fired to Van Doren.

The blood tasted salty in his mouth, and he heard an Aggie say, "More where that came from, pal." He shook his head as Brewster helped him to his feet, and there was Yeager standing near, with a tiny smile that said it knew a lot. *He doesn't know a thing,* thought Joe; *the hell with him.* He called the deep pass to Brewster, who raced down from the flank.

Aggies came from everywhere, putting on the heat. He cocked it back. *One moment, please, a moment more.* Then he let it go. A ton of sturdy Aggie beef sent him crashing to the ground, so that Joe was not aware that other Aggies, fleet of foot, caught Brewster on the five-yard line. "Go away," Joe told an Aggie. "Go blow a tuba in the band." His name was in the air.

Van Doren took a hand-off to the three. Joe heaved a happy sigh as Brewster, much inspired, squirted through to score. Joe held the ball and Brewster sent it spinning through the posts. *We're halfway there,* Joe thought, *and this is really living.*

Aggie boys hit back at State, but not so far or hard enough. Van Doren brought the kick back. Joe saw the eyes in the huddle—eyes that were full of hope, friendly eyes, eyes that said, "We're with you, Joe." He sent Brewster through for six; he passed to Thorndike, a boy of promise; and when Brewster hit again for nine, the Aggies had enough. They called for time on their own thirty-three.

Once more in the huddle Joe saw the eyes. "Hit me," Yeager said. "I can outrun the halfback." Instead, Joe sent Van Doren over tackle; then passed to Thorndike for a first down. "Hit me," Yeager said again. "I tell you—"

"Just say one thing," Joe snapped. "Say you need me. Say it sweet."

Yeager dropped his eyes. "All right. I need you."

Joe called the deep pass to Yeager. He faded back, watching the big guy fake the halfback, then leave him with a burst of speed. He threw the pass almost between the arms of a charging Aggie tackle and hardly felt the impact of the ground. The crowd's noise told him Yeager scored.

The final drive took fourteen plays. Joe faked and passed and lashed his playmates into fury. It was Brewster, going all the time; Van Doren too. Joe laced in three passes to Yeager, who never could quite break away. *This one's for Brewster,* Joe thought, saving the blast in Brewster's legs for the last hundred inches. Another pass to Yeager made it to the ten, from where Van Doren butted to the three. Joe whirled and faked, then jammed the ball in Brewster's belly. "Bon voyage, pal," he said, and Brewster took it through. The try for point was just a touch, the frosting on the cake.

The dressing room was full of steam. Old grads full of other things mingled with the boys. Joe Mitchell leaned back against the wall, legs stretched out along the bench, feeling the sweat, still warm, running down his chest.

Palmer shook his hand and said, "I wish I had your arm," then added, "Arm? I wish I had that other thing"—he tapped his chest. There were many hands to shake.

Dressed again, he walked with Brewster down along the avenue, in silence rich with memories of the day. *Now it's like it used to be,* Joe thought.

Then Brewster said, "You gave me that last one, Joe. I won't forget it."

"Do one thing," Joe Mitchell said. "Lend me a dime."

"A dime? You want a dime? What for?"

"I have to call a girl I know," Joe said; "I have to call a girl about a horse."

Talk about coming through the back door. For some years I'd been dying to get out of sports because the sports beat had come to seem like an overfished lake. The break came one evening when I was having dinner at Cliff Warling's place out at Green Lake, then one of the best restaurants in town. What Cliff proposed was a subsidized "about town" column, something that would give stay-at-home Seattleites a hint that going out after dark was not a mortal sin. Cliff's belief was shared by some sixteen fellow restaurant owners—representing about all the decent eating places we had then. They included, among others, Walter Clark, Jimmy Ward, Pete Canlis, John Franco and Vic Rosellini; they also numbered among them no less a personage than Eddie Carlson, then an executive at Western Hotels—later to become Western International Hotels and then the Westin chain.

The idea was simple enough, but full of entrapments. The restaurant guys would run a list of small ads for their places; the ads, in a two-column format, would be stacked down the page, top to bottom. Next to it would be my column, also two columns wide, also top to bottom. They would pay me $100 a week, and the column would appear each Tuesday.

Nobody in editorial command at The P-I thought that I rated, or that the paper needed, an about-town gossip column. But here was the aforementioned back door into non-sports writing. I specified that I would not take money from the restaurant guys, noble as they might be; everything would have to be handled through The P-I's payroll department; so, in effect, I got a $100-per-week raise. In each case, I said, I would not necessarily plug their restaurants. If something newsworthy happened, fine, but the whole idea, as they had proposed in the beginning, was to drum up interest in downtown, or at least after-dark, Seattle.

Have you ever tried to educate a bunch of restaurateurs in the editorial process? It took some doing, but they were fine. The only one who gave me any trouble was Pete Canlis. He once called a meeting about my alleged independence. After a lot of talk, Pete exploded, "Hey, I got it! This guy doesn't give a damn whether he does the column or not." That wasn't at all true, but if Pete and his cohorts thought so, fine. The column, called "This, Our Town," went on and, rather amazingly, I thought, began to pick up readership. I was doing the three-dot stuff in my spare time while working in the sports department. In due course, somebody looked up and said, "If this thing is so popular, why don't we make it three times as popular?" So "Watson's Needle" in the sports pages was cut back to twice a week, and I began writing the about-town stuff three times a week under a subtly different column name, "This, Our City." Many a free drink followed.

"This, Our Town" Debuts

Seattle Post-Intelligencer, August 14, 1956

A SMALL PARTY OF WILDLY OPTIMISTIC CITIZENS is willing to bet that I can write a weekly, non-sports column that will keep people awake for as long as three minutes. Many bets have been made to the contrary—mostly by sports readers, who contend that my stuff is the next best thing to Nembutol. Betting odds are now 6–5, take your choice. Editors of The Post-Intelligencer are understandably joyous about this new experiment. They argue (and rightly) that people who don't read my stuff on the sports pages have been getting off too blamed easy. Hardship, they say, toughens up a reader. This column, only a few words old, already has much in common with those produced by Walter Winchell, Ed Sullivan, Herb Caen and Cedric Adams. When I say "much in common," I mean it will appear in a newspaper. For the most part, this column will touch on general topics, like books, plays, alimony, dining, starving and up-to-the-minute trends in bee culture. Don't worry. It will be the kind of a column that children can read—if you force them to. There will be only an occasional reference to sports, and their names will be spelled correctly. And now, let us all bow our heads and make the best of it.

ARTISTS AND WRITERS: Singer Pat Suzuki, who has kept one night club open practically by herself, is being scouted by Herman Diaz of RCA Victor. A local record album of Suzuki's best numbers has been held up as a result of big-time interest . . . The Vancouver Sun owns a newspaper in California, where tired Canadian staffers (ulcers seem to be the vogue) are shipped for three–four months "rest" . . . Expectant fathers are expecting fringe benefits from a national news weekly. One of the guild "conditions" being argued in current contract negotiations is a yearly, one-week "paternity leave."

NO WAY OUT: A classified ad of a recent morning read: "Tobacconists! Don't sell any more tobacco to nuclear physicists or electronic engineers." The background: John Thomas, P-I's classified ad manager, says the man who placed the notice figures that tobacco is a stimulant and, if it weren't for tobacco, the A-bomb and H-bomb and possibly Elvis Presley would never have been invented. Logician Jim Faber pointed up the real rub: "But who," he demanded, "will get the Russians to quit smoking?"

ACTRESS JANE DARWELL'S steady return to the Cirque Theater started with a lawsuit. Back in 1950, Jane skipped out of a contract with Gene Keene, Cirque mgr., who went to law school. To settle, Jane offered to come up "for expenses" the following year. Agreed. Out of potential litigation sprang a firm Keene-Darwell friendship and frequent returns to Seattle for long runs . . . Topical crack by Al Cummings, the bearded one: "You don't need a vacation, you need a change of anxieties" . . . Bob Woolson, of the Transit System, recalls that his grandfather, Albert Woolson, last survivor of the G.A.R., who died a few days ago at 109, regularly smoked eight cigars a day—supplied, for advertising purposes, by a famous manufacturer.

HORSE LOVERS: A. S. Barnes, publishing house, announces for its fall list a yearly catalog of race horses for many, many years back—bound in buckram, stamped in gold and jacketed in acetate. Price for 1940 edition: $55. NOW how much do you love horses? . . . The boys at Walla Walla (graduate school) had a big festival, complete with fireworks, scheduled for July 4. The "coming out" party was discovered by officials and nipped . . . One more note from behind the brick wall: A killer sentenced to life (he's from a neighboring county) is presently digging his way out of his cell. He's using razor blades to cut through the floor and has cut away about yea-much. "We don't worry," yawned a guard. "As long as we know where he's digging, we can watch him."

ADDITIVES: Wm. T. Waggoner, owner of Shanty I, is sole heir to a $300 million cattle and oil fortune; said to own 2,700 oil wells. Let's see how it looks, stretched out: $300,000,000. Wistful afterthought: If they don't let Shanty in the Harmsworth, he's liable to buy up the Detroit River ... Nicolas Poppe, prof. in UW's Far Eastern Dept., is the only former member of the top-level Soviet Academy of Sciences living in the U. S. His recollections would freeze your spine ...

FOOTNOTE on Waggoner $$$—family fortune was established by grandfather, who came to Texas when land was nothing down and a nickel an acre. Once, after his cattle barony was established, Waggoner and a Texas friend, Burk Burnett, another wealthy rancher, got into an argument over religion. Heated words flew. "I'll bet you," challenged Burnett, "fifty thousand dollars you can't recite the first line of the Lord's Prayer." More to the argument, then: "I'll double that bet—make it a hundred thousand." Both ranchers wrote out their checks for 100 grand apiece. "Now," started Waggoner, beginning his recitation, "Uh—Now I lay me down to sleep ... " The stakeholder stared in open-mouthed amazement as Burnett roared: "By thunder, he did it! Pay him off."

WRIGGLING GROANER Elvis Presley amounts to an epidemic. In Boston, a disc jockey is offering seven (7) hairs from Presley's head for the best letter telling what the writer would do with this lavish prize (I could suggest) ... Teenagers reportedly are soaking Presley records in water before playing—they sound even sexier when warped and waterlogged ... In Memphis, teenagers are saving paper cups of water, drawn from the pool where Elvis took a dip. Had enough? Okay, let's go out and kill ourselves.

Mrs. Kid Matthews, who filed for divorce a week ago, called it off and returned to Harry's corner ... If you're making a confidential call to Olympia, don't bet that it's confidential—tap, tap, tap ... While S. S. Sayres maintains a steady silence about plans for Slo-mo IV and Gold Cupping, a rival owner cracked: "Stan will wait until everybody guesses he's going to run—then he'll run."

"This, Our City" Debuts

Seattle Post-Intelligencer, May 18, 1959

THIS COLUMN WILL BE ABOUT A LOT OF PLACES, mostly Seattle. It also will be about people, mostly males and females . . . From time to time, it will include some very bum jokes, like the one about the woman who bought 300 pounds of steel wool. So she could knit a stove . . . At the risk of being technical, I'd like to say that, except in cases of emergency, the column will be printed in black ink on white paper, Mondays, Wednesdays and Fridays, regardless of the weather, unless I am under it . . . Whose idea was it to run this column three days a week, instead of one? Well, a lot of people have disclaimed any responsibility for the decision, including C. B. Lindeman, the publisher; Ed Stone, the managing editor; Oscar Merritt, the business manager, and others too timid to mention. It just sort of happened. Does that answer your question?

TWICE EACH WEEK, on Tuesdays and Thursdays, a sports column of mine will appear in its usual place next to an advertisement saying, "Amazing New Discovery For Men Over 40!" This has no significance . . . The reduction in sports columns will deprive our reader of many genuine laughs, since my famous football predictions will be discontinued . . . In this new venture, we'll try not to overmention such names as Gordon Clinton, James Carey, Al Cummings, Pete Canlis and Rutherford B. Hayes, our 19th President.

SINCE THIS COLUMN will appear three times a week, you have a right to know what kind of person you are dealing with . . . I am six feet tall and practically uneducated, except for three years at the UW, where I majored in Sand Piling and Finger Painting . . . Politically, I kind of admire Adlai Stevenson, who once said, "A funny thing happened to me on my way to the White House" . . . In the matter of religion, I'm sort of a utility infielder in need of coaching . . . I don't drink as much as I used to, but don't let that statement fool you . . . I am hard of hearing, overweight and extremely disorderly. My desk looks like a mare's nest.

MORE ABOUT the author of this stuff: I have two children, a wife, a sports car and an old Mercury I'm trying to sell for $600. That's too much money, and I advise you not to buy it . . . I'm very absent-minded. In 1951, in New York, I walked into the wrong hotel room, where a woman was half-undressed. I still write her thank-you notes for not screaming . . . My face looks like I'd just been stuck with the check for a party of eight, but I'm kind of a happy guy inside . . . As far as organizations go, I'm a non-joiner. The only organizations I belong to now are the American Newspaper Guild (AFL-CIO) and the Huckleberry Hound Fan Club.

GETTING BACK TO this column business: Flat promises are hard to keep, but we can practically guarantee that at least six Seattleites per month will get their names misspelled here . . . In the past, we've had the right stewardesses working for the wrong airlines, the wrong models working for the right department stores, but around here we don't call them mistakes—we call them Freudian slips . . . If you are planning to have a divorce, don't expect to see your name here. We don't deal in divorce news, unless you become hilarious about it . . . Other forms of indoor sport: We will not deal in the kind of item that goes, "What left-handed lawyer, initials P.J., whose wife thought he was working, huddled at El Gaucho with a shapely blonde last night?" We won't use such an item, but we will wish him luck.

TO DATE, WE HAVE received stuff from such exotic places as Tehran . . . Mexico City . . . Paris . . . Spain . . . Tel Aviv . . . Ballard. And lately, we've added a Point Barrow correspondent, Guy Okakok, a full-blooded Eskimo with 13 children . . . A word more on Guy: He writes for the Fairbanks News-Miner and his stuff goes something like this: "Ruth Ahnagee died early this morning. Ruth never did come back after she got unconscious, for hours" . . . Every once in a while, we'll throw in a bit of wisdom from one of the great philosophers to give the column a little class. My idea of a great philosopher is the former pitcher, Lefty Gomez, who once said: "I owe my success to clean living and a fast outfield."

THIS COLUMN will be, as I say, about people. And it will be about screwy signs, jokes, puns, pets and poets; about lushes, thieves and girls you wouldn't introduce to Grandmother. It will be about Grandmother, too . . . It will deal with High Society and low lifes, and people with terrifying authority, like cops, judges and small children . . . It will be dedicated (if at all) to the proposition that the world, and This, Our City, isn't so grim or dull a place as some of us jerks try to make it . . . In searching around for a credo, or some such lofty declaration, there doesn't seem to be one. I'm faintly embarrassed to paraphrase an epitaph, written by H. L. Mencken years ago, which kind of sums things up—

"IF, AFTER I DEPART this space, you ever think of me, or have thought to please my ghost, forgive some sinner and wink your eye at some homely girl."

That's a hell of a way to start a column—with an epitaph. It's the penalty for being disorderly.

One day, out of the blue, my old friend Henry MacLeod, managing editor of The Times, offered me a chance to come back to Fairview and John. It was tempting, and I almost went, because I had a high regard for Henry. But The P-I laid out the red carpet—what did I want to stay? I said it wasn't dough. I wanted to get the hell out of sportswriting; I wanted to write a so-called "general interest" column five days a week; and I wanted a full-time assistant to help process the alleged news items that came by mail, over the transom or via press agents.

Mostly the columns were three-dot pieces. This was a form first popularized by Walter Winchell in New York. Winchell used this rat-a-tat style, first in print and then later on his Sunday radio shows. He was the most powerful writer in America, to the extent that even Franklin D. Roosevelt cultivated him to counterbalance the bad press he was getting from 80 per cent of the nation's newspapers. The three-dot form spread all through newspaper-dom. John Lardner called it "boilerplate journalism," the reference being to the three dots (like rivets) that separated items, no item having much relationship to the one preceding it. Its greatest practitioner was Herb Caen of the San Francisco Chronicle. Caen was witty, literate and urbane, and he had a conscience, a point of view. He far surpassed Winchell in both style and substance. Caen was my own role model.

Yet I was never comfortable with the three-dot style. It required, in addition to interesting items, a boiled-down way of making complicated stuff seem simple. As the columnist Jim Murray once said, "It's almost an art form in itself. It's a knack of saying something in a way that makes you believe it's the only way it can be said." You had to do it with what seemed like spontaneity and you had to ram it home, like a rivet gun.

"This, Our City" Expands

Seattle Post-Intelligencer, November 19, 1962

MUCH CONFUSION AND CONTROVERSY raged around this space last week. Veteran readers thought they detected the old Watson Touch in some items, which scanned aimlessly, went something like this:

"Diabetes is a subtle disease that creeps up ominously, so watch out for it . . . I have heard of a clinic in Switzerland that is supposed to be able to treat multiple myeloma . . . The 'blood tests' required before you can get a marriage license in most states are aimed only at venereal diseases. They are a good thing . . . "

Stand by for clarification: what you were reading there was Dr. Joseph G. Molner, M. D., who took over this space during my absence, and, frankly, I feel lucky to get it back. Anyway, there were a lot of irate calls, not from readers who missed my stuff, but from irate readers who screamed things like: "What's with that Watson, saying venereal diseases are a good thing?" Honest, I didn't write that. I was away from the desk setting fires for insurance.

Meanwhile, a Master Plan evolved from all this confusion. It was decided that this column should be printed six days a week and Dr. Molner would appear on another page. You see the logic?

"If we run Watson six days a week," decided a promotion expert, "that will make the readers sick. Then they'll turn to Dr. Molner for advice. A perfect tie-in."

SIX DAYS A WEEK: Barring flood, hurricane, war, famine, pestilence and an author's hangover, this thing, will, indeed, appear six days a week. Add up all those disasters and compare them to a steady diet of Watson and what have you got? Not much to choose from. As usual, this will be a column in depth. I mean it will be 18-1/2 inches deep. After a long consultation of editors, it was decided that there will be no basic change in format, meaning it will continue to be printed black-on-white, instead of vice-versa.

Actually, the column you are reading now will appear Mondays through Fridays. Sunday, beginning December 2, there will be a sort of general feature, which will appear in the Pictorial Review, unless it gets crowded out by the U-Bild It column. The editor of the Pictorial section, Bruce Penny, says he plans to use lots of pictures and cartoons, so you'll get off easier on Sundays. I suggest that you read it before going to church, then say a little prayer of forgiveness.

SIX DAYS A WEEK? Tomorrow, being Tuesday, we'll have an item about—no, better save that. Six days a week! A lot of people think a column like this has an "army of informants" and, in a sense, that is true. Most of my army consists of Pfc. Roy Edenholm, who raises the flag on The P-I Building, then comes down to help out on the phone.

A word about Pfc. Edenholm: One morning he raised the flag upside down and this called for a summary court-martial in Publisher Lindeman's office. But Pfc. Edenholm was saved by a presidential order. The president of the Hearst Corp. called long-distance and, during the subsequent excitement, Pfc. Edenholm made his escape.

Glad he did, too. Pfc. Edenholm has been a tower of strength in the past. Three times he has been punched in the nose by people who thought they were punching me. He is, in all seriousness, a talented fellow whose stuff frequently appears in the sports pages under his own byline. He's a pleasant, productive man on the telephone, with an uncanny ear for sensing a phony or a bill collector.

SIX DAYS A WEEK: This column started half-a-dozen years ago as a once-a-week entry, then about three years ago one of the editors suggested running it three times a week. The suggestion was adopted and, though it cost the editor his job, his successor felt that pulling the column out would give subscribers violent withdrawal symptoms, like quitting the weed. Now it's up to six a week. It is this sort of creeping pestilence that inspired Rachel Carson to write *Silent Spring*.

Using a flabby definition, I was once a sportswriter. There is, therefore, a temptation to bid a tearful farewell-to-sports column, which is hereby resisted. Tearful partings imply tears on both sides, and the sporting fraternity is noticeably stoic about my leaving 'em for good. Curiously, no down-memory-lane anecdotes come to mind, but don't relax; with 18-1/2 inches to fill every day, a fellow can stir his memory with a mixmaster to fill out a few lines.

Actually, the only sports note that I remember, at the moment, doesn't concern anything that took place in a ballpark or a stadium. It concerns a press conference, held by Mr. Branch Rickey, the well-known linguist, who was outlining a plan for giving baseball to the Hottentots, or somebody. It was a dazzling display of double-talk, but sportswriters, bless them, are a notably cantankerous lot. When Mr. Rickey finished, logic seized the intellect of one of my colleagues. He rose to protest, saying: "You are absolutely right, Mr. Rickey, but I disagree with you."

Meanwhile, let us dwell not on the past; rather, let us dwell on the future, which, I have on good authority, lies ahead.

"Go forward, Watson," said Managing Editor Stone. "Scour the city for stories, feel the pulse of the city. You are free to write about anything. You are free of sports."

He doesn't know how free I really am. Now I no longer have to mow Royal Brougham's lawn. Free at last . . .

As a consequence of circumstances too tedious to go into, I ended up, in the early 1980s, writing two columns a week for The P-I while working for another company, Pacific Institute, where I wrote motivational textbooks. Then came a parting of the ways with The P-I, and, eventually, with the other company. Which brings us up to one fine fall day in 1983, when I sat at lunch with three editors from The Times: Jim King, Mike Fancher and Alex MacLeod. They offered me a job, and I couldn't help but remember that I had almost dangled Alex MacLeod on my knee when he was a child. It was Alex's idea to hire me. "Full circle," I thought, since Alex is the son of Henry MacLeod, for whom I had worked at The Times so many years before.

Return to The Times

Seattle Times, October 30, 1983

SINCE YOU ARE HELPLESS SUBSCRIBERS to this newspaper, you at least have the right to know who you are getting mixed up with here, since I probably will lead you down some strange paths as the weeks go on.

You are not getting a debutante. I worked here before, from 1946 until the winter of 1950, at which time I excused myself to go on a minor errand, promising to return right away. That was 33 years ago, and I apologize for the delay.

For what scant interest it may hold, an explanation will ensue. I was waylaid by the blandishments of some people who worked for William Randolph (The Real Article) Hearst, known more readily today as "Pop." The Hearst people had their headquarters at 6th and Something. Wall, I believe.

"The Chief" was alive in those days, and you could see chicken feathers flying all over the Denny Regrade when the teletype rumbled out, "The Chief suggests . . . "

I was young and innocent but not so innocent that I would write anything favorable about Orson Welles in *Citizen Kane*. You could end up in one of Mr. Hearst's Bolivian tin mines for a sin like that.

Those early years at The Times were pleasant. Truman was president, we were only fighting one war at a time, and Hugh McElhenny was just beginning to draw a nice salary as a University of Washington halfback.

In those years, I worked under a managing editor named Russell McGrath. He brought a Cromwellian ethic to the Times stylebook, and he ran a good paper when you consider that he did it mostly by memo.

One of the strictures he applied (this was not in the stylebook, but in his head) was the use of the word "blood" in Times news columns. It was a forbidden word, possibly because he felt our readers, however they may have suffered at times, did not bleed. As a result of this ban on the word "blood," and because I covered lots of prize fights, I developed considerable skill in the field of euphemisms.

"Mr. Mac" wore a green eyeshade at work. On him, this eyeshade took on the likeness of those spiked helmets worn by Prussian generals when they invaded another peaceful Balkan country. But he was a good man and a kind one, though his memos could sting.

I truly learned the meaning of his authority when I did a sparkling interview with a wrestler named Gorgeous George, who was big box office in 1949. Gorgeous George, always the villain of wrestling's rehearsed vaudeville, affected the demeanor of an 18th century English fop; he wore festooned robes, entering the ring to the strains of "Pomp and Circumstance."

My glistening interview never appeared in print, but one of McGrath's memos hit my desk like a righteous thunderbolt. "Watson!" it said. "The sacred pages of The Seattle Times will never be used, by you or anyone else, to advance the sordid fortunes of this perfumed lout."

How I finally returned to The Times is a rather complicated deal. Somehow, during negotiations for the joint operating agreement between The Times and the other paper at 6th and Something, a side deal was struck. It was announced that The Times would give up 16 obsolete IBM typewriters in exchange for several barrels of ink and a columnist to be named later. The latter is me. And since you had nothing to say about this trade, further identification is in order—a half-full disclosure, so to speak.

I was born here, raised here, and never regretted any of it. I know a lot of people, but only a handful of millionaires, and I spend an inordinate amount of time with the boys on the curb. My acquaintances include people who are dangerously close to being intellectuals, more lawyers than seem absolutely necessary, and more bookmakers than are good for me.

I am free of debt, except for a $618.23 Visa card bill, which I wish they'd stop grumbling about. I own a 1973 Fiat Spider, a 1971 GMC truck, a 1973 camper, a 1969 Cessna airplane and a 1980 dog. All of them, including their owner, register high mileage. In fact, I have an old Casey Stengel quote stenciled on my office door, a message of defiance: "Most people are dead at my age, and you can look it up."

The dog's name is Tiger. He is a French poodle (runt, Miniature Div.) who has traveled with me all over the Western United States in one or another of these ancient vehicles. You'll be hearing more about him.

Occasionally, when the old psyche needs therapy, Tiger and I take the Cessna out and bore a hole in the sky, high enough so we can admire the clouds, the greenery, the great waters and the ruggedness of this most beautiful of all countries.

Tiger has only one fault as a copilot. Just before takeoff, when I've got the throttle jammed to the firewall and we're almost up to rotating speed, Tiger paws impatiently at my white knuckles on the throttle. There is no mistaking the signal. He wants his stomach scratched.

Politically, I am firmly to the left of the Sheriff of Nottingham but safely to the right of the McNamara brothers, who once blew up the Los Angeles Times. (Readers were more critical in those days.)

The last I heard, this column will appear twice each week, Tuesday and Sunday, or perhaps vice versa, and selective subscription cancellations on these days are not permitted.

Oh, I almost forgot. I am also the president and chief executive officer of the tax-exempt, nonprofit organization known as Lesser Seattle Inc. Our stockholders are legion. Our mission is to drive out tourists and would-be immigrants—in short, to keep Seattle unspoiled and unsprawled. Toward this noble ideal, our KBO agents work day and night.

What is a KBO agent? The answer to this acronym will come in due time, once we get to know each other better and I can bootleg it past a Times copyreader. This here is a family newspaper, friend, and the spirit of Russell McGrath still lives.

Part 2
Names in the News

The dailiness of column writing does not allow such prestigious malignancies as "writer's block." I don't know what one is, frankly. All I know is, when the time comes, you deposit your seat on a chair and begin to expound. Mostly you have delayed so long that there is no alternative. The hole in the paper is there; you do what is necessary to fill that hole, anywhere from 800 to 1,000 words, most of them forgettable.

Only the people are memorable. They're the natural resources a columnist uses to make his allotted portion of newsprint interesting. They're also the reason the job is seldom dull, often fun and usually educational. I've talked to, or rather, listened to, hundreds of people—perhaps thousands—in the course of the column-manufacturing business. Most have made some impression; some have had profound impacts.

I wouldn't testify that I have done justice, in the writing, to any of them. Columns are not full-scale biographies. Columns are written under time pressure, which is to say, against a deadline. On only a half-dozen occasions in 50 years have I completely funked off. The rest of the time, muse-less or not, I got the stuff done. In that sense, I am a disciple of the author-economist, John Kenneth Galbraith. He was invited to teach a semester of writing at the University of California. The idea was to hold seminars for undergraduate students who wanted to learn about the craft.

Galbraith, the author of more than 20 books and dozens of essays, was well qualified. "There was, however, a major difficulty," he wrote. "It was that I could tell everything I knew about writing in approximately half an hour."

In his essay "Writing and Typing," Galbraith warned of the dangers of alcohol, hanging out too much with other writers, excessive windiness and other pitfalls. One of his cautionary notes has stayed with me; it has, indeed, been a part of my allegedly creative life.

Said Galbraith: "All writers know that on some golden

mornings they are touched by the wand; they are on intimate terms with poetry and cosmic truth. I have experienced those moments myself. Their lesson is simple: they are a total illusion.

"And the danger of the illusion is that you will wait for them. Such is the horror of having to face the typewriter that you will spend all of your time waiting. I am persuaded that, hangovers apart, most writers . . . are about as good one day as the next. The seeming difference is the result of euphoria, alcohol or imagination. All this means is that one had better go to his or her typewriter and stay there regardless of the result. It will be very much the same."

Galbraith then hammered home his point: "Don't wait for the golden moment. Things may well be worse."

In telling you that my pieces were written under deadline is not to set up an alibi in advance. They would be just as good, just as bad, if I had written them at any other time. Bellyaches, a cold or a hangover do not wash as alibis.

In March 1959, I took a pleasure trip to Sun Valley, the ski resort, with a young friend, Jerry Gray. Jerry was a good companion, very knowledgeable about skiing—a sport which I only half-mastered a few years later. But this trip had no purpose except to feel some sun and walk in the snow. I had no idea how quickly I would be back at work.

On our first night, Dorice Taylor, the Sun Valley publicist, had a small cocktail party at one of the tables. It was then we saw Ernest Hemingway sipping a drink and chatting with the barkeep. I knew that Hemingway lived most of the year in Ketchum, the little town next to Sun Valley. And there he was, white beard and all, rough winter clothes and laughing freely as he talked. He looked like all that I had read about him.

Abruptly, at Dorice Taylor's invitation, Hemingway arrived at our table. Once he began to talk and tell stories, I knew that the vacation was over. That night I shipped off a modest news feature to The Post-Intelligencer.

A Drink with Hemingway

Seattle Post-Intelligencer, March 4, 1959

SUN VALLEY, IDA. — The old man with the beard stood at the end of the bar drinking his favorite drink (Haig and Haig, on the rocks, with lime) and exchanging banter with resident and visiting skiers.

This is Ernest Hemingway country. Off and on, since the late 1930s, Hemingway has come here to write, and he is here now, working on a new book. "Papa is wonderful to everybody," said Dorice Taylor, the long-time public relations director for Sun Valley. "The only time he resents people is when they get too pushy at the wrong time."

Hemingway came over to the table. Obviously this was the "right time"; it was Saturday night, and Hemingway had stopped by the Sun Valley Lodge before going home to dinner. He was in a good mood.

Papa's hair is white now, and so is the beard. He was dressed in a red-checked shirt, a white washed-out vest, rather tight-fitting pants and comfortable beige-colored boots. He carried a ski jacket to the table. "I can't stay long," he said, apologetically. "I'm supposed to be home soon or I'll get in trouble." He stayed for perhaps a half-hour, rising once to leave, then saying, "Oh, well, just once more. I can loaf a while longer."

He talked and laughed a lot, speaking in a sometimes inaudible murmur, about his books and the movies that have been made from them. Somebody asked him if he saw the second film version of *A Farewell to Arms*. "About 20 minutes of it," he said. "I couldn't watch any more." Clearly, his opinion of Hollywood has not mellowed with the years. He was not at all happy with the way the late Tyrone Power played Jake Barnes in *The Sun Also Rises*. "Maybe it's not right to talk about the dead like this, but that's the way I feel," he said. "And that guy they had in there as the bullfighter, he was no good. You know who did a good job in that picture? Errol Flynn did a good job."

Hemingway is a sportsman in the broadest sense of the term. He is an avid boxing fan, an expert on bullfighting, and, until 1952, he was a steady skier at Sun Valley. He now hunts bobcats in the jagged Sawtooth Range of the Northern Rockies. One of his closest friends was his old hunting guide, Taylor Williams, who passed away recently. Hemingway was a pallbearer at Williams' funeral, and the veteran guide died owning the only existing corrected galley proof of the manuscript *For Whom The Bell Tolls*.

"Where did you write *For Whom The Bell Tolls?*" somebody asked Hemingway.

"Part of it in Cuba, part in Kansas City, part of it here."

"What part did you write here?"

Hemingway laughed. "The part with all the snow in it," he said.

Somebody told Hemingway that I had once written his obituary, when he was believed killed in a plane crash in Nairobi. "You did?" he laughed. "You know, I got obituaries mailed to me from all over the country. Bill Corum wrote half a column about me before he discovered I was still alive. I think Bill must have been drunk when he wrote it because he got pretty sentimental."

Abruptly, Hemingway began talking of boxing.

"That Utah fighter, that Fullmer is a bum," he said. "He doesn't know how to fight. He clubs with his left, like this"—Hemingway made several short, awkward motions to demonstrate— "how can you hurt anybody hitting like that?

"Did you read Bill Heinz's book on boxing? That was all about Jack Hurley and Matthews. Damn good book. Matthews knew how to fight. What was the name of that book? That's right, *The Professional*. Damn good book."

A man came and whispered in Hemingway's ear.

"Mary just called," Hemingway announced, tossing off the last of his drink. "Looks like I'm in trouble. After all, I'm supposed to be working up here. I just went out for a walk, and now I'm in trouble."

Two days after our first encounter with Hemingway, Jerry and I bumped into him again. He invited us for a drink. This time, the conversation turned to Cuba and Castro. Two months previously, on New Year's Day of 1959, the dissolute dictator Fulgencio Batista had fled Cuba in the face of Castro's advancing revolutionaries. In those early days of his power, Castro had not yet proclaimed himself a communist, although other Latin American dictators— and right-wingers generally— were deeply suspicious.

Hemingway had lived and worked in Cuba for many years and so was regarded as something of an authority on the country. Hundreds of reporters had tried to get his views on Castro and the revolution, but he had not spoken. Suddenly, here I was, a vacationing sports columnist from Seattle, which was hardly an international media center, hearing the great man's opinions about a subject that was Topic A in most of the world's capitals. I had no pencil nor notebook. So I listened carefully, hoping my memory cells were not overloaded with long-ago box scores.

When our conversation was finished, I rushed back to my room in the lodge and typed out notes of what Hemingway had said. Then I packed to return to Seattle so that I could write the story. In the lobby, I ran into Hemingway again. "Of course, I'm going to write it all," I told him, "except for the part you asked me to withhold." (He had expressed doubt that Castro was strong enough to carry out the revolution but didn't want to be quoted on this since he wished to return one day to live in Cuba again.) "I didn't take any notes," I said, "but I put some together after we talked. In fairness, I think you should see those notes before they are published." Hemingway smiled. "No," he said, "I think you will probably get it right."

It was an international scoop. The wire services picked it up from The P-I and sent it all over the world. Unfortunately, in the writing of it, I tried to ape Hemingway's style. That was a bad idea.

A footnote: I never saw Hemingway again. But I heard from a friend who knew him that he had liked the story and had been relieved that I had quoted him accurately. Accolade enough for a reporter: I had got it right.

Hemingway on Cuba and Castro

Seattle Post-Intelligencer, March 9, 1959

SUN VALLEY, IDA. — It was early afternoon and the bright, high sun was melting the snow to slush on the walk to the Challenger Inn. The skiers were on the slopes and the village was nearly empty. This was a good day for skiing and now was the time to go out and give it another try. But the figure coming down the main walk on the west side of the village was unmistakable—tall, white-bearded, with steel-rimmed spectacles; he was carrying a brown sack with some papers inside.

We had met Ernest Hemingway two nights before and he remembered. We went inside to a place called The Ram for a drink. The other night we had talked about boxing and skiing and bad movies and good books. Hemingway had said, jokingly, because he was in a good mood, that he had given up skiing "after we bent that airplane," referring to his two near-fatal plane crashes in Uganda, East Africa, four years ago. He had told a wonderfully funny story about a doctor surveying a gash behind his left ear who had picked up a bottle of gin and said, "Gordon's is as good as anything for this." "He poured gin over my head," Hemingway said, laughing. "It goes to show that gin is good, inside or out."

But now it was early afternoon and there was no more thought of skiing. The mountains would always be there, but a chance to talk with Hemingway doesn't come with every snow. "Look, I'm all through working," he said, "and I don't mind talking. Anything you want to talk about is all right."

So we talked about Cuba and the Castro revolution—the first time that Hemingway has commented on this historic event for any American newspaper. Hemingway, who has fought in two wars, observed first-hand the Franco revolution in Spain and has written about all three, called the Cuban uprising against dictator Fulgencio Batista "the first revolution in Cuba that really is a revolution." Hemingway said he has "great hope for the Castro movement" and added that the public trials and executions of former Batista officials are necessary. "They are doomed anyway," he said.

Hemingway now lives in Ketchum, Ida., with his wife, Mary. He is busy finishing his latest novel in the wild, white, mountainous country of Sun Valley, the nation's foremost ski resort. The famed American novelist has lived much of his recent life in Cuba. *To Have and Have Not*, a hard-bitten but compassionate book, begun in 1933 and finished in 1936, had its setting in Cuba and part of it was written there. *The Old Man and the Sea,* his most recent success, has as its central character an aging Cuban fisherman.

"I believe in the cause of the Cuban people," he said, during a relaxed hour-long talk. "They have had changes in government before in Cuba . . ." Hemingway shrugged and waved his hand. "But these were just changes of the guard. When the new ones got in, they went right on stealing from the people."

The tall, white-haired, bearded writer, who has won both the Pulitzer and Nobel prizes for literature that spanned the past 30 years, spoke intently of the country he loves. "Some of Batista's officials and police officers were good, honest men," he said. "But a lot of them were thieves, sadists and torturers. They tortured kids, sometimes so badly they would have to kill them." Hemingway described how the bodies were found—horribly mutilated. He catalogued in unprintable details the methods of torture used by Batista police. He described the graft and corruption, citing the case of one high official who stole 40 million dollars in six years.

"These trials and executions are necessary," Hemingway said. "If the government doesn't shoot these people, they will be killed for vengeance. The result would be personal vendettas in every village and town.

"What would happen to these Batista men if they were allowed to return to their homes?" he asked. "The people know who the bad ones are. Sooner or later, they would take revenge on them. They are doomed anyway."

Hemingway said the Castro movement depended, in large part, on its promise to the Cuban people that Batista men responsible for the atrocities would be punished. "The government has to carry out its promises," he said. "There was a lot of criticism over the shooting of Batista officials. So the Castro government began conducting public trials and executions. People abroad began to yell, 'Circus!'

"But the government had to do this to show it was in control, to give people a respect for law and order. It is to avoid the village vendettas that would be sure to come if Batista men were turned loose. If the government doesn't shoot these criminals, they would be killed anyway. They would be killed for vengeance. Then there would be a wave of killings, back and forth.

"It would be very bad, very bad," he said. "If people can justify killing men for atrocities, soon they would justify killing for a debt, or some other minor reason. Unless the government conducts these trials and executions, the man seeking justice who killed one of these criminals would become a criminal himself."

Hemingway talked of the Cuban revolution with scarcely a pause. He went on: "When the executions are over, I believe the government should ban capital punishment. Shooting a man is not necessarily the right punishment. People say that because a man dies before a firing squad bravely"—Hemingway gestured with his huge hand—"that doesn't mean anything. A lot of bad men have died wonderfully."

The 59-year-old novelist, who probably has seen more of war and death than any writer alive, paused for a moment. Then he continued, citing the case of a man who had been executed only a few days before. "I know him," he said. "If they shot him a hundred times it wouldn't be enough punishment for the terrible things he has done."

Hemingway said that he believes the Cuban labor laws, under Batista, were good. "But the unions were closed to a lot of workers. Others couldn't get in. They were closed, and a lot of people couldn't get work.

They were actually going hungry." He mentioned the case of a father who had sent his three girls to normal school. "They were qualified to teach school," he said, "but they couldn't get a job because they didn't have graft money. They had to pay $2,000 to buy a teaching job. Cuban kids," he added, "have a right to education."

Hemingway went on to describe company plantations where workers were denied the right to own, or work, the land. "If they wanted to plant truck gardens during the off-season, they weren't allowed to," he said. "They were forced to buy food in company stores. American companies have some 800 million dollars invested in Cuba. Some of them behaved well. United Fruit and the Hershey Sugar Co. were good. Others were not so good, and others were drawn into the pattern before they realized what was going on. They came to Cuba and thought this was the accepted way of doing things."

He repeated: "I have great hope for the Castro revolution, because it has the support of the Cuban people. I believe in their cause."

He spoke of returning soon to Cuba to live. "Cuba has been good to Americans," he said. "It's a wonderful place to live. I lived there and worked there. *The Old Man and the Sea* was about a Cuban fisherman, and it was written in Cuba." Hemingway's voice was lowered, then he added, almost shyly: "It was kind of a good book."

Hemingway has a fine ruddy face and his smile gives warmth and confidence across a table. He sipped his Scotch and lime slowly; his working day was over and he seemed relaxed and happy. He said he works in the mornings, writing in longhand, and that his new book is nearly completed. He told of how, each morning, he goes back and cuts and changes and adds to the work of yesterday. His writing hand was marked by several ugly scratches.

"My pet owl," he said, chuckling. "I've been training him. He didn't mean to scratch me. He was just trying to stay on my hand. I was going to train him as a decoy for crows . . ." Hemingway chuckled again. "But I got too fond of him. I like the way he sits on my hand"—Hemingway held out his scratched hand to show where the owl sits—"He sits there and stares right back at you. I like owls. They look you right in the eye. They don't take any guff from anybody." He stopped talking a moment, then added: "I guess I'll turn him loose when the weather warms."

Hemingway's face brightened at a sudden thought. "He had a better winter than any owl around here."

The huge, roughly dressed writer has become a legend in Sun Valley, where he has lived, intermittently, since the early days of the village, and where he wrote parts ("the parts with snow in it") of *For Whom the Bell Tolls*. He loves to fish and hunt with a few close friends, or with an occasional visiting celebrity. His late friend and hunting guide, Taylor Williams, died owning the only existing corrected manuscript of *For Whom the Bell Tolls*. When Williams died, his attorney, Everett Taylor, called Hemingway and offered to return the manuscript. "No, it belongs to him," Hemingway said. "I wanted him to have it. The manuscript can go to his family." The attorney put the manuscript in Williams' estate, placing a "nominal" value on it, which can mean it is worth one dollar or $10,000. (The original manuscript of *Death in the Afternoon* recently sold for $13,000.)

I mentioned that I had spent some time with Jack Dempsey, and how I marveled at Dempsey's patience, the way he answered the old, old questions, the same questions about fights never forgotten. "That's why it's difficult to ask you questions—they must be the same questions, over and over."

Hemingway shook his head and replied seriously. "No, I don't circulate much," he said. "I have a private life. I can't have a lot of people around when I work. Guys like Dempsey," he added, "have two lives, a private life and a public life. Most of them hate their public life, but Dempsey likes his. He needs his public life. He needs people." Hemingway thought a moment. "Nobody will ever hurt Dempsey. In a public life, nobody is really close."

Hemingway has friends, many close friends, and many people love him. But dimly you remembered something he wrote when he accepted the Nobel Prize four years ago. "Writing at its best is a lonely life," he said then, "for he (the writer) does his work alone and if he is a good enough writer he must face eternity, or the lack of it, every day."

But his life has been full of doing. He has seen wars and revolutions, watching people live well, or meanly; people dying heroically, and meaninglessly. His life's work recorded events and people and emotions as he saw them, in violence and peace, on three continents.

"Would it be off-limits," I said, "to ask you about your new book, what it's about?" Hemingway looked back for a long moment. He dropped his eyes, murmured something, then spoke loudly enough to be heard.

"If you talk about it," he replied, almost apologetically, "you lose it. Something happens to it. You talk about something you're writing, or plan to write, and suddenly it's gone. You've ruined it by talking. The book is a very real thing. To the writer, the book is more real than the reality around him."

An hour had passed. He had talked of many other things: Of sportswriters like Frank Graham, Red Smith and Jimmy Cannon, of reporters like Bob Considine; he had talked about John Lardner and about Jim Lardner, who was killed in Spain while Hemingway was there reporting, storing up the emotions and experience that came alive in *For Whom the Bell Tolls*. He had talked about the new Spanish bullfighter, Antonio Ordonez; of Harry Greb and Gene Tunney; he had talked about fishing, of hunting bobcats and shooting magpies, in language sometimes soft and subtle, but often blunt, never pompous and always concise.

For a few brief moments, one thought of all the things that lay between Hemingway, the writer, and you, the reader. It was an acquaintanceship of long standing, developed off the rich, clear pages of books that had shaped American literature, books that opened windows to the art of saying what is truly felt. One recalled the magnificent episode in *For Whom the Bell Tolls,* when El Sordo fought fascists from the hilltop . . . The calm sense of peace and dignity when Nick Charles fished in the "Big Two-Hearted River" . . . The epic short story, "Snows of Kilimanjaro," where a writer died with his talent wasted . . .

There came to memory the tragic, hopeless love between Jake Barnes and Brett Ashley, and the wonderfully definitive bullfight passages in *Death in the Afternoon* . . . All of these and other people came alive in his books: Robert Jordan and Harry Morgan, Rinaldi, Lieutenant Henry and the beautiful Catherine Barkley . . . Francis Macomber, who found courage and maturity too late, and "the beautiful red-faced Robert Wilson."

When Hemingway failed, as the critics sometimes said he did, he failed in the grand try; he had no shoddy goals, and critics had no effect on him, anyway. He wrote and lived as he pleased. He still does. And always he left claw marks on the hands, looked the world in the eye, and took no guff from anybody.

"I promised to meet Mary in an hour and a half," he said, putting on his coat at the door. "I'm afraid it's an hour and a half now. I have to go."

Hemingway is slimmer now. And he is much older than when he wrote *Green Hills of Africa*. But if someone asked him, as Kandisky did, "And what do you want?" he would still reply, as he did in 1935: "To write as well as I can and learn as I go along. At the same time, I have my life, which I enjoy and which is a damned good life."

A little more than two years after I met him in Sun Valley, on July 2, 1961, Ernest Hemingway shot and killed himself at his home in Ketchum, Idaho. When I heard the news, I called The P-I's managing editor, Ed Stone, at his home and begged him to send me over to Sun Valley. "I know something about those people over there," I said, "and I once knew Hemingway and I know some of his friends."

When I got there, landing at the Ketchum airport, I was in the middle of a mob scene; it seemed like every writer on earth was already there.

The Hemingway friends, and his wife, Mary, kept insisting that Hemingway accidentally shot himself while cleaning a shotgun. Most of the newsies were accepting things that I refused to accept. Here was a man who, in life, was attracted to shooting, who had a magnificent gun collection and knew guns intimately. He was an authority on guns. A guy like this could kill himself accidentally?

In Ketchum, I had a reunion with one of the best friends I ever had, in or out of journalism. Barry Farrell had recently left The P-I and joined Time Magazine. He was then based in Time's San Francisco bureau. I told Barry what I thought, and he called his bureau chief in San Francisco. His bureau chief was an extremely nice man.

He told Barry, in effect, "It's easy for me sitting down here with my feet on the desk to tell you what to do. But since Hemingway lived a wild, dangerous life, involved in three wars and the Cuban revolution, I think it's important to know some things. Death was a theme in a lot of his writing. I think it's terribly important that we learn how he died."

So Barry and I worked as a team. We interviewed villagers—from bartenders, to Hemingway's hunting pals, to maids, to waitresses, to his typist. Finally, through some shameless flattery of one of the officers involved in the investigation, we learned the truth. I could not attribute the story to the officer then, and the commitment not to use the man's name is still binding.

This was the first story saying that Hemingway's death was not an accident but a suicide. Mary Hemingway held out for a long time, but many months later she told people that her husband had died by his own hand.

Hemingway's Death Is Suicide

Seattle Post-Intelligencer, July 7, 1961

KETCHUM, IDA. — Ernest Hemingway, who shot and killed himself with a simultaneous blast of two shotgun barrels, deliberately ended his own life, The Post-Intelligencer learned yesterday.

The noted author, whose death has been described as one of "accidental shooting," was found Sunday in his Ketchum, Idaho, home lying on his back with the shotgun across his lower legs.

The manner of Hemingway's death has been the subject of international speculation. His immediate family, including his wife, Mary, and all of his close friends have steadfastly maintained that the author's death was accidental.

However, it was learned authoritatively yesterday that Hemingway, who recently returned from the Mayo Clinic in ailing health, placed the shotgun muzzle in his mouth and deliberately killed himself.

The suicide occurred in a small 10-foot by 12-foot foyer in the southeast corner of Hemingway's large living room. He was found lying on his back at a cross-corner angle in the small room, which served as an entranceway to the author's home.

Since Sunday, when Hemingway's death was first announced as a shooting accident "while cleaning a shotgun," all details of his death have been denied to reporters who converged here from many parts of the world.

Not even the make of the gun was revealed.

However, The Post-Intelligencer learned that the death weapon was a silver-inlaid, double-barreled shotgun with a hammerless, tandem trigger mechanism. Both barrels had been fired.

The 12-gauge hunting gun was an Angelini & Benardon, made by W. C. Scott and Sons of London. The make of the gun was described on the right barrel.

On the left barrel was inscribed "55 Victoria Street, London, Scott's Improved Bolt, Monte Carlo B."

On Monday, Blaine County authorities said the death certificate would read "self-inflicted gunshot wound in the head," but Blaine County Coroner Ray McGoldrick refused to say whether Hemingway's death was an accident or a suicide.

"I wasn't there so I don't know," he stated at the time. "Maybe the truth will never be known. No one saw it."

Mrs. Hemingway stayed in seclusion until the funeral yesterday, while none of the author's several relatives, including three sons, Patrick, Gregory and Jack, would discuss any details of the author's death.

Following the funeral yesterday, Blaine County Sheriff Frank L. Hewitt described the physical appearance of the Hemingway living room and drew a rough sketch of where the body was found.

"I was called to the Hemingway home Sunday at 8:10 in the morning," said Hewitt. "I arrived about 8:25.

"Mr. Hemingway was lying in a small foyer which leads into the living room. On the other side of the foyer wall, facing the living room, is a gun rack. Mr. Hemingway kept eight hunting guns in the rack.

"Mr. Hemingway was lying on his back in the small room. His head was in one corner, his feet in the other. Nothing had been touched when I arrived."

Like other officials in Ketchum and Blaine County, the sheriff parried all questions pointing to the subject of suicide.

But the staunch refusal of all law enforcement officers and Hemingway's family and friends to admit the possibility of suicide has not abated the curiosity of the multitude of reporters and photographers swarming about Ketchum and the nearby resort area of Sun Valley.

However, inquiry by The Post-Intelligencer along other channels disclosed that the author's death definitely was a suicide. Thus ends speculation, which may well have plagued Hemingway scholars for years to come.

At the urging of her friend, Dorice Taylor, a week after her husband's death, Mary Hemingway invited a small gathering of newsies to the Hemingway home, about a mile out of Ketchum.

Mary Hemingway Talks

Seattle Post-Intelligencer, July 9, 1961

KETCHUM, IDA. — "It had been a calm, good-natured dinner," Mary Hemingway said. "It was Saturday night. We had come home early. We went upstairs, and I went into the bedroom while Ernest was cleaning his teeth.

"I was sitting on the edge of the bed," she went on. "Suddenly a song came to my head. It was just a silly little song called 'Tutti Mi Chiamano Bionda' (Everybody Tells Me I'm Blonde). Just a silly little Italian folk song.

"I thought of it and said to Ernest, 'I have a present for you.' He stopped cleaning his teeth and listened. When he had finished, he came into the bedroom and we sang the last few lines together."

Mary Hemingway paused. "All this," she added, "made me feel that in some incredible way it was an accident."

Mrs. Hemingway looked around at the people gathered in the large living room of her Ketchum, Idaho, home where she talked about the legendary author who had shot and killed himself early last Sunday morning. For a full hour, "Miss Mary" Hemingway discussed their life together, their plans to travel, her husband's unpublished manuscripts, his habits, his religion, his attitudes and—most important to her—the most infamous legends that have been reactivated since his death.

Their final hours together, she said, were peaceful and happy. She described the five-day automobile trip across the country, from the Mayo Clinic to the Hemingway mountain home in Idaho. "We crossed a bridge over the Missouri River," she said, "and Ernest looked down and said, 'An inch deep and a mile wide.' In Montana, we stopped to watch some quail cross the road. The traffic wasn't bad, as we expected, and we took some side roads, to see the scenery. We got up early to travel. Ernest had always been a 5 o'clock man. We arrived early Friday afternoon, and on Saturday Ernest went for a long walk with George Brown. He loved to walk. They saw a deer. That night he took us to dinner at the Christiani restaurant in Ketchum, and we sat at his favorite table and had a lovely time."

That was the way it ended: a slow, pleasurable return home, a good day, a leisurely dinner and the final gift of love, a "silly little Italian folk song," sung together in the quiet of their bedroom. Next morning, Ernest Hemingway was found dead, a double-barreled shotgun lying across his lower legs.

Hemingway's widow is a small woman with a trim, attractive figure, a person of quick movements and keen, incisive speech. In agreeing to discuss her husband's life she refused to elaborate on the manner of his death but repeatedly volunteered that it had to be "some sort of incredible accident."

To bolster the story, she said that Hemingway (she referred to him as "Ernest," using the nickname "Papa" only twice) had suggested a trip to nearby Hailey to pick up some unfinished manuscripts which were left in a safety deposit vault in the First Security Bank of Idaho. The manuscripts, Mrs. Hemingway revealed, were placed in the vault before Hemingway's final trip to the Mayo Clinic on April 25. "With that in mind," she said, "it's hard to think that he could have had any plans except plans to write."

Mrs. Hemingway also refused to discuss the nature and degree of her husband's ill health, except for a brief written statement: "It was hypertension (high blood pressure) which did not respond properly to the usual treatment of that disease. If you want further elucidation, you could ask Dr. George Saviers of the Sun Valley Hospital, his physician here, or Dr. Hugh Butt at the Mayo Clinic, since I make no pretensions of being a medical expert."

Mrs. Hemingway revealed that "Papa" left "a great amount of unpublished work—none of it ready for publication, all of it needing polishing. "There is some poetry, but I don't know the title. There is a wonderful, witty thing about the early days in the Bahamas—or maybe it's Bimini—which was part of his writing about the sea." An unpublished work often described as a treatise on "the land, sea and air" exists. It was intended to be a collection, of which *The Old Man of the Sea* was to be a part, but Hemingway was persuaded to publish the latter as a complete novel.

"He had no plans to write a 5-pound or a 10-pound book," said Mary Hemingway. "He was planning three volumes, and I think that among his manuscripts I'll be able to find most of this.

"He was never eager to publish," she went on. "Why should you be in a hurry to move up from a 75 percent tax bracket to a 95 percent bracket?"

Which of his many works did he like best?

"That's really an impossible question to answer," she said. "He always regarded the last thing he had written as his best. Momentarily, he liked whatever was finished, and he was always trying to make his next work better than the last."

Mrs. Hemingway revealed that she and her husband planned to go to Cuba, later on to Europe ("Venice and southern France, which he liked") and return to Idaho "in time for the duck season." She added: "His plans were to live in places he liked best. Once we visited Italy—I think it was in 1948—and planned to stay for two days. We stayed for nine months and traveled all over the *Farewell to Arms* battleground."

Mrs. Hemingway granted the informal discussion with newsmen ("Please don't call it a press conference—that sounds so pretentious") with the purpose in mind of clearing up what she says are glaring inaccuracies about her husband. "I read where he had bluffed with two queens at poker and took $25,000," she said. "That's incredible. Ernest was never a big bettor. He would bet on Saturday night TV fights, a pigeon shoot or the World Series, but these were only $1 or $2 bets. In Cuba, he'd occasionally bet with the servants—you can see that would not amount to much. When we would visit a casino in Las Vegas or Monte Carlo or Havana, Ernest would put down $50 or a $100, and if his number didn't come up, he would walk away."

Mrs. Hemingway was particularly disturbed by one story which said that after the author had seen the motion picture version of his short story, "The Killers," he had said, "Get me to the bathroom." "That's ridiculous," she said. "He was perfectly capable of getting anywhere he wanted to go." She added that, contrary to such reports, Hemingway thought highly of the screen version of "The Killers." "He thought it was a brilliant job," she said. "The best of all the films done of his works. Being a perfectionist himself, he didn't like some other film versions of his works."

Mary Hemingway also objected to published accounts of their two 1954 plane crashes in Africa in which Hemingway was pictured as coming out of a "crocodile- and elephant-infested country with a bottle of gin in one hand and me in the other—It was not true, and he didn't like the image it portrayed. He regarded it as too theatrical."

Of his Catholic graveside services, Mrs. Hemingway volunteered the information that the author was raised as a Congregationalist. "Then, when he went to Italy to join the ambulance corps," she recalled, "they wanted to know, 'What religion?' He said, 'Anything,' so he got what amounted to a Catholic dog tag, and later he sort of became a Catholic. His second wife, Helene, was a Catholic, and Ernest practiced Catholicism for a while. When he won the Nobel prize, he was presented with a beautiful gold medal. He gave it to the Virgin de Cobre shrine in Santiago de Cuba. I don't know if it is still there."

Throughout the long discussion, Mrs. Hemingway remained composed and calm as she reviewed her life with "Papa," whom she married in Havana in 1946.

The Hemingway home here was purchased two years ago from millionaire Bob Topping for $50,000 and is regarded by local residents as "a steal at that price." Five zebra skins serve as scatter rugs in the 40-by-20-foot living room; a gun rack near the foyer where Hemingway committed suicide contains seven guns, each in a canvas case. Wall-length magazine racks hold virtually every current publication, and many book shelves are filled. Decorations include several Spanish porcelains depicting bullfight scenes with appropriate legends, such as "Pase de Muleta" and "La Codiga."

On one wall is a working map of Idaho's Sawtooth mountain range, and on another, next to the foyer, is a photographic reproduction of an early Picasso. The one photograph in the room is of Archie Moore, the prizefighter, shown with Hemingway's own trainer, George Brown. On it is the inscription: "To my friend Ernest Hemingway from Archie Moore, the ol' mongoose."

The living room is commanded by a huge, rough-stoned fireplace; next to it is a built-in 27-inch television set, which, said "Miss Mary," "is seldom in service."

"He watched the boxing matches, baseball and football," she said, "and, of course, he watched the inaugural. But he never looked at the rest of it."

Mrs. Hemingway herself is a writer. She was born and raised in Minnesota, worked on a newspaper in Chicago, and later became one of the few women war correspondents for Time and Life magazines. She talked freely of the many places she had visited with her husband, who taught her to become an expert huntress. Through the years, she had carefully guarded his working privacy, and local intimates of the family credit "Miss Mary" with keeping "Papa" on a good and productive writing schedule. Hemingway liked to maintain a tongue-in-cheek pretense that "Miss Mary" kept him on a tight leash, but this was always regarded as one of "Papa's" jokes.

When the question came, "What are your plans now?" Mary Hemingway answered: "My plans seem of no consequence whatever. Write? I do indeed. It's like breathing. It's like having plans to breathe."

At one point in the discussion, she looked about the room and said, "We had a very pleasant life together." And then, at the finish, as the people rose to leave, she volunteered one last corrective remark on her husband. Speaking quite firmly, she said: "The one thing that is always wrong when people speak of him is that they don't know what a quiet, soft-spoken, very gentle and thoughtful person he was."

Tears came abruptly, and "Miss Mary" turned away.

Supreme Court Justice William O. Douglas died on January 23, 1980. Some weeks after that, I made a pilgrimage, a very private one, by driving over to Goose Prairie, where he had lived. Goose Prairie is well up into the Cascades, a farmlike place with mountains and forest around and a wood-frame house, the windows of which overlook a meadow below. I found the entrance gate unlocked; the place was empty. I felt no qualms about invasion of privacy because this visitation would not be written about (until now), and my presence there was solely to pay my respects to one of America's greatest men. At the rear entrance, I found a sign that I knew would be there. It said "Honest Lawyer, One Flight Up." It would have been easy to take that sign as a treasured Douglas memento, but I disturbed nothing. Inside a kind of toolshed and garage was an old Plymouth with a fine coating of dust. I went back down the road to the highway, closed the gate, turned left and drove home, thinking of the time, in 1969, when I first wrote about Douglas. In 1975, when Douglas announced his retirement from the Court, The P-I reprinted those four columns in an updated form.

Justice William O. Douglas – I

Seattle Post-Intelligencer, November 13, 1975

SOME YEARS AGO, A YOUNG ATTORNEY set out on a mission to find Supreme Court Justice William O. Douglas at his home in Goose Prairie. With only slight poetic license—to protect Justice Douglas' privacy—he recorded the mission as follows: "Justice Douglas' home is located 50 miles out of Yakima, off the ninth dirt road on the left before you reach a sign saying 'Goose Prairie Cafe.' You then drive through a large mudhole, up the road until you come to a meadow. Across the meadow is a large gray house.

"At the back of the house is a sign stating 'Honest Lawyer—One Flight Up.' Go up the back stairs, knock on the door and Justice Douglas will be there."

The young attorney never recorded whether his hand shook as he knocked. But well it might. Young lawyers rarely knock at the back door of a legend. Justice Douglas is all of that. Only a handful of Supreme Court judges, living or dead, have had Douglas' impact on the Court's legal decisions—and American society at large.

Appointed in 1939, he served on the Court for 36 years. His majority opinions and ringing, eloquent dissents would fill a long shelf in a law library. His books on the law, on liberty, on conservation, hiking and travel are staggering in number. *Who's Who* lists him as the author of 19 books; librarians put the total closer to 30.

Twice he was promoted as a vice-presidential candidate, once by FDR in 1944, again by Harry Truman in 1948. He was mentioned for the presidency in 1962. He has always been controversial. Calls for his impeachment as a Supreme Court Justice were numerous, because he had been fearlessly outspoken, caustic, and even scathing. (The Nixon administration, using then Rep. Gerald Ford as the catalyst, tried to have him impeached in 1970.) But in case after case, he has come down hard on the side of individual rights and liberties.

His colleague on the bench, Justice Hugo Black, once said of him: "I suspect that he must have come into this world with a rush and that his first cry must have been to protest against something he saw at a glance was wrong or unjust."

As a youngster he did, indeed, see much that was wrong and unjust. Crippled by polio at the age of four, his withered legs were the object of ridicule by other children. To strengthen his legs he devoted himself to hiking and climbing the Cascades—and as a result, American got one of its most eloquent conservationists. He won a scholarship to Whitman College. He worked his way through high school and college in stores, cold-storage plants, orchards, and as a waiter, janitor and field hand. He once lived in a tent while attending Whitman.

To get to Columbia University Law School, he traveled as a custodian of a trainload of sheep to Chicago; the rest of the way he hopped freights and arrived in New York virtually broke. Knowing this, another justice said of him: "He came to know poverty and fear, and with an idealist's fervor, wanted to rid the world of them."

He later practiced law, taught at Columbia, then taught business law at Yale. As a part-time project, he produced a monumental eight-volume study that, in the words of one biographer, "documented the manner in which the equity receiverships were operated for the profit of the bankers at the expense of investors."

In 1936, at the age of 38, he was appointed to the Securities and Exchange Commission; less than two years later he was its chairman, and (to say the least) he hit the banking community and Wall Street like a ton of bricks. In one speech, delivered before the New York Stock Exchange, Douglas described the Exchange as a "cross between a casino and a private club," referring to some of its practices as those of "financial termites." Early on, conservatives knew their man.

A series of banking scandals, followed by reforms, developed during Douglas' tenure with the SEC. Then in April 1939, as Roosevelt sought liberal appointees to the Court, Douglas became an associate justice; at 40, he was the Court's youngest member in 125 years. For a long time the phrase, "Justice Douglas dissenting" became a familiar one, but with the development of the "Warren Court" in the early 1950s, he was found among the majority in a series of far-reaching decisions that have changed the direction of American society.

Justice William O. Douglas – II
Seattle Post-Intelligencer, November 14, 1975

DURING A LONG CONVERSATION with Supreme Court Justice William O. Douglas six years ago, he covered many wide-ranging subjects in response to questions. One of these questions involved the nature of the Court itself; how, by its majesty and institutional permanence, by the nature of its responsibilities, it affects the men who sit on this ultimate tribunal in the U.S. What happens to a man once he is elevated to the Court, once he is settled—for life, if he chooses?

"Very often a man changes when he becomes a member of the Court," said Justice Douglas. "It is why presidents are so frequently disappointed in their appointees. Take Warren (the late Chief Justice Earl Warren). In public life, when Warren was governor of California, he was a conservative person. He was used to dealing in pressures, resisting pressures, working for political support, compromising.

"But on the Supreme Court, there is no pressure—not of that kind. Of course, there is pressure. There is internal pressure: your own reading of history, the law, and social issues. So what happens then is that you gradually begin to see the *real* Earl Warren, the *real* Bill Douglas. You're not afraid of being fired, or offending some political group. You can be your own man."

Few Courts in American history came under the kinds of attacks leveled at the "Warren Court," of which Douglas was a member for 16 of his 36 years on the Supreme Court. (The Warren Court began in 1953 and ended with Warren's retirement in 1969, a few weeks before this interview took place.)

Much of the criticism of the Warren Court came from thoughtful judicial scholars, who thought the Court went too far in exercising power for reform. Most of it, however, was the rantings of the "impeach-Warren" mentality; Douglas' own impeachment was called for several times by ultra-conservatives. Only a year after this interview, Pres. Gerald Ford (then an obedient hatchet man in the House for Atty. Gen. John Mitchell and former Pres. Nixon) tried to get Douglas impeached,

Douglas spoke then of such attacks on the Court.

"These people have a point of view and a right to express these views granted by the First Amendment," he said. "I suppose the solution to attacks on the Court lies in education. We get so little of this in public schools. We are faced with the problem of how to run a multi-racial, multi-religious, multi-ideological society. Starting, say, at the junior high school level, in 50 years we might get some results."

As he spoke, Justice Douglas' face was active and expressive. Seeking a word, or a phrase, he would brush his hand quickly over his rumpled hair; a quick movement—no more—and always the cold, blue eyes, alive with his thoughts.

"It should be done," he added. "People should be taught what the Court means. What we've got in this country is something precious, something unique. Nothing like it anywhere in the world. We have a tremendous opportunity to get rid of the rancor—not all, perhaps, but some. To get rid of it all would take three times 40 years. But it's not being taught in the schools.

"By God," he went on, "I only got it by osmosis, this respect for the Constitution and the courts. And when you get it by osmosis, what do you get? You get it by the prejudices of the older folks."

It was mentioned that somebody—perhaps Chief Justice Warren himself—had said that if the Bill of Rights were put to a vote today, it would be defeated. Justice Douglas nodded. "There were some polls taken on this about 10 years ago," he said. "They took the Bill of Rights around for people to sign, and they shied away, suspicious of 'a document.' But if the Bill of Rights were put up for public debate—in open forums—I think it would be passed today.

"What people have to realize is what the Bill of Rights is all about. When the government gets on the backs of people—well, once it gets on the little guy's back, it's on yours, too. That's the way fascism grows. I'm not saying it's growing here. I'm saying that's the way it grows."

▼

Justice William O. Douglas – III
Seattle Post-Intelligencer, November 15, 1975

IN THE YEARS 1964 AND 1966 came the famed Escobedo and Miranda decisions, which revolutionized the process of criminal trials. The two decisions, Escobedo vs. Illinois and Miranda vs. Arizona, each by 5–4 majorities, found the U.S. Supreme Court ruling that a suspect must be informed by the police of his rights to silence and (in the case of Miranda) that the Constitution's demand for "due process of law" required an opportunity for every arrested person to see a lawyer before being questioned by the police. The decision further ruled that the state must provide a suspect with a lawyer if he is too poor to hire one.

The subsequent outcry has scarcely ceased. Cops have complained of being "handcuffed," editorial writers have wrung their hands, charges of "coddling criminals" have been leveled at the courts. As though anticipating a question on these decisions, Justice William O. Douglas shifted in his chair, ran his hands over his unruly hair, and began talking.

"Now, crime is a terrible problem, we all know that," he said. "But it happens that the FBI is able to live under the Miranda decision. That is because the FBI is smart, energetic, well-trained and well-paid. They have their advanced methods, their academies and all. But on a lot of levels, local levels, they don't pick the smartest or the best people or the best-trained to be policemen. They just pick the biggest guy. And they like to take shortcuts with the law. People get aroused about criminals, so police take shortcuts.

"It makes me think of the way they run courts in the People's Republic of China. Here, you've got this big hall, and they have hundreds of people in this room, and the police say, 'This man is guilty—what should we do with him?' So the people yell, 'Hang him!' Now that's a helluva way to run a courthouse. That's what we're trying to escape here."

These two decisions were among several that had a massive impact on the legal and social fabric of the nation. As Anthony Lewis of The New York Times pointed out, the Warren Court "set the United States on a new path in race relations, wiping out the legal basis for discrimination." Lewis wrote:

"By imposing the rule that all citizens must be represented equally in state legislatures and the national House of Representatives, the Court eliminated the rural bias from American politics. It wrote what amounted to a new constitutional code of criminal justice, one restraining the whole process of law enforcement from investigation through arrest and trial, and applied the code rigorously to state and local activities formerly outside federal standards. It greatly broadened the citizen's freedom to criticize public figures, and the artist's to express himself in unconventional, even shocking ways; it greatly restricted governmental authority to penalize the individual because of his beliefs or associations."

In virtually all of these cases, Justice Douglas ruled (and frequently wrote the opinions) for the majority. In one dissent, Justice Douglas alone, among nine justices, found worthy of consideration a plea by three Dallas youths that high school boys have a right to wear their hair long. "I suppose," said Justice Douglas, and one can almost hear the sigh in his words, "a nation bent on turning out robots might insist that every male have a crew cut and every female wear pigtails. But the ideas of 'life, liberty and the pursuit of happiness' expressed in the Declaration of Independence, later found specific definition in the Constitution itself, including, of course, freedom of expression and a wide zone of privacy."

Of all the decisions, Justice Douglas considered the reapportionment case—"one man, one vote"—the most important of the Warren Court. "That," he said, speaking softly, "broke up the rotten boroughs. It broke the stranglehold of the little cliques, particularly in the South, where three or four men decided what was good for the people. In some places, it changed the party in power." Justice Douglas paused, then laughed. "I remember in Arizona, a man told me—he was a Democrat: 'All I've got down here is a bunch of goddamned Republicans, and I can't get any appropriations.'

"But that decision—the reapportionment decision—catches up all the minority groups, the blacks, and it gives them tremendous voting power in the urban centers."

Justice William O. Douglas – IV
Seattle Post-Intelligencer, November 16, 1975

THE WORDS OF SUPREME COURT JUSTICE WILLIAM O. DOUGLAS, when read in notes or set in type, often give an impression that they were spoken at the top of his voice, a voice made shrill with indignation. Far from it. Justice Douglas' speech is soft, thoughtfully conceived, with a Western flavor and a tendency to use mild expletives. Now he was being asked, "What is the overriding—the single greatest—problem facing the nation today?" One was thinking of racial turmoil, war, environment.

Again, the voice came softly. "Well, you see the—well, I suppose in the simplest terms it's the disappearance of the university in the scholastic sense of the term. Some of the schools are good, but so many have disappeared in the scholastic sense.

"Instead, the university has become the heartbeat of industry, the heartbeat of the military-industrial complex. The tragedy of this is that no group of scholars is sitting apart, debating the dangers of what we are doing. Instead, we have a bunch of goddamned technocrats telling us how the goddamned thing works. And the technocrats aren't adequate critics of each other. A lot of what they do is secret; the students can't even get in. What we need are more people to study, debate, think, and try to give us directions.

"Now, who's sitting back and really thinking about disemployment, for example? How many people can private industry take care of in 10 years? These are the kind of big, staggering problems we have to face. The tragedy of the schools is that they're feeding on federal research funds, or trying to attract large private funds, to do special things. They're doing that instead of producing a community of scholars, of people who debate and try to reason where we are going."

The prolonged delays in implementing the Court's desegregation decision were, in Justice Douglas' opinion, predictable. "At the time of the desegregation decision, I thought that if the Court—my successors on the Court—succeeded in two generations in seeing the decisions come about, that would be good. I thought then, and I still think, that a quick solution is impossible. Under our constitutional system, there's not much that can be done. Johnny Jones has to bring a suit. Then Suzie Jones has to bring a suit. We don't have the power of the Interstate Commerce Commission, for example, to say all the states and all the schools should do so and so. It's inherent in our system that there'll be that delay. Our attitudes are deep-seated, and it takes a long time."

On his 70th birthday, Justice Douglas delivered a speech in which he said he saw no major role the Court could play in overcoming "the political bankruptcy of my generation." He called the elections of '63 "irrelevant to the problems of the people," and added: "Great tides are running all over the world. Young people are growing up to the dawning realization of the awful condition in which my generation has left the country."

What of the future of the Court? "The big decision before the Court will be in the area of what the government is doing to the individual," he said. "That's the classic conception of the controversy—is government doing something to the person or his property? For example, can the Pentagon send a man to Vietnam? That is a justifiable question.

"In property, Harry Truman seized the steel mills so he could carry on the Korean War. That was a justifiable question. He said he could. The

Court said no. It's what the government does to an individual or his property which represents the issues that would come before the Court."

The man who might have been president shrugged off the past. "Politics was never my dish. I never had a feeling for it. Running for office is something that has to build a fire in a man. God knows, I was promoted and pushed. FDR wanted me to run as his vice-president in 1944. Harry Truman wanted me to run with him in '48. Truman once told me, 'By God, Bill, you certainly missed the boat.' " Douglas chuckled. "Well, I missed *his* boat. I suppose we might have been elected." With a laugh, he dismissed it. "Then I'd probably have been the heir apparent—and I'd have had the privilege of running against Eisenhower."

B ill Gates was Seattle's first billionaire. His pictures and many stories about him appeared in various computer journals. But a columnist, being nosy, had to know more about him. What's he like personally? How does he have fun? It took three weeks to even get to Gates, but we ended up spending a pleasant two hours together. I was pleased when a Microsoft official told me, "Bill was really quite excited about this interview. You see, he grew up in Seattle reading your column." Could it be, in some measure, that I had inspired him? Are there royalties due for this?

Bill Gates – I

Seattle Times, July 29, 1990

IN COMPUTER TRADE CIRCLES, HE'S KNOWN AS the Whiz Kid; his employees call him Bill; and his family bestowed on him the name of William H. Gates III, so his family calls him Trey.

Most of the rest of us refer to Bill Gates as "that kid billionaire over in Bellevue." That is only two-thirds correct. He launched his career to the stratospheric billions when he was in his early 20s, which makes him, even at 34, something of a kid. A billionaire he surely is, but he isn't from Bellevue. He lives in Laurelhurst, and his corporate headquarters is in Redmond.

Visiting Bill Gates is like entering a well-kept college campus—tasteful, low-rise architecture, flowers, well-manicured lawns, guides or security guards to tell you where to park and how to get to where you want to go. Buildings are designated by numbers. After checking my appointment, one of the pleasant guards went to a wall-mounted telephone, returned and said, "You will find Bill Gates in Building 8, right next to this one."

My appointment with Gates was for 12:30, and a young dark-haired guy named Marty Taucher came out to greet me. "Bill is running a little behind today," he said, "so it will be a few minutes." While we sat on a sofa and waited outside Gates's office, Taucher filled me in on Microsoft. "This complex is 221 acres," he said. "There are 15 buildings here, but we are building two more new ones. The actual software manufacture is done in our plant in Bothell's Canyon Park. Here we have 3,500 employees and about 5,000 employees around the world. I was the 426th person hired here." There are nine people in Microsoft's public-relations department.

"Does everybody call him Bill?" I asked.

Taucher grinned. "Yes, he's Bill. That seems to fit best. We're a fairly informal company."

Many of the employees you see at Microsoft are in their 30s and even 20s. "This is a young company and we've grown fast in a new industry," Taucher said. "We look for computer programming superstars." Taucher said that Microsoft recruits intensely, making it sound like nothing so much as the NFL's draft of college football stars. "We recruit from 20 leading technical schools around the country," Taucher said. "We have a fine pool of talent, because we go in for this aggressive recruiting."

Taucher ducked out and went into Bill Gates's office, unannounced. When he returned he said, "It will be a few more minutes." It appears that Gates's day includes a succession of meetings. He seems to be programmed down to the minute. "Bill comes into the office about 9," Taucher said, "and usually stays until 11 at night."

"But the rest of you go home at 5," I said. Marty rolled his eyes. "Not around here," he said. "We work long hours, too, and frequently on weekends."

Along with its support staff, Microsoft is made up of whiz-kid programmers and marketing and sales people. Microsoft recently introduced Windows 3.0, and sales took off like something launched at Cape Canaveral. About 500,000 programs have been sold in two months, far above even Gates's projections.

Then Taucher volunteered, "You came in on the right day. In a few minutes, at 1 o'clock, we are announcing our corporate sales for the year. More than $1 billion." It turned out to be $1.18 billion—which made Microsoft the first computer software company to exceed $1 billion. Its quarterly profits were up 76 percent from $45.4 million last year.

I had done some reading on Bill Gates before meeting him. This is not hard to do, because he is a cover boy, or centerfold, for dozens of business and computer publications. As it develops, Bill Gates is far more than a computer whiz. Business Week described him as having "the right blend of youthful energy, technical acumen, intellectual breadth and business savvy to adjust as his company matures." Make no mistake, he runs this company. His title is chief executive officer, although he recently hired Mike Hallman away from Boeing. Hallman is president and chief operating officer. Bill Gates seems to have an instinctive feel for running a business, which is why Microsoft has grown while many computer-whiz entrepreneurs have failed. According to Business Week, he has prospered in the turbulent, volatile, savagely competitive business of software development because "he has staying power." As Microsoft grew, Gates began bringing in professional managers. One former Microsoft exec said, "He learned at a young age that you've got to give up power to get power." That overworked and loosely defined word *genius* gets floated around when Gates is the topic of conversation. Certainly, he was dazzling teachers and friends and parents when he was an eighth-grader at Lakeside School.

In a few more minutes, Marty Taucher led me into Gates's office. Seattle's only billionaire and perhaps one of the 10 richest people in America has a small, cluttered office that would do credit to a sloppy newspaperman. He was warm, friendly and smiling. He wore no tie, wrinkled slacks and soft shoes. His hair is sandy and tousled, and his frame is spare and active.

With his thin, scholarly face and large horn-rimmed glasses, he looked like the teacher of a science course I once flunked.

This is the first of a series on Bill Gates. Who is he, really? What does he think? What are his values? Who are his friends? Stop by this space Tuesday.

Bill Gates – II

Seattle Times, July 31, 1990

HERE WE ARE, STANDING IN THE SMALL, cluttered office of William H. Gates III, known to his family as Trey, known to his friends, associates and 3,500 Microsoft employees as Bill.

He is 34, the Northwest's first and only billionaire, one of the richest men in America. Flat out, you can say he's a genius. Not only is Bill Gates a computer wizard, his business acumen is 3.2 degrees sharper than mustard. On the very day I saw Gates, his company reported fiscal year sales of $1.18 billion—the first computer software company to exceed $1 billion. Yet here he was, casually dressed, tousled hair, soft shoes and an easy smile. What do you ask a guy like this? So I blurted something out: "Suppose nobody had invented computers, suppose computers didn't exist. What would you be doing today?"

He seemed to like the question.

"Something related to science, probably," he said. "Math, physics, medicine. Those are the things I enjoy reading about. People I admire work in those fields." Gates added: "Pure science has an appeal for me because you can tell if you really did something or not. You know who does good stuff. One of my favorite people is a guy who died recently, Richard Feynman. Feynman was a prof at Cal Tech, kind of an unusual guy, who had his own way of thinking about things. He was also very good at physics."

We were off and running. There would be no silly questions about girlfriends, being an eligible bachelor, how much money he really has—trivial junk like that doesn't matter. "What kind of stuff do you read?" I asked.

He liked this question, too. "A lot more history and biographies than science," he said. "About every fourth book I read is a science book. Science books take longer to read. A book on the molecular biology of genes took me a year and a half to read. Some of the stuff I read is like *Barbarians at the Gate,* which everybody read. Now I'm reading this Picasso thing. In history, I get interested in an era, like the making of the atomic bomb. There's about 10 great books on that. Biographies: Napoleon. FDR. The magazine I spend most of my days reading is the Economist, a British news weekly. It's incredible. I read that more than Scientific American."

Bill Gates is an incurable workaholic. He comes to his campuslike Microsoft headquarters (15 buildings, 221 acres) at 9 a.m. He goes home at 11 p.m. When does he find time to read? He reads some at work, of course, or at night when he goes home to Laurelhurst. "I'm a fast reader," he said. "I always thought about taking one of those speed-reading courses, but I'm fairly high up on their scale even without that." Even though he reads computer magazines at a breakneck pace and rapidly devours current events, he truly savors reading. On the heavier stuff—science, for example—he slows down.

"You've got to make sure you're paying attention," he said. "You find yourself moving along and then saying, 'Wait a minute, did I really understand that or did the words just fly into my head?' I read an hour almost every night. It's part of falling asleep. Like anyone who loves books, if you get into a good book, it's hard to go to sleep. I like to get seven hours of sleep. Even though it's fun to stay up all night, maybe taking a red-eye flight, if I have to be creative I need seven hours. I can give a speech without much sleep. I can do parts of my job that way, but in thinking creatively, I'm not much good without seven hours."

Thinking creatively. Computer stuff. To invade Bill Gates's thinking on his own intellectual turf, one would have a better chance of learning Sanskrit than computer language. In workaday terminology his speech is splattered with "randomness" (a confused or haphazard situation) or "bandwidth" (the amount of information one can absorb); being young, he uses "cool" a lot, or "super," or "gee whiz," and there is a genuinely boyish quality about him when he says he had "the funnest" time when doing something.

Who are his friends? Paul Allen, his co-founder of Microsoft, now owner of the Portland Trail Blazers basketball team, is still one of his best friends, even though Allen has split off from Microsoft. Some of his friends are kids he knew in high school; many are in the computer business.

"It's interesting," he said. "I live in Laurelhurst, my family lives about a mile away. My little sister lives a half mile away. I have another sister in Spokane. I'm very close to my family. For a guy my age, I spend more time with my family than anyone I know. My parents are a lot of fun. My dad," he said, referring to William Gates Jr., a prominent Seattle lawyer, "ran the United Way campaign last year." He speaks of "my mom" with abounding affection. She, of course, is Mary Gates, a former schoolteacher, a director of First Interstate Bank, a civic activist and a member of the UW Board of Regents.

"I recently built a place on Hood Canal," he said, "where there's a house for each of us. I'm there with my family every other weekend. I'm close to Paul Allen, who started Microsoft with me. Paul got cancer, Hodgkin's disease; he was gone from work almost two years. I guess he decided life was short. I had pushed him pretty hard. He wanted to go out and prove he could do his own thing. I tried to convince him to do that within the context of Microsoft, but he decided to do it himself. About 90 percent of his wealth is in Microsoft stock, he's on our board, he gives us good ideas. Now he's got the Portland Trail Blazers, and one of the

funnest things I've done is go with Paul to all those NBA playoff games.
I went to Portland and Phoenix and Detroit and got to know some of the
players. We had a wonderful time."

Bill Gates – III

Seattle Times, August 2, 1990

JUST THE FACT—A RARE FACT, TO BE SURE—of being an authentic billionaire
changes your life forever. You are an instant celebrity, whether you like
or not. You are an irrevocable celebrity, doomed forever to be different
from thee and me.

Such wealth is an assault on your senses, your values, your privacy,
your view of the world, your feeling of security. Such wealth distorts
virtually all relationships, all normal human contact. Many old friends
are lost along the way, and your sense of contentment, the epicenter of
your existence, must come from a few close friends and your family. Some
billionaires have allowed these relationships to be destroyed. Bill Gates,
the billionaire owner of Microsoft, the nation's largest computer-pro-
gramming company, appears to be a heartening, perhaps even an
inspiring exception. There is a lot of the kid in him yet, something of the
little boy, a youthful enthusiasm that it's easy to find engaging. Here he
is on the subject of recreation:

"If you look through my CD collection, you'd see that I like Western
rock. And I probably know the songs of more musicals than most people.
I have almost a complete collection of songs from musicals. I like modern
rock. I go out dancing, to the normal dance places. I get down to the
Pioneer Square area, places on the East Side. It ends up being a time when
we're celebrating product shipments as much as anything. Or when we
have a sales meeting. That's a chance for me to get out and see my own
city."

If you go out dancing, you probably have seen Bill Gates without
knowing it, because most people don't recognize him on sight. He has
managed, somehow, to retain a certain degree of anonymity. "I don't get
recognized very much," he said, as we talked in his office at the Microsoft
headquarters in Redmond. Sometimes on a plane flight people recognize
me. Not just people from Seattle, but businesspeople who use computers.
Sometimes they come to my seat—they come politely, nice people—and

have some computer-related story. Or they just want to say hello. But if I go out to dinner it would be fairly unusual for someone to recognize me—and extremely rare that someone would bother me."

A vagrant thought occurred as Bill Gates talked on. No matter what room he ever walked out of, the space would suffer a profound brain drain. Yet there is nothing arrogant about him, nothing elitist. "Suppose," I asked him, "that Ken Behring walked in here and offered you a chance to buy the Seahawks football team?" With Gates's net worth sometimes pegged as high as $2 billion, the price of the Seahawks would be chicken feed to him. Not even hesitating, Bill Gates said, "No, even if I had a lot of free time, I wouldn't buy the franchise. First of all, it doesn't fascinate me. Being the owner of a sports team is a strange thing—because you're not really creating anything. You just own something that already exists. It's fun if I create a good software product. Like we created Windows 3.0, and that was a lot of fun. Certainly, there's an element of ego in getting up, demonstrating it, having people respond positively. The involvement I have here meets whatever needs I have for ego satisfaction. My job gives me all the public exposure I need."

Gates talked about his friend and Microsoft co-founder, Paul Allen, owner of the Portland Trail Blazers basketball team. "But if I had free time, I'd spend it funding a research center, or working with biotechnology," Gates said. "I'd rather put myself into something like that where I have unique interests. The truth is, I get much of my fun by being Paul's friend. Actually, I don't know how much fun I'd have going to those Trail Blazer games without him. You start going, you learn the players' backgrounds. You meet them, you see them lose, it's one of those addictive things. I had fun doing that. Why was I using my mind like that? Well, it's fun." Bill Gates paused a moment, then added: "I think you're allowed to have some random facts in your head."

Where does he see himself in the community? Not now, perhaps, but 10 or 20 years from now, a man of immensely powerful wealth. The name of the late Ned Skinner popped up immediately. Along with the names of Jim Ellis and the late Eddie Carlson. Clearly, Gates admires the doers, the movers, the shakers, who have enriched Seattle's history. "Seattle is a community that *has* people like Ned Skinner," he said, "business leaders who played a positive role. Seattle is a community where people know each other, can pull together." He mentioned Forward Thrust, United Way, the World's Fair—things in which the power hitters took a positive stand. "I admire the way people do these kinds of things. As I get older, and I'm not tied down in here 24 hours a day, making things happen, I expect to be one of those kinds of people. I don't see any circumstance where I'd move to another city. I grew up here, my business is here. So I expect to be one of those people, where there's a problem in the community, and they want someone to serve . . . I'd know other people in the community, and I'd want to play some kind of role."

The interview, if that's what it has to be called, was over. As I drove out of the Microsoft campus, the names of Ned Skinner, Eddie Carlson, Jim Ellis and many others kept recurring. Young Bill Gates wants to be like them. I think we've got a pretty good billionaire on our hands.

Due to the steadfastness of Senators Dan Evans and Slade Gorton, the Reagan administration finally had to swallow hard and accept William Dwyer as a federal judge. Though they didn't understand, and never will, it was that sorry group's finest act in office.

William Dwyer

Seattle Times, June 21, 1987

BY THE VERY NATURE OF THOSE long-running "new development" type of stories, something gets lost in their almost daily repetition. What gets lost, usually, is the nature, the vitality, the juice of people involved.

No better example exists than the case of William Dwyer's nomination more than a year ago to the U.S. District Court bench in Seattle. This is truly one of those long-running "development" stories. In the beginning, Dwyer's nomination—hailed by most of the legal community— seemed assured. Then politics got into it, then anxiety, then bitterness; charges of broken promises have been hurled. As of now, Sen. Dan Evans is threatening to hold up other of the Reagan administration's judicial appointments unless Dwyer's name is again submitted for the judgeship. At one point in this sorry, interminable serial, President Reagan himself called Dwyer to congratulate him on his seemingly assured appointment.

Now it emerges that Dwyer's nomination is encountering an almost faceless, but fierce, opposition from the political far right. At the same time, his supporters include not only a majority of the legal profession, but Republican and Democratic partisans as well. They are almost passionate in their belief that Dwyer is an outstanding candidate for the federal bench. A sampling of the flood of local letters to the Justice Department on Dwyer's behalf reads like a who's who of business and civic leaders, attorneys and judges. They include letters of support from Republican Norm Maleng, King County's prosecuting attorney, and Seattle Police Chief Patrick Fitzsimons.

So what we have here is a kind of "polarization" of opinion. On the one side is an unprecedented cross section of informed supporters—of all political shadings—urging Dwyer's appointment. On the other side is a faceless, ideological cluster of ultra-conservatives spreading false rumors and lies about an outstanding judicial nominee.

What gets lost here, as these running story developments unfold, is the man himself. Who is Bill Dwyer? What is he? About all we are really told is that he is considered an outstanding judicial candidate and that he is a "liberal" Democrat. Giving Bill Dwyer the shallow label of "liberal" is to say of melody that it amounts to a symphony. There are many bars of music that make the man.

Curiously, in the 14 months since Dwyer's nomination for the federal bench, only one in-depth story has been written about him in the local papers. This was a profile that appeared in The Times on March 14, 1986. In it was included one tribute by attorney Lem Howell: "If there was one lawyer in the State of Washington that any lawyer or any judge would want to be their lawyer, I think it is Bill Dwyer. He's a man of total integrity, he's honest, he's bright, he's capable, he's hard-working, he's well-respected, he's reasonable."

Aside from divine revelation, that's about all you can hope to get from a lawyer—or a judge.

I have known Bill Dwyer for more than 30 years, and I have often said (in moments of presumption) that he is the best friend I have. That may not be reciprocal, but no matter. Those of us who claim his friendship talk about him a lot. We see him as a richly shared experience, and some of us, I think, feel rather sorry for people who don't know him as well as we do.

His own unspoken, private integrity is balanced by a tolerance and compassion that make him an easy mark for those in need of help. A number of friends refer to him as "the godfather," using it as a term of almost familial endearment. Years ago, some of us called him "Destructo," a nickname that is hazy in its beginnings, but one that stuck. Once, when he brought in a settlement against American League baseball owners who capitulated and put back a franchise stolen from Seattle, a mutual friend called to exult: "We don't call him Destructo for nothing, do we?"

Bill Dwyer has an almost lethal wit that he rarely turns against others, using it mostly in self-deprecation; he shuns pomposity. Today, he drinks sparingly, if at all, but there was a time when he liked to sit up into the tall hours, spinning stories and enjoying the confidence of the cups. He may be all lawyer, but within him is a romantic, a writer and a poet—a man who can quote great swatches of Shakespeare and other writers he admires. Material possessions mean little to him, even though his law practice has brought him moderate wealth. "Money is good for only three things," I have heard him say. "It should buy good food, a good place to live and the freedom to travel. All else is superfluous."

An astonishing amount of his varied practice has been pro bono work—legal service for free. Though he has brought in enormous settlements in antitrust cases, he is not, as Charlie Burdell Jr. was quoted as saying, "a person who will sell his talents to the highest bidder." He has defended Black Panthers, disbarred lawyers, small theater owners and other people who need help. "He's very much a defender of the human spirit and the freedom of the human spirit," says his friend, Jim Wilson, legal counsel to the University of Washington.

There is more to say of him, to be sure: A writer of surpassing skill, a creative legal scholar, an innovative teacher of the law, a devoted father and husband—all things that should not be forgotten in the numbing, repetitive sameness of developing stories about his judicial appointment.

And always, of course, there is the pleasure of his company. The air becomes less troubled when he is around. Good things happen when he is near.

Warren G. Magnuson was any columnist's dream, and I wrote several about him, in Washington, D.C., and here at home. During his senatorial campaign one year, I flew to Yakima with him, just to watch the old boy in action. He was feted and fed from the moment of arrival, giving speeches along the way. He also visited a nearby Indian reservation. That evening I sat with him in his small hotel suite. He began drinking his favorite: vodka and water. He had a speech scheduled that evening, at 7, to an audience of farmers and ranchers—always a tough crowd. As speech time neared, I thought he had blown it. On the walk to the church basement, where some 50 people waited, it became clear Maggie had taken on too much fuel.

He attacked his audience. He was not insulting, but he was a bit hostile, and I thought, "Oh, man, he's losing this crowd." But as the evening wore on, the vodka wore off. The audience turned from being critical to being somewhat neutral, as Maggie answered more and more questions. It was now getting along toward 9:30, and plainly he had won them over. He stayed until past 10 o'clock talking to small groups.

It had been a long day; and his schedule was a killer. But here he was, still talking to the few citizens who stayed to the end.

As we walked back to the hotel, I said, "Why do you do it, why do you stay so long? Even if you won them all you'd only get a few votes."

"Because I like it," he said. "I like getting out among people like that. You get to know them that way. You find out what's on their minds." A remarkable man.

Senator Warren G. Magnuson

Seattle Times, December 6, 1983

THE SENATOR AND GERMAINE LIVE in their house atop Queen Anne Hill, where they can watch a beautiful part of the world go by—the harbor of Elliott Bay, the moving ships and ferries, the young people who stop in front of their home to lean on the balustrade at Eighth Avenue West to view the harbor, the islands and the Olympics beyond. It is a house with a warm feeling. Not at all pretentious, but softly carpeted, with period furniture, a large kitchen and a hallway where the senator's own paintings hang.

The paintings are by no means Louvre quality, but you might want to own one of them, even if you did not know they were painted by Warren G. Magnuson.

Days for the senator and his wife are busy. Many ordinary people still can't get it through their heads that Maggie is no longer the most powerful man in the U.S. Senate, so the telephone rings constantly. Germaine takes most of the calls. "They call wanting something done," she says, "and when you try to tell them that Warren is not in a position to do what he used to, they say, 'But nobody can take his power away.' They think all he has to do is pick up a phone. I try to get them to call their congressman or that man who took Warren's place, but some of them don't even know who their congressman is. Sometimes," she laughs, "I feel like I'm giving civics lessons. And, of course, Warren is a doer, and it makes him feel . . . well, because he can't do those things for them." The heavyweights call, too. The Mondales and the Glenns and the others who want to be president. Senators drop by from Washington, D.C., and, of course, the local Democrats. "Sometimes I feel like the Godfather," Maggie chuckled, "a political Godfather."

I explained that I did not come to talk about the big hitters, the national power brokers, the long-gone presidents he had known and worked with. How did it all start? What was it like before he became president pro tem of the Senate, fourth in line to the presidency, with No. 3 on his Washington, D.C., license plate? That is over, of course, but what was it like as a kid?

He came here from North Dakota when he was 19, he said. He intended to go to Stanford, but he stopped here and liked it. He got a job as an oil wiper with the American Mail line, then shipped out to the Orient and stayed a year. When he returned, he went back to North Dakota, worked a summer in the harvests, and he and a buddy "rode the blinds" to Seattle. "That's when I joined the IWW," he smiled. "I became a Wobbly." It was outright extortion, not conviction. The Wobs who also rode the blinds made the two kids cough up $5 apiece to join the International Workers of the World. "If they'd known we had the rest of our savings in our shoes, they'd have knocked us on the head for it. I've still got my old Wobbly card around here somewhere."

He decided to enroll at the University of Washington, but he needed money, so he went out to see Enoch Bagshaw, the hard-bitten old football coach, and Baggy said, "Well, I'm always looking for football players," and got him a job delivering ice. He was a young, tough kid, a good athlete, and Baggy was then fashioning the Husky Rose Bowl teams of 1924 and 1926. "I was small, but they had small quarterbacks in those days. George Guttormsen played ahead of me, and so did a fellow named McGee. I was on the supervarsity. We learned the other team's plays, and on Wednesday we'd go up against the varsity, and, Jesus, they would slam us around! There was no grass, just dirt, and when the rain soaked the field long enough, when it dried, it was like cement. I made the squad, though, and I got to play two minutes in the Rose Bowl."

He finished law school in 1929, "and I always was a good student, I was Order of Coif, the highest law-school honor there was." Al Schweppe was his law-school dean, and he took the required Latin from the famed UW professor Edmond Meany, the fellow they named the hall and later the hotel after. Maggie remembers how beautiful the UW campus was then and how a neighborhood bulldog adopted him and followed him to class. "Meany got so he liked the bulldog, and he would let him sleep under the desk during lectures," Maggie said. "Can you imagine anything like that happening now?"

The Depression came and Al Schweppe got him a job as secretary to the Municipal League. Later he became an assistant U.S. attorney and then King County prosecutor. He seems to take pride in the fact that he personally handled his own cases as prosecutor. "(Norm) Maleng and Chuck Carroll never tried their own cases, but I tried them all. I had Russian Mary, a tough old gal who killed a guy in Hooverville. I defended a guy once in the famous Black and Tan murder—you remember the old Black and Tan up on 12th and Jackson? Well, I defended the killer, and you could do that in those days. His name was Moultray, Percy Moultray, and it was a cold-blooded killing, but I got him off with second degree. He didn't even want parole. He loved it in the penitentiary, and he became foreman of the leather shop and he would send me wallets every Christmas." As a U.S. attorney, Magnuson tried lots of bootleg cases. "Particularly Whatcom County," he said. "We had a list of cases this long, because Whatcom County was a great moonshining place. Every day at 3 o'clock the judge—I think his name was Judge Nueter—would recess the court. Even if a jury had been out only five minutes! And finally I caught him in the Leopold Hotel and said, 'Judge, what are you doing, dismissing those cases at 3 o'clock?' He said, 'Young man, don't you know that's milking time in Whatcom County?' "

He warmed up as he talked, forgetting to relight the cigar he rolled in his fingers. I had a faint impression that Germaine rationed his cigars. And, as he warmed up with these old stories, he laughed more about the memories, and it was easy to forget that this man, at one recent time, almost ran the U.S. government as chairman of the Senate Appropriations Committee. Nothing requiring money happened without his permission.

"Now I tried a murder case once involving an Indian killing up on the island of Oona in Alaska," he went on. "You want to hear about that? One Indian shot another Indian over a woman, and I sent a U.S. marshal up there to Oona to bring her down to testify. Now, when you are a good lawyer and you have a witness like that, the first thing you want to prove is that you have a reluctant witness, so I set out to prove that she did not come to Seattle of her own free will. So I put her on the stand and asked her, 'Do you know this marshal sitting over here?' Well, she didn't know. Then I asked, 'Did he come to your house and serve some papers on you?' She didn't seem to understand. After about eight or nine questions like that, I got desperate, and I said, 'Tell the court, did this man subpoena you?' Her eyes brightened up and she said, 'Yes, once in Oona and twice on the boat.' Jesus, that poor marshal! We had to adjourn the court."

When he was King County prosecutor, Maggie tangled with the Rev.

Mark Matthews because he allowed beer sales on Sunday. "You remember Doc Matthews? He was Seattle's Moral Majority then. He came with a bunch of preachers and said he would ruin me politically if I didn't stop beer sales. I said, 'Do you want me to enforce all the Blue Laws?' He said, 'Yes,' so the next Sunday I shut down beer sales and the ball games and the theaters and the racetrack. Joe Gottstein went crazy. The next week old Doc Matthews came back and said, 'That's enough, maybe you'd better call it off,' and we got to be pretty good friends after that. Of course, they couldn't have ruined me politically because my district was the 37th, which took in downtown, and all the restaurant guys liked me."

Maggie is the man who found Joe Gottstein the property on which to build Longacres. As a state legislator he tried to permit cocktail lounges in Washington state some 15 years before they came to pass, and he also introduced a bill in the Legislature to permit the 18-year-old vote, "and look how many years it took to get it. Mike Mansfield and I made it a federal law and that made *all* the states put it in.

"You know, I never really intended to run for Congress that first time back in the '30s. I had an offer from George Vanderveer to practice law with him. He was a great lawyer, and I would have made a fortune, wouldn't I? But I talked to George before I filed, and he said, 'Go ahead, do it for a couple of years. That will be good experience for you, and then you can come home and work with me.' And I went back there for what was supposed to be a couple of years and ended up staying 44 years. So beginning in 1930, when I was special prosecutor, and then the Legislature and then prosecuting attorney, and chief assistant district attorney and then Congress and then the Senate, I was 50 years in public office. The longest of anybody in history around here."

In the spring of 1990, I took my 1978 motor home and my 1980 dog, and together we explored some of Idaho, Utah, Nevada, Arizona and, finally, New Mexico. We stopped in Santa Fe. Through a mutual acquaintance who knew him well, I sought a chance to talk to one of the arch-villains of my memories, John Ehrlichman. At first, I was told, Ehrlichman didn't want to talk to me because I had been rough on him in print—right in his then-hometown of Seattle. Both of us, it turned out, changed our minds.

John Ehrlichman - I

Seattle Times, May 6, 1990

SANTA FE, N.M. — It had snowed the night before in this artsy, craftsy, touristy, sometimes precious, but altogether laid-back town in northern New Mexico. Because of the 7,000-foot altitude, there is cold and snow, and we had abandoned the motor home for the warmth of a motel room. The phone rang at 8 a.m. It was John Ehrlichman, and he was laughing. "I thought some malevolent force from Seattle brought in this terrible weather."

It was my first encounter with John Ehrlichman, who, in some ways, can be counted as one of Seattle's most notorious citizens. The John Ehrlichman I remember—strictly from viewing the Watergate hearings on TV in the early 1970s—was snarly, tough, snappish, arrogant, with the audacity to lecture Congress before the so-called Ervin investigating committee. He said that some of Sam Ervin's Senate colleagues showed up drunk on the Senate floor. He was combative, quite unattractive in demeanor and manner. So many of us hated him then. He was Richard Nixon's point man, his hired gun, his advocate. He was President Nixon's counsel on domestic affairs—and, therefore, one of the most powerful men in America.

Some of us smiled when Watergate unfolded. We made vengeful, bitter jokes. We said that the boys in the White House, including Ehrlichman, were suddenly taking an interest in prison reform. Lord, how we hated those people—suborners of the Constitution, liars, cheats, break-in artists—an administration that had its dread little "enemies list" and set the IRS and the FBI on its perceived enemies. Among those who protected Richard Nixon, the most suspicious, reclusive and devious of our presidents, were Ehrlichman and Bob Haldeman, Chuck Colson, John Dean and the Attorney General of the United States, John Mitchell.

That was about 18 years ago. This morning in Santa Fe, when Ehrlichman called, things were much different. I had arranged the call through a mutual acquaintance. We made a date for lunch at a place called The Pink Adobe on the old Santa Fe Trail. Ehrlichman is 65 now, but tall and straight. He wears a well-manicured salt-and-pepper beard. He came across the street, smiling—smiling, for God's sake!—a tall man with long strides, wearing an open sports-shirt, slacks, and a sky-blue sweater with a small food stain on it. What happened to the well-tailored, lofty fellow we saw on TV? The Ehrlichman who once said of L. Patrick Gray, embattled FBI director, during Watergate, "Leave him twisting slowly in the wind."

For a while we talked about mutual friends in Seattle. Ehrlichman talked of his old law practice in Seattle. He had fought and won two big environmental cases, barring commercial development on Guemes Island and Port Susan. He became an expert in real estate law and in land usage. The thing that strikes you now is his proclivity for laughter and his gift for the subtle phrase. He is as unassuming and friendly as the waiter who pats him on the shoulder and apologizes for taking so long. The trappings of power are long gone but not the sense of humor that made him unique among Nixon's dour men. Now he can even laugh about Watergate.

He talked about leaving Washington—Nixon had resigned, but the scandal was in full bloom—and how he was taking his family home to Seattle. "We were flying for the first time on a commercial flight instead of Air Force One," he said, laughing. "And one of my children, maybe Jody, said, 'Why Dad, this is absolutely terrible.' "

Curiously, with his telling of that anecdote, you found yourself *liking* the guy.

Watergate took a terrible toll on John Ehrlichman—it cost him his marriage, his freedom, his civil rights, his respect in the community. Not only did you like him for the casual, easy conversation, you began to think in pluses. After all, here was a guy, sitting at this table, who had reached career heights that few men ever scale—then he crashed. Yet he picked himself up, summoned forth some inner strength and carved out a successful new career in the toughest of all rackets—that of a free-lance writer. Fewer than 5 percent of all writers can say that.

He taught himself to write. He has written several books, most notably *The Company* and *Witness to Power*. He writes for magazines, for journals, for newspapers, whatever. Most recent of Ehrlichman's work was a highly readable, sensitive story in Parade magazine on the life of ordinary Soviet citizens. He brings to writing some of the qualities that made him disliked in Washington—diligence, total sobriety and the kind of iron self-discipline it takes to be successful. He writes at home, in his pink adobe house overlooking Santa Fe, doing it all in longhand, using a clipboard and legal tablet. "I can type, but I can't think when I type," he says. He doesn't think his writing career is anything special. He thinks the same thing about a career in government and business. "If you're halfway bright and you have a certain diligence, you are going to do all right in government," he says. "But only about one-tenth of 1 percent have these qualities."

Ehrlichman is equally unimpressed with many leading business executives, especially the third-generation richniks who inherited their wealth. He knows hundreds of chairmen and CEOs; many he met during his White House days, but quite a few more recently through his yearly lectures at Stanford. "I expected guys like Henry Ford the 3rd or 4th, or whoever, to have their daddys' ramrod backbones and steely eyes," he said. After taking a good look at them, he concluded they weren't like their ancestors. "Then I decided that competition in business isn't all that tough, either."

John Ehrlichman – II

Seattle Times, May 8, 1990

SANTA FE, N.M. — Ernie Gann, the famed writer and pilot, titled one of his books *Fate Is the Hunter*. You are the quarry, fate is the hunter; fate always enters into the decisions you make. Whether you are an airline pilot, as Gann was, or a political operative, as John Ehrlichman was, fate has much to do with what happens to you.

This thought intruded as we sat over lunch with Ehrlichman here. About 18 years ago, Ehrlichman, as domestic counsel to President Nixon, was one of the most powerful men in the U.S. Businessmen and politicians came to him as supplicants. He met with Nixon almost daily. He was then thought of as arrogant, somewhat aloof, even cruel at times. If he was arrogant, he had much to be arrogant about—a brilliant planner, a doer. He was Seattle's most visible and shining alumnus on the national scene. Ehrlichman was a man about whom Theodore White, the chronicler of presidential campaigns, would write: "He was one of those indispensable individuals who could translate policy, once set, into programs and actions. His shop was one of the few at the White House where ideas were seriously entertained—good ideas, too, on energy, on land-use policy, on urbanization, on preservation of the American environment."

But something went terribly wrong. Ehrlichman made a fateful decision that would cost him years of disillusionment, sorrow and punishment. Ehrlichman's White House position, as well as his ability, attracted attention. "A very large company offered me a good job in New York," he said.

"As corporate counsel?"

"Just say it was working for a big conglomerate," he replied.

So, toward the close of Nixon's first term, he turned in his resignation as the President's domestic adviser. "I explained my reasons, but Nixon asked me to stay on until after the 1972 election." His eyes flashed briefly when somebody said, "That was a mistake." He stayed too long and soon was caught up in the squalid doings of Watergate—eventually convicted of conspiracy, obstruction of justice and two counts of perjury. He spent 15 months in prison, his life shattered, his integrity in shambles.

Fate is the hunter.

When he tried to leave Nixon's White House late in 1972, he was explaining now, "I felt I had become part of the problem." As Nixon's domestic adviser, he had stepped on too many big toes. For example, he opposed plans by the secretary of the Navy and the Army chief of staff to build a luxury military hotel in Hawaii. "It was to be all suites," Ehrlichman said with a smile, "so there was no doubt who this hotel was for: officers, not enlisted men. Another thing, they planned to finance it with PX profits, which was outrageous. That money was supposed to go exclusively for the well-being of military families." He managed to change some of the worst features of the scheme, but from then on the Pentagon began to end-run him.

"Do you communicate with Nixon now?"

Ehrlichman's face darkened. "No," he said. After a long pause, he added: "I think the last time I was in contact with him was when I tried to subpoena him for my trial in 1975. In his new book, Nixon distorted the facts about resisting my subpoena. In his book he says he didn't want to testify against his aides about what happened. But that is precisely what I subpoenaed him for."

Of all the president's men, none turned more savagely against Nixon than John Ehrlichman. For weeks, he said, in preparation for his trial, he listened to the infamous Oval Office recordings, the so-called "smoking gun" tapes. Ehrlichman had been a loyalist to the end. But in listening to the tapes, he found to his horror—and deep, disillusioned hurt—that Nixon was saying exactly the opposite things on tape that he had been telling Ehrlichman in private. "He was working both sides of the street," Ehrlichman said.

Ehrlichman was convicted on all counts. During his trial he told how Nixon had misled and deceived him and, at one point—talking about his dismissal from Nixon's White House—he burst into tears. But the evidence against him was overwhelming. He refused to appeal, and, on Oct. 28, 1977, he entered the Swift Trail federal prison in Safford, Ariz.

Upon his release and subsequent book tours, people would say to him, "You're not the person I expected to meet." And he told the Chicago Tribune: "My answer to that is that I never was the person everybody saw in the Watergate hearings." But his image, he said, "was set in concrete. It bothered me enormously for a while—what people thought of me. But I made myself stop caring because I knew I couldn't do a thing about it, and I knew it was going to tear me up if I tried."

Whatever he did, he did it well. The John Ehrlichman today—sitting in a Santa Fe restaurant, casually dressed, smiling, poking fun—is an enthusiastic man. He is eager for every day to begin. He is a respected novelist and journalist. He is close to his five children, a stepson, seven grandchildren (soon to be nine). He has forged a pleasant, enduring marriage with a vivacious and charming woman. He is a respected celebrity in Santa Fe, a man who is at ease with himself. And he does have some strong opinions.

John Ehrlichman – III

Seattle Times, May 10, 1990

AS YOU MAY HAVE GATHERED if you read our two previous pieces on John Ehrlichman, there is far more to this man than his implication in the scandal of Watergate. Yet his public image, as he puts it, "was set in concrete," and there was nothing he could do about it. Ehrlichman is a pragmatist, a superb administrator, a man with humor and warmth, even with a dash of the poet in him. It would be a sad thing, indeed, if John Ehrlichman is remembered only for his part in America's most far-reaching and poisonous political scandal.

We talked over lunch for nearly two hours the other day. Ehrlichman talked about his boss, Richard Nixon, and his disillusionment over Nixon's deviousness. He talked some about writing, about his family, about the agony of going to prison, about his new life in Santa Fe.

Now he was talking about government itself.

Ehrlichman thinks that, like most bureaucracies, the Executive Office is badly structured. At one point, he said, he convinced President Nixon that he should institute a "four-pointed cabinet"—for economic affairs, human resources, natural resources and community develop-ment. "The idea, among other things," he said, "was to reduce duplication. As one example, it's ridiculous to have departments such as the National Parks and the Forest Service doing essentially the same job. But the idea never got anywhere. The president can go before Congress and tug his forelock, but if entrenched bureaucracies don't want to change, nothing is going to happen."

As Nixon's counsel on domestic affairs, Ehrlichman had more success in promoting environmental issues than in reforming the Executive Office. "In the 1960s, environmental action was dead," he said. "Two environmental bills had been drafted by the staffs of Sen. Scoop Jackson and Sen. Ed Muskie of Maine. President Lyndon Johnson didn't want to get involved and, well, he finessed it . . . he pulled back." When Nixon took office in 1969, Ehrlichman encouraged him to back Sen. Jackson's environmental bill. "Nixon didn't like Muskie, but he did like Jackson. We got on board with Scoop, and the National Environmental Act was passed."

Though he didn't use the word "disaster," it was plain that Ehrlichman has a very low opinion of the Reagan era. "When the Reagan people came on in 1980," he said, making a broad, sweeping gesture with the palm of his hand, "they completely wiped off all domestic issues, like erasing a blackboard." Like many of us, Ehrlichman is appalled by the results. I mentioned a column that appeared that morning in the Santa Fe New Mexican, a column by Anthony Lewis. The theme is that the harsh judgment of history is quickly closing in on the Reagan presidency. "I read it," Ehrlichman said. "There was one part of it of which I said 'Amen.' That was the part about the wholesale takeovers and junk-bond maneuvers that took place in the 1980s.

"Now, any alert hands-on president would read his daily briefings about what was going on. A hands-on president would have demanded, 'What's going on out there?' And he would have done something about it." Then he added, with some pride: "When I was in the White House, we sent at least two pieces of important legislation to Congress each month."

"Who was Deep Throat?" I asked, abruptly. The reference was to Bob Woodward and Carl Bernstein's mysterious high government source, who tipped them off to Watergate scandals and even guided their investigations. "I've heard it said that Deep Throat was you." Ehrlichman burst into laughter. "I wasn't it," he said. Then he added: "I suspect that Deep Throat was a composite. It so happens that Bob Woodward and I have the same publisher. So does Sy Hersh, the New York Times investigative reporter." Sy Hersh, Ehrlichman said, told him that the original draft of *All The President's Men,* the best-selling book by Woodward and Bernstein, had no Deep Throat character in it. Sy said he heard from editors there that the publishers felt the book needed a gimmick to spice the book up. "Sy swears that it was only in the second draft that Deep Throat appears."

For one who has been savaged by so much of it, John Ehrlichman has a notably benign view of the press. "I feel, though, that the press plays a role that I approve of. Lots of guys like Jack Anderson perform a valuable service in informing people about what's going on." He believes that the true, the definitive books on Watergate are yet to come, that good reporter-historians are at work on them. "I look forward to these books," he said. "There is an awful lot about Watergate that I never knew was going on."

In one of John Ehrlichman's books, *Witness to Power*, there appears this passage: "I was wiped out. I had nothing left that had been of value to me—honor, credibility, virtue, recognition, profession . . . It was all gone, and it seemed hopeless to expect that I could ever get any of it back."

We talked some more about what those years cost him—marriage, salary, public acclaim, profession—all gone. Would he ever get into politics again? "No," he said, "and I couldn't if I wanted to. You see, I have no civil rights. I can't vote, I can't run for office, I can't be on a jury, I can't even own a hunting rifle." Only a full presidential pardon can get his civil rights back. "Yes, I've applied," he said. "The application is back there, somewhere deep on the bowels of government."

When John Ehrlichman got up to leave, you thought of his spiritual toughness and how he has changed. It is easy to say, "Well, they all change when they fall from grace." But not all of them change. Not even most of them. But John Ehrlichman did change, in deep, meaningful ways, and he is now at ease and at peace with himself. He has changed all that—his own somber judgment in *Witness to Power* about losing honor, credibility, virtue, recognition and profession. It is nice to see that now, as a better man, he is getting it back.

On June 16, 1993, Dave Beck became 99 years old. He was one of the few people I knew who felt that John Ehrlichman should not have been sent to prison. I remember how he stuck up for Ehrlichman at the time and concluded our conversation by saying, "I just called to tell you that June 16 is coming up. That's my birthday. I'll be eighty-eight, by God, and I'll outlive the lot of you." His prophecy will probably prove correct.

Dave Beck

Seattle Times, June 20, 1991

IT SEEMS LIKE I HAVE KNOWN DAVE BECK for 100 years, although that is impossible, because Beck himself was only 97 last Sunday.

My first meeting with Dave was with Charlie Burdell, the late, great Seattle attorney, who had performed legal miracles on Dave's behalf. Charlie defended Beck during his trial in federal court in Tacoma. Anyway, Charlie got Beck off on a number of charges, but Dave did go to McNeil Island in 1962. He was convicted on two counts of filing false income-tax returns for the Teamsters Union; he was convicted on a state charge of misusing $1,900 from the sale of a union-owned Cadillac. He served half of his 5-1/2-year sentence, and, later, Gov. Albert Rosellini gave him a state pardon, and then, in 1975, Gerald Ford granted him a full presidential pardon. For those of you who like your history with neat little twists, Burdell's assistant in the Beck trial was a young attorney named William L. Dwyer, now a federal judge in Seattle.

Because he liked Dave, the Beck defeat hit Charlie hard. Burdell and Dave and I used to meet for breakfast up at George's Cafe, a fine Greek place that got wiped out by the freeway.

So on his birthday last Sunday—Father's Day—a few of Dave's family and friends had a small dinner party for him at Canlis. I dropped by to pay my respects and left. Later, one of Dave's close friends, Dick Klinge, laughed as he told me about Beck's 97th birthday. The Teamsters, it seemed, had invited Beck to their big international convention this year. This event is held once every five years. Klinge remembers: "Dave told them he couldn't make it this year, but he said he'd be sure to attend the next convention. By then he'd be 102."

That Sunday evening, I thought a lot about Dave Beck. In those days, the full fury of anti-labor papers, radio and TV, plus magazines, particularly Time, made Dave seem like Public Enemy Numero Uno. There had been the televised Senate rackets hearings, with Bobby Kennedy snapping at him like a tousle-haired terrier. Kennedy's hostile posturing had not a hell of a lot to do with the public good. He was out to get his brother elected president. He exploited Beck to make the Kennedys look moral, upright and crusading. A lot of money has flowed into Swiss banks since then. In the 1970s and 1980s, we developed a species of genuine, purebred sleaze bags—money grubbers, power brokers, inside traders, corporate-takeover artists and big-bucks swindlers.

The next morning I called Dick Klinge and said, "You know, these guys today make Dave Beck look like a St. Mark's Cathedral choirboy."

"They sure do," he said.

And speaking of St. Mark's Cathedral, if it weren't for Dave Beck, who stepped in and saved it, the lovely old building would today be some kind of an owl sanctuary. Dave had power—big power then—and he used his muscle, meaning persuasive power, and his own money to save it. He was Seattle—all Seattle—the original rain-soaked kid. As a young boy, he shot rats for bounty near the University Bridge to bring home money to his mother. He delivered papers all over First Hill. He would get his dinner in the free-lunch saloons because a kindly cop let him do it. He ran errands for the whores in the old Skid Road district (now Pioneer Square), and it was only later that he found out (to his mother's horror) that he was running dope for the hookers.

When he became International Teamsters president in the 1950s, he had to spend a lot of time in Washington. The Washington sophisticates were appalled, then amused, because Dave proudly showed off his Elks pin at formal dinners. They could not figure him out when he said, "I'd rather lean against a lamppost in Seattle than own this whole goddamned city."

When he made Teamsters president, he took $8 million of union funds in Indianapolis banks and transferred the money to Seattle First National Bank. In those days, this was one great shot in the arm for the local economy. He loved being accepted in the business community. And it hurt him, after McNeil Island, when he had continuing tax troubles, that business leaders kept their distance from him. He once confided to me, "I put all that Teamster money in Seattle First, but now I can't borrow a plugged nickel from them."

He had power and money then. He raised money and used his own money to build swimming pools for the YWCA, and again for the YMCA. He helped Seattle Pacific College and Ballard General Hospital. He raised money for the Ryther Child Center and, of course, for the March of Dimes. He raised money, but used a lot of his own, to buy a big house up on Capitol Hill. This house was to be used by parents of servicemen who couldn't afford hotels when they came to visit their sons during World War II.

Along with Sen. Warren Magnuson, Beck had much to do with founding University Hospital. He raised money for servicemen, the Associated Boys Clubs, Seattle University, also for the United Good Neighbor Fund, now United Way. He used Teamster money to build affordable housing for World War II service veterans. Not many people know this, but Dave Beck, because he loved baseball and because he thought baseball was good for his city, succeeded in persuading millionaire brewer Emil Sick to buy the old Seattle Indians. Sick built a modern new ballpark and the team, rechristened as the Rainiers, entered the glory years of pennant-winning baseball in Seattle. Beck seldom missed a game.

Father John Sneeringer came to Dave and told him that his school, Bellarmine High, was literally broke and might have to close. Dave raised $24,000 to bail the school out. Back in 1953, Children's Orthopedic had just opened its new hospital out on Sand Point Way, but there remained the enormous task of moving the children from their old Queen Anne Hill quarters. Once again, the muscle. Literally hundreds of union taxicabs and many trucks descended on the hospital. They moved the kids and all of the hospital equipment in 48 hours. Gratis.

Dave is still garrulous, bombastic and often domineering, and his speech as always, is salted with "damns" and "hells," but he would never, never use the kind of four-letter words that are so much in vogue today. He never smoked and never drank, although now, at his doctor's suggestion, he might sip a little wine before dinner. He still climbs aboard his exercycle each morning, but he has given up the long brisk walks he used to enjoy. He naps a lot during the day. "The old man has slowed up a bit," Dick Klinge said, "but he's still quite a guy, still one hell of a man."

Figuratively, Hazel Wolfe always takes my breath away. Literally, it would be the same, if I were ever foolish enough to attempt matching steps with her.

Hazel Wolfe

Seattle Times, May 6, 1984

ABOUT EIGHT YEARS AGO, when the local pro football team got its name, Seahawks, which really are ospreys, I called up the secretary of the Seattle Audubon Society. Surely, an expert's opinion was needed, and that is how I first met Hazel Wolfe. What she said then endeared her to me for all time: "Oh, yes, I saw the headline about some Seahawks. At first I thought it was a new sighting!" I would like to report that I have seen a lot of Hazel since then, but finding Hazel in one locale is not easy. She isn't always in when you call.

Hazel Wolfe, who was 77 when I first met her, frequently went off to climb a mountain or run some rapids. She is an accomplished canoeist, a confirmed backpacker, and when I caught her for lunch shortly after the Seahawks episode, it was only by luck. Hazel was leaving the next day to go snowshoeing near Leavenworth in Chelan County. And when we did talk, she revealed her plans to camp that spring on the north slope of the Brooks Range, inside the Arctic Circle. She said she wanted to see some caribou and grizzlies and moose and maybe find some nesting birds.

So when I heard the other day that a gifted lady named Susan Starbuck is writing Hazel's biography, I figured there is a very thick book in the making. Hazel, you see, is a lovely wisp of a woman who seems to be imbued with some cosmic energy that gets her involved in all kinds of projects, causes and enterprises. She was the guiding spirit behind the Audubon Society's publication and sale of natural history guides, *Trailside Series*, now widely distributed in schools and libraries. In addition to the Audubon Society, she is a leader in the Federation of Western Outdoors Clubs; she belongs to the Sierra Club, Friends of the Earth, The Wilderness Society, the Washington State Parks Association and was one of the founding members of the Washington Environmental Council.

She doesn't dillydally in this stuff. She has a sharp intelligence and a paralegal background, and she is well-informed about almost any issue you can name. She also has a spicy wit. A reporter once called Hazel to ask how far south the gray whales had migrated, and Hazel told him: "They went as far as Olympia, got one whiff of the Legislature, turned around and headed north."

Hazel was born into poverty in British Columbia, but her life soon developed into a full and joyous existence. As an eighth-grader, she actually introduced girls' basketball to Victoria. When the headmaster told her sternly that "girls don't play basketball," she replied: "Of course they don't, because we have no ball." Then the headmaster played what he thought was his trump card. He told Hazel to go find enough girls to play, then he might give them a ball. What he didn't know was that Hazel already had lined up the teams. "He was stuck," Hazel said, delighting in the memory.

Even at the age of 10, she was concerned with the problems of "the people in my little world," and she always had this dream of doing things in a greater world to help others. And the other day she said: "It is good to be able to say in the closing years of my life that most of these dreams have been realized. Most of my adult years I have been engaged in struggles to preserve civil liberties, to promote health programs, better housing and a better environment. That is, the preservation of wilderness, wildlife and natural resources, also to provide urban parks, clean air, unpolluted water and recreational opportunities for city people. I seem to have come full circle, except that my neighborhood has enlarged to include the whole world, and the people of my childhood extended to include all people everywhere. My dreams have not changed."

One feature of Hazel's impact on the community is that she never, never was regarded as "just another little old lady in tennis shoes." Earth shoes or hiking boots, maybe, but never tennis shoes.

In her constant quest to enlarge civil liberties and promote a better environment, opponents found her to be fair and reasonable. When she won the prestigious Sol Feinstone Environmental Award from the State University of New York in 1977, those urging her nomination included state bureaucrats and officials in the timber industry. While setting this down, I can anticipate a couple of letters coming in, letters that say, "Didn't you know that Hazel Wolfe was once a communist?" Yes, I know that. So do many others. None of us gives a damn. For many years, from 1947 to the early 1960s, the U.S. government tried to have Hazel deported. She had her difficult times and legal battles, but Hazel won. "I quit the party in 1944," she says.

Now in her 80s, she never seems to run out of steam, her life force still going at full throttle as she throws her frail body into this cause or that. She is now the editor of the newspaper Outdoors West. She is helping to build a coalition to oppose the selection of Hanford as a repository of radioactive waste. She is, in her own words, "cooking up a storm" against a huge 500,000-acre irrigation project in the East Columbia Basin, what she calls "a dangerous, costly boondoggle." She is active in politics and is on the advisory committee of a proposed global environmental conference projected for 1985, in Portland. "And several odds and ends as they arise," she adds.

Most important, perhaps, is that she does not live in fear. "Much of fear is based on something nonexistent, or remote, at best," she says. "So I refuse to keep off the streets at night because of possible muggers. I refuse to stay out of the woods because of bears, or away from deserts because of rattlesnakes. Above all, I refuse to live in fear of death. Long ago I was convinced that death will not go away. So I analyzed it and faced it. Like most things in nature, death is a gift. As sleep is nature's gift at the end of a day, so is death the final sleep at the end of a lifetime."

And thus Hazel will go on being Hazel, alert to the rich, rewarding—often funny—vagaries of life, ever ready to tackle a cause or a project that will make life better. And several odds and end as they arise.

▼

I first met Yasser Seirawan when he was an irrepressible kid of 19. He captivated me, as he did so many others, and we became friends. He never became the world champion in chess, but his talent took him to within a rung or two of that exclusive level. Today, he lives in the higher realm of international chess, much honored throughout most of the world, though not in his hometown.

Yasser Seirawan
Seattle Post-Intelligencer, February 17, 1980

THE WORLD OF MAJOR CHESS—the stratosphere of Grand Masters—bears the image, not undeserved, of eccentricity, mental aberration, grimness, hostility and despair. Bobby Fischer, the world champion of the early 1970s, now lives as a recluse in Los Angeles, refusing to play. Boris Spassky, the Russian destroyed by Fischer, lives as an expatriate in France, no longer a folk hero in the Soviet Union. A great American champion of the 19th century, Paul Morphy, lived out his life as a paranoid recluse in New Orleans. Wilhelm Steinitz (1886–94) became demented and died as a charity patient. The game is replete with wild behavior, bitter feuds and one-upmanship. Not all Grand Masters are like this, of course. But in this game—a war of intellects on a 64-square battlefield of knights, rooks, bishops and destructive queens—there is a brooding air of almost spiritual intensity.

Into this world now comes a kid of 19, a boy full of laughter and the juices of fun, a kid out of Garfield High School who can say, in a spirit of innocent bewilderment, "My rise is as meteoric as Spassky's. It's unreal." His name is Yasser Seirawan. He is of Syrian descent, but as American as the nearest Pizza Haven. The day we talked, in fact, pizza was very much on his mind. "Tonight is all-you-can-eat night at Pizza Haven!" he exclaimed happily. "All the pizza you can eat!" His nickname is Yaz, and he laughs a lot, telling stories of meeting girls, playing basketball, surfing and going to movies. Is this the new kid on the block of Grand Master chess? Is this the American who will one day take the measure of Anatoly Karpov, the world champion from Russia? "Uh-huh," he nods, matter of factly.

Yasser Seirawan: Except among chess buffs, virtually unknown in his hometown. He lives in Seward Park, and his dad works at Boeing. He doesn't train much. He loves to party and eat and tell stories and go to movies. He is the antithesis of those brooding chess masters who devote hours each day to memorizing complex openings or studying the Nimzo-Indian defense. Will he be the next world champion of chess? "Uh-huh," he said, and why not? Only a few weeks ago he tied for first in the prestigious Hoohoogovens Tournament in Holland. In doing so, he beat Victor Korchnoi, the No. 2 player in the world. "I was surprised. *He* was surprised," laughs Yaz. "Unreal."

Unreal, indeed, and what about this kid who (via chess's immutable point rankings) will be among the top 10 of the world's chess masters next year? At age 10, he was hustling pool and surfing in Virginia Beach, Va. At 11, he arrived in Seattle, where he turned to chess "because Lake Washington is too cold to swim in." He began winning almost instantly, small tournaments, then bigger ones. One of the first to see his promise was Arnold Garcia, a local real estate investor, who staked him to expenses, much the way people underwrite a promising golf pro. "We don't need you here any more," Garcia said. "It's time to ship you out." The victories piled up; at age 16, he won the American Open against 600 entrants, including many Grand Masters. By now he was in demand, here and in Europe; tournaments vied for his appearances, and finally, Garcia said, "Yaz, you don't need me any more."

Chess is not profitable in the U.S., so, to make money, he hustled the chess clubs in New York, playing "blitz" chess (all moves in five minutes) against the Times Square chess hustlers. In a memorable two days he posed as a rustic from Seattle and blitzed them for more than $1,000 in bets. "At the end," he said, laughing loudly, "they brought out their best man. He looked like Jackie Gleason in *The Hustler*. He was all barbered up, wore a three-piece suit and he had short, fat little fingers. I was so entranced by his fingers I lost concentration and he beat me the first game. Then I beat him four straight and he quit. Oh, it was wonderful! Oh, how I smiled!"

He hustled in Yugoslavia, where he was the guest of Grand Master Ljubimir Lubojevic, the nation's No. 1 hero. He won more than $3,000. Just as they did in New York, the Yugoslav hustlers brought out their best—Lubojevic himself—to play Yaz. "When he saw me," laughs Yaz, "Ljubimir almost fell down laughing. 'So this is how you spend your evenings!' he cried." The two went off together, leaving the Yugoslavs, schooled in ploys of "blitz" chess, agape.

By now, he could never get away with that. Unrecognized in his hometown, Yaz is a European celebrity. TV cameras crowd him. He is feted in England, Sweden, Norway, Holland; the Soviet Union treats him as they once treated Van Cliburn. "They give me black caviar from Odessa—the *real* thing!" he cries. Soon he will be back playing among the 120 Grand Masters of the world, "and I must start training, I gotta get my act together."

L ike Yasser Seirawan, Sonny Sixkiller was an engaging 19-year-old with a memorable name when I wrote about him.

It is given to aging writers to feed off the innocent energies of the young.

Sonny Sixkiller

Seattle Post-Intelligencer, June 4, 1971

I DON'T MEAN TO SOUND EXCESSIVELY DRAMATIC, but the other day I had lunch with a legend. Don't get me wrong, I've had lunch with legends before, some of whom even picked up the check, but most legends of my acquaintance are in their 40s, run to fat, and are comfortable among a wide circle of admirers, including themselves. The legend I had lunch with is remarkable in one respect—he is only 19 years old. Certain presidential candidates would be overjoyed to get the publicity he will get this fall. Magazine cover stories; that sort of thing.

How do you get to be a legend at 19? A good start is to choose your parents wisely, of the right Indian nation, and go through life with the marvelous name of Sonny Sixkiller. The late Arthur Brisbane, a daily pundit, once took notice of "Lefty" O'Doul, the baseball player. Pondering O'Doul's career (Lefty was somewhat of a legend himself), Brisbane asked, "How can a man fail in life with a name like Lefty O'Doul?" The same question could be asked about Sonny Sixkiller—it's a name with zing, the "it" quality; once having been introduced to it, nobody will ever say, "Pardon me, I didn't quite catch your name the first time."

There have been great Indian athletes before Sonny Sixkiller, of course. Greater ones than Sonny—and a fellow named Jim Thorpe readily comes to mind. "You, sir, are the greatest athlete in the world," the King of Sweden told Thorpe, after the 1912 Olympics. Thorpe excelled at just about everything that requires muscles. In his era, Thorpe could do about anything. At football, he was merely the greatest of his time. But his name, Jim Thorpe, had a Waspish ring to it; without a picture of the high cheekbones, the black hair, the long nose, the dark eyes, you could guess Thorpe to be an Irishman, or even English.

But never Sonny Sixkiller. To a certain kind of white mind—usually found buzzing over typewriters, or in editors' chairs—the name Sixkiller connotes predictable word responses, such as tomahawk, massacre, teepee, uprising, arrows, scalping and hey, let's hear a good war-whoop from Sonny. To all of this, Sonny uses the phrase, "It gets pretty old."

He is alternately fascinated and repelled at the blaze of attention. On the one hand, he guards his privacy fiercely—living quietly a mile off campus. "The people I know," he says, "I want them to consider me— well, me. Not the ball player. Just me. I don't mind meeting new people. But I like to go to a place where it's private." That's one side. The other is the warm feeling of knowing you are *somebody*, the chicks crowding around, the feeling of importance, the offers and invitations—finally, the ultimate money all this implies.

So you put up with the 6-Killer sweatshirts and even learn to endure the banal "Ballad of Sonny Sixkiller," and make a stab at answering the fan mail. And Sonny admits, "You have to be flattered by it all." It helps not to read the newspaper, too. "I don't want to read about it," he says of any game. "I know what happened. I just save the sports pages and take them to my Mom." Being Sonny Sixkiller, celebrity, you are constantly asked about trivia. About freshman football, for example, before coach Jim Owens installed the wide-open, pro-type offense. "We used the Y-formation then," he says. "And it stunk, it really stunk." Quarterbacks who lead the nation in passing can say things like that; second-string tackles wouldn't dream of it. Chalk up another plus for fame.

The next invasion of Ft. Lawton or occupation of Alcatraz will have to make a go of it without Sonny Sixkiller. He identifies with Indian causes, but he doesn't get in there. He was honorary chairman for the Save Ernie Crowfeather Drive, a fund-raiser for a kidney machine. But that's about it. "Sonny Sixkiller can fish anyplace he wants," went the gag last fall. But you won't find Sonny at a fish-in protest. His life in Ashland, Oregon, was almost middle class; he has never seen a reservation.

But he is different—not so much as an Indian; more like a new breed of non-conformist athlete. More easy and relaxed. The black hair is long and growing longer. He resents having to move into the UW crewhouse this fall, commonly called "the zoo" or the "ape house." He quit his fraternity. "Not because I didn't like them," he says, "but I just don't like dorm-style living."

"We're not mad dogs like they were six years ago," he says, referring to the super-discipline and crewhouse living. He laughed at his own exaggeration. "You know, crew cuts and all that. We're different. I want to do what I want, I want to live the way I want." Right now he wants to gain weight. "I'll eat better now that summer's coming on," he grins. This summer Sixkiller will drive a Coke truck in Bellevue, and you can't get any more American than that.

The novelist Tom Robbins is probably the best we have around today. I first knew Tom when he worked nights on The P-I copy desk to earn support money while he wrote his first big hit, *Another Roadside Attraction*. Any conversation with Tom has a good chance of veering in an interesting direction, like the time we earnestly discussed comic strips.

Tom Robbins

Seattle Times, February 2, 1986

TOM SAID THAT THE FIRST WORDS HE EVER WROTE, at the age of 5, were "Harold Teen," the name of an old comic strip, now in cartoon heaven, or wherever defunct cartoons go. "I carved the name 'Harold Teen' on my mother's French doors at home in Blowing Rock, North Carolina," Tom said. "As far as I know the words are still there." Then he smiled: "I write for posterity."

Tom, of course, is novelist Tom Robbins, and his millions of fans will assure you, yes, indeed, he writes for posterity. In fact, some people worship Tom. To date, Robbins has written four novels: *Another Roadside Attraction, Even Cowgirls Get the Blues, Still Life With Woodpecker and Jitterbug Perfume. Roadside,* a slow starter because people were slow to discover Robbins, has now sold more than 2 million copies. His latest, *Jitterbug Perfume,* was on The New York Times best-seller list for 12 weeks, and he's about as rich as any writer deserves to be.

He's easy to be with, Tom is, and we spent a wonderful afternoon talking about—believe it, you Robbins worshipers—comic strips. Yes, we talked about "Blondie and Dagwood," "Dick Tracy," "Mary Worth," "Apartment 3G," Walt Kelly and "Pogo," "Joe Palooka," "Doonesbury," "Andy Capp," "Krazy Kat," "Skeezix," "Maggie and Jiggs," "The Katzenjammer Kids"—some still with us, others gone to that great comic page in the sky. At times it got to be a trivia game. Who did Snuffy Smith edge out of the strip? Barney Google, of course. What was Barney's horse named? Sparky, or Sparkplug. Who was Joe Palooka's fight manager? Knobby Walsh.

"Krazy Kat," Tom said, emphatically, " 'Krazy Kat' is the only strip I can unequivocally say was a work of art. The 'Krazy Kat' strip followed no rules except its own. It was philosophical in content with enough ambiguity to be open to various interpretations. It had a whimsical and mystical quality that has influenced today's up-and-coming cartoonists." For folks born too late in this century to know George Herriman's "Krazy Kat," the characters were the Kat (kind of dumb), a very smart mouse named Ignatz, and a slow-witted cop named Officer Pupp. Ignatz frequently ended a panel by beaning Kat or Officer Pupp with a well-aimed brick.

"Let's take Harold Gray and 'Little Orphan Annie,' " I said. "Daddy Warbucks was a right-wing fascist. International financier. He had Punjab around, a sort of giant Oriental strongman, who carried a curved saber and killed off Annie's enemies. He may have been our first terrorist." Tom said that Harold Gray, Annie's creator, was ultra right-wing himself. "And 'Dick Tracy,' " he said. "Tracy represents a sort of police-state brutality. The cops are always right. Both strips had, or have, a sort of Germanic Expressionism about them. 'Orphan Annie' bordered on the psychotic."

The most popular strip, the most read today, is about "Blondie and Dagwood." I ventured that Dagwood, who goes back some 60 years or more, was really our first suburban character in a cartoon strip. "Dagwood," Tom said, "is man at his worst. He's the ultimate henpecked husband. He is dominated by Blondie and mocked by his kids and tyrannized by his boss, Mr. Dithers. For years and years, Chick Young did Dagwood, then his son and a couple of assistants continued the strip when Young died— exactly as Dagwood Bumstead has always been. It must be genetic." It is Tom's belief that Dagwood's sustained popularity comes from the fact that so many people were imprinted by Young's drawings and jokes at an early age. "People tend to hold on to those things that have continuity," he said.

Walt Kelly and "Pogo." Satire on social and political questions. "Krazy Kat" defied authority, and so did Pogo, but Kelly's alligators and bugs in the Okefenokee swamp never threw bricks. They were gentle creatures, particularly Pogo himself, who spoke out against mankind's cruelty and sophistry.

"Beetle Bailey" and Sarge and General Halftrack came out of the

Korean War. The strip is a bludgeoning parody of the Army. The Army brass (particularly in the early going) was enraged by the strip's portrayal of Sarge as a gluttonous bully and Halftrack's image of a pathetic, ineffectual Army bureaucrat.

Somewhat sadly, Tom thinks, comic strips have been in a long decline—ever since the 1950s, with the arrival of "Yogi Bear" and "The Flintstones," drawn by two Hollywood film cartoonists named Hanna and Barbera. "Cartooning always had a junk-food character about it, but the strip had soul and the juice of humanity. The new humor, 'Yogi Bear' and 'The Flintstones,' was something only the very young or the very stupid would laugh at. Fast and economical, very bland." Another point of decline came not so long ago when the newspapers, to save space and newsprint, began shrinking comics down. "There is some good drawing being done, as in 'Steve Canyon,' " Tom said, "but the reproduction is so small it scarcely matters."

Yes, one longs for the colorfully drawn "Katzenjammer Kids," defying parental authority, and "Li'l Abner," featuring Daisy Mae and Moonbeam McSwine, whose leggy, busty figures, scarcely concealed by their ersatz hillbilly costumes, must have aroused the libidos of millions of pre-adolescents.

"If I owned my own newspaper, I'd throw out at least half the comics and bring in some of the new, exciting young cartoonists," Tom said. "Then I'd restore the comics to their former size so you could appreciate good drawing. It's interesting to note that two of the good young cartoonists, Lynda Barry and Gary Larson, are from Seattle. Gary Larson does 'The Far Side.' You know, comics, particularly older strips, have always had vitality and energy and humor. The kind of thing I've tried to get into my novels and take to a higher purpose."

Writing about Emmett Day Jr. was a joy because I had discovered a little-known young man whose talent had begun to take hold on a nationwide scale. He was an altogether delightful human being, as well as an artist of surpassing talent. Three years after I first met him, a mutual friend, Maggie Brown, told me that Emmett was dying, "and he'd like to talk to you to get some things off his chest." I could not write this second, and final, column about Emmett without crying.

Emmett Day Jr.

Seattle Times, July 18, 1989

IN WRITING ABOUT DEATH, as he frequently did, Ernest Hemingway spoke about "it"—death itself, what he termed "that necessary business" at the end. No one escapes that "necessary business," which is indiscriminate and respects no talent.

We should all grieve because "it," the impending necessary business, is close for Emmett Day Jr., possibly the greatest talent Seattle has ever known. Back in April, doctors told Emmett, who has lung cancer, that he could expect to live two more months. It took the doctor 15 seconds to tell him. Emmett is now one week past the estimated deadline. He is 41.

I wish you knew him. I wish everyone knew him. For it is a rare thing to encounter such a person as Emmett Day, who has transformed craft into art. I once referred to Emmett as a throwback to the 16th, 17th and 18th centuries. Like the craftsmen-artists of those ages, Emmett created his own designs, pondering each piece as an act of subconscious vision. He fashioned with fine woods like rosewood, cherry and ebony. He was skilled in metallurgy, using gorgeous inlays of gold and silver he mined himself. Within the past couple of years, collectors from everywhere came to view these incredible pieces of art—bookcases, jewelry boxes, cabinets, tables. And many of them paid breathtaking prices for the unique creations.

His life stands for something profoundly important. He has revolutionized craftsmanship, taking it one giant step into the esoterica of fine art. Nothing exists that in any manner approaches Emmett's 21-karat-gold-and-Cuban-cocuswood concert flute. It has been played by such world-famous flutists as James Galway and Julius Baker. Galway is an internationally celebrated soloist; Baker is the principal flutist for the New York Philharmonic. Both pronounced the flute flawless.

"It was made as a piece of art," Emmett once said, "and it was my incredible fortune that it was perfect." This rare object has been purchased by a local patron and given to the Seattle Art Museum. It will, on occasion, be played by Scott Goff, principal flutist for the Seattle Symphony Orchestra.

And the piano, of course—nothing like it anywhere. When he conceived the piano, Emmett sat and studied at the mechanism, the strings, the innards of a 1928 Steinway grand—conjuring up his vision of what this piano should be. Six weeks later—Emmett worked very fast—he had melded rosewood and brass, Makassar ebony and refinished ivory, into a unique grand; nothing like it ever was, or will be. When the "it" became a dark presence in the Emmett Day household, the piano went up for sale. Debra Winger, the actress and a patron of Emmett's art, found a wealthy buyer in California. The piano sold for $75,000 and will be shipped to the buyer when the time comes.

And when "it" came to the household, Therese, Emmett's wife, had all the other pieces, the jewelry boxes, the cabinets, the tables, and other rare pieces, removed from the Northwest Gallery of Fine Woodworking in Pioneer Square. "I don't think Therese will ever sell them," a friend confided.

Seeing him there, lying on his sofa, it all seems so terribly wrong. He is young and has seen so much of his work acclaimed, then suddenly, the promise of goals tomorrow will not be kept. "Remember the climber who said he simply climbed the mountain 'because it's there,' " he said. "Well, I made my things because they weren't there. I knew that if I didn't make them they would never be here and I very much wanted them to be here."

Emmett Day is a man of almost staggering complexity, a man of multiple gifts, and not the least of these is the gift of bravery. This handsome, vibrant man can still smile. "I feel strangely complete about my work," he said. "I have no real desire to keep on topping the last piece, although given more time I imagine that would have happened."

Seeing him lying there, terribly tired, going through that "necessary business," one could not but help remember Hemingway's Robert Jordan, in the final pages of *For Whom The Bell Tolls*, talking to himself to relieve the final pain: "I hate to leave it is all. I hate to leave it very much and I hope I have done some good in it. I have tried to with what talent I had."

Now Emmett Day was saying:

"What I miss and what I feel was near was having the chance for a body of work to make a larger difference. My work is not about furniture as art—that's nonsense, and can be argued indefinitely. I see my work as a very tiny antidote to the enormous tide of the soulless production I see slowly washing away people's connection with quality. My work is about adventure, passion in living, and a love of this Earth's materials."

Part 3
This, Our City

It took a while for me to get over my inner rage because of a sense of inadequacy that I thought I found in Seattle. My hometown. Big deal. I thought of Seattle as backward, slow to catch up, a dull city far out of the mainstream of what was going on in America. This was a narrow view, shaped from a seat in the press box, formed admidst not very imaginative athletes, a world somewhat limited to the jockstrap-snapping environment of dugouts and dressing rooms. So for a long time, as a young fellow too impressed with his own talents, I wanted out of here. I wanted to leave Seattle, a very minor league city, and get caught up in the excitement of big-time sports—Los Angeles, Chicago, New York, St. Louis, even Pittsburgh, for God's sake.

But I was lucky, fortunate in the sense that both papers I worked for, The Seattle Times and The P-I (long after The Star), sent me to cover events in far places. At the time, I had sense enough to realize that all I was seeing around me on these travels were airports and press boxes. So I would do the corny, the touristy thing. I would take guided bus tours through any large city I happened to be in. Or I would just take a city bus, sometimes a cab, or go for long walks. I exulted in the food, especially in New York, where a thing like a thick pastrami sandwich at the Carnegie Deli could send me reeling down the street with joy. You could not get pastrami in Seattle, not in those days.

But, over time, I began to see other things, too. I visited my first ghetto in New York. The Hollywood scene began to pall. Sacramento was a drag, and in Pittsburgh, the summer heat, fueled by humidity, was unbearable. There were thousands of dirty, treeless streets, immobilizing traffic snarls, garbage cans on sidewalks, and what seemed, then, an insane hurry by people to catch up with something. I hung around a lot in those cities, making friends, listening and drinking too much. In those days, I had a head like an oaken bucket.

It took a while, but I finally woke up. There were a couple of

125

chances, none very serious, to take sportswriting jobs elsewhere. Frank Graham, the splendid sports columnist for The New York American, once warned me, "Kid, don't come back here. It's a dying business in New York." Red Smith, the Hall of Famer then with The New York Herald Tribune, was equally kind, although he warned me off in a more subtle way. Sports Illustrated made a mild pass at my undoubted genius, but I had come home to Seattle once too often. I had arrived home by train, by bus and by airplane. In Seattle, you had clean air, views of water and mountains; the people were civil; it had everything except urban sophistication. And in a very few years my revelation hardened into an unspoken credo: "This is a goddamned paradise compared to where I've been."

In time, I began to write about the city and the people that give it substance, humor and character. Gradually, I got away from the jockstrap beat, and now I could write about Seattle itself, with all its shortcomings—and perhaps do something about them.

A Mature City

Seattle Post-Intelligencer, January 31, 1971

IN JUST THE FEW YEARS I'VE BEEN SCRIBBLING this column, it seems to me I've seen good signs that Seattle was becoming more mature as a city. Not so long ago you couldn't buy a drink on weekdays, let alone Sundays, a good restaurant was hard to find and people actually took Seafair seriously. We've come a long way, I think. We had major league baseball and blew it—but at least we *had* it. The SuperSonics, a major league basketball show, are one of the city's prime entertainments. Opera, thanks to Glynn Ross, ranks with any in the land; the Rep is a first-rate company, not to mention ACT and a few other attractions that didn't exist a few years back. "In Los Angeles," they used to say of us, "it's the smog. In Seattle, it's the smug."

Yes, things are definitely better. It used to be that a crisis in UW football merely meant fire-the-coach; now a large segment of people want the coach fired but for deep sociological reasons that even have the better brains on the campus baffled. Lately, the news that we might inherit pro football resulted in only modest hysteria. Forward Thrust got knocked on its tail by the voters, but this seemed to be more a revolt against higher taxes than a blithe unconcern with the quality of our environment. Indeed, we have become increasingly sensitive to what is happening to the town around us, as witness the valiant fights here and there to block I-90, save the Market and preserve old landmarks. All in all, a better city than it was a few years ago; definitely, progress has been made.

However, these modestly sanguine thoughts, which I've harbored for some time, were shaken in recent days. As we all know, 1970, with its Boeing layoffs, was the kind of year we should have sent back to the factory. Unemployment zoomed, jobless pay increased, crisis seemed to pile on crisis, and the shock waves hit just about everybody. What we were—and are—is a "company town," and there is little to argue against that fact. Boeing employment plunged from 100,000-plus to less than 50,000, and, of course, we had to man the lifeboats. Even the humor got a little sick, as a Boeing joke made the rounds: "I hear they're hiring people at Boeing so they'll be sure to have enough layoffs before Christmas."

Out of all this came an understandable nervousness among the business community. The SST, once just an interesting—even dramatic— piece of hardware, had become our salvation. Our very survival depended on the SST. It was going to be the "psychological" boost that would revive Big Daddy of The Duwamish—bringing him back to his former benevolent, job-giving, life-giving self. A few weeks ago, an SST ("Seattle Stands Tall") campaign got going on a local radio station. As such campaigns go, it is harmless enough. It features local business leaders exhorting the citizenry to "stand tall," as though standing on tippy-toes, head high, eyes straight, heart pure, will somehow lessen all those unemployment lines and make the cash registers jingle again. Football-type pep talks from our leaders; but just remember, nobody ever died for dear old Rutgers.

The other day, in a spirit of fun, I printed a joke about people here boycotting Wisconsin cheese—because a Wisconsin senator, Mr. Proximire, was leading the fight against the SST. It was a joke, and not a very good one, but I never dreamed anybody would take it seriously. What happened? Last week, three Seattle business leaders kicked off a campaign to sell the SST nationwide. "Truth Squads" would carry the word to the nation about the SST. Money would be raised to fight the battle of getting the SST for Boeing—and Seattle. Part of the campaign, I learned with surprise, was a serious effort to boycott Wisconsin cheese. Bumper stickers would be sold featuring tasteless messages like these: "With Hams Like Proximire Who Needs Wisconsin Cheese?" and "Laid-Off Aerospace Workers Say Sen. Proximire Lies About SST, Boycott Wisconsin Cheese."

Haven't we learned anything from the Boeing debacle? Isn't it time we thought of ourselves as a many-industry town, a city that has learned how perilous it is to depend, entirely, on one Big Daddy? Aren't there other ways? The SST (Uncle Sugar giving it to Big Daddy) isn't going to bail Seattle out. Moreover, the SST is a highly complex question; many serious thinkers have doubts about its value. Supersonic flight is a national—even an international—issue. Opinions on it are by no means unanimous.

That is why I worry about this whole huckstering business. A mature city doesn't go out hustling something as complex and important as the SST, as though we were trying to grab off some Seafair business. The whole campaign—cheese and all—is embarrassing. This is not, one might add, the way to make Seattle stand very tall.

▼

Homage to Seattle

Seattle Post-Intelligencer, January 7, 1979

SOMETHING IS THE MATTER THIS MORNING, friends, so it's fair warning—if you hang around me, you'll be branded with guilt-by-association for consorting with a fellow who's in a good mood. Definitely subversive, good moods. Maybe it's the weather, crisp and cold, giving us skies that are blue and clear, mountains etched skyward, pristine white peaks rising gloriously and—[Ed.'s note: calm down, Watkins, you're acting like a buffoon]. So be it. Let us revive a phase from the 1960s, "If it feels good, do it," and today I feel like saying a few nice things abut the city that still squirms, a bit uncomfortably, under the title "the nation's most livable." As it happens, I just finished reading an old copy of the magazine Mother Jones, in which author Ray Mungo treats us to a catchy quote from an anonymous promoter: "When the end of the world comes, Seattle will still have one more year to go."

Little things help. Despite all the money they've poured into it for rehabilitation, the Pike Place Market is making a strong comeback. Day by day it's taking on more of the splendid character of grubbiness that once made it glorious—unstructured, uninhibited, inefficient, a restful island of push, shove and babble, a relief from the Saran-Wrap-set-to-Muzak in the world outside.

At the other end of the spectrum is Rainier Square, of which not enough praises have been sung. Unlike so many underground shopping centers (Vancouver's for one), Rainier Square has held steady against the tendency to club you with commercialism, the way so many such contrivances do.

Seattle is still a city of fine neighborhoods, with a sense of place and community, and one of the hottest places right now is—downtown. Apartments and condos on the drawing boards, with housing on the way in Pioneer Square, condos in the Central Area, a concern for the houseboats, and almost explosive activity on the Regrade. Within one four-block radius downtown, you can find a plethora of small restaurants—French, Russian, Czech, Mexican, Vietnamese, Swedish and Native American. The city is still small enough so strangers exchange "good mornings" on street corners, pedestrians admonish fellow pedestrians about jaywalking ("be careful, you might get hurt") and it's a rare walk downtown when you don't bump into somebody you know.

A city where you can still poke around, finding new places and people—tiny specialty shops, elegant junk places that pass themselves off as "antique" stores. An enlightened Parks Dept. that gives us indoor tennis, concerts in the parks, kite-flying competitions and no signs that say "Keep Off The Grass." Small blessings, to be counted at leisure: Army-Navy stores where they've never heard of Calvin Klein; marvelous old-fashioned hardware stores that still keep going; a waterfront that still has working docks and isn't totally given over to cutesy shops and boutiques; and, for that matter, you can still pull into a few parking lots that aren't run by Joe Diamond.

More good news today: For the first time in 25 years, you can go to a public library on Sundays. Starting today, in fact, four branches—Ballard, Columbia, North East and West Seattle—will be open in the afternoons, and the library folks are still pushing to get the big one downtown open on Sundays. A small thing, but mine own: This lover of potatoes seems to detect a new interest in the noble spud, where hash browns—such as you'll find at the Athens Cafe at 2nd and Blanchard—are lovingly and properly prepared; no potato should endure the indignity of flash-freezing.

Seattle, a city that long ago became too big for its bridges, but still, somehow, retains a small-town character. Going big league in sports and restaurants, opera and theatre, yet definitely out of the mainstream of dizzying fads and fashions; for the most part liberal and tolerant of neighbors and offbeat lifestyles. Maybe the man was right—when the world ends, Seattle will still have one more year to go. Enjoy.

If I once thought Seattle was Dullsville, USA, it took a few years to realize that I was the one of slow wit and sorry comprehension. As the great Mark Tobey once remarked, "It isn't always the place, you know. It's the people in it." Seattle, as I discovered over the years, was rich in character and characters. It was full of unusual people. No city on earth could replicate Dorothy Bullitt, who not only brought us pioneering quality television but set a standard for general integrity that helped make us what we are today. Ivar Haglund was a funny little man, who came out of Seattle's bohemian past and became, literally, a world figure by the mere act of merchandising mollusks. Henry Broderick was unusual and different, and so, in a more colorful way, was Rudi Becker, who knew every corner of the city intimately and prowled its precincts in a pickup truck. On the surface, Gracie Hansen looked like an 1890s madam, but she, too, had her warm and generous and most respectable side. The whole damned city was a gold mine for any writer who paid attention to the people.

Dorothy Bullitt

Seattle Times, March 6, 1984

DOROTHY BULLITT HAS THIS WAY OF SPEAKING which makes you pay close attention to what she says, not because everything she says is important but because a certain word or phrase has a way of making her point and the rest of it doesn't even matter. Listening to her you think of the Mark Twain edict: "The difference between the right word and the almost right word is the difference between the fire and the firefly."

We don't need to put too fine a point on it, but she can engage you, this woman with the deep, almost baritone voice, who has had such a profound effect on this city. On politics she says, "I am sometimes tempted to say a few things now and then, but I don't belong to either party. I don't take part in any of it. It is sometimes hard for me when I am feeling resentment, as I do these days, and I have to be very careful."

There you hear a statement rich with implications that tells you all you need to know. And she can talk about her girlhood, the growing-up-wealthy among those who had coming-out parties and deb-balls and formed their values from tilting proper tea cups. "My friends had a different life, friends that I had grown up with. They went the usual way and did the usual things."

Oh, damn, she is a remarkable woman! We talked for almost two hours, and sitting there in her small office, inside this glass-slab building that is the KING-TV headquarters on Dexter, I felt awfully glad that she did not go the usual way and do the usual things.

Dorothy Bullitt was born in 1892, so depending on her birthday, at this minute she is either 91 or 92. It doesn't matter. What matters is, she did not throw those years away on frivolous, self-gratifying indulgences, the way so many of the early airheads did. She played a much tougher game than that, and so she made a better city of us.

Her husband, the late A. Scott Bullitt, was a strong, gregarious man who ran for U.S. Senate and then governor, losing both times, but he was well liked by Republicans, even though he was a powerful Democrat. Scott Bullitt was the man Warren Magnuson came to when he wanted to enter politics. This was in 1928, and Bullitt paid Magnuson's way to his first Democratic convention.

Within three years, Dorothy Bullitt lost her father, her husband, and her brother, and because her father's will left her with the real estate side of the legacy, she thought she was being thrown to the sharks. She didn't know anything about real estate, and it was the bottom of the Depression. One of her properties, the Coliseum Theater, was busted, and when a man from Los Angeles came to see the empty theater, she thought, "Oh, one of those hot-shot Los Angeles people, he will take the skin right off my back."

But they developed a sound, trusting business relationship, one which existed for a long time with only a handshake for a lease. And she took over management of the 1411 Fourth Avenue Building and competed for tenants with other real estate interests downtown. She watched the hustlers come and go, but it was said of Dorothy Bullitt that she never forgot those who stuck by her.

Her father had build the 1411 Fourth Avenue Building, and she managed that, even to inspecting the toilets. She was proud of this building because, she said, her father had designed it carefully for the people who would work there, putting stringers under the floor so the women who did the filing did not have to stand all day on hard cement.

She first got interested in broadcasting when she and her husband sat up until 2:30 a.m. and heard the king of England speak on their old Atwater-Kent radio. She thought this to be terribly exciting, but it wasn't until the late 1930s that she acquired KEVR, both AM and FM, because a tenant in her building wanted to unload it. She remembers that it was such a terrible station that the Hooper people, who did the ratings in those days, graciously sent back the former owner's check because they found that nobody even listened to it.

She picked off Channel 5 in 1948 for $375,000. It was the only channel in town, and there were only about 6,000 TV sets in the entire city. When somebody asked Saul Haas, who owned KIRO, why he didn't get a television channel, he is said to have replied, "No, no. We will let Mrs. Bullitt have television as long as there are only 6,000 sets. But when there are 50,000 sets, then I'll do it."

But suddenly the FCC froze all new licenses. Nobody could get one. "So then you had a monopoly in this town for five years," I said. This seemed to please her. "Yes, we did. That was what made us."

William Randolph (The Real) Hearst owned 25 percent of KING-TV for a while. The Hearst people wanted to buy the whole thing, but she wouldn't sell it all, and they agreed on 25 percent, even though she was told, "Mr. Hearst doesn't buy parts of anything."

The Hearst executives, she said, always dealt fairly and sensitively with her, even thought the old man had the reputation of being a piratical sensationalist. Some years later, when Channel 8 became available in Portland, she went after that. Her arch-foe was the huge Westinghouse Corp., and the Westinghouse lawyer behaved before the FCC hearing examiner like a histrionic trial lawyer. But Dorothy Bullitt had some things going for her—a detailed knowledge of the TV business and a good track record for public service with KING.

But one day the Westinghouse lawyer hauled in a pile of documents on a wheeled dolly. Right into the damned hearing room! Dorothy Bullitt saw that these documents were labeled "Hearst," and she knew that Westinghouse was going to send up some rockets about William Randolph (The Real) Hearst's penchant for sex, blood and sensationalism. "They were smacking their lips over Hearst," she said.

So she immediately left the Washington, D.C., hearing room and went to New York. She ended up buying back Hearst's 25 percent interest, making the Westinghouse case against Hearst instantly obsolete. "It was a bloody thing, but we went through it," she says of the 11-week hearing. "I had been brought up under the thinking that Hearst was dreadful, that he was a dreadful man who ran a dreadful business. But they were certainly decent to me, awfully good."

What marked Dorothy Bullitt as a TV owner was her commitment to independence. No mouth-breathing yahoo who bought ads ever kept her from putting something on the screen if she thought it belonged there.

Like her late husband, she is a civil libertarian as it pertains to broadcasting, and she will say, "Yes, he taught me that way."

KING-TV may have flopped around in its own incompetence sometimes, but it had that commitment. Dorothy Bullitt's commitment. She set a standard.

You might get arguments out of the Mormons or out of the Fisher family that they, too, are "committed" and "responsible," and that is true. But she set the standard. As a result, Seattle and the Northwest gets some of the best television to be found anywhere in the country. People who travel to other cities come back and tell you this.

So her friends "went the usual way and did the usual things," but Dorothy Bullitt, to use the words of Robert Frost, took the road less traveled. And that has made all the difference.

▼

Ivar Haglund

Seattle Post-Intelligencer, January 19, 1975

PERIODICALLY, IN TRYING TO REASSURE MYSELF about the city, I check to see if the Ballard Bridge is still there, if the seagulls are giving Chief Seattle a bad time, or if somebody has made off with the statue of Governor McGraw. Now and then this inspection tour of old Seattle artifacts includes a visit to Ivar Haglund, the famous balladeer of Pier 54, who sells a little fish on the side.

Ivar is not always easy to find, for reasons I think I've mentioned before. He has a house on Magnolia, an apartment on Portage Bay, three restaurants with an office in each, and no requirement to be in one of them at any specified time. Ivar is short and, in a phrase dear to scribblers like me, rotund. His picture would make a splendid centerfold in Reader's Digest.

Ivar is also famous for not following the advice of Mark Tobey, the famed painter. Tobey and Ivar were friends in the Depression 1930s, and, on occasion, they would get together for private musicals, Tobey on the piano, Ivar on the guitar. When Tobey learned that Ivar planned to open a restaurant back in 1938, the great man was outraged. "No, no, not a restaurant, Ivar!" he stormed. "You are destined to play the guitar!"

Today, several restaurants later, Ivar is one of the few people in Seattle who can afford a Tobey painting. He doesn't own one, by the way. But he does own some expensive art, including four paintings by another old friend, Kenneth Callahan, whose work is not purchased with clam shells.

The way Ivar was telling it over a plate of black cod this week, he really blew it with Callahan. The two of them, friends since 1931, would get together periodically. One day Callahan took Ivar down in his basement and showed him three paintings. "I'd like you to have one," said Callahan. "Take your pick."

"I don't want one of those things around," Ivar responded. "I wouldn't understand it if I had one."

Ivar winces at the memory, too pained to guess what the painting might be worth today. "So I ended up buying four of them after Ken became famous," he says. "That part I understand."

Ivar, as you may know, got his start by opening an aquarium on Pier 54 in 1937. He likes to say, "I got so hungry I ate the show," but it wasn't quite like that. "My brother had a couple of aquariums down in Oregon, so I went down and visited him for a few days. That made me an aquarium authority. I caught some fish and put them in a glass tank. In those days, you charged a dime for adults and a nickel for kids. The first year, 60,000 people came to my aquarium. I thought, 'My God, this must work.' "

The second year, he got a 15-minute radio spot on KOMO, singing and playing his guitar. "I was sandwiched in between the Salt Lake Tabernacle Choir and a program called 'Invitation to Learning'; in other words, I had 15 minutes between two programs on Sunday afternoon that nobody listened to. But the next year, 100,000 people came to my aquarium, so I figured there must be something to this advertising. So I took a three-month trip to Mexico."

The rest is history. Ivar came back and, over the protestations of Mark Tobey, opened a fish-and-chips joint. Today there is nobody on the West Coast—possibly the nation, even the world—who sells more cooked fish than Ivar Haglund. At his Salmon House alone, last year he sold 250,000 pounds of salmon. If clam juice were oil, they'd make him an honorary Arab.

But his chief fame, in the early years, was that of a balladeer—one of the few in America at that time. Singers like Burl Ives, John Jacob Niles, Earl Robertson, Pete Seeger and Woody Guthrie considered him a compatriot. He even went on tour a couple of times himself, with an improbable road show backed by the West Coast Lumberman's Assoc., as part of its Keep Washington Green campaign. The group also included such writers as Stewart Holbrook and Jim Stevens as speakers, with Ivar singing ballads.

In the years since, he has become a compulsive collector of artifacts, trivia and decorations for his restaurants. He long has been devoted to the central waterfront. He once laid out $10,000 to paint the old firehouse red; he put up flower baskets along what was then Railroad Ave., and, most recently, led the fight against retiring the fireboat *Alki*. Lately, he steamed full bore into the bazaars of Portugal, Italy, Yugoslavia and waypoints, returning with pottery, carvings, Gucci scarves and other items that fill up the wall space of the already jammed Acres of Clams.

When I asked him where he was born, he said, "On Alki Point . . . You can also put it down that I went to West Seattle High School and the University of Washington. My major was nuclear physics and guitar playing."

▼

Henry Broderick

Seattle Post-Intelligencer, May 9, 1972

"I'VE BEEN STUDYING SEATTLE FOR 71 YEARS, and I haven't graduated yet." The man who awaits his diploma is, as you may have guessed, Henry Broderick, the best 91-year-old harmonica player I have ever heard. Lunch with Henry is always a joy since he makes you feel so young—not by comparison, but through his matchless spirit and sparkling sense of humor.

The talk started out on a sort of "state of the city" theme but quickly shifted to other subjects. One sensed that Henry, who gets asked about Seattle so often, was slightly bored with the subject. Or he's written so much about Seattle himself, via his annual Christmas books, that he isn't about to give any choice stuff away. Writers tend to be jealous of their material.

Over the years I have collected a fair number of Broderick stories, but each time we meet there are a few I haven't heard. He spins a good yarn, and his friends come from all corners of life. He was a good friend of the late Maurice Chevalier, and it was the great French entertainer who told him, during a four-hour bull session: "The trick to living is knowing interesting people. Not important people, but people who are interesting. But there's another side to the coin," Chevalier added. "You can't hold interesting friendships unless you yourself are interesting."

Henry grinned happily as he remembered the words. "The odd thing is," he said, "that I have had that philosophy all my life. My interests have always been outside the world of business. You have to know and cultivate and meet new, interesting people all the time. And, in turn, you have to be interesting yourself."

Henry is all of that. A Seattle pioneer in a sense—he came here in 1901 from Minneapolis—his life has been full of odd paradoxes. During his early years, for example, he used to buddy around with Bill Boeing when the founder of the great airplane company had only seven employees in a shack on Lake Union. Notwithstanding that association, he never flew in an airplane—not until he had reached the age of 90.

Prior to that, when Northwest Airlines came into Seattle, the firm's president, Croil Hunter, looked up Henry for guidance. He was so impressed that he later asked Broderick to serve on Northwest's board of directors. "I don't think you want me," replied Henry. "Your meetings are held in St. Paul, right? Well, how would it look if a Northwest Airlines director traveled to St. Paul on the Great Northern Railroad?"

It was typical of Henry that he took his first plane ride at 90. He flew to San Francisco to attend a get-together with Chevalier; Louis Lurie, the California capitalist; and Jake Ehrlich, the late San Francisco criminal attorney. "Now I fly all the time," he grins. "I tell people I like airplanes but I'm afraid of trains."

He has never owned a car. He rides every place in taxicabs, spending $2,000 to $2,400 a year on them, and figures he isn't too far behind the game. One night a driver asked for his credit number. "I really don't have one," said Henry, "but if you want to check me out, call your dispatcher." The call was made, and the dispatcher replied: "Broderick? Listen, driver, if he wants your cab, *give* it to him!" Not many years ago, Henry was seriously ill in Providence Hospital and a call went out for blood. No less than 27 cab drivers arrived as donors.

His friends have made up a cross-section of the worldly and humble. He carries on a lively correspondence with Erskine Caldwell. He once played the harmonica for Madame Schumann-Heink, accompanied by Meredith Wilson. Gypsy Rose Lee was an old friend, and, beginning with Nellie Cornish's famed school in the 1930s, he has sponsored and helped dozens of people in entertainment and the arts. He has a Chinese goddaughter, a talented painter, who lives in Sacramento.

He used to prowl the night spots and visit the Skid Road more than he does today. "Today's Skid Road bums," he muses, with a twinkle, "are of very poor quality compared to what we used to have. We used to have a more interesting collection of bums down there. We even had a lady bum. She was a college graduate and operated a Russian typewriter."

Henry's favorite story on himself concerns a Sunday, cold and blustery, when he decided to work. Looking out of his elegant, paneled office at 2nd and Cherry, he spotted a poor old guy rummaging through a garbage can. Henry crumpled a dollar bill in his hand and went out. He poked his head down into the garbage can and began foraging about, then pulled up the dollar bill. "Hey, look what I found," he said. "A dollar! Look, you were in this garbage can first, so why don't you take it?" The bum smoothed out the bill in his hand. "Yeah," he said, "I guess some rich bastard threw it away."

Rudi Becker

Seattle Post-Intelligencer, January 27, 1963

The energy expended on practical jokes, in this country alone, exceeds the combined energy that goes into the production of napalm bombs, erasers and prayer books.—H. Allen Smith

THE TERM "PRACTICAL JOKER" is elusive of definition and the range of practical jokes covers a broad spectrum from downright crude and cruel to gently amusing or instructive. And whether we admit it or not, there probably is a strain of the Katzenjammer Kids in all of us.

Some people would call Rudi Becker a "practical joker." Rudi is a big (6-4), intelligent, good-natured fellow who may well be, by certain definitions, a practical joker. But he insists that he never pulls a joke that might hurt anyone; he prefers to think of himself as a fellow adept at giving "the mental hot-foot."

Rudi probably is the town's most inventive prankster. He is a sales engineer for Olympic Prefabricators, a local construction outfit. Rudi sums up his prankster credo as follows: "I look at it this way—a lot of people, myself, fortunately, not included, lead a dull, humdrum life. If I can provide a little something of interest to them, fine."

Rudi provided "something of interest" to an impatient motorist one time. Becker's pet peeve happens to be people who, the instant a traffic light turns green, shatter the nerves with a honk of the horn.

So he got hold of an old, but fearsome-looking, blunderbuss and wired it up to a loud air horn. Inevitably the victim came up behind. He was impatient, he was in a hurry, and he drove a fancy convertible with the top down. At the change of the light, he honked fiercely.

Rudi, also in a convertible, stood up. He reached down, picked up the gun, slowly and deliberately he aimed it at the honker's chest. As his pasty-faced victim pressed back in his seat, an unbelieving look of horror on his face, Rudi pulled the trigger. Out came a loud air-horn blast, which even under normal circumstances would turn a victim to glue.

Becker calmly sat down, put his car in gear and drove off, leaving the honker in a pallid state of seizure.

Rudi doesn't always need elaborate weapons to deal with honkers. Once, when he was stuck on the Ballard Bridge, the man behind Rudi kept laying on the horn. Rudi got out, lifted the man's car hood, reached in and ripped out the horn wires. Then, towering amiably above the honker, he announced pleasantly: "There. Your horn was stuck, but now it's fixed."

Many of Becker's stunts bear no relation to the so-called practical joke. Sometimes he just likes to stimulate presidents of large corporations.

For example, he once bought a box of toothpicks that advertised "750 toothpicks" on the cover. With his friend, Joe Johnson, Rudi emptied the box, and the two began to count. They came up with 742 toothpicks. They found that six of the 742 were bent and four were broken in half.

Off went a stern, formal letter to the company. Back came an abject, almost fawning letter of apology from the company president, along with eight boxes of toothpicks.

Rudi once provided "something of interest" to a few humdrum lives along 2nd Avenue. He got hold of some Sea Dye, waited until the rain clouds boiled in, then drove slowly down the street spreading the stuff liberally around. In a few minutes, thousands of citizens lined the curbs, open-mouthed, as the rain hit the Sea Dye and turned all of 2nd Avenue a brilliant green.

His favorite gag occurs in bars. He enters a bar carrying some plastic bags filled with soda water and several raisins. The raisins, resting on the bottom, gradually pick up seltzer bubbles and rise to the top. As soon as the bubbles pop, the raisins sink to the bottom, and the whole process is repeated over and over.

"These," Rudi explains to the curious, "are Chinese Diving Oysters. They feed by raising up and down, collecting plankton."

To demonstrate further, he asks the bartender for a glass of water. The bartender is cued in advance and gives him seltzer. After a few raisins have gone up and down, no sales pitch is needed.

In a few minutes, Rudi sells his plastic bags full of "Chinese Oysters" for whatever the traffic will bear. Then he calmly takes the profits and deposits them in the nearest Milk Fund bottle.

Education, of course, is the cornerstone of Becker's real "practical jokes." A "Dump No Rubbage" sign on his property near Carkeek Park had no effect—at least not on one lady who dropped off a huge pile of stuff. Rudi went out, rummaged through the pile, found an old blouse with black sequins, a green scarf and—most helpful—a cluster of gasoline credit card slips that indicated the lady had recently returned from a trip to San Diego.

Rudi checked the phone book and went into action. "Hello, Madame," he announced over the telephone, "I'm going to ask you three questions, and if you can answer them correctly you will win a valuable prize."

"Oh, a quiz show?"

"You might say that," replied Rudi. "Are you ready? Very well, here's the first question: Do you own a blouse with black sequins?"

"Yes."

"Congratulations, Madame. You've answered the first question correctly. Now for the second. Do you own a green scarf?"

Excitedly: "Yes, yes." At least I *did* own one. I threw it away yesterday. Am I still qualified?"

"Yes, Madame. Now for the third question. Did you recently make a trip to San Diego by car?"

"Yes, yes! Oh, do I win? Do I?"

"You certainly do, Madame," replied Rudi. "You win 90 days in jail or a $300 fine, unless you get out here and remove all that junk you dumped on my property."

These are just samplings from Rudi Becker's anti-humdrum existence. We will have more later. Meanwhile, Rudi noticed that a certain cigarette company advertises recessed filters that put the tobacco "a quarter of an inch away" from your mouth. Rudi measured. He found that it's only 7/32 of an inch, a clear error of 1/32 of an inch.

He is now composing a letter to the company president.

Gracie Hansen

Seattle Times, January 15, 1985

TO APPRECIATE ANYTHING WRITTEN ABOUT GRACIE HANSEN, you have to go back to the Seattle that existed before the World's Fair. It was the Seattle of insularity—a plethora of Blue Laws, no Sunday booze, a low boiling point in the morals department, a bit wary of outsiders, more or less ruled by a narrow downtown oligarchy.

Oh, we were going to have a World's Fair, all right. We were going to smother 'em with science. A scientific exhibition, that's what it would be, and it would draw millions from all over the world, including scientists, and some of America's biggest corporations would lay money on us to show their wares. It promised to be as dull as a temperance lecture.

I remember that Westbrook Pegler, the old right-wing curmudgeon, came to town about then, and somebody asked him about nightclubs and serving booze on Sundays. "Sure, you've got to have booze on Sunday. Listen, boy, you can't run a World's Fair like a Methodist camp meeting," Peg said.

The landlords were sleazing it up by kicking their regular tenants out so they could rent apartments at stiff prices when the Fair started. There was a general jockeying and elbowing for space to run some restaurants and merry-go-rounds on the fairgrounds, and the parking lot Shylocks wondered how much the traffic would bear.

But, down inside, nobody was quite sure if the thing would have enough sex appeal to draw the big crowds everybody wanted. Then all of a sudden she arrived on the scene.

Gracie Hansen. Who? Whom-hell's she? She ain't out of Vegas. She's outta what? Morton? You mean that little town up by Mt. Rainier? What's her track record? Oh, sure, she ran a thing called the Morton PTA Follies. Oh, fine. Hey, what this fair needs is a Billy Rose, for Pete's sake. She began to get publicity. Lots of it. And when the lovely housewives of Seattle opened their papers and saw pictures of Gracie, what they saw was . . . Well, there were a lot of pursed lips and straightened backs, and Gracie got a good going over at the Women's University Club.

And when the men saw Gracie's pictures! Geez. She looks like a fat madam out of a whorehouse, all those feathers and junk jewelry around her neck, and enough blue mascara to camouflage a battleship. But when Gracie said she would put on a topless dancing revue, then the boys in the WAC and the College Club simmered down and let their wives do all the caterwauling.

Topless dancing? You mean kind of bare-breasted like in Paris and Vegas? Not kind of, dearie, Gracie smiled, the real jiggling, unsupported bra-less articles. Right out of Hollywood. Maybe some of them could even dance.

So Gracie Hansen's Paradise International began going up on the corner of Fifth Avenue and Mercer Street, where those grass mounds are today; and letters pro and con began appearing in the papers; and even some editorialists wondered aloud how our mossbacked City Council and the cops would deal with this . . . this woman, this little five-by-five who looked like she came out of a casting stereotype for Barbary Coast.

What this archetypal sin-and-satin house mother turned out to be, of course, was a very moral lady. She looked the part of a latter-day Sally Sanford, but she knew all the Ten Commandments by heart, and she was, in large part, a creature of here own publicity.

In this endeavor, she was helped along by two sharp Seattle press agents of that era, Guy Williams and Bob Karolevitz, who understood the nuances of the game they were playing. They fine-tuned Gracie by getting her outfits designed by John Eaton, a local designer of some renown, and that's where all the ostrich feathers and baubles came from. They worked on Gracie's racy little one-liners, and Gracie was very good at this because she was quite witty herself. Then they went to Huling Bros. in West Seattle and made a deal to have Gracie driven around in a big, fat, brightly colored Buick. And, on each door, they had artist Bob Todd paint a picture of a large, luscious apple. The exquisite touch was that they had Todd draw each apple with one bite out of it. Original sin, right?

While the carpenters were still hammering away on Gracie Hansen's Paradise International, Guy Williams went down to Hollywood with Gracie to book the topless review. They hooked up with a show-biz type named Barry Ashton, who came up with the girls and choreographed the show.

Then Guy Williams had a seizure of inspiration. He knew that once you've seen a lot of bare breasts, you really can't top them with an encore—not without getting thrown in jail. Besides, when you've seen several dozen of these titillating mammaries you've seen 'em all. Repetition sets in, and guys start looking at their watches.

So he signed up a dog act. The dog's name was Louie, and his owner-trainer was a fellow named Bob Williams (no relation to Guy). Louie looked to be part, or mostly, basset hound, and he had these long ears, short legs and big soulful eyes that mooned around the stage. Bob had trained Louie by reversing commands, "Up and at 'em, Louie, old boy, you're a bundle of energy tonight!" And Louie flopped down in a state of torpor. It went on like that. And pretty soon people were falling off chairs and spilling their whiskey sours, they were laughing so hard.

So what you had was a bosom bazaar and Louie the dog, with Jackie Sounders in the orchestra pit. On opening night, Guy Williams went outside the exit so he could hear the crowd and get a feeling for its reaction to the show. He did that several times and finally came to the conclusion: "Seattle is a wonderful city. The whole town is slavering to get in and see the bare chests, but they all come out talking about a trained dog."

What Williams and Karolevitz had in Gracie was a beautifully attuned performer. They put her on the speaking circuit, and she never failed because she could read the house like a sheet of music. She never hit a discordant note; her double entendres were gentle and witty, and Gracie never slipped into vulgarity, so the city that once scorned her came to love Gracie. She became synonymous with the World's Fair, like the Space Needle and Belgian waffles. And that is why, when she died last week, you read and heard so many nice things about Gracie Hansen.

Origin of the Space Needle

Seattle Times, July 29, 1984

WELL, JUST 25 YEARS AGO, that spindly-legged symbol of Seattle got itself conceived on the blank side of a paper placemat in a coffee shop in Stuttgart, Germany.

That was in 1959. The gestation period compares favorably with that of an elephant, since the period of conception, from placemat to reality, took only until April 1962—the opening of the Seattle World's Fair.

The funny thing is, the man who dreamed up and actually named it the Space Needle was afraid he'd get laughed out of town. He confided his idea to only a few close friends, whose derision, he figured, he could withstand. "When I came back with that idea," Eddie Carlson was saying, "I wanted to find somebody who'd listen to me without cutting me off by saying, 'This is the craziest thing I've ever heard of.' So I got hold of Jim Douglas, an old friend. I knew Jim's mind, and I knew Jim would listen to me. I didn't know if he'd agree, but I knew he'd listen." At the end of a long lunch at the old Olympic Hotel's Marine Room, Jim Douglas said, "Let's go see John Graham."

Now understand, children, these guys were talking about something that today is so successful, so much a part of Seattle, so well-known throughout the world, that the wonder is there was any hesitation at all. As Mel Anderson once put it, when the Space Needle began to attract hordes of people: "You know, those guys could have run into some hard luck that could cut their profits—they might have struck oil when they dug the foundation."

Eddie Carlson is one of the best yarn-spinners I know. Eddie's delivery isn't flashy, and he tends to be too self-effacing, but he loves telling a good story. He has a dramatist's sense of pace and structure (beginning, middle and end) plus a fine sense of irony and an orderly succession of facts. It might also be added that this 73-year-old chairman emeritus of UAL Inc. has a bold imagination. It all began, he said, in Stuttgart, when he and his wife, Nell, and their close friends Virginia and Webb Moffett took a pleasure trip to Europe.

The foursome was taken to dinner in a two-story television tower with a restaurant on top. "The place was loaded," he recalls, "and I was fascinated to see in a city like that, that was the place you had to go."

He got up early the next morning and went down alone to breakfast. The coffee shop, as you'd expect, had paper napkins and paper placemats. Eddie was deeply involved in the Fair; the Russians had just fired off Sputnik, and the Fair cried out for a theme, "and I remember sitting there alone in that coffee shop, turning over one of those placemats.

"Then I began drawing this tower and putting a circle on top of it, and I thought, 'If we could do something like that, build something like that, we'd have this big tower and we would call it the Space Needle.' " Then he bought a postcard and mailed it home to Ewen Dingwall, who was the director of this somewhat limping, altogether uncertain, often-derided thing we called a World's Fair. As nearly as Eddie can remember, the postcard said something like, "I've got this idea for building a tower—this could be the symbol for the Fair."

From there, Eddie and Neil and the Moffetts went to Paris, which has, to be sure, the most famous tower on earth. "I began to see the Eiffel Tower through different eyes, and then I thought of the Television Tower in Tokyo and about the Empire State Building in New York. And the thought threaded through my mind of how great towers have forever been an attraction for people."

So all of this spacey thinking led to that lunch with Jim Douglas, the developer of Northgate. When the two of them found John Graham that same afternoon, they outlined this idea that grew on a placemat, and Graham, one of the city's biggest construction men, finally said, "OK, I'll prospect on this thing." But "this thing" didn't take shape right away. Eddie Carlson went to The Times and pushed his idea at Ross Cunningham, the political editor. Ross was receptive but noncommittal. From there Eddie went to Howie Odell, then a county commissioner, and, as Eddie says today, "Nobody in the public sector wanted to tackle this thing."

Well, the end of the story is they went out and recruited some big hitters. They got Norton Clapp and Ned Skinner and Bagley Wright and Howard Wright Sr., and by now, of course, they already had John

Graham. "I suspect it was Graham who pulled these people in," Eddie says. Then they had to get special legislation from the city to buy enough land, privately, to build a private facility on public grounds. They had the clout for this, you'd better believe. Where the Space Needle now stands was an old firehouse, which had to be relocated. And finally they began digging and dumping concrete.

You may have heard the rest. About 5,850 tons of concrete went into this great big hole—the support and anchor for 3,700 tons of structural steel. Up it went, to the height of 605 feet above the ground and $4.5 million in cost. People gawked and exclaimed, "This thing actually works!" The Eiffel Tower and the Taj Mahal possibly excepted, this has become the most photographed man-built edifice in the world.

Eddie Carlson's eyes sparkle when he tells the next part —how the Space Needle builders, the Pentagram Corp., asked him if Western Hotels (this was before it became International, then Westin) would build a restaurant on top of the Needle. That amounted to a cool $600,000, in 1960 dollars, and Eddie, having dreamed this far, said, "Sure."

Not if a man named Troy Himmelman could stop it. Himmelman, father of Lynn, and S.W. Thurston ran the Western Hotels of the 1960s. Nobody went around committing $600,000 of corporate money for a nutty scheme like this.

Eddie laughs at the memory, the scene of them sitting around the Western Hotels boardroom. "When I told them what I'd done, that I'd committed $600,000 to this project, Himmelman exploded," Eddie said. "Troy said, 'Why this is the most ridiculous thing I ever heard of!' So I said, 'Troy, that's fine. If that's the way you feel, I'll organize a syndicate on my own and we'll put the money up ourselves.' Himmelman looked at me a long time, and said, 'If that's the way you feel, I move that we go ahead with the deal.' I knew what he was thinking: 'If this little guy thinks it's that good, it must be all right.' "

That was the end of it, Eddie recalled, although not quite. The original Pentagram group splintered off; Bagley Wright and Ned Skinner and Norton Clapp later sold their equity, which grew to considerable value, and used the money to build the downtown Bank of California Bldg. The Space Needle itself (and the restaurant) is now owned by Howard Wright Jr. and George Schuchart and their families. A young man named Rod Kauffman, who now runs the property for them, says that, since the Needle was opened, more than 25 million people have paid to ride the elevator skyward. Thirty-five percent of those, or 8,750,000 people, went up to spend Lord knows how many millions to dine.

"It's a funny thing," Eddie Carlson says, "but I haven't the faintest idea where that original placemat went, and Ding never saved the original postcard. Another funny thing is, I called it the Space Needle that morning in Stuttgart, and nobody ever tried to change the name."

O ur city truly came of age, I think, in 1971, when its good citizens arose en masse to save our most precious treasure— the Pike Place Market. I was lucky enough to wave a few pom-poms, cheering on the troops.

Pike Place Market

Seattle Post-Intelligencer, November 1, 1971

AT THIS WRITING, THE POPULATION OF SEATTLE is pegged at 530,831, a number mentioned here only to point out that all but about 31 of us are confused by the issue of the Pike Place Market. Tomorrow is the day we vote. For weeks now, the city has been split over an initiative that would create a seven-acre historical district—one its proponents, who ask you to vote "yes," say will save the Market. Other interests, mainly downtown businessmen and real estate developers, say that by voting "no" they will save the Market. Everybody wants the Market saved, and isn't that nice?

Since 530,800 of us are confused and 31 of us understand the issue, a clarification may be in order. I always remember with particular joy an editorial in the Brand G newspaper, one that lamented the fact that the Market initiative was confusing to the voters. It never occurred to them, it seems, that the first and highest duty of a newspaper is to clarify and inform. But so much for that.Well, you ask, whose gang is whose?

Those who are asking you to vote "yes" on the initiative to create a seven-acre historical area around the Market have been with us a long time. They are the Friends of The Market. Lately, they have been joined by another group called Alliance for a Living Market. This may seem confusing, but it isn't. Their goals are one and the same. In some instances, the same people belong to both groups. The point is, Friends of The Market was in existence long before this flap ever began. Some of Seattle's finest citizens belong to it. They raise money in bits and pieces. They put on small parties and auctions and sales to keep going. They have long maintained a headquarters in the Market. If one man alone typifies the spirit of the Friends of The Market, it is Victor Steinbrueck, whose sketches and prose on the Market are classics of a minor sort.

Now for the other group. This is called the "Committee to Save the Market." It was formed only a few weeks ago by a large ad agency, retained by the downtown business interests and the Central Park Plaza Corporation, who are saying they plan to put in a $100-million development in the Market area. According to their viewpoint, a seven-acre historical site would seriously cripple their project. Their project, of course, depends in large part on $10.5 million in federal Urban Renewal funds. Mayor Uhlman and most of City Hall are sided with the downtown business interests. The Stimpson ad agency is going to great and expensive pains to convince us that only the Central Park Plaza Corporation can save the Market.

Planned for the Market area are some 1,400 apartment units. Also a 500-room hotel. Also a 4,000-car garage. Leaving aside the fact that Seattle, today, cannot fill the apartments and hotels it already has, such as project, if it is ever realized, would have such an impact on the Market area that it's doubtful if the Market we know today would survive.

By now you must know how I will vote tomorrow. I will vote for the initiative by voting "yes" to make a seven-acre historical site of the Market area. This does not mean I think all is black and white. It does not mean that I think the Central Park Plaza real estate developers are bad guys. They are not. They are out to make a dollar, and, unless something has gone awry in the American system of doing things, there is nothing wrong with that. It's just that I would like to see them make a dollar some other way. Several of them are good friends of mine. It is to their credit that they have never tried to stifle the many pro-Market things I have written.

The Market, to me, is a living thing. It is a babble of voices, different languages, different accents. It is the incredibly beautiful displays and colors of vegetables; its very tackiness is part of its charm and a living reassurance that things are not all plastic in this Saran-wrapped world. The Market is the smell of beer and fresh bread and fish; it is the noise of feet shuffling along the stalls, the cry of the hucksters, the popping of bags, the laughter in the air, a bar of the music that makes a city.

Make no mistake about it, the Market is world renowned. It has been written about, lovingly, in London, Paris, New York, Los Angeles, Chicago—indeed, all over the world. People know about Seattle because of the Market, and I am desperately afraid that any giant project of parking lots, hotels and apartments will destroy this fragile thing that has made Seattle famous. One of the world's great artists, Mark Tobey, haunted the

Market and did some priceless paintings of its unique character. If I remember anything in my life, it will be the time, three years ago, when I visited Tobey in Basel, and we walked along the Rhine while he talked of painting, colors, philosophy and humanity. Quite abruptly he interrupted himself and exploded on another subject. "I have solved it," he said. "I have solved the problem of the Market. Leave it alone. Let them go ahead and build their silly buildings, but leave the Market alone. They *can* leave it alone. Don't they know," he added, "that the Market is the very soul of Seattle?"

The most remarkable folly in our city's history (always excepting freeways and viaducts) was the absurd thing we allowed to arise in the very heart of downtown. Well, you can't win 'em all.

Westlake "Park"

Seattle Times, February 24, 1987

THE OTHER DAY I AMBLED OVER TO FIFTH AND PINE to examine a hole in the ground. Peering into that hole, then looking up at the sky, it seemed to me that a funny thing is happening on our way to the next high-rise.

We are talking, of course, about the beginnings of a new Westlake Mall, that 21-year-old bone of contention in downtown Seattle. Already assured—unless there is a big switcheroo in plans—is yet another office-building high-rise, smack in the center of Seattle's most elegant shopping core.

But as I say, something funny is happening to this scheme. More and more people are viewing this hole in the ground, then looking skyward, and some of them are saying, in effect, "Hey, why not leave it the way it is—fill in the hole, plant some grass and trees and enjoy the open space."

The idea, however tenuous, is catching hold at City Hall. One councilwoman, Jeannette Williams, is having second thoughts about another huge downtown office structure and shopping complex. The other day a Seattle Times editorial writer mused on the virtue of a public square at Westlake. And, on the same day, The Weekly came out with a not-so-whimsical editorial entitled, "A Westlake Whimsy," and subtitled, "Why shouldn't Seattle's loveliest block be a green oasis?" Noting that

Seattle powerful downtown interests are adamantly in favor of more office and shopping development at Westlake, The Weekly adds: "But an awful lot of people who have walked by the square and seen what it looks like with the buildings demolished are saying it sure does open up a lot of light and views. It's not intimidatingly large. The facades of Frederick's, The Bon and the Times Square building look wonderfully unified in all that exposure. Is this not a rare last chance to have a public green space downtown, in the most populous and lovely block in the whole Northwest? Do we really want another office building and mini-Bellevue Square on that site?"

It was only a day or so later that I got a call from Marjorie Steinbrueck, Victor's widow, insisting that I go over and see Westlake Mall now that some of the buildings have been cleared out. "You know," she said, "that is what Victor wanted all along—a grand open space, a place for everybody, at Westlake Mall."

Of course, it's impossible, isn't it? As the old fight manager Jack Hurley used to say, "It's too late already." The Rouse Company, developer of the Mall, owns the Westlake property, having paid $11 million for it. Contracts are signed. It's their ball game. Doug Jewett, the city attorney, was quoted elsewhere that it would cost "tens of millions of dollars" to satisfy the developer. He said a buy-out would be "totally unfeasible unless people are willing to spend sums of money that are beyond my comprehension."

That seems like a lot of money to spend for an acre of grass, doesn't it? But still . . .

The same kinds of objectors said we couldn't put a lid over the freeway, thus creating an immense "Central Park" in downtown Seattle—now ripped apart by that same freeway. The Kingdome, priced at $40 million, was once regarded as a scandalous waste of money.

The easy way out for the Pike Place Market, rickety and unsanitary and even unsafe in 1970, would have been to turn it over to private developers. They would have torn it down, replaced it with sanitary office buildings and high-priced apartments—without spending a public nickel. What would we rather have today? A park over the freeway, or this monstrous varicosity within the city? A Kingdome of today, or no Kingdome at all? A Seattle without the Pike Place Market?

Maybe, as Hurley would say, "It's too late already." But viewing that big open space at Westlake, even as the rubble is being removed and the hole grows deeper, is kind of an inspiring sight.

Makes you hope a little, anyway.

Vice Squad Follies

Seattle Post-Intelligencer, January 18, 1979

THE PROBLEM ARISES IN THIS URBAN PARADISE, sometimes called "the nation's most livable city," over the correct attire to be worn by a policeman when he is negotiating a short-term lease with a prostitute. Ever since I can remember, police vice agents, posing as lustful tourists, or whatever, have negotiated such leases at public expense. That is, they pretend to rent prostitutes. They go though the charade of making a deal before making a bust (that is street slang for arrest; nothing more). The short-term rental racket has long been of concern. It is of particular concern to what, for lack of a more definitive term, we call "the better elements" of our society. So the police use undercover agents to trap hookers. I have always felt there was a danger here of cost overruns. Public money is easy to spend, and the temptations must be euphoric. Looked at another way, it would be tantamount to ordering a county commissioner to spend his evenings in a roomful of paving contractors.

But enough of unsupported speculation. One prefers to visualize the vice squadder heroically feigning the hots and allowing himself to be taken to the place of proposed assignation. At the moment of climax (the term is used here only to describe a dramatic arrest scene), the officer gives Speech IV, Section B, Police Manual of Conduct: "Put on your clothes, madam, for we are going to the police station and not to your promiscuous bed. As you can see, I am fully dressed with all buttons functioning tightly. This money I pretended to offer you belongs, in fact, to the taxpayers of the municipality to obliterate the devilish temptations of your ilk. You are under arrest."

I'm sure we all thought of it that way, but now what has happened? I tell you, friend, this was one shocked columnist who read some accounts in the papers this week. Stunning revelations came out of discussions between Police Chief Vanden Wyer and Mr. Bob Royer, deputy mayor of Seattle. All about the question of robing, or disrobing, among vice squad agents making a pinch (that is street slang for arrest; nothing more). Vanden Wyer came out like a monk against disrobing. He said he "halted operation" when some officers took off their shirts in the company of prostitutes. The Chief did not say if he burst in the room and halted the pinch (slang term again), but he seemed to speak from first-hand knowledge.

Deputy Mayor Royer had a vastly different view. He said he understood the cops would strip to their underwear to make a pinch (again, street slang). He said he understood "they have an underpants rule, that they can strip but they can't drop their pants." He said the police came and "specially asked for an exemption to undress all the way." He said, "They took off everything. They even indulged in fondling."

From there on it was Parental Guidance all the way. Royer said that even though the police indulged in "fondling," they didn't give up their essence in protecting the law. "But there was a nearie, as I recall," Royer said, "and we were concerned." Chief Vanden Wyer denied all. He said that, to his knowledge, his officers "were not totally stripped." He said there was no fondling. He denied there was—in Royer's words—"a nearie." No nearie. No fondling. He said these stories may have gained credence because a studio dancer, under investigation, made a "sudden outreach." Police anatomy was violated, which goes to show the nightly terror involved in trapping prostitutes.

Clearly, this is a matter for the Police Guild. If disrobing is outlawed, only outlaws will disrobe. The Police Guild must prepare for another initiative campaign. It sponsored (and helped pass) an initiative that prescribed how officers can shoot people, and with what bullets. A prominent Police Guild member sponsored an initiative to de-citizenize homosexuals. Plainly, another initiative is called for—if we unshackle police with guns, we should undress them in the cause of morality. A new code, Police Against Prostitutes, known as PAP, requires signatures to get on the ballot. Fight outreach with outreach, stop fiddling with fondling. Trapping hookers requires naked force. At the least, PAP would include a Police Academy course in Anti-Blushing, special emphasis in suave pants-dropping, plus defensive tactics against "sudden outreach." And Initiative PAP would establish a new Policy Review Board, made up of prominent, respectable ladies, who would critique disrobing and fondling techniques. Law enforcement requires citizen involvement.

The erection of a new esprit de corps among our anti-prostitute commandos is critical. For only then can citizens sleep soundly at night, knowing that a nearie will not go too far.

Seattle Stoics

Seattle Post-Intelligencer, June 7, 1974

"SEATTLE IS A GREAT, VIBRANT CITY," said Peter Rozelle, the reigning deity of the National Football League, shortly before the league owners put a

$16 million bargain special on the franchise. Vibrations came swiftly. It was instantly noted that local hopefuls, anxious to partake of the NFL's action, began to vibrate alarmingly on their way to the bank, reeling out their lines of credit. However, this should not concern us.

If Washington-bred capitalists cannot fill the NFL's wheelbarrow with doubloons, Peter has them elsewhere. There are always a few multi-type millionaires around, basking in the shade of their oil wells, or insurance conglomerates, ready to invest in sporting livestock. Texas and Oklahoma are full of them.

What does concern us, however, is a name for the team. With only two years to make a decision, there is no time to waste. This is not a name-the-team contest, or an invitation to start one. I have a name already picked. Conceding my vast expertise in the field of nicknames, it is necessary that I act alone. This is the name I have chosen: The Seattle Stoics.

Think about it; roll it around on your tongue; visualize it in a headline. And then consider: The name "Stoics" is original and unique. For perhaps the first time in the often-sordid history of naming athletic teams, this one is symbolically pure. Utterly appropriate to the team we will have—and the fans who will support it.

The name "Seattle Stoics" is not banal or trite. It does not invade the already depleted ranks of animals, birds, fish or fauna. Thousands of teams have ravaged the animal kingdom—to the point where tigers and lions, cougars and bobcats, coyotes and wolves, are on the endangered species list. There is little left except Musk Oxen, Aardvarks and Duckbill Platypi.

"Stoics" is a name that makes no concession to weapons of destruction, such as Bombers, Missiles or Rockets. It makes no pretense of violating nature's sound barrier, as in SuperSonics, and it does not kowtow to regional chauvinism. People are certain to argue that Seattle Kings, for the salmon, is a name indigenous to the Northwest. Perhaps it is. But, however noble the King salmon may seem, it is, finally, a fish. A slippery fish.

These are sensitive times. The name Seattle Stoics cannot possibly offend ethnic minorities, as would be the case if we tried Eskimos, Cossacks, Mau Maus and Sasquatches. I hear the latter already have consulted the ACLU.

Consider the Seattle Stoics: The name, the designation, has its origin in the ancient, philosophic pursuit of human dignity. It was formed on Hellenic soil in the 4th century B.C. The name Stoics implies—indeed, proclaims—the noblest of human virtues: moral fiber; strength of mind; patience in adversity; intelligent existence; noble aspirations; the spiritual substance to dare and endure. The philosophy of stoicism is well defined in the Encyclopedia Britannia: "No idle gratification of curiosity, no theory divorced from practice, no pursuit of science for its own sake, but knowledge realized in virtuous action, the learning of virtue by exercise and effort and training."

Here is the stoic in the words of Webster: "Not affected by passion or feeling, manifesting indifference to pleasure or pain." Somerset Maugham described the virtue of a stoic: "The courage which enabled him to bear perhaps the most dreadful of human afflictions." And Harold Shyrock said, "a stoical person is one who does not allow a 'mere pain' to interfere very much with what he is doing."

Make no mistake about it, the new Seattle team is going to suffer much pain and bear "the most dreadful of human afflictions." The NFL will see to that, by giving Seattle its cast-offs, and pain will come, perhaps for years, in the form of 38-7 or 42-14 defeats. A high degree of stoicism will be needed to survive the first few seasons. Indeed, the name Seattle Stoics is part of the city's heritage. Solid sports fans, not mere dilettantes but those with a kinetic feeling for jockstraps, have stoically endured second-class status over the years. They have been involved with more losers than Elizabeth Taylor. Stolidly—yes, stoically—they have suffered the pain of losing basketball, hockey, Husky football, and a baseball team that left in a blaze of bankruptcy. They endured—again, stoically— agonizing delays in getting dry, warm facilities that would attract major league events.

And, finally, when the first game is played, when the fan queues up for his first ticket and the man says, "That will be $15, please," he will suffer yet another dreadful affliction. He must be a true Stoic.

We Can Do Better

Seattle Times, July 28, 1991

STATE OF THE CITY . . .

Need I say it once more? Seattle long ago became a citified sex symbol, lusted after by travel writers, knot-headed developers, chintzy urban "analysts" and big, bold schemers. We are the darlings of Easterners and

Californians, a curiosity for magazine writers, a magnet for novelists, artists, painters and people just trying to find a job and a decent place to live.

Sometimes I think we have thrown our youth away, but no matter.

We love every minute, every word of it. But, in all of our civic breast-beating, not many of us (or visiting writers, either) are prone to give enough credit where credit is due. Enough credit, that is, to the guy who made this city beautiful. I refer, of course, to God. It was God, or one of his gifted aesthetic subcontractors, who gave us the water, the trees, the coolness, the gentleness, the hills and mountains, the sense of openness and space. Nothing we have done has improved on any of this. Because we proliferate and urge more people to come and enjoy, all we have done is nearly ruin what we already have.

But it's too late now; perhaps it was always too late, so we must make do with the city as it now is.

The latest of the magazine pieces about us (there seems to be one every week) appeared in the July issue of the Atlantic, a monthly, a generally good look at us by Ellen Posner. The titles are on target: "A City That Likes Itself," with a revealing subtitle, "By plan and by chance, Seattle is both urban and livable—and very agreeable for visitors, too." Posner's piece is illustrated by a breathtaking color photo of the Seattle skyline, as viewed from West Seattle. The colors (likely the picture was taken near sunset) are a blend of blue, gold and white, subtle shadings, an awesome forest of skyscrapers.

I rather wish she had talked to Jonathan Raban, one of England's great travel writers who has moved here to live. In his book *Hunting Mister Heartbreak,* Jonathan has a perceptive sentence: "If you had the bad taste to look at Seattle from the back, all you'd see would be plain brick cladding and a zig-zag tangle of fire escapes."

Travel writers seem to love skyscrapers, because they never mention what horrible damage these glass-steel-concrete-marble monsters do to the street life below. You walk among them many times, as I have, and you find their monstrous scale, their huge, rich fronts, their sterile lobbies, their covered escalators, their total physical dominance, placed, as they are, side by side . . . make you feel like an ant or one of our celebrated slugs.

This is not to belittle Posner. She has a very good section on our waterfront—not critical, but skeptical. She is restrained about our architecture (I think it's hideous), and she examines better than anyone else ever has the freeway-lidding convention center. She concludes, right-fully, that its very location is admirable. She should have been here before it was built. Then she could have witnessed the pounding Jim Ellis, who is Mr. Convention Center, took from people who wanted it, Lord forgive them, out by Seattle Center.

She writes of the "hard-to-avoid talk of turning Seattle into a 'world class' city," whatever that means to people prone to talk like that. And in this vein she adds, "There is the temptation to capitalize on further tourism, which is already the third-largest industry here—and which, it has been said, is to the life of a city what prostitution is to love."

Tourist-hustling, tourist-pulling has always been, it seems to me, akin to whore-mongering. But since every city does it, I guess it's at least as respectable as a state lottery.

Posner is admiring of Seattle's "citizen-generated efforts" to improve the city, its willingness to raise money for amenities like parks and other urban needs. But we can do better. Pending an end to the recession, we need even more bond issues, more public money to mitigate some of the clumsy damage we have done to this burg.

One admirable project is Times columnist John Hinterberger's idea for a wide swath of a mall, à la Europe, leading from downtown to the southern end of Lake Union. A great idea. Go get 'em, Hint.

Which brings us near the end of today's spasm. Before signing off, I would like to apply for the job of Seattle's dictator. Fear not, I would be a benign dictator. A tyrant with a heart, that's me. As dictator, I would go forward on Hinterberger's plan, but there would be more—even if I had to steal the money. I would raise enough dough to add more fountains to the city, many more fountains—don't let them kid you about a water shortage in Seattle. Along with these fountains would be statues, dozens of statues, many likenesses of people who made the city great. Make up your own list.

And cops. Maybe 100 or 200 more cops, whatever's needed. If we are so damned beautiful, livable and desirable, let's make every corner of this city a safe place to be. All urban life is dangerous these days. We may not be "world class," but we sure are urban.

Part 4
Lesser Seattle

Most great revolutionary movements, failed or successful, began in bars. Our own freedom-loving forefathers plotted to overthrow the British in the taverns and tea houses of Boston. The French Revolution was born in the bistros of Paris. Robert Emmet schemed against the British crown in a dingy little bar in Dublin.

So it was with Lesser Seattle. The seminal meetings of this mighty, yet benign, movement were held in the bar at Victor Rosellini's famous old 610 Restaurant, at the corner of 6th and Pine. This was in the 1950s.

Each day at noontime there gathered a crowd of advertising men, photographers, artists, freelance writers and newspaper people. It was a joyously witty and inflammatory group, the kind that viewed chest-beating boosterism with amusement and skepticism.

They included such luminaries as Marlow Hartung, Jerry Hoeck, Jim Neidigh, Bob Woolson, Mel Anderson, several reporters, a couple of columnists and the indomitable Guy Williams, a fellow of gentle but rapier-like wit. Any self-important humorless burgher entered among us at his peril. All substantial civic uprisings are ignited by the excesses of the ruling power structure. In this case, it was a large, well-financed organization called—my right hand to God—Greater Seattle Inc.

It seems almost quaint from this distance, but Greater Seattle, composed of industrialists, real estate tycoons, insurance magnates, politicians and like-minded chest-thumpers in the holy cause of Progress, was designed to "put Seattle on the map." It was boosterism of a kind that would shock George F. Babbitt. More people, more industries, more tourists—those were the things we must have to allow the Queen City to fulfill her destiny.

Then suddenly, in a dark corner of Rosellini's 610 bar, there came a quiet voice of reason. It was the voice of Marlow Hartung, an advertising artist of surpassing talent. Like the rest of us, Marlow was weary of Greater Seattle hoopla and the notion that bigness equaled goodness. "What we really need," Marlow said, "is a lesser Seattle. I like Seattle just the way it is." It took off from there. I could scarcely wait to get to a typewriter. But what did we have to fight with?

We had no money. We owned no newspapers or TV stations. Most of us, in fact, worked for the power structure. But we had one great weapon, a weapon that could render ridiculous the whole gross assumption of Greater Seattle. Our weapon was humor.

Ah, dreams of glory. I thought of Carl Sandburg's great line in *The People, Yes* when he said: "And the laughter of the people, foretokening revolt, carries fear to those who wonder how far it will go and where to block it."

So I became a conduit for the Lesser Seattle movement. We poked fun at bigness and grossness. We developed stories and themes and jokes that parodied and spoofed the whole notion of rampant, mindless growth.

From the beginning, it became apparent that Lesser Seattle had touched some kind of civic chord. People liked Seattle as it was, a city blessed with water, mountains and greenery that added up to incredible beauty. Most of all, we had space and elbow room, things we would not lightly surrender.

So over the years the Lesser Seattle movement grew. I must have written more than a hundred columns satirizing bigness, chiding grossness, ridiculing the notion of more tourists (who might return to live here) and greater development. Then we noticed a peculiar thing. New-comers soon wanted to join our ranks. In other words, the last person to move here became the first to join Lesser Seattle. Each wanted to be the final immigrant.

Lesser Seattle has its poets, its songwriters, its historians and even its own official prayer. Our ranks and our spirit are ever-growing. And finally, an unsung heroine named Susan Gerrard came up with the official Lesser Seattle motto: "Have a nice day—somewhere else."

No Lake Washington Bridges

Seattle Times, December 22, 1957

GENTLEMEN, THERE JUST HAS TO BE A WAY OUT of this long-standing second Lake Washington Bridge beef, and, as usual, I am not at a loss for suggestions.

Plans for paving the lake, while inspiring, are in themselves controversial, and so are suggestions for turning Mercer Island around to make it fit the mainland. And so, for that matter, is a suggestion to recommission the ferries.

A splinter group, or radical wing of Lesser Seattle Inc., has formed a new committee called the Society Against Progress. Its suggestion for solving the bridge controversy is at hand and duly noted. To be brief, the Society Against Progress, or SAP, has come out in favor of destroying the existing Lake Washington Bridge. They want to start over.

But the trouble with Lesser Seattle Inc. is that it can't even get along with itself. Each member thinks he is the president, but as a matter of fact they are all wrong. I am the president.

Now the trouble with radical wimps, like SAP, is that they talk a great bridge-wrecking game, but basically they are mere theorists who would destroy the best of the old order while trying to establish a new one. Babes in the woods. Bums! Mind you, I am not out of sympathy with these SAPs—if there is one thing that splits Seattle wide open with controversy, it's our unholy urge toward progress and more progress.

And that is why it's absolutely necessary that we start over by dismantling the existing span.

Well, while the theorists babble over their martinis, I have been working on the problem in an orderly, practical way. I have asked for and received sealed bids from nationally known wrecking companies; the contract has been awarded to the East Texas Wrecking & Pillage Co. The East Texas Wrecking & Pillage Co. has a good reputation in its field. This is the outfit, you may recall, which arranged the Dallas tornado last spring. They offered to do the same for Kirkland and Bellevue, which would certainly solve the problem. But the bidding clearly specified dismantling the existing Lake Washington Floating Bridge.

Their bid was $337,634.18 and the date for completion is set at January 28. Unlike the planners of SAP, my scheme would preserve the best of the old order, namely the pontoons. Each of the pontoons that keep our bridge afloat would be taken out, refurbished, powered with Rolls Royce engines and entered in the Gold Cup. During the winter, naturally, they could all try for new speed records over a measured mile course. The resulting noise would drive East Side residents away and it would be only a matter of time until we had a nice, tidy little town again.

This plan is cheap, it is practical, it is set for execution. The East Texas Wrecking & Pillage Co. is ready to start work on a moment's notice.

Why fight over Evergreen Point, Montlake and Sand Point? Let's purge ourselves of Lake Washington bridges for all time.

▼

Love That Rain

Seattle Post-Intelligencer, December 26, 1969

WELL, MAYOR WES UHLMAN HAS BEEN in office less than a month, but I am now ready to help him try the untried, or even think the unthinkable. What triggered this outburst of selfless devotion to the cause of a Better Seattle was a few lines of type on the back pages of the other morning's paper, and I quote: "Yes, folks, the Weather Bureau tells us it will rain today, tomorrow and it will probably rain on Christmas. In fact, we've already had over six inches of rain this month, almost half an inch more than normal with nine days to go. So far this year Seattle has had 34.51 inches of rain. That, too, is about half an inch above normal."

Where other mayors have failed, Mr. Uhlman can succeed. As I've said before, the mayor of Seattle should appoint a Committee on Rain— in order to best exploit our most important product. The duty of any Rain Committee should be clear: get the most out of our moisture, utilize every drop of our wetness; stop muddling around our mud puddles and get out there and sell.

First, of course, will have to come a radical departure from our present defensive attitude about Seattle's rain. We must learn to take pride in it. Veteran citizens remember when rain was considered more or less a nuisance, but not much more. We even took pride in it. At one time the Washington Huskies were known as the "Sun Dodgers," out of pride in our thick, black clouds. But over the years, our attitude changes. As transportation improved, citizens began to travel more—worst of all, in winter—and they became corrupted by sunshine. The discovery that places like Phoenix, Palm Springs and Hawaii had sunshine all year round sapped the spirit of our citizenry. They returned home with wild tales of sunshine in December and January, thus eroding our confidence that this was the best of all possible cities. We became a bunch of pebble-kickers, mumbling apologetically to strangers things like, "Aw, shucks, sorry about this rain and all . . . "

The time has come to change that. The Committee on Rain could enlist the help of what is euphemistically known as "the media." We could, subtly at first, but with greater intensity, propagandize the virtue of wetness. Since most people think we are all wet anyway, the job shouldn't be too hard.

Having created a booster spirit about our soggy climate, the Rain Committee could then utilize the best brains in our community to make Seattle a self-sustaining city. What we do best here: We get rain better than almost anybody. Boeing, of course, makes us virtually a one-industry town. The dangers are less if we use rain as our principal industry; after all, you can't blow a big federal contract on 34.51 inches of rain.

What then? Well, Boeing would be gradually phased out of the airplane business and turned into a huge galoshes factory. We would, in short, advertise our rain to the world by becoming to rain gear what Grand Rapids is to furniture. New, quality lines of umbrellas, boots, rubbers, sou'westers, hoods, parkas and whatnot could be exported steadily. But since (as you've notice in the past few months) everybody here needs rain gear we could prosper by selling it to each other. Buy Seattle!

Technologically, we are in great shape, with a bundle of skilled technicians already lured here by Boeing. They could, no doubt, develop a cheaper, more efficient brand of windshield wiper, thus assuring steady subcontracting work with General Motors, Ford and others. Seattle could someday proudly proclaim itself "The Windshield Wiper Capital of The World." Tried and tested in our own climate.

The Committee on Rain would travel extensively—especially to places like California, the East and the Midwest. Texas-style, they could boast about our rain to a point where nobody would want to come here. Those damned Californians are overrunning us now, and the trend must be stopped. Keep Seattle small and comfortable by inserting large, institutional ads in Life, Look and Holiday proclaiming: "If rain gets you down, stay away from Seattle."

As I see it, the idea is foolproof. Seattle will continue to grow, of course, because there are always a few nuts who like rain. The trick is to be selective. We could attract many beautiful girls by pointing out that a wet, damp climate enhances the skin, rather than shriveling it. Our suicide rate is one of the highest in the nation. But we can be No. 1. Subtly, we could lure a better class of suicide here. Let two or three international celebrities knock themselves off in Seattle during a gloomy December and we'd have it made. They couldn't keep us off the front pages.

Using our rain properly, we could become a proud, distant, forbidding community. Seattle's explosive growth could be slowed. Then someday, if things work out right, we may actually be able to find a parking place.

▼

Man the Parapets!

Seattle Post-Intelligencer, September 18, 1977

IT USED TO BE THAT WHEN I HEARD THESE THINGS, I'd respond in mock anger, but secretly I was pleased when some national publication or newsletter referred to us as "Seattle, Ore.," or had ships sailing into "Spokane, Wash." Good, all to the good, I would think, secretly, never letting the Chamber of Commerce in on my seditious thoughts. Elsewhere, we knew—the nervous legions of Lesser Seattle Inc.—that people thought of Seattle as a small enclave of rain-soaked sods, way up there on the map someplace, just a short cab ride from Alaska.

When a New York cabbie once asked me, "Seattle? That's near Westport, isn't it?" I knew we were safe . . . An occasional story about us in the Butcher's Quarterly, or the Saturday Review, did no harm. I was also heartened by the story of the Eastern lady who announced that she was "flying out to Seattle." "Oh?" replied a friend, archly, "on your way to where?"

But gradually, the battlements began to weaken. A story here, a travel piece there, extolling our virtues started what the sociologists call an in-migration. It was a trickle of Ivy Leaguers, at first, but they—being elitist and snobbish—were content to call us "small town" and "dull." An Ivy League Mafia even infiltrated our government, but no real harm done. They were non-violent and none of them (to my knowledge) tried to raid the treasury, or steal a city bus.

But suddenly, overnight, our line of defense began to bend. We became "major league" in sports, although this wasn't too bad; your average Eastern sports fan regards it as a scenic and exhilarating experience when he doesn't get mugged in a subway. But Billy Graham came last spring and brought us major league religion. Meanwhile, inexplicably, larger publications discovered us. Such terms as "natural beauty" and "preserved environment" and "scenic ambiance" and "plethora of good restaurants" surfaced to describe Seattle. Suddenly, it seemed, traffic problems became more serious; "elbow room" was a phrase you heard less frequently. Then we began to mutter: "Too many blank-blank tourists in town!"

An alarming article in Harper's (or was it the Atlantic?) called us "America's most livable city." It caught on. As a city, we were livable and full of lovable people. Paradise beckoned to mosquito-bitten Midwesterners, those pushy Easterners, and we were, in a phrase of the day, becoming

"Californicated." "We've got to keep them out!" I snapped to a C of C official. "Watkins," he said, patiently, "you have a no-growth mentality." "You mean I've stopped growing mentally?" I asked. "That happened a long time ago," he replied. "What I mean is, you are anti-progress. Progress: more people, bigger buildings, high-rises, large developments. What made America great."

That did it. It is time to staff the parapets, ladies and gentlemen—be you Lesser Seattleites or not. To the breastworks, troops. Get thee to the ramparts and keep the bastards out! Our weapons are not bullets, but bad news. Let the word go forth, at this time and place, that Seattle is dark, ugly, rainy, unfriendly and probably beyond saving. Scare off the invaders. What we need is a long, dreary, storm-ridden, sopping winter. Let us pray. I do not advocate anything so drastic as an earthquake. This department is against all forms of natural disasters, such as Wayne Larkin for mayor, but the invasion is imminent.

The powerful "Eastern establishment" press is in a conspiracy to overcrowd us. The NY Times extolled our cultural sophistication, the Washington Post raved about us only the other day. Next, they may re-enlist Woodward and Bernstein to dig up the scandalous news that this is a good place to live. We must fight on the beaches, we must fight in the bars, we must fight on the landing grounds (raise fees at Sea-Tac).

Let us fight in the churches as well. Let us pray that the Mariners go on losing, to avoid national attention; regard every Seahawk fumble as a patriotic sacrifice for our city's oblivion. Be surly in victory, malevolent in defeat. Snarl at strangers, glower at outsiders, write plaintive, complaining letters to our neighbors abroad. Let us dirty the streets, neglect our parks, magnify our problems. In short, we may have to destroy the city in order to save it.

Defend the City!

Seattle Post-Intelligencer, December 11, 1977

NOW, TROOPS, IT WAS NOT A VERY GOOD WEEK for us, and signs of a crisis appear on the horizon. Everybody out on the parade ground, while your cerebral leader, Gen. E. Watson (known affectionately as Old Dud and Thud), prepares you to defend our frontiers. As you know, the news is grave. After an entire year of media hype about Seattle and Northwest virtues, what may have been a knockout propaganda blow was struck this week. It is one thing to be praised ("livability," "America's No. 1 city," etc.) by such lightweight publications as New West, Vogue, Sunset, NY Times, Washington Post and the East Plerrisy, N.J. Advocate-Item. It is quite another thing to be praised by the pompous, statistics-spewing prose of Time, the weekly newsmag—circulation 4.25 million, for crissakes!

Time's cover features Gov. Dixy or the willow goldfinch, our state bird (it's hard to tell which). The story is lathered with superlatives about our lifestyle, our beauty, our appeal, our accessibility and friendliness, ad nauseam. And take this damaging quote from William Ruckelshaus, a late-coming carpetbagger who has no empathy with us Lesser Seattleites: "People are simply more civil, more pleasant out here."

"Well, there goes the neighborhood," you say to yourself. Visions of latter-day Okies, Crackers, smog-bound Los Angelenos, Arkies, and other migrants from distant peat bogs blacken the imagination. You see them selling out, packing their belongings in motorhomes and clogging the East Channel Bridge, trying to get at us. Hordes of developers, speculators, loan sharks from elsewhere line up to take out licenses to rape, plunder and pillage. One even envisions Howard Cosell co-hosting editorials with Lloyd Cooney.

Hear me out, troops, and I won't let you down. Old Gen. Dud and Thud has a plan. The other day I was reading a story about Liechtenstein, done by the Los Angeles Times. It appeared here in the Brand X paper, so I'm sure you missed it. In order to stay small we must think big, and Liechtenstein, a tiny principality near Switzerland, has much to teach us. For starters, Liechtenstein charges $25,000 a year just to live there—as long as you are childless, over 60, and cannot procreate. About 20 years ago, they sold citizenships for $18,000, but threw that out when more people applied than they wanted.

In Liechtenstein citizenship is voted on by the people, and applicants must then be approved by parliament, concurred in by the reigning prince. Nearly everyone gets turned down, for Liechtenstein is determined to remain small. There are 45 factories in tiny Liechtenstein, but no more.

"Foreigners," meaning non-Liechtensteiners, must renew their visas every year. People who have lived there for generations are regarded as "foreigners." Naturally, they cannot vote or have any say about what goes on. Pollution is nonexistent; working plants are designed like villas or chalets; no foreigner is allowed to buy property. Liechtensteiners are prosperous and self-sufficient; they even get snockered on home-made schnapps, which they keep in bottles labeled "Holy Water." Since we regard our keep-'em-out campaign here as co-educational, I hesitate to mention that Liechtenstein doesn't let its women vote.

Therefore, considering the damage done by Time, we need a broad, malevolent, comprehensive defense plan. Enact legislation similar to Liechtenstein's. Forthwith and right now, lay a residence tax on newcomers—maybe $10,000 a year, for starters. Harass them, inspect their luggage like surly U.S. Customs inspectors; let off your aggressions by being rude and boorish to "foreigners," who will be defined by an Unwashington Activities Committee. Censorship in wartime is acceptable—and we are defending our borders against Paradise-seeking hordes—so visas must be denied to all "unfriendly" correspondents from outside publications determined to praise us. Outside relatives may visit, of course, but only on a strict quota system, with a rigid visa policy.

Now, time is growing late, and we must toddle up to the barricades. Spring will soon be here, with the invading forces of campers, trucks, mobile homes and moving vans not far behind. But victory will be ours, troops. Keep them out, and one day we will celebrate our splendid state with plenty of elbow room to raise our glasses with a toast of Holy Water.

▼

Welcome, Tourists

Seattle Post-Intelligencer, July 17, 1978

YES, WELCOME, TOURISTS, TO SEATTLE, still basking in the limelight, thumbing its press clippings as "the nation's most livable city"—a rather meaningless title bestowed on us by magazine editors who like to rate things. We are big on elbow room, clean air and water, scenery, and prolonged rains. You have come at the right time, tourists. We are just going through our annual euphoria, a seizure of self-love and tourist-dollar volume, brought on by periods of intermittent dryness. We call it summer. We have made some progress over the past few years in the area of civic sophistication, whatever that means, and I guess it means more things to do—major league opera, major league baseball, football, basketball and soccer, good theatre, some splendid restaurants, and enough outdoor amenities to keep you healthy.

Tourists, I wish I could give you a general guideline on Mr. Typical Seattle, so you'll know him when you meet him. For starters, I'd say your average Seattleite is a pretty good guy, all in all. This goes for Ms. Seattleite, too, but we'll use the masculine gender so we don't clutter things up with a lot of Mzzzs and "persons" along the way. Your average Seattleite relies heavily for social guidance on his church (which he doesn't attend much) and he is quick to support Worthy Causes, so long as these causes have, in themselves, an aura of acceptability and a reasonably certain tax write-off. In general, he is polite, helpful and extremely hospitable, ready to start up his backyard barbecue at the first sign of friendship.

To be perfectly candid, the average Seattleite is probably a myth. If he's been here more than five years, he's a native; if he came here before World War II, he's a pioneer. He rarely carries an umbrella, partly because he's defensive about our constant drizzle, partly because he considers this most practical instrument as effete. Mention that you once ate at Antoine's or Sans Souci, and he'll immediately boast about Seattle's "many fine restaurants"—but if somebody offered him pâté de fois gras, he would probably call the FBI. But in all fairness, Victor Rosellini, who should know about these things, having traveled the nation as president of the Nat'l Restaurant Assoc., calls Seattle "number one in eating among medium-sized cities."

Some of us think that "Mr. Seattle" is, in reality, an elderly lady, of Protestant convictions, profoundly content with herself and dedicated to believing that fun is paid for with generous tithes of conscience. That is probably wrong. But it's notable that many of us attend "prayer breakfasts" before venturing to the day's commerce, chilled Chablis lunches and a hard run at the city's zoning laws.

A lot of you, tourists, have come here this summer to visit the treasures of the Kid King*—so this may be our best "tourist season" ever. Our itching palms are extended in welcome. But be it known that I, as the self-appointed pres. of Lesser Seattle Inc., hope you will go away in due time, preferably after your last traveler's check is cashed. Lesser Seattle-ites—and this is a growing underground movement—do not want you to come back and live. You see, more than our scenery, we cherish our parking places, golf courses, tennis courts, fishing spots, picnic grounds and fairly uncrowded neighborhoods.

We, of Lesser Seattle are non-violent by nature, so do not be alarmed. The worst we will do is snarl at you now and then, just to keep in practice, and all of us are practiced in reciting to you rain statistics, cloud-cover days, storms, high winds and rising prices. So if you will promise to go

---

*The King Tut-treasures exhibit was in town.

home, like good people, promising never to return, except as visitors, I will tell you how to deal with Mr. Seattle himself. A Seattleite, as I say, is a pretty good guy—a sucker for flattery about his city. Just tell him how lucky he is to live here. Tell him how great the mountains are, rave about his domed stadium, gasp loudly over the scenery, remark on how "friendly" everybody is.

Point out that "a little rain never hurt anybody," finger your sincere tie and proclaim to him how awful those "other" cities are compared to his. Ladle it on thick and you've got him. In short order, you'll have a free dinner, a boat ride, a visit to his vacation home and the keys to his second car. Any smart tourist can take him.

President Speaks

Seattle Post-Intelligencer, February 18, 1979

Report to Stockholders,
Lesser Seattle Inc.
Subject: Sinkable Bridges

YOU ARE ALL AWARE BY NOW of the stimulating event that took place last Tuesday morning at the entrance to Hood Canal. As your president, I suggest that all members of Lesser Seattle give Mother Nature a standing vote of confidence; she has earned a place on our Honorary Board of Directors. While you have all been rejoicing over our good fortune, your president has not been idle. I have burned several candles and offered up sacrifices to Mother Nature. These sacrifices have been in the form of old news clippings in which public officials have advocated "a permanent cross-Sound bridge in the cause of progress." In satiric reference to conventional folly, I have regularly intoned that canard heard so often: "Trust the engineers—they know how to get things done."

We should dwell, briefly, on the good fortune that has fallen to the people and creatures of the Olympic Peninsula, now that the bridge is gone. Fewer people will congregate at Dungeness Spit to watch the birds copulate; clams, oysters and fish should get a breathing spell; Port Angeles will have to undergo fewer humiliating comparisons to Victoria, and Hurricane Ridge deer will eat less Wonder Bread, cast out by tourists; UW faculty takeover of Port Townsend may be slowed, and the old milltown atmosphere should benefit.

What of Trident? One thinks of those enormous subs trapped at Bangor like so many killer whales, unable to get out through the wreckage of the bridge. These are all pleasurable fantasies, to be sure, but as your president, I think Lesser Seattle should go on record as being in favor of rebuilding the bridge. But this time, they should built it carefully—and slowly. About 25–30 years should be a good timetable.

The disappearance of the Hood Canal Bridge shows what can be accomplished with a little luck. Does any red-blooded Lesser Seattleite fail to dream of a giant rock slide at Snoqualmie Pass? Mother Nature accomplished the Hood Canal sinking with no injuries or loss of life; surely, she can do the same at Snoqualmie Pass. One envisions it happening, with no injury to anyone, at precisely the right time: just after the last resident has traveled safely over the pass, leaving on the other side a convoy of Winnebagos and other highway battleships, bound here from all over the Midwest.

The true paradise of Lesser Seattle cannot fully be realized, of course. A few outlanders will always trickle through, to work at Boeing, or whatever; but we can hope to minimize what sociologists call in-migration. We can never achieve out-migration, but we can try to achieve stay-put-migration. What we need, then is a good rock slide at Snoqualmie Pass (the other side of the ski areas, to be sure) and then something to the south, down around Portland, to block I-5. Lesser Seattleites no doubt have some creative thoughts on this. By partially blocking the east, then the south, we can cut down on in-migration immensely. And with the Hood Canal Bridge gone we have a splendid, relatively unpopulated recreation place—a whole peninsula—available to those natives who will take a little trouble to get there.

As your president, I urge Lesser Seattleites to work constructively at home. Let us take care of our own. Instead of fretting about the Hood Canal Bridge, let's do something for West Seattle. Rebuild the bridge for the folks over there. For starters, a Lesser Seattle campaign should be mounted immediately. The goal: to take the $64.2 million being proposed for a giant convention center and use that toward fixing the West Seattle Bridge. An enormous convention center at the foot of Queen Anne Hill, as now proposed, exceeds even our past imaginative plans for self-destruction.

It is not enough, Lesser Seattleites, to create bumper stickers saying "Tourist Go Home" and the like. They are fun, but they grow tiresome.

Moreover, a comfortable, manageable number of tourists is acceptable. But to keep ourselves Lesser, rather than Grosser, we must discourage rampant invasion. When Vice Premier Deng caught a cold here, we were lucky. So with the Hood Canal Bridge. If the outside world gets the impression that we are a sniffling disaster area, so much the better. And we've got the engineers to prove it.

A Letter to Outsiders

Seattle Post-Intelligencer, September 10, 1981

AS OUR LESSER SEATTLE MEMBERSHIP GROWS, we find that some of the recent converts have trouble grasping our style. Our KBO agents report that Lesser Seattle's newer members, like most everybody else, tend to procrastinate in our critical letter-writing campaign. These are letters in which loyal Lessers write to friends or relatives they don't want to see, subtly discouraging their in-migration, as the demographics boys put it. Agents of our KBO, or Keep the Bastards Out, report that our be-rude-to-tourists program went quite well this summer. But they also say that the recent good weather tended to make our members complacent. "The problem is not illiteracy," reports one agent. "It is well known that Lesser Seattle members are far above the norm in basic intelligence. A recent check showed the big-growth, pro-development Grosser Seattle people scored far below our own members in I.Q. tests. The problem with our own people is that they put off writing to Aunt Minnie, Cousin George or whomever, urging them not to come to Seattle. You, as our President, must show them by example what to tell people who might want to move here. Perhaps a sample letter, which they can copy and mail, would increase the volume." As president of Lesser Seattle, I can not shirk this duty. Here, then, is a sample of what you might send.

Dear (aunt, uncle, cousin, old buddy): We are thrilled to hear that you and the five kids plan on visiting Seattle with an idea toward moving here. Even if Uncle George doesn't have a job, I'm sure you can park your trailer in our beautiful Volunteer Park until he can find work and buy a house. You might be told by the police to move on, but you just don't take any lip from our cops. You tell them visitors have rights. You dare them to throw you in jail. They won't do it, of course, because everybody knows the jails are so crowded out here that we have weekly commencement exercises for the "graduates" they turn loose on the streets. Boeing isn't hiring right now, but don't let that discourage you. Our Port Commission at this very moment is busy trying to wipe out a boat marina so they can rent the space to a rock-crushing plant. The Port Commission says this new rock-crushing plant will provide as many as 15 new jobs to our economy. How's that for progress?

The Port Commission, you may be interested to know, gave us our grain terminal. The grain terminal hasn't won any architectural awards, but when you consider that it provides maybe 12 or 13 jobs, who cares if somebody's view gets blocked? Of course, a few people here think the Port Commission's heads should be the first rocks to go into our new rock-crusher. That is a local joke. Ha. Ha.

I am sure you heard about our big "million dollar salmon derby" last weekend.   You will notice, however, that nobody won it. Some 25,000 fishermen fished to win the million bucks. Even though we know you want to come out here partly for the fishing, we have to tell you that the "million dollar salmon derby" was a big fraud. The salmon they tagged in Puget Sound was really brought here from Alaska. You see, nobody catches salmon here because all the salmon are gone. The Indians took half of them and the rest were killed off by pollution and big dams. So you might as well leave your fishing tackle back there. You won't be needing it.

The housing market has remained bullish here. That's because we've had a massive influx of PLO terrorists who are driving real estate prices out of sight. They are nice enough people, I guess, but we prefer our Moonies and the Doukhobors who are becoming a force in our community. Since you are such swell folks, you'll be tolerant if our Seattle neighbors appear to be rude, dirty, irritable and hostile to strangers. We attribute this to our recent three-day dry spell. Whenever we get a protracted drought like that, people behave boorishly.

Recently, a Seattle paper ran a big story on "killer fleas" in Seattle, but don't let that bother you. Killer fleas are old stuff to us. Killer fleas and caterpillar explosions. We have also learned that our great influx of Californians has brought in some

Medflies. So, what with the killer fleas, the caterpillars and the Medflies, you might hesitate about coming. Don't worry. Plans already are drawn up to spray the entire city with some powerful pesticides that are guaranteed to kill all three. Which reminds me, you'd better not bring your three cats along until the spraying is over. They plan to spray as soon as it stops raining.

Since two of your kids are ready for college, I should encourage them to enroll at the University of Washington. Since Boeing isn't hiring much, the Engineering Dept. is offering some courses keyed to local needs. Instead of aeronautical courses, they now offer a curriculum that includes Introductory Roof Repair, Mud Slide Prevention, Bridge Disaster Procedures, Flood Sewer Main Prevention, Lava Evaluation and, most recently, Understanding Earthquakes. It has just been discovered that we are sitting on a hitherto unsuspected earthquake fault. I'm sure you're looking forward to the excitement of living in Seattle.

Though I began writing about Lesser Seattle in 1957, it wasn't until 1989 that, without trying, I struck columnar gold. I happened to spoof immigrant Californians, who responded with glorious vitriol. The uproar kept me supplied with material for months. So dizzying was the effect that at one point I stepped over the line and referred to Californians as "nitwits." What seemed at the time to be playful stereotyping came out rather mean in cold print, and I am truly sorry. By now, I assume, our immigrant Californians are solid Northwest citizens, some of whom, no doubt, have joined Lesser Seattle.

Tears for Californians

Seattle Times, July 20, 1989

"FEAR AND LOATHING LURK BENEATH placid San Diego," begins a turgid story in the usually restrained New York Times, under a headline that reads "Wary residents ever mindful of 'Los Angelization' of San Diego." The fear, it is reported, comes from apprehension that San Diego will be "consumed like cancer by its relentlessly hip neighbor to the north, Los Angeles."

Plainly, San Diego loathes Los Angeles. A recent L.A. Times survey fueled this loathing by reporting that nearly 50 percent of L.A. County residents hate the place themselves; they consider moving elsewhere, and "a goodly number cited San Diego as the best destination." A San Diego Union columnist, Karla Peterson, has suggested "border checkpoints" to ferret out automobiles for tell-tale signs of 'LA-lien activity.' "

Lesser Seattle Inc. grieves, more or less, for the plight of San Diego. But in a mood of civil detachment, we see this as a grosser vs. lesser fight between two California cities. We in the Northwest, however, have no time to sympathize with one California city against another. We are alarmed by the whole blinkin', bloody, over-bloated state of California.

Horror stories abound. Californians, trapped in elbow-to-elbow congestion, yearn for more breathing room. As developers chew into their living space, they become nervous, intense and neurotic. They long for wide-open spaces, preferably a space in which to park their cars. So what is happening? I will tell you what is happening. Because this crowding has led to obscene real estate prices, they sell their homes for $500,000 and head for Seattle and environs. Here they buy homes for $200,000 or $300,000 and settle in with cash to spare. These are usually two-car, even three-car, families, and they are cluttering up the once pristine Northwest landscape.

Lesser Seattle Inc., of which I am founder, president and CEO, has always advocated outright hostility toward these sun-kissed barbarians. Keep them the hell away from here, we say. "KBO" is our motto—"Keep the Bastards Out."

Our KBO guerrillas are doing effective work. More and more, we see plaintive letters in our gazettes—from newly arrived Californians who claim they are being discriminated against. They charge us with rudeness, with Northwest chauvinism, with downright prejudice.

Music to our ears. Yet, as we have advertised, Lesser Seattle Inc. is a corporation with a heart. We are nonprofit and devoted to public service.

For example, we Lesser Seattle patriots recently established our own "outpatient facility" to assist the unfortunate. That is to say, the wretched refuse from California cities are given counsel and guidance.

Our trained staff of para-professional KBO agents minister to bruised California feelings of being unwanted in Puget Sound country.

"Do not despair," we tell them soothingly, "you are wanted—back in California. Here is a road map. Take I-5 southward and don't stop till you see the first palm tree."

As I say, Lesser Seattle grieves for those fearful San Diegans. We are not without sympathy as they face the invading hordes from L.A. In fact, we sympathize with all Californians. That is why we have formed a separate Lesser Seattle cheer-up group of dancers and singers known as the Crocodilettes.

I will not describe their bodies, for that is sexist. But all of our Crocodilettes have broad, ample cheeks and copious tear ducts. At the first sign of depressed Californians, those who feel unwanted in the Northwest, our Crocodilettes unleash a flood of crocodile tears on their behalf.

We are shipping a canister of crocodile tears, along with some bottled rain water, to the beleaguered San Diegans. Indeed, to all crowded Californians.

All of us in years past have felt the sting of California's sarcasm. "Rain city," they would sneer. "The rust capital of the world," they would snicker. "Three days of summer," they would chortle.

But all that has changed. Now they want to get away from each other and come up here, perfectly willing—even eager—to endure a little dampness in exchange for elbow room. They now whimper because we don't love them.

Bring on the Crocodilettes. I say the game is up, and I say the hell with them.

Fight Californication!

Seattle Times, July 30, 1989

YES, FRIENDS AND NATIVES OF LESSER SEATTLE, the invasion of California nitwits to the Northwest has now reached epidemic proportions. The term "hordes" is now used to describe the horrendous influx of sun-bleached barbarians to our shores.

Only this week USA Today ran a cover story headlined "Locals fear the 'rat race has followed' "—locals meaning us, and the rodents, presumably, meaning those neurotic Californians.

It has been going on for weeks. Since last April, your Lesser Seattle president, namely me, has been deluged by calls from publications asking for interviews on the California quandary. News outlets such as The Atlantic magazine, USA Today and U.S. News and World Report are onto this migratory epic. Only last Wednesday, U.S. News sent a veteran reporter from San Francisco to interview me. I agreed to the interview only on condition that he head straight back to San Francisco when his journalistic mission was complete. Before I finished pounding his ear, the veteran reporter's eyes were puddling in sympathy. He promised to get out of town immediately.

USA Today, meanwhile, cited documentary evidence that the crisis is real. Using a colorful graph, this national paper cited figures from U-Haul International showing that the California-to-Washington plague is up 129 percent. Similar evidence came from driver's license figures and the Household Goods Carriers Bureau. I can also report that Lesser Seattle's membership has increased by 112,380. KBO recruiting stations are swamped with volunteers wishing to join our urban, anti-growth guerrilla fighters. At one recruiting station, KBO aspirants spontaneously burst into song: "Out, out, out! Keep the Bastards Out!"

Something drastic must be done.

For starters, we must levy a stiff head tax on Californian immigrants. They are the true scourges of our Northwest way of life. They must be dealt with severely. You see, in virtually all these stories about disillusioned Californians, fed up with smog, traffic jams and crime, there is a common thread. Because they have made a human zoo of their environment, they want to come here.

Because they are overcrowded, their real-estate prices are grotesque. So they sell their shabby, fixer-up houses for, say, $500,000 to $600,000. Having price-gouged their dwellings to such obscene levels, they then buy a house up here for, say, $150,000. They pocket their windfall profits and buy themselves an extra car or two and start the overcrowding process all over again.

As author Tom Robbins told USA Today, "The rat race has followed them here."

So we need a tough, even punitive, tax on invading Californians. Once they arrive here, a windfall excess-profits tax should be assessed on them—the difference between what they sell in California and what they buy here.

Now a Californian is not hard to spot. Usually he is arrogant, even about the sun-kissed place he has ruined. He sniffs at our rain. He decries our "provincial ways." But we can deal with such a California boor. Let him try to dodge our immigrant head tax. He will try, to be sure, but modern technology can bring him to heel.

The other day, you may have noticed, a federal judge dealt with a multimillionaire Saudi Arabian named Adnan Khashoggi. This Saudi counterpart of many Californians is free on bail—charged with fraud in his business dealings with former Philippine President Ferdinand Marcos. The judge ruled that this suspect must not flee the country. The court decreed that he must wear an electronic bracelet around his ankle or wrist. In this way, authorities can monitor his whereabouts at all times.

So it must be with Californians. Each immigrant from California should be made to wear such a bracelet. This way we can follow his migratory habits, the way biologists can monitor the travels of anadromous fish. Such electronic surveillance can guarantee a Californian's good behavior. We can monitor his mating habits, his banking proclivities, his general behavior, until he becomes an acceptable (i.e., humble) citizen. For a given probationary period, our California immigrant will be forbidden to step onto a golf course. To test his mettle, he will not be allowed to buy an umbrella or a raincoat. In certain areas of downtown Seattle he will be permitted to park his car only on alternate Wednesdays or Thursdays, whichever comes first.

Those are a few conditions we can put down. If the immigrant wants to escape the hellishness of California congestion, so be it. But let him not profit at the gates of what he thinks is paradise.

Californians Are Pussycats

Seattle Times, August 6, 1989

HAVING RECENTLY TICKED OFF EVERY California-to-Seattle immigrant who can read (a surprising number can), this department wishes to go on record as being neutral on cats. Especially if they are neutered.

It is wellknown in the column racket that if you want to get lots of mail, you denounce cats. This is supposed to impress your employers. I didn't expect that insulting California immigrants would have the same effect. But it did. Anti-Watkins diatribes are being collected, filed alphabetically and separated according to scatological content. They will then be shipped to the Kennedy Library.

Meanwhile, I will take an evenhanded attitude toward cats.

As unfortunate readers of this space know, I like to write about animals. Within the past year, I have written about llamas, gorillas, horses (the kind that race), harp seals, extinct mammals, and two kinds of elephants—both endangered. My pure-hearted literary efforts on behalf of animals have yielded a combined mail count of zilch.

I have also written about my dog, Tiger; some say with excessive frequency. As long as I give Tiger a good press, there are no complaints. But utter one word of even affectionate criticism, and owners of small dogs are heard from.

Small dogs are about on a par with cats when it comes to attracting mail. I remember vividly that Mike Royko, a columnist whose stuff appears in The Times, once wrote an essay denouncing small dogs. He said they were useless, too cute, messy and meddlesome. He said they were good for only a few things. One example, he said, was to attach the small dog to a broom handle and use it to dust under the bed.

Intentionally or not, Royko attracted a ton of hate mail.

As for cats, some people think they have eight lives too many. Others would put the number at nine. I do not share this extreme view. But a dilemma occurs, as I try to be neutral about cats, and the dilemma plainly is this: Every time I think of a cat, it reminds me of a migratory Californian. The two animals have much in common. For example, cats, like Californians, have a way of getting underfoot, of taking over, like demanding guests at a party to which they were not invited. Let any cat show up at your doorstep, and he, she or it expects you to make room for it, no matter how much trouble this may cause. A cat, like a migratory Californian, can be terribly self-centered. It never occurs to the cat or the Californian that people can get along perfectly well without them.

Comparisons are easy. Californians deride our rain, scoff at our clouds, make large, impolite noise about our general weather. A Californian, like a cat, doesn't want to get his feet wet. This is not to say that all Californians are like cats. Some Californians are like the duckbill platypus, inoffensive, slow-moving creatures, acutely aware that they have much to be humble about. But many Californians tend to be narcissistic; they never tire of telling you that they live in Hippville, in Lotus Land, and that anyone who doesn't live in San Francisco or Los Angeles is merely camping out.

Of course, all that is changing, which is our problem. The Californians have overfilled their litter boxes, and now, like migrating cats on a doorstep, they come here expecting to be cuddled and loved. In fairness, it must be said that many of us Northwesterners have our phobias, too. Where Californians are concerned, we have a thing called ailurophobia, which is a fear and suspicion of cats. The effect is the same.

A prominent 18th century naturalist, Count de Buffon, may have anticipated our present migratory infusion of unwanted Californians. The count wrote that a cat "appears to have feelings only for himself, loves only conditionally and only enters into relationships (with people) in order to abuse them."

That is all I have to say on the subject today. I hope I have not offended any cat-lovers.

"Seattle Dryrotta"

Seattle Times, August 13, 1989

QUITE A FEW LETTERS—bales of them, in fact—have arrived in this stately think tank at Fairview and John. They were written by residents, former and present, of a very large state, the name of which will come to me if I dwell on it long enough.

Perhaps you can think of the state's name: It is just south of Oregon, has 28 million people in it, lots of smog and almost no sense of humor.

Letters came in describing your inoffensive correspondent as being "full of hate," "bigoted," "racist," "discriminatory," "cantankerous" and "negative." One author compared my pristine Lesser Seattle prose to "rhetoric used by witch hunters, lynch mobs and anarchists." Another said he could scarcely wait until I croak, "and then the rest of us can have a good time dancing on your grave."

Having people dance on my grave is not entirely displeasing—especially if some of the dancers are nubile, well-tanned surfing bunnies. My only fear is that those bacchanals might become a big tourist attraction—thus defeating the purpose of Lesser Seattle.

It appears that those Californians—ah, the name came to me—did a stretching exercise in a reach for paranoia. They somehow equated Lesser Seattle's long-established, tongue-in-check campaign to keep Seattle moderate, sane and uncrowded . . . they equated that with racism.

That's racist? Frankly, I didn't now that Californians are a race. Can it be?

For the record, my tolerant instincts toward Californians have cost me real money. Only the other day I turned down a $75,000 advance from a large Eastern publishing house. They wanted me to bring out a new book of old Polish jokes, changing all the Poles into Californians.

Californians need to have humor labeled for them. Once some-body, perhaps a mischievous Seattleite, tells a Californian he has just been insulted, there is the very dickens to pay. The mail, as I say, was incendiary. It came in such outraged volume that two U.S. mail carriers were treated for double hernias. Three Times editors, manning the phones, are being treated for acute ear overload.

"You'd better leave town, Watkins," one of them said. "Hide out somewhere." Good advice, but where? For a brief moment, I considered moving in with Salman Rushdie, sought by Muslim death squads, under a fugitive rent-sharing agreement.

Quite a few letters complained to The Times about using my picture in the column. They called me fat, ugly and cruel-looking; they said it was bad enough to publish my satiric drivel, but the picture is too much for any subscriber to bear. Let me explain: The picture which The Times runs is not a likeness of me at all. It is a fake picture. You see, when we run my real picture, too many readers think that Robert Redford is writing the column.

Plainly, transplanted Californians have a need to be loved, appreciated, understood and even cuddled. So now we have good news for you. Lesser Seattle Inc.'s board of governors, having conferred with Amnesty International, has decided to let you in—provided you don't urge any other Californians to come here. We have too many of you now.

The vote on whether to grant you amnesty (no punitive head tax, no electronic tracking devices, no further discrimination) was taken by the full membership of Lesser Seattle. We voted 284,408 for, 284,407 against, letting you become citizens and property owners in the Great Northwest. This exception applies only to ordinary migrants, not to California developers. Escapees from that miserable, overcrowded state are allowed in under strict conditions. Remember, no urging other Californians to come north. No smart cracks about our rain. In addition we expect you to commit the following chant to memory. It was written by a lady named Susan Moss, a calligrapher, poetess and essayist. Moss is anti–big growth. Her chant is called "Seattle Dryrotta."

Here are your initiation instructions: Each morning, bow down and face south, where you came from, for your Mecca is the land of smog and sun. Then recite "Seattle Dryrotta" until it becomes part of you. Live up to it. Cherish it. Feel fortunate that you are here.

Now all together, California immigrants:

> *Go placidly amid the volcanic ash and remember what peace there may be in car-pooling. As far as possible, be on good terms with your neighbor when the sun shines.*
>
> *Fish only when the Fisheries Department allows and drink only that which is mountain fresh.*

*Do not concern yourself with ferry schedules, for the ferries are as
perennial as the grass, though somewhat more expensive to walk on.*

*You are now a child of the Northwest, no less than the slugs and
the clouds; you have a right to be here. And whether or not it is clear
to you, no doubt it will be raining tomorrow, as it should.*

*Therefore be at peace with the Sasquatch, wherever you happen to
run into him. And wherever your hiking boots take you, be at peace
with your soles.*

With all its gray cloudiness, this is still a beautiful world.

Strive to stay dry.

▼

A Friendly Guide Service

Seattle Times, September 5, 1989

YESTERDAY WAS LABOR DAY. I love to slip in little scoops like that; it keeps
the competition on its toes. Anyway, Labor Day marks the winding down
of the tourist season. Tourists have been among us now for weeks, like
great hordes of Visigoths, plundering the city's parking lots, beaches,
restaurants and information booths. But a few such tourists remain, and
Lesser Seattle Inc. would like to prove once again that it's a corporation
with a heart. Therefore, as is our annual custom, we intend to be friendly
guides to the remaining tourists in our city. Since it's almost time for you
to go home, tourists, you will want to see all the sights you can before
leaving—for Nebraska, California, Illinois, or wherever you came from.

Lesser Seattle's guide service is like no other. It is courteous, helpful,
lint-free, clean-living and dedicated to your pleasure; the Convention
and Tourist Bureau gnashes its teeth in jealousy over the Lesser Seattle
guide service.

Let us begin . . .

You cannot have visited Seattle without a stop at the Space Needle.
The view from atop the Needle is breathtaking, and no doubt you will be
so taken by Seattle's beauty that you will wish to return here and buy
property. That's a problem we have with it.

If you are staying in the downtown area, the Space Needle is just
north of you. The easiest way to get there is to travel south. Go south on
Second Avenue, a one-way street, until you come to Columbia. Turn right
on Columbia, which takes you onto the viaduct.

Keep heading south on the viaduct. Note the beautiful cargo cranes on your right. Keep driving. Continue driving until you come to the first airplane factory you see. Soon you will be on Highway 99, a breathtaking vista of gas stations, junk yards, fast-food emporiums, used-car lots and hot-pillow motels. Enjoy this vista to its fullest. After a while you will come to a place called Tacoma. You will find the natives there to be hospitable, more so than here. Stay in Tacoma as long as you can. Sooner or later you will see the Space Needle. We plan to dismantle it and give it to Tacoma since Tacoma needs tourists more than we do.

Another dazzling Northwest attraction is Bellevue. Drive east until you see eight million cars backed up in a total stall. You have now reached the Evergreen Point Bridge. I advise visitors to Bellevue to pack a picnic lunch. It will take you several hours to get across, especially if you head for Bellevue at 5 p.m. To revive an old phrase, Seattle is a place that has grown too big for its bridges. When you get to Bellevue, apply for citizenship.

Yet another exciting Seattle attraction is the grain terminal, slightly north of our central waterfront. Its spires, stairs, huge silos and crossbars have an unreal beauty about them. Very unreal. Getting there is easy. Take the Mercer Street on-ramp to I-5, heading north. In about 25 minutes you will come to a dazzling jewel of a vacation spa called Everett. You will be so captivated by Everett's beauty that you will forget all about the grain terminal. Stay there forever if you like.

The West Point sewage treatment plant is a "must see" for any tourist. It is an architectural triumph. Beauty flows out of function, and West Point functions well. To get there, you take a ferry to Bremerton. Drive south from Bremerton and keep going until you get tired. Write if you find work.

And so ends another of our Lesser Seattle travelogues. Let us close off your visit with a heartfelt Lesser Seattle slogan, meant to express our good wishes for a safe and speedy journey to wherever you came from.

Have a nice day—somewhere else.

I n the fall of 1989, following a summer of uproar by immigrant Californians, The Times sent me south, as somebody said, "to consort with the enemy." The journey was made with Tiger, my poodle, in our 1978 motorhome.

We met many wonderful Californians, but by now we had a publicity circus on our hands. Day after day, it seemed, I would be sought out for interviews—mostly by California newsies in print, radio and TV. Some of them came with preconceived notions that Lesser Seattle was a serious hate movement. It was a busy few weeks, and for a time I became an instant national celebrity. Even the London Times and the British Broadcasting Company tracked me down.

Missing the Point

Seattle Times, October 8, 1989

LOS ANGELES — "Tell our listeners about Lesser Seattle," the voice chirps."Is it true that Lesser Seattle wants to drive all Californians out of the Northwest? Is Lesser Seattle a profit-making venture? What are the dues? How does one join? Why are you in Los Angeles?"

These are the voices of pack journalism.

Everywhere Tiger and I travel here in California, the media people hunt us down. Tiger is my flea-plagued poodle. We have been interviewed by at least eight radio stations. We have TV programs in the works, and ABC's "20/20" has us down for a sound bite.

The Chicago Tribune, the L.A. Times, the San Diego News (or Union, I forget) have run stories on disillusioned Californians moving to the Northwest. Time magazine interviewed us. So did Newsweek. The Wall Street Journal wants quotes. Both wire services have called. So help me Hannah, we got a call the other day from New York—a publication called Physician's Lifestyle. The lady who did the interview said, "I'm thinking of moving to Seattle myself. Would I be welcome?"

The reason we are getting all this national press is because, early last summer, I enraged a bunch of California migrants to the Northwest by suggesting they go home. These sun-kissed transplants went ape, having somebody write letters for them demanding my head on a platter. Then other media types picked up the "California migrants" story. Most of them had a preconceived notion of what the story is.

Suddenly I was being pursued by pack journalists. Pack journalism is when everybody wants the same story with the same angle at the same time. All of them ask the same questions, over and over, expecting solemn, revealing, statistics-laden answers.

Here in the Lotus Land of Southern California, I have suddenly developed a kinship with John Ehrlichman, of Watergate infamy, and

Bobo, the late, impotent gorilla of Seattle's Woodland Park Zoo. They were subject to pack journalism. Anybody who acts strangely, or illegally, is caught up in it. Mr. Ehrlichman and Bobo aside, there are hundreds of other species who are victimized by hordes of reporters asking the same repetitive questions.

So they ask, "How many members in Lesser Seattle?"

I say there are 320,621 members. "Is that an up-to-date figure?" "Of course it is, I just made it up." "Really? Is that ethical?" "No, but it's up-to-date."

Most of the nation is after this story, and most of the nation—or the nation's media—is taking it seriously. Finally, you get tired of the same questions, so tired that you make up bizarre answers to break the monotony. To one interviewer (radio, as I recall) I explained that Lesser Seattle was a three-martini concept. I stumbled on it while I was drunk in a bar. That was back in the Pleistocene era of my youth, I explained. "I have since abandoned this loathsome habit," I told him.

Having laid the groundwork, I also told him that Lesser Seattle was really meant to be a Looser Seattle. "Seattle used to be uptight," I explained, "We wanted to loosen it up. This was back in the days when the town was so drab our only call girl had a pull-down bed."

I told another interviewer: "Back in the 1950s, Seattle was so uptight they closed the bars at 8:30 p.m. That was so Boeing workers wouldn't get too hung over to build airplanes."

To yet another interviewer I explained: "Actually, Looser Seattle was invented by three old ladies in a loft out in Ballard. They wanted some action." "Is Ballard a state of mind?" he asked. I said, "No, it is a neighborhood. Bellevue is a state of mind. Depressing, but a state of mind. Looser Seattle wanted to create a gambling hell in Ballard."

I don't know if I qualify as a satirist, but people just go on missing the point. Three distinct dangers await the satirist:

The first danger is that he will be understood.

The second is that he will not be understood.

The third—worst of all—is that he'll be taken literally.

The life of a satirist is hard.

Meanwhile, I have three more Lesser Seattle interviews scheduled this week. I think I will say that we enjoy terrorizing property-rich Californians—we dress up in Sasquatch suits and perform fertility dances on their newly acquired lush green lawns.

▼
━━━━━━━━━━━━━━━━━━━━━━━━━━━━

Berating the Ratings

Seattle Times, October 26, 1989

WELL, AS PRESIDENT OF LESSER SEATTLE, I can tell my constituents that I am sitting here in one big major-league snit right now. It all began when USA Today called from someplace in Virginia and wanted to know about the "Places Rated Almanac," put out by some publishing house that seems to specialize in horror stories.

"The Places—what?" I said.

"The Places Rated Almanac," the reporter said. "They just rated Seattle No. 1 among American cities."

I said, "Oh, s—!"

"We can't use that," USA Today said. "Couldn't you—uh, sort of clean it up a bit?"

So I said, "Oh, God, not again!"

"That's better," he said. "As the Northwest's leading sourpuss on the subject of growth and tourism, we wanted to get you on the record."

That was Tuesday afternoon. Yesterday morning I had a message on the answering machine to call CBS News in New York. Since I am deafer than a mouse caught in a spin dryer, I slept through the call—which came at 6 a.m.

Then Channel 11 called for a Lesser Seattle reaction to this latest atrocity against our city. I started to use a series of words beginning with "f" and "s" and "a," but I realized I was talking to a nice young lady named Diane Robinson. As it happens, Diane is the niece of Earl Robinson, the famous songwriter and balladeer. So when Diane arrived, I spouted off at great length about nitwit editors [Editor's note: Watkins often uses redundancies], demented publishers and assorted mouth-breathing circulation jerks who do these city rankings. Then I spluttered some stuff about our Convention and Tourist Bureau. By now, these growth-boosting yahoos were dry-washing their hands over another free windfall of publicity. "Seattle's No. 1!" they were chanting.

Then United Press International called. The guy was wonderful. He let me use a whole week's worth of four-letter words, none of which will make the wires, but at least they cleansed my soul.

Then it was KIRO. This team was led by Monica Hart, a newscaster on TV. Because Monica is an absolute knockout, I calmed down and dusted off a few long-neglected good manners I acquired in Miss Million's third-grade class at Lafayette Grade School. I babbled on to Monica and after she left, a radio station called. I said the editors of Places Rated Almanac would themselves rank below used-car salesmen and junk-bond dealers in a list of buck-hustling scams.

Then Janet Myers from KING 5 showed up. She said the world was breathlessly awaiting my curmudgeonly reaction to Seattle's being ranked No. 1.

I won't test your boredom tolerance much more by telling you what I said in each interview. Capsulized, they added up to this:

"The whole thing is phony. They rank cities and get a bundle of free publicity from local media. They cash in on it. They don't give a hoot what city ranks No. 1, or No. 296.

"Furthermore, they wouldn't know a decent city if they saw one. Their ratings are superficial, irrelevant, nonsensical. They rank Yuba City, Calif., at the bottom, but Yuba City is a wonderful place. I just came from there.

"Seattle has become a metropolitan Marilyn Monroe. The media can't get enough of us. We are becoming, like poor Marilyn, a sex symbol among cities. Automatically, we're No. 1 in the glamour department.

"If this keeps up, in 20 years our traffic jams, smog, crime and overblown egos will be the death of us. If I were dictator of this town, I would sentence all members of tourist bureaus, chambers of commerce and assorted booster groups to 1,000 hours each of community service.

"They would be forced to explore Pioneer Square and upper First Avenue and find out what real poverty is. I would force them to know every homeless person by name.

"I would make them take courses in architecture and planning so that we never again would have a grain terminal, a Columbia Center, or a dozen other towering, sterile edifices built by blockhead developers. I would put them to work moving traffic on the Evergreen Point Bridge."

At the end of the day I felt much better. Blowing your stack in public can be fun.

Man-in-the-Street Speaks

Seattle Times, February 4, 1990

HAVE YOU EVER BEEN A MAN-IN-THE-STREET? In this age of multiple TV news shows, a man-in-the-street is not hard to be. Stand on any corner, wait long enough, and along will come a TV crew, which will spot you. They will interview you about something.

They also favor 6-year-old children. Let the waterfront viaduct collapse, say, and camera crews go looking for reactions from ordinary citizens. They will ask an adult, "Tell me, sir, what was your first—your initial—reaction when you saw all that cement crumbling?" Or to the 6-year-old, "You saw what happened—all that cement, smashed cars, people getting killed. What did you think when you saw that?" The 6-year-old usually giggles and says something like "Hey, that was neat!" The adult is probably overwhelmed by all this attention. Pleased and over-whelmed.

I grant you, your first television interview is pretty heady stuff. You become a neighborhood celebrity. You call up all your friends and relatives and say, "Hey, catch Channel 5's evening news. I'm on televi-sion!"

As I say, with the proliferation of television and radio field interviews, you are a dead immortal cinch to become a man-in-the-street interview. Don't let it go to your head. You see, I have been a sort of man-in-the-street specimen since early last summer. To date I have been interviewed by no fewer than 18 radio stations, here and in California, even including the BBC. I have been on four California television shows. My right hand to God, Channel 4 in San Francisco sent a crew up for another interview only last Wednesday.

To date, I have been on "Good Morning America" and Peter Jennings' "World News Tonight" on ABC. I have been interviewed by CBS, NBC and CNN. Also stations in Vancouver, Los Angeles, San Francisco, Sacra-mento, plus four local channels. Another is due on Dan Rather's "CBS Evening News."

Heady stuff . . . for a while.

But it's all about the same things: What is Lesser Seattle? (A frame of mind, a concept.) Do you really hate California immigrants? (No.) Are you winning the battle of Lesser Seattle? (No.) Do you hate developers? (Yes.)

When the BBC came, I figured England was far enough away so that I could say anything. I told the BBC, "Tell all those Brits back home to stay there. We had to fight two wars to get rid of you people. Tell Margaret Thatcher if she'll keep her Brits out of Seattle, we'll get her face carved on Mount Rushmore."

Heady stuff, indeed. But after the first 10 or 12 interviews you become bored listening to yourself. Once I was on Larry King's show and Larry asked me about Lesser Seattle. I prattled on and soon a glaze came to Mr. King's eyes. You could almost hear him saying to himself, "Oh, God, how did I get this sap on my show?"

Pretty soon you get punch-drunk from so many interviews, like an old fighter who begins shadow boxing every time he hears a bell. I am Pavlov's dog in the presence of a microphone. Conditioned response— every time I see some unlucky citizen with a tape record, I walk up and start babbling.

A lot of the recent interviewers want to know about the Berlin Wall. Was Lesser Seattle really serious about buying the Berlin Wall and putting it around Seattle to keep the outlanders at bay? "Of course," I say. (After so many interviews, you will say anything, the more outrageous the better.) "Certainly we're serious about buying the Berlin Wall. It comes complete with barbed wire and machine gun parapets. We can hire some out-of-work East German border guards to keep California developers away."

A friend of mine began to keep a scrapbook of print interviews. These include stories in the Los Angeles Times, the San Francisco Chronicle, Editor and Publisher magazine, the Chicago Tribune, San Jose Mercury News, Wall Street Journal, Time magazine, The New York Times, USA Today, Orange Coast Daily Pilot in California, The London Times, The London Telegraph, The Weekend Australian, The Suddeutsche Zeitung and a magazine called Physician's Lifestyle.

Those are a few. This scrapbook of stuff about Lesser Seattle has now grown thicker than a pro-growth booster's head. The San Francisco Chronicle article referred to me as "an old poop." A radio interviewer from California called for my reaction. "How do you like being called an old poop?"

"Not at all," I said. "I have never cared much for euphemisms. I prefer to be called the real thing."

The Price of Progress

Seattle Times, January 13, 1991

BACK ABOUT THE TURN OF THE NEW YEAR, USA Today listed its "ins" and "outs," nebulous things that people are allegedly turned on or off by. Seattle was among the "outs." After more than a decade of puff pieces about us, suddenly people were getting tired of us.

Known in these parts as a no-growth curmudgeon, I was interviewed by a local TV station to get my reaction to the glad news. This happens quite often, probably, in the vain hope that I might say something witty for a sound bite. What I said, in effect, was neither witty nor profound, much less worth listening to. I said Seattle had received entirely too much national magazine publicity over the past 15 to 17 years.

The danger in this, I prattled, is that as a city we get fatheaded. We tend to believe all the saccharine sheep dip they print about us. These press notices, usually hooked up by editors with a "best in the nation" mentality for circulation building survey-type stories, have a bad effect. Here in Seattle, reading all this puffery, we begin to think in effect, "Hey, we're OK—don't fix what ain't broke." So we ignore and fail to do anything about genuine problems that are coming upon us.

There is hope on the horizon.

Only last week the New York Times Magazine, something of an editorial trendsetter, ran a long piece entitled "Seattle—Too Much of a Good Thing?" For starters, it described us in glowing terms. It spoke of affluent crowds "among the gleaming skyscrapers" and "the fashionable indoor malls" of downtown, filled by "young, sharply dressed up upwardly mobile Seattleites."

The author, Jon Bowermaster, continued: "The whole scene is an advertisement for the good life. I feel like I've stumbled onto the set of a credit-card commercial." So far, it sounded like just another Seattle puff-piece. However, it was far from empty praise. Bowermaster's mission was journalism, not puffery. He spoke at length about our warts and wattles. He wrote about Rainier Valley's "street hustlers, crack dealers, whores and gang boys, eager to begin their day while the commuters are heading home. Up and down Pine and Pike streets, from Capitol Hill to the Alaskan Way Viaduct, clusters of young toughs—of a variety of ethnic groups—gather on street corners."

He talked about embattled Seattle cops "ever since Seattle became a favorite stopping-off point for gang members—Crips and Bloods—from Southern California . . . Teen-age prostitution was already a problem downtown, and soon crack houses proliferated." He spoke of the dangers "on the corners near the Pike Place Market. Patrols were beefed up, more of Seattle's first-in-the-nation mountain-bike cops were deployed."

There is more of everything, he wrote: "Traffic congestion around Seattle is so bad that on many summer days a haze clouds Mount Rainier from view. Every day the city is becoming more and more like the Southern California megalopolis it so detests."

Bowermaster quoted David Bricklin, an environmental lawyer in Seattle: "We have virtually no mass transit—no rail, no segregated busways. We are just now trying to develop a plan for mass transit from Seattle out into the suburbs, but that's a decade away, at best."

You've read all this before in national magazines, haven't you? It all sounds familiar. Just change a few streets and place names and you are reading about Cleveland, Detroit, Milwaukee or any one of a dozen cities in the Rust Belt.

So after 15 years of "most livable city" hoopla, we're getting ours. Things are become worse and, if The New York Times is indeed a trendsetter, you'll be reading more such stories about this jewel-like Emerald City. It's about time.

Back in 1982, a book was published about Seattle. It contained a plea to preserve and protect the best that is Seattle—its beauty, its charm, the safety of its citizens. It contained this passage:

"A city is a place where streets, parks, buildings, vistas and boulevards make up the controllable environment in which we live. We can make of it what we wish.

"We must ever be wary, alert to trade off carefully, aware of the cost to be paid for certain forms of progress we are offered. Every monstrous scheme or structure exacts its price, the penalty of visual blight and loss of human scale.

"What we have must be fiercely protected, firmly enhanced, constantly improved . . . Any prediction about Seattle—what are the chances?—will depend on how willing we are to shoulder the burden, not only in money, but in time, concern and often painful involvement.

"These are the costs you and I should be willing to assume."

That was written at the height of our "most livable city" euphoria.

The author's name will come to me if I dwell on it long enough.

Part 5
Gullible's Travels

Back in the good old days—gad, it seems like forever ago— we were all pleasantly corrupt in the newspaper business. It was the era of freebies— free drinks, free lunches and dinners; most important of all, it was the era of free trips. It seemed then that airlines almost tracked you down to hand out nice free tickets to places like England, France, New York City, Honolulu and virtually all of what the Japanese military used to call the East Asia Co-Prosperity Sphere. So I took these freebies like everybody else, although usually an editor or a publisher got the choice ones before anything trickled down to me. I got a few freebies, I confess, but much of the time I traveled on my own. Or by the generous sweat of a few newspaper bean counters. In those days, too, it was always wise to stay on good terms with the travel editor, who got first crack at tour trips.

"Inaugural Flight" freebies were best. One I got from SwissAir got me to Denmark, France, Switzerland and Italy, with a few side trips thrown in.

All I needed to do in order to pass the freebie test was to take an "inaugural flight" from Geneva to Amsterdam and return, without seeing anything except the airport. One luxurious freeload came through the Japanese Foreign Office, a two-week all-expenses tour of Tokyo, Kyoto, Osaka and Hiroshima. This one went through a publisher and two editors before I turned up last in line. Another good one came from Scandinavian Airlines, which not only included the required inaugural flight but, once that was accomplished, let you go almost anyplace in the world that SAS flew. When I was offered this one I said, "No, I need two tickets, because I have this friend who wants to go." Sure enough, we got two tickets. The next freebie step was to call Bill Dugovich, who handled public relations for what was known in those days as Western International Hotels. So my friend and I traveled almost the whole world with nice luxurious free quarters so we could rest up from the rigors of flying first class.

But mostly it was catch as catch can. And mostly, The P-I caught the checks. All freebies ended when I went back to The Seattle Times, which long before had become a freeloader's wasteland; no more junketeering, The Times paid or you didn't go. Looking back on it, I never felt much corrupted by free airline tickets and I don't think anyone else did, either. Newspapermen, especially columnists, are noted for their monumental ingratitude. We wrote what we pleased.

All this wasn't enough, was it? No, I had to buy first a truck camper, later a big trailer and still later a motorhome. Tiger, my dog, loved them all and we met some wonderful people in campgrounds. And always there was that column hole to fill, so you wrote when and where you could, and when things got desperate, I would say, "We need a column today. Do something cute, Tiger."

Bussing the Blarney Stone

Seattle Post-Intelligencer, April 11, 1977

SOMEWHERE IN IRELAND — It all began last December when the phone rang and the voice of Margaret Seidelhuber came on the line. "This is Balloon Travel Service, right across the street in the Grosvenor House," she said. "We are forming a tour to Ireland in March. Dr. Giovanni Costigan was scheduled to lead it, but we find he is unable to go. We are looking for somebody who is reasonably well known who can take his place. Do you have any suggestions?" "I accept," I said.

There was a long, skeptical pause, before I outlined my credentials as a tour leader. "I know nothing about Ireland," I explained, "but I don't get airsick and never steal hotel towels."

That's the way it began. But later, by a fantastic stroke of luck, it turned out that Dr. Costigan, the retired UW professor and famed authority on Ireland, actually could go. As soon as this news leaked out in The P-I's travel section, the stampede was on. The tour group finally totaled 53, about double the size of the average tour group. The list included Dr. Costigan and his wife, Amne; and John Murphy, of Balloon Travel, with the skill and proper name to handle details (he seemed to have relatives in every town). Margaret Seidelhuber herself went along, and, of course, your correspondent, who didn't steal a single towel.

The tour was a winner, start to finish, largely because of John Murphy's efficiency and Dr. Costigan's encyclopedic knowledge of Ireland. Giovanni has, of course, lectured extensively on the country for years; his book *The History of Modern Ireland* is readable and scholarly. He gave three lectures before we ever left Seattle and, seemingly, there is scarcely an hour of Irish history he doesn't know. Each day of sightseeing was preceded by an invaluable and eloquent Costigan lecture.

The first stop was Cork, and one small incident made you revere the Irish forever. You know about customs—cold, a trace of suspicion in the air; bored, unsmiling agents letting weary lines wait as they process luggage. Well, the Irish customs are a bit different. One of our group, Tracy O'Day (she owns the Irish import store Wee Bit O'Ireland, on Occidental), asked an agent where to put her bags. "Put them over there," the agent said, cheerfully, "and I'll give 'em absolution all at once."

The Irish are naturals at tourism. Friendliness, humor, warmth and a willingness to help come naturally to them. And this is no blarney, even if we did kiss the Blarney Stone, right outside Cork. No easy task, by the way. To get at it, you climb endless, dark stairs in ancient, forbidding Blarney Castle. Once up there, you lie on your back, grasp some iron handholds, bend your head far back, upside down, and kiss it.

Now you have done it, and, according to legend, you are forever blessed with the gift of eloquent speech. You become, in effect, a sort of Rotary raconteur, holding audiences rapt with your fluid rhetoric. "You feel like an orator now?" somebody asked when I straightened up. "Only out of breath," I gasped, eloquently.

Parading for St. Patrick

Seattle Post-Intelligencer, April 12, 1977

CORK, IRELAND — We all know him, don't we? He's the Irishman who surfaces, rather brashly, often drunkenly and loudly, each March 17 all over America. Seattle has its share of "stage Irishmen," and some who aren't even Irish at all affect thick "Oirish" brogues and carry on a bit much for St. Patrick's Day. Bars, especially those with Irish names, do a heavy business, much of it in Irish coffee—for which the Irish all over the world have much to answer for. "It's the only drink I know," said a friend one time, "which combines to spoil three perfectly good ingredients."

And of course there are St. Patrick's Day parades, marches and hijinks. Well, I'm here to upstage all my Irish acquaintances. While you, presumably, were having a hell-raising time in Seattle, I marched in a real St. Patrick's Day Parade—in Cork. Most all of us did, the 53 on this smashing Balloon Travel Service tour of Ireland—led by the famed Irish historian Dr. Giovanni Costigan. Greatest parade I've ever seen. Nobody drunk. Nobody loud. Just a wonderful mass celebration, religious in flavor, simple and ceremonial.

St. Patrick himself was real enough. But as Dr. Costigan, in one of his splendid morning lectures, told us before the parade: "Much of St. Patrick is legend and stories and myth." He was born in 389 A.D. That was 21 years before the fall of Rome, and on this day we marched to honor him in Cork, it was the 1,516th year of his death.

According to the "traditional" version, he was born in South Wales; poor and unlettered as a boy, he was kidnapped by pirates and sold into slavery in Ireland. He escaped six years later. At some point he had a vision, or a dream, that he was sent to earth to Christianize the people. He made his way to France, where he studied for 21 years, then returned to Ireland at the age of 43. And he did, indeed, bring Christianity to Ireland. He left only a thin autobiography, written in Latin, and through centuries of tortured Irish history he became, as Giovanni said, the stuff of legend, stories and myths.

And we all know for a fact, don't we, that he drove the snakes out of Ireland? Drove them off the cliffs and into the sea. We also know, as Dr. Costigan pointed out with his own Irish smile as he quoted Sean O'Casey, "that the snakes took 1,500 years to swim across the Atlantic and emerge in the form of Tammany Hall."

So on this lovely morning in a soft rain, 1,516 years after St. Patrick's death, we marched to honor him—wearing real shamrocks on our coats. There were no expensive floats, but there was a donkey cart; a flat-bedded truck with home brew equipment and burning turf; and a vehicle put together by John O'Brien & Sons, clothiers, advertising "complete Confirmation outfits." Those of us, "The Seattle Set," carried our own banner, and we were applauded warmly along the two-mile route. "Mother!" cried a child in the crowd, "I didn't know people from Seattle are so *old!*"

We marched down McCurtan St., turned left at Bridge St., crossed the River Lee, and on past the reviewing stand. The principal industry in

Ireland, one must conclude, is the production of children. Children everywhere. We walked in a sea of freckles and red hair and laughing faces. And everywhere along the route they applauded these strangers from a far corner of the U.S. that most had never heard of.

It was festive, yes, perhaps 50,000 people, from all over County Cork, lining the parade route. Not a drunken Irishman in sight. They had just come from Mass. The pubs, that afternoon, would be closed for two hours in observance of a Holy Day. That night there still was no revelry, but a lovely thing happened. A young girl named Kathy Dennehy came to our hotel with her guitar. She came and sang "Hail, Glorious St. Patrick" for us, the first verse of which goes like this:

Hail glorious St. Patrick,
Dear Saint of our Land.
On us thy poor children
Bestow a sweet smile.

Looking for Mt. Fuji

Seattle Post-Intelligencer, April 15, 1970

TOKYO, AS IN JAPAN — Well, for one thing, it's big. No matter how much you hear about the people being smaller, they still add up to the world's biggest city—unless you believe Mao Tse Tung, the eminent Chinese demographer, who claims 12.5 million for Shanghai. But this is Tokyo, and nobody quite agrees how big it really is. Some say 12 million, some say 11.3 million and others peg it higher than that. (Tokyo: bigger than London, much bigger than New York, and you could put one and a half Los Angeleses in it.) Give or take a million here and you wouldn't notice the difference.

Tokyo, the giant city of Japan, which stretches as far as the eye can see. That, by the way, is a bad cliche and a worse description. As I write this—with a view from the 15th floor of the New Otani Hotel—the eye can see about 600 yards. The more defensive Japanese call it "hazee," but in any language it's smog, thick, eye-smarting smog, mingled with a few low clouds, the kind that made Los Angeles so famous you can scarcely find it.

"One of these days you will see Mt. Fuji," a Japanese friend assured me. "Of course, it will depend on the length of your stay. Perhaps you should come back at the New Year to see Mt. Fuji. That is when the factories close down and the air is clear. Then you will see Mt. Fuji."

Tokyo: The most cosmopolitan of all Asian cities, and one of the most cosmopolitan in all the world. The top hotels, the Palace, the New Otani, the Okura, the Ginza Tokyo and many others, are jammed with English, American, French, German and Spanish visitors—to list only a few. "I've been here two weeks and I still haven't had a Japanese dinner," an American said, half in complaint. The reason is obvious enough. Tokyo has some 33,000 restaurants with 70 different styles of cooking, including an abundance of that fine old American tradition, bacon and eggs for breakfast.

From the time you arrive at Tokyo's Haneda Airport, the first thing that strikes you is the ineffable courtesy and politeness of the Japanese. To one who has been snarled at in French, growled at in Austrian and denounced in New Yorkese, the cheerful helpfulness of Tokyoites comes as the first of many pleasant culture shocks. And the upraised Tokyo palm is almost nowhere in existence. No tipping is expected from cab drivers, waitresses or anyone else among the people who serve you—one exception being a porter, who expects a few yen for wrestling your bags.

What am I doing here? A good question, if you bother to ask it at all, and deserving of a short explanation. Your correspondent is in Japan as a guest of the Japanese Foreign Office. Assignment: Write what you learn about Japan, preferably in English. It all began a few weeks ago when the distinguished Consul General of Japan, Mr. Shigemi Hayashida, of Seattle, extended the invitation to everybody's favorite morning newspaper. The next thing I knew, I was checking passport and visa, getting myself punched with needles, then put aboard a JAL flight out of Vancouver, happy as any other tourist in a happi-coat.

Before that, there was the little matter of an "itinerary." "Arrangements," Mr. Hayashida explained, "have to be made far in advance in Japan at this time of year. Very crowded." Since Japan is a country of 102 million people and I know none of them, the itinerary had to be confined to "areas of interest." I listed a few of these, and out of this humble list came the most remarkable document since the prospectus that founded the United Nations. Spelled out in dazzling detail were rounds of appointments, rail, plane and taxi schedules, hotel reservations, departure times, arrival times, tours, trips and still more appointments.

The fellow who makes all this fall miraculously into place is a young man named Akihiro Aoki, a rising careerist in the Foreign Office. Mr. Aoki is a strong, intelligent, square-set individual, whose English is excellent, but whose Japanese must be superb. A few words from Mr. Aoki and doors open, redcaps appear, food is produced and insurmountable linguistic blockades tumble swiftly. A fine gentleman, Mr. Aoki; with friends like this, you make no enemies. When Mr. Aoki is busy elsewhere, Mr. Kato arrives, equally proficient, polite and patient.

Mr. Aoki can produce miracles, but one thing he can't produce is Mt. Fuji. It's out there someplace, enveloped in the "hazee." "It's a little like your Mt. Rainier," an American in the lobby was saying. "Been to Seattle three times and I still haven't seen it."

The Fading Geisha

Seattle Post-Intelligencer, April 20, 1970

TOKYO — "And so, even when you know all the facts, the geisha remains exotic, mysterious, tantalizing, desirable. She is woman—only more so." The foregoing was written by Walt Sheldon, whose excellent guidebook *Enjoy Japan* was picked up in the arcade of the Palace Hotel, across from the Imperial Palace near the center of Tokyo. To say that the geisha is woman, only more so, is absolutely true. What is also true is that as a particular kind of woman, she is less so now. For the traditional geisha—trained for years in a centuries-old tradition—is dying out.

For casual travelers to Japan, the geisha is a financial decision. The costs of an evening of entertainment with two or three geisha can have an unsettling effect on your balance of payments. Only the Japanese—the affluent Japanese, with an open-end expense account—can afford her. Moreover, the true geisha doesn't like to entertain Westerners—too many misunderstandings. And unless you have a well-heeled Japanese friend willing to spend a small fortune on you, the chances are almost nil that you'll ever see a real geisha party.

The geisha, like other traditional art forms, is dying out as Japan's industrial pace accelerates. "As the new generations come up, fewer young men are interested in geisha-type entertainment," my friend John Randolph was saying. Randolph, a former AP bureau chief and longtime foreign correspondent here, has lived in Japan since the early 1950s. "The young Japanese—well, he'd rather get some slick chick and play golf, or something. Of course, some of the geisha have kept up—they're good at golf, too—they can put on a pair of slacks and go out and keep up with anybody.

"But generally speaking, the classical side of geisha is deteriorating. It takes years to train a geisha—in the arts of music, repartee, serving, entertaining. Recruiting is difficult, because now they have laws that kids must go to school. Attractive young girls are trained up from childhood, or their early teens, and there are very few parents who will go along with that now. I doubt if in all Japan there are more than 500 true classical geisha, certainly no more than a thousand."

The other night we drove through the Tsukiji district, of Tokyo, a series of little places cowering among the tall, modern concrete buildings. There is no such thing as a geisha "house," of course. There are places, not unlike sororities, where geisha live, but they do their entertaining in restaurants. Ten years ago, in the Tsukiji district, the geisha places dominated; now they're being shoved aside as land values skyrocket. Another famous geisha area, the Akasaka district, is now largely taken over by nightclubs, cabarets and restaurants.

As part of the tradition, geisha still ride to and from their parties in rickshaws. As we passed a couple in one of the dark narrow streets, Randolph said, "There's been a lot of nonsense written and believed about the classical geisha. In the first place, they're basically entertainers, and they do live in a somewhat Bohemian world. Some of them wind up as mistresses to wealthy Japanese. But the type of entertainment they provide is pure Japanese and very classical—they sing, serve, dance, engage in repartee. A true geisha party is something like a church supper with racy jokes.

"But it's not an orgy, or anything like that. At 10 or 10:30, everybody goes home separately. No touch, no hanky-panky. The men probably go off to a cabaret, and where the girls go, that's their business."

Of course, there are levels of geisha. There's the "country geisha," which is a euphemism for a pick-up in a hot springs town. Some of these girls, if they have any talent, move into Tsukiji or Akasaka. Another name might be "pillow geisha," rather untalented girls who pretend to be geisha. "With some honorable exceptions," said Randolph, "many are high-class prostitutes—but not all. We must not libel a perfectly respectable working girl."

But for all of this, the ancient, honorable profession of the geisha is dying out. One of the prime centers for geisha training in Kyoto has been taken over largely by night clubs, and the girls with names like "Miss

Peach Blossom" and "Miss Pine Tree" written on wooden slabs in front of the house have located in another, poorer district. Nothing traditional in Japan—not even the geisha—can hold firm against rising real estate values.

"The modern geisha," Randolph concluded, "is very much around. But she's a long, long way from the classic geisha. In 10 to 15 years, I suspect the geisha will be just another ordinary entertainment girl who puts on a kimono. It's almost that now."

Camping with Tiger

Seattle Post-Intelligencer, August 7, 1981

ON THE ROAD — Well, it's time to stop playing Walter Cronkite with Tiger and go into my John Steinbeck number on traveling with a dog. Tiger gets bored with my truck cab broadcasts, but he makes a good show of listening. Smart dog. He knows where the old supper dish comes from. Anyway, this is being written in what you might call an "urban campground" up at Tarr's Resort at Baker Lake. To get to Baker Lake, you turn left just before Concrete and then drive to hellandgone into the woods. About the time you give up and are ready to turn back, you are there. In all, we've logged maybe 750 miles poking around in Western Washington, leaving a trail of garbage, literary and other, in our wake. We are once again surrounded by RVs, ranging from cruising to dreadnought class, plus trailers, tents and a few campers like ONB*. Strangely, I've lost my po'-folks complex among all these rolling battleships. I suppose if you enter Broadmoor enough times, you begin to feel at home.

Tarr's Resort is democratic, make no mistake. It is crammed with kids and dogs and plenty of people who have been coming here for years. Tiger has to be on a leash. He doesn't like it much, but when you play in somebody else's park, you play by their ground rules. This is being written in the camper, which makes a great office, by the way, once you get the electricity hooked up. I forgot to mention Elmer Fudd. He is our mascot. Elmer Fudd is a doll, a character out of Disney, who looks a little like W. C. Fields. Even Tiger, who will chew anything with stuffing in it, doesn't

---

* *Old National Bank—ONB—owned the Watson camper, until the loan was paid.*

grab Elmer Fudd and shake him. He seems to know that Elmer is our good luck talisman.

Earlier this evening I took Tiger for a walk down to the lake. Mt. Shuksan, all 9,127 feet of it, rises up quite white and beautiful, beyond the opposite shore. I shared a bench with two Canadian gentlemen. You can spot Canadians by the way they say "aboot" instead of "about." One wore a red-and-white-checked shirt, the other was stripped to his underwear top and around his neck was a bright strap holding a 35-mm camera. We got along famously. We cussed out the governments of both our countries; this is fun when you do it on an international scale.

"Met a writer like you once," the checked shirt said. "Ran across him just out of Death Valley. He had two burros and a sulky, and he was walking—walking, mind you—from Arizona to Vancouver. Said he was going to write a book about it." "Guess there's a book in that all right," I said. "You do meet all kinds," said the Canadian. "No offense intended, of course."

Tiger and I were walking back toward ONB and GMC, our cozy little gas guzzlers, when we came upon a shed with a carcass hanging down from a cross beam. It was an open-sided shed, and four guys were watching while another of them washed down the skinned carcass with a hose. I couldn't tell what the carcass was, but its head was cut off and one of the men pointed to show the others where the bullet went into the neck. They were good ol' boys. You could tell by the way they talked. Finally I asked, "What is that thing?" "That? Oh, that's ol' George's wife," one of them chortled loudly. This got a big laugh all around, except from me. After they got through cackling, good ol' boy style, the man said, "It's a bear. George shot it." Nearby was George's truck with two hungry-looking bear dogs and a gun rack in the cab that carried three rifles. Later I asked a woman who worked in the camp, "Is bear shooting legal?" "Legal on Saturdays," she said.

The whole episode made me despondent. I couldn't figure out what the hell harm a bear would do anybody way up here. Tiger must have dug my mood, because he didn't even beg to have his tinkle ball thrown for him. That's quite something when you consider Tiger's mania for chasing balls. Or maybe he was despondent over the day's developments for a different reason. You see, Tiger fell in love with a beautiful female cocker spaniel. He has a good eye. She was a gorgeous buff color, and she was off her leash. I let Tiger off his leash and right away, of course, he began behaving like King Farouk.

The cocker spaniel thought he was insane. But she tolerated him, the way some women tolerate an overly amorous first date, hoping that after his ardor cools, she can discover some good in him. This was not the case with Tiger. In the heat of passion, he breaks his thermostat, and when the cocker's lady owner came along, Tiger was still trying to score. In my own cowardly way I tried to disown Tiger, turning my back on this awful scene, pretending I didn't know him. The lady wasn't fooled. "This your dog?" she said. "Yes," I said lamely, "I guess it's the French in him."

She disentangled the two dogs and carried hers off, saying, "Being French is no excuse." I thought about that for a while, too. I'll bet the guy with those two burros didn't have that problem.

Journey's End

Seattle Post-Intelligencer, August 16, 1981

DEAR P-I EXECUTIVE COMMITTEE: I hope this interoffice memo reaches you gentlemen before you set the business agenda at your next prayer breakfast. I realize you are all terribly busy making Important Decisions, but I hope you have found a few spare minutes to read the paper. If you did, you will know I have been out "on the road," as we say in camperdom. My 1971 GMC truck and my 1973 camper and my 1980 dog, Tiger, have been out foraging around the countryside looking for material to write about. In case you missed any of this exciting stuff, we called it "Travels With Tiger." My stuff was very well received, according to people back in the office who are authorized to open my mail. I will quote one excerpt from a particularly glowing letter: "Once you pick up a column by Watson on his 'Travels With Tiger' it's hard to put it down, unless you have a table handy."

But for now, maybe I can rough in a few numbers for you. My GMC truck has its good days and its bad days. On the straight and level, it gets about 10.3 miles per gallon—if it is having a good day. If it is having a bad day, this drops to about 7.9 miles per gallon. There's no telling. On a couple of occasions I almost missed deadlines since I spent so much time at the Self-Serve gas pump. Oil consumption followed a similar pattern, and I have those receipts, too.

So in case some of you on the Executive Committee were too busy to read the paper, I will fill you in on what you might call the highlights of our trip. One highlight was a Maine lobster dinner at the home of Torre

Dybfest, who owns the Farmhouse Inn near LaConner. Torre told a friend, who was visiting Boston, to bring him back "about 5 pounds of live lobsters." The fellow misunderstood and instead brought back 50 pounds of live Maine lobster. This put Torre up to his backside in live lobsters. So he threw a big dinner party to eat all these lobsters. Since he was practically stopping people on the street to find enough guests, I got invited. So 10 or 12 people sat down with lobster and nothing happened. Everybody looked at everybody else. Dead silence.

Nobody there had ever eaten a fresh, whole lobster before. They didn't know whether to smash the shell with a hammer, jump up and down on it or call up the local fish warehouse to send a man out. But, fortunately, one lady present had lived in Boston. So she went patiently around the table showing us how to crack the claws with our teeth and push the lobster meat out of the shell with our thumbs. That was one highlight.

Another highlight occurred in Twisp, Wash. Tiger and I checked into the Winthrop Inn, which is run by Mildred and Butch Hardy. We stayed there a couple of days, then hit the road again, during which the GMC came down sick and needed some kind of appendectomy. It got towed to a garage at Twisp. Lo and behold, a car pulled up and here was Mildred Hardy to say I had inadvertently overpaid her. She said she would save a room for me (this was a busy weekend), and I could have it free. She said she heard about our truck problems, and she offered to take me around on any errands I had to run. She drove 11 miles, Winthrop to Twisp, to see if I was okay. Now, I ask you, revered Executive Committee, when you stay at all those plush Sheratons and Hiltons, did you ever get treatment like that? I like small towns and the people in them.

Also, in case any of you read these pieces, you might think I overwrote about Tiger, my dog. He is undersized and oversexed. Thus, we ran into some embarrassing moments at various campgrounds and way stops. In fact, I have just received a picture, forwarded over here, showing Tiger trying to commit an atrocity on a female dog five times as big as he is. This picture, I am sure, was taken by the Channel Town Press in LaConner. I suspect the editor, Al Pentz, is behind this. Anyway, if you get a discreet note asking The P-I to cough up a little in exchange for the negative, don't pay it. Tiger's reputation as a canine satyr is so well known that it's useless to try to suppress this picture.

To get to the point of this memo for your business agenda, it is hotter than billy-old blazes over here, with temperatures hitting between 102 and 108. The inside of our camper is a sauna. So it's impossible to concentrate when the sweat pours off your face and shorts out the old

Satellite 2001 cliché-mixer. What I ask is this: In order to write this deathless prose, I have to find a "vacancy" sign once in a while at a place which advertises "Air Conditioning." So the motel bill will be a little higher than budgeted. I kid you not, revered Executive Committee. It is so hot over here in the semi-Inland Empire that I saw a dog chasing a rabbit and they were both walking.

So I will be back in Seattle tomorrow. You'll be pleased to know that The P-I sells big over her. You have to get to the store early to find one. They sell right out and then you are stuck with the Spokesman-Review. That is roughing it.

▼

Tora, Tora, Tora

Seattle Post-Intelligencer, October 20, 1975

HONOLULU — The way we planned it, we were sitting over breakfast in the Ilikai Hotel's coffee shop, and it was Sunday, the sun was bright and the room alive with aloha shirts, with a few hangovers in evidence. Nobody was much alert to anything this early Sunday morning, and it was easy to imagine the same conditions over at Schofield Barracks and the quarters near Ford Island, smack in the middle of Pearl Harbor. Much the way it was on Dec. 7, 1941.

"It's your mission," said Art Wildern, Lt. Col., Army Air Force, Ret. "How do you want to fly it?"

Wildern shoved the chart at me. It was a brightly colored, low-altitude aeronautical chart of the Island of Oahu. We were going to "bomb" Pearl Harbor, Wheeler Air Force Base and the Schofield Barracks. On the charts were marked all the routes—all coming in from the north, then spreading around Oahu.

There were seven routes—traced in red, blue, green, orange, blue-green, brown and reddish brown. Four of the routes split off at Haleiwa, a little town a few miles southeast of Kahuku Point, the northernmost tip of the island. The color lines were coded—orange for Mitsubishi A-6 M2 Type 21—the famed Japanese Zeros. The others were dive bombers and high-level torpedo bombers. The routes split once more as the planes neared their targets.

Exactly the way it was—the precise bombing routes of Pearl Harbor—nearly 34 years ago. And it was Sunday.

"What about the radar station?" I asked. Art Wildern checked the chart. "Right here," he said, pointing to the little town of Kahuku, with a little point sticking out. "Okay," I said, "let's take the fighter route through Kole Kole Pass, then cut over to the radar station, then come back and take the bomber route into Ford Island off the east shoreline."

Wildern raised his thumb and little finger in the air. "The airplane's all ready," he said. "I rented us a Cessna 172, and we're set to go."

We cleared Honolulu International Airport and climbed to 3,000 feet, turning north toward Wheeler Air Force Base. That would be the first target. Would we make it? You'd better believe we'd make it, because Lt. Col. Art Wildern, Ret., had flown 106 missions over Europe in World War II. He had received 19 Air Metals and the Distinguished Flying Cross. But more important than all that—at this moment—was the fact that Art Wildern's other qualification is historical.

As a resident of Honolulu, he had made an intensive study of the Japanese raid on Pearl Harbor; he knew exactly how, when, and with what, the Japanese inflicted the greatest defeat on another power in the history of modern warfare. He was "director of air operations" for the filming of *Tora, Tora, Tora,* the semi-documentary film account of the Japanese attack that began World War II for the United States.

Not many fliers in Honolulu would be permitted to do what Art Wildern was doing this day. The air controllers, both civilian and military, knew him well. He handled ground communications, I did the flying. We flew over the mountains on the west side of the island, over an enormous ammunition dump, then made a 180-degree turn. "There it is," he said, pointing. "That's where the Zeros came through—Kole Kole Pass. Stay low, and a little to the left."

We were on an exact heading of 90 degrees, just as the Zeros were 34 years ago. Through the pass, I throttled back, got down lower, over the pineapple fields, and there it was—Wheeler Air Force Base and Schofield Barracks. It was 7:55 a.m., the exact minute, 34 years ago. "Some of the original hangars are still there," said Wildern, pointing. "Just as they were then."

From there we flew on up to Opana Pt. There was nothing macabre about this. It was just that we wanted to say I'd done it, flown the same routes of this most incredible surprise attack in military annals.

We were over the radar station now. On Dec. 7, 1941, two Army privates, operating an experimental radar screen, spotted the Japanese planes some 140 miles out. When they telephoned headquarters they were told to forget it. "We're expecting some B17s from the States," they were told. "That's what you're seeing." The two privates shut down the radar and went to breakfast.

Later we came down the west side of Oahu on one bombing route, then cut over and picked up another, heading 40 degrees. Right off the nose was Ford Island. We were at 800 feet. You could still make a faint outline of the sunken *USS Arizona*, over which was a monument, now visited mostly by solemn-faced Japanese tourists snapping pictures. On the other side of the island was the upturned hull of the *Utah*. "See the oil slick from the *Arizona*?" Wildern said. "They estimate that oil dribble will go on for 100 years."

Pearl Harbor: "The day that will live in infamy." 2,341 Americans killed. 1,102 men entombed in the *Arizona*. Almost half the U.S. Pacific fleet destroyed. A stunning, crippling victory for Japan, but Admiral Isoroku Yamamoto would say that morning: "I fear all we have done is to awaken a sleeping giant and fill him with a terrible resolve."

▼

There is a yearly rite known as baseball's spring training, and while it is alleged to get athletes into condition, its real function is to give many people a reason to go and soak up six weeks of sunshine. Such are the perks of a columnist with a baseball background.

Spring Training Bliss

Seattle Post-Intelligencer, March 20, 1980

PHOENIX — Today we will talk about heaven. Not the kind of euphoric, misty-clouded, peaceful Nirvana we are supposed to collect on in the afterlife—provided, of course, we follow God's by-laws and don't steal too much money or covet our neighbors' wives or hot-wire our neighbors' cars. I get ecclesiastically confused, at times. A different kind of heaven. There is, I am convinced, a heaven on earth, brief periods of blissful tranquillity when your work, your dough, your geography and chemistry flow into a confluence that can best be described as happiness. Aphorism coming up: The secret to finding happiness is knowing when you're happy. Parson Peter Raible can have that one for the theme of his next Sunday sermon.

To begin: Phoenix, Arizona, itself is not heaven. For large parts of the year it's a sun-blistered hell, but now, in March, it's pretty okay, if you can put up with constant sunshine and 75-degree temperatures. Not to knock Phoenix too much, but like any Sun Belt city which has blown its seams with too many immigrants, it is a sprawled-out nothing of a city; a sort of urban desert within a real desert, but with occasional green spots, with pools of water, and nearby Coke machines. These are called motels.

People pay thousands of dollars to come down here and lie by the pools at these motels, trying to forget the frozen pipes back home. I'm getting it all free, thanks to the practically peerless P-I, and I'm getting paid to write about baseball, a game I love. (I love writing, too, but I love not writing more.) Anyway, the work, the dough, the geography and the chemistry are now in confluence. Do I hear the rustle of angry letters in the mailbox? "Dear jerk: Stop bragging about that soft job you've got while us poor people stay here in the rain." Tough beans, baby. Next summer when you're out camping near a beach, I'll be locked in a stinking hot office trying to recycle clichés. Let's play it as it lies.

Right now I'm staying at a place called the Ramada Inn, on East Van Buren, a few miles from the Mariners' training camp in Tempe. Each day, in the interest of professional diligence, I go up to the ballpark and catch Darrell Johnson, the Mariner manager, in a spare moment. I get out pad and pencil and say, "How's the team looking?" He usually says, "Not bad," and thus ends another long interview. Then I go back to the Ramada Inn and sit by the pool.

The tennis courts. Outside my door are two tennis courts which are never crowded. The Ramada Inn attracts conventions of John Deere Farm Machinery dealers, who don't seem to play much tennis. Right now I'm up to three sets a day and stand even, 9 games to 9, with my buddy, a fellow newsie, who does even less work than I do. When we get bored with our courts, we go up to the Fiesta Inn, where Mariner executives stay. The other evening I lost to Mariner Pres. Dan O'Brien, 6-3, but not even this spoiled the day. Sometimes I go to the Arizona Athletic Club, which we get to use because Rene Lachemann, a Mariner coach, belongs to it. The pool there is ultra scenic, being landscaped with daughters, wives or mistresses of prosperous members.

You have heard of a U-bat-'em machine? That's a batting machine, where you get pitches thrown to you by a heavenly device that never hits you in the back with a fastball. The Mariners have one. The Nirvana of any washed-up bush league ex-player like myself is to stand in at one of these machines and hit till the blisters blossom. Not only that, status goes with it. Mr. Johnson, the "American League Manager of The Year" in 1975—none other—has promised to feed this machine for me. He has also promised not to laugh at what he sees.

Across the street from the Ramada Inn is a dog track, but on weekends the track's parking lot turns into the world's biggest garage sale. It's called a Swap-a-Rama. Garage sale freaks like me go crazy. Acres of stuff (some of it hot, no doubt) are displayed for sale. Aphorism coming up: At a garage sale, you never know what you can't live without until you see it.

Thus, the blissful confluence of words, dough, geography and chemistry has wrought a temporary state of happiness. Baseball, tennis, hot sun, girl-watching, junk-swapping, free U-bat-'em. Men of the cloth will lay you 8-5 that I'll never get into heaven. But right now, it can wait.

▼

The Pink Pony

Seattle Times, March 25, 1986

SCOTTSDALE, ARIZ. — This Arizona Cactus League cluster of cities (Mesa, Tempe, Scottsdale, et al.) must add up to the cholesterol capital of America. Barring a few carnivorous centers in perhaps Texas, Wyoming or Colorado, the area centered by Phoenix is the citadel of red meat–chompin' joy and delight. One expert estimates there are more than 150 steakhouses in the Valley of the Sun. They seem to compete to see who can turn out the biggest slab of beef.

Just to confuse you a bit, studies show that Arizona is considerably below the national average for deaths by heart attacks—in which cholesterol is suspected of being the prime villain.

Anyway, one of these places is called the Pink Pony. It is the hangout and gathering place for hundreds of players, scouts, managers, coaches, executives and baseball writers attached to such teams as the Cubs, the Giants, the Angels, the A's, the Brewers and the Mariners.

In Sports Illustrated recently, Ron Fimrite skillfully summed up what the Pink Pony is like:

"Now it is spring again and the Pony has emerged from hibernation. As surely as the cactus flowers are blooming, so is this flourishing little restaurant. What a life it leads.

"For 10-1/2 months of the year, it's just a good place to get a stiff drink and a thick steak. Then for six uproarious weeks, it metamorphoses into the hottest spot in the desert. Its tables are alive with famous people. Its walls hum with gossip, tall tales, fond recollections, hare-brained schemes.

"It becomes baseball's command post, its private club. Spring is a time for renewal and hope, and the Pony is the storehouse for those commodities."

I've eaten at the Pony at least six times this spring.

Bill Rigney, former manager of the Giants, the Twins and the Angels, is a Pony regular. So are such people as Lou Boudreau, Bob Lemon, Leo Durocher, Herman Franks, Gene Autry and the famous broadcaster Harry Carey. The Mariners' broadcaster, Dave Niehaus, would as soon succumb to tonsillitis as miss out on the Pony during spring training.

The Pony, which has flourished for 36 years, is owned by Charlie and Gwen Briley. Charlie probably knows more baseball celebrities than any "civilian" in the country. His friends range from such late greats as Dizzy Dean and Rogers Hornsby to such living greats as Ted Williams, Pee Wee Reese and Ferguson Jenkins. On one evening a smattering of the Pony crowd included Lemon, Boudreau, Ernie Banks, Eddie Matthews and Mickey Mantle—each a member of baseball's Hall of Fame.

The Pony is as unpretentious as an old fielder's glove. No ferns in planters, no palm fronds, no sawdust on the floor, no self-conscious decorator gimmicks. It's as straightforward as a fast ball under the chin. It is a low-ceiling place, seating some 200, accommodating another 50 at the bar; it is a place of comfortable booths, and the noise level when crowded—the Pony is always crowded in the springtime—is miraculously muted; no clang, no din, no music. As you enter, you look off to the left where the bar is festooned with cartoons and caricatures of famous players and managers. Many of these were done by Gwen Briley herself. Against the back bar wall is stacked a row of souvenir World Series bats.

And the food. You can read Charlie's simple menu in a minute. It has seafood, to be sure, and calves' liver and onions broiled, and fried chicken and prime rib. The steak—ah, well, the steak. Ballplayer's fare, thick and juicy—U.S. prime, corn-fed beef, aged a minimum of six weeks.

When I dropped by to talk to Charlie one quiet mid-afternoon, he told me: "I've got a standing offer—I'll give anybody $10,000 if he can find one smidgen of tenderizer in my kitchen. In 36 years, I've only served the best meat money can buy."

Charlie claims to have 25 Hall of Fame players as good friends. He is a tall man, ramrod straight, and uncompromising as to what constitutes proper behavior. You will always find him there, standing at the end of the bar, sipping a beer, while he eyes the tables of famous grazers.

On any given evening, there will be a huge cluster of executives and owners. Gossip of deals and pending trades is all part of the conversation, and as Don Sutton, the well-known pitcher, has said of the Pink Pony: "They ought to hold the winter meetings there. On an ordinary night there are enough general managers in the room to make 15 trades."

▼

Here Today, Gone to Maui

Seattle Post-Intelligencer, April 10, 1979

MAUI — This not-so-clever column heading is meant to draw your attention, however reluctant, to the mischievously lazy doings of your correspondent, Kid Gullible the Traveler. Maui is Hawaii's second largest island, and "Here Today, Gone to Maui" is the first favored among T-shirt slogans. Another one is "I Got Lei'd in Hawaii." I saw this one on the chest of a haole girl in the Wailea Beach Hotel where I'm staying. She may have been all of 13 and the product of indulgent parents. And for sure, all parents, honeymooners, conventioneers and other seekers-after-sun can only find this a great place to indulge in. And with good reason. It is the latest resort area in Hawaii (more than $60 million, and growing) whose elegance helped earn for Maui the Time Mag accolade of "the last paradise with panache."

Here today, gone to Maui: So here I am, seated on the lanai of an opulent room, within spray distance of the white sand and surf, nibbling that exclusive delicacy of Maui—found here and no place else—a special breed of potato chip, sipping a coconut milk drink, the name of which I can neither spell nor pronounce. Bathed in warm air, watching whales surface off the beach, catered to by room service, 11 tennis courts and 36 golf holes awaiting, life as sweet and gentle as the famed Maui onion; as I keep telling my editor back home, "Man was made to live like this."

To get here you drive through a somewhat tacky resort strip, appallingly misnamed "the Maui Gold Coast," and eventually end up at Hawaii's first planned resort city. Once sand and brush, Wailea Beach is now green—exquisitely green with manicured golf courses, strategic plantings, curved streets around expensive condos (a whiff of suburbia), the towering volcanic height of 10,023-foot Haleakala in the background (the world's largest volcano, obligingly dormant), soft trade winds, distant sound of surf—and my God, Watson, how you do run off about this place! A few miles away rise the contours of Kahoolawe, a waterless, uninhabited island which the military uses for maneuvers and bombing practice. There are protests about this, of course, but for now the description of Kahoolawe by my friend Dick Johnston works best: "An island that's no good for anything which the Navy uses to prepare for World War II."

This kid is not trying to scare you off, but don't come around Wailea trying to impress people with a big roll of food stamps. This is Elegantsville, U.S.A., latest jewel of the 50th State, "destination resort" of what the travel people call the FITs (Free Independent Travelers). Some 500 hopeful FITs showed up last year to draw lots—for Pete's sake—in order to buy 148 condos that sold in the neighborhood of $150,000 to $230,000, which gives you an idea of the neighborhood. According to some accounts, the lucky winners needed bodyguards to fend people off—those unlucky FITs who were saying, "Hey, buddy, I'll give you $40,000 more for that condo than you paid for it." Real estate prices have taken off here like something launched from Cape Canaveral, and somebody figured out that leisure housing in Wailea is rising at the rate of about $2 per hour. "It's a striking example," notes travel writer Tom Horton, "of a legitimate way to make money in bed."

My own hostelry (it's just for rent) is the Wailea Beach Hotel, a sort of 1 and 1A entry with the Intercontinental Maui, the new Hawaii favorites in the Luxury Derby. They are tastefully low-rise, about a 3-wood shot apart; yet another low rise, to be built by Japan money, is scheduled a bit farther down the beach. All of this is owned by Alexander & Baldwin, one of the legendary Hawaii Big Five companies, all of which got launched by the acquisitively spiritual nature of the early New England missionaries to Hawaii. Several versions of this are popular in the islands, the shortest one being: "The missionaries came to do good, and they did extremely well." In any case, A & B owns the 1,450-acre Wailea complex. A year or two ago, they were nervous enough to fly in clusters of travel writers to draw attention to their wondrous works, but now they get nervous only if you're late checking out. The occupancy rate is in the high 90s.

On the way to this splendid leisure spot, you pass thousands of acres of A & B sugar cane fields, the over-billed "Maui Gold Coast," and a huge billboard that heralds the news "Jesus Is Coming Soon." He may well arrive any day, but I hope he has a reservation.

▼

Fisherman's Tale

Seattle Post-Intelligencer, June 27, 1968

GENEVA, SWITZERLAND — Before beginning this insufferable chronicle of Permesso No. 124 (or how to get fouled up in three countries in one day), let me plant an alibi. My downfall began in one of those eye-catching calorie houses known as a Swiss delicatessen, on the car trip down from Basel to Geneva. It seemed like an ideal day for a picnic. Loaded down with pâté, veal loaf, a roast poulet and a bottle of white wine, I pulled off the road about 30 kilometers north of Lausanne, headed the trusty Hertz up a road by the river—and settled down on the bank for a feast.

That's when the sinister stranger arrived. He had a fly rod that cost maybe 250 Swiss francs. His boots were rolled immaculately. He had on a pretty Swiss fishing cap. His fishing jacket had about 16 pockets; the jacket, too, was immaculate, and underneath the jacket he wore a stiff, starched white shirt, and a red striped tie. I mean, he was a beautiful thing to behold, and I shudder to tell you what he cost me.

He could cast, and he could catch them. He was good. And right there, the awful power of suggestion took over—what a way to spend a day! Fishing in a Swiss mountain stream. Checking in a few hours later at the Hotel de Russie, I searched out the impeccable, English-speaking concierge. "A fishing license," I said. "Tell me where I can get a Swiss fishing license." The concierge could not have been more startled if I'd said I was Joe Gandy looking for a stadium site. Clearly, he was dealing with a madman.

Failing there, I headed for the tourist office. Two young girls giggled at my request, then gave me an address across town. After a staggering hike, a lot of confused questions and answers, I finally wound up at the Pêche Sportive, Rue du Rhône 19, where, miraculously, the proprietor spoke English.

"Fishing in Switzerland for tourists can be difficult and expensive," he explained. "The license is 55 francs. That is only good for the Rhône River. And of course you have no tackle, and I do not rent tackle. Why not give up this silly idea? We have some very nice museums in Geneva."

By now, the memory of that pretty Swiss fisherman, hauling in those trout, was too much. I insisted. "Very well," sighed the Pêche Sportive proprietor. "I will sell you an outfit." Exactly 92 Swiss francs later, I owned a fly rod, reel, floating line, a selection of *mouchesragot* nymphs, assorted other flies, a can of red Swiss angleworms, and a few sinkers. "Take this road," he said, pointing on the map. "Go through this portion of France, through the Mont Blanc Tunnel, and you are in Italy. The proprietor of the Edelweiss Hotel will sell you a fishing license, and for a fee, he will let you fish the hotel's private stretch of river. You cannot fail."

Through customs at the French border, then the Mont Blanc Tunnel, 12 kilometers long, and a round-trip toll of 32 francs. The Italian customs man viewed my fishing outfit suspiciously. "Anything to declare?" he asked. "Only my ignorance," I said. Twenty minutes later I was at the Edelweiss Hotel, armed with 33,250 Italian lire. The proprietor of the Edelweiss thought I was insane; he directed me to City Hall, which, it turned out, doubled as a schoolhouse.

Inside was all Italian bureaucracy—and no English spoken. After 30 minutes of guessing, gesturing (I made a very good fly cast, to demonstrate) and waving, they got the idea. What came out made me want to sit on the schoolhouse steps and cry. Fishing, it seemed, was legal only on Thursdays and Sundays in this province. Today was too late and tomorrow was Friday.

After an early dinner (only 5,900 lire, with wine), I drove down the road—and ran smack into another Edelweiss Hotel. "Of course we have fishing," smiled the English-speaking proprietor. "The room is 3,500 lire, the fishing is 3,000 lire. You may fish a kilometer of this river. Breakfast is 2,000 lire."

That night we had a sort of celebration in the bar. The crazy Americano, overwhelmed by gratitude for the fishing, agreed to show the bartender how to make a dry American martini. Everyone in the hotel gathered for the performance. I made a superb martini: 5-1, ice cold, gin and dry vermouth—unheard of in this hotel. Proudly, I held up the martini and passed it around. One woman looked positively ill; the men all shook their heads. The way of the Peace Corps must be hard.

The weather the next day was lovely, and I fished away happily, interrupted finally by an indignant growl from behind. He looked like a leftover of Mussolini's invasion of Ethiopia—army khaki, army cap and all authority. He was the game warden, and he was sore. As he marched me up to the hotel, I thought of making a break for it, like a Hemingway hero, diving into the river. And the headlines, "American Arrested for Illegal Fishing!" "The license is required, even on hotel property," explained the concierge. "Give him 3,000 lire, and you will go free."

That is how I got Permesso No. 124, signed by Il Presidente, G. Cornilo. Back in Geneva, I reported to the man at Pêche Sportive, who agreed to buy my rod back at half price. "Very strange," he sighed. "I have sent so many people to that hotel, and you are the only one who has never caught a fish."

An Innocent Abroad

Seattle Post-Intelligencer, May 3, 1976

HONG KONG — Well, here we are, all those tourists, going broke on the money we save shopping in Hong Kong. You hear them everywhere in the Miramar Hotel. In the lobby, a lady: "I got this darling bag from Paris today—only $160 American, and that wasn't what he was *asking* for it, either. I talked him down $10." In the elevator: "Look at this jade ring— only $900 Hong Kong. That's just $180 American. How do I know it's good jade? Well, the guide book said it was a reputable store."

Do I make myself clear? Hong Kong, the biggest shopping center in the world; bargain basement of the universe; never pay what they ask, always haggle a bit. It's amazing. How these people go on, surviving, actually staying in business, after we sharp American tourists get through driving our hard bargains. They beg to be taken. At the airport lovely Chinese girls hand out a book called *Bargain Guide to Hong Kong*, complete with maps and addresses. Yes, you can go broke saving money in Hong Kong.

Well, you actually can save money in Hong Kong. Cabs are cheap— incredibly cheap by American standards, although the rickshaw, the cheapest ride of all, is fast disappearing. Wander the back alleys. You can still get a tooth filled cheap—by an ancient Chinese dentist, using a foot-pedal drill. And Dr. Yat Sun, the noted Far East physician, will probably remove your appendix for a small fee if you knock on his door.

After six days here, I am, of course, an expert on Far Eastern commerce. I'm amazed that the State Department hasn't hired me by now. But seriously, folks, you *can* get good bargains in Hong Kong—and you don't have to scour the city to do it. In fact, there are quite a few stores, called "fixed price" stores (that means no haggling), where you can get your money's worth. I'm not talking about Gucci shoes, or Joy perfume, fine Swiss watches or super Hitachi stereo stuff; this runs to rather ordinary—but often good, frequently beautiful—things native to China.

Minute Men or Birchers, if any, are now invited to leave the room. Super patriots may grit their teeth. But what I'm talking about is the stuff imported from Mainland China—Red China, if you please. Yes, there are several places here which sell things from the Workers' Paradise—such as China Products, Ltd. and China Merchandise Emporium, Ltd. Both of these places are Hong Kong–owned, but the goods are strictly Red China.

Visit a small department store—four floors of everything from ping pong paddles to bootery; baby cribs to tennis balls. Silks, beautiful silks—at competitive prices, if not lower—and leather and jade and cookware and ivory carvings. On and on. A consumers' paradise, courtesy of the Happiness Boys of Peking. And dear old Richard Nixon, who made it possible for us to bring it all home.

None of this comes with a foolproof Watsonized guarantee. But I did shop there with an experienced American woman, a long-time resident of Southeast Asia, with an eye for prices and bargains. "This is where I shop," she said, "and this is where my friends shop. The prices are low—perhaps lower than most, and the quality is there. Especially the silks—as good or better than any silks in the world, including Japan's.

"You see," she went on, "the mark-ups here have become terrific. Yes, you can find bargains anywhere. But I've seen Americans buy things like hair dryers here and pay more than they'd pay at home. Of course you can haggle in these shops. But they start high, so they can come down to what they want. No, friend," she concluded, "the day of fantastic bargains in Hong Kong is over."

So I spent half a day in one of these stores with my knowledgeable companion from Hong Kong. She touted me on some things, warned me off others. I bought a 12-place, complete setting of splendid stainless steel flatware; under $25. An intricately hand-crafted, finely detailed stick-pin—only $8. All in all, a pleasurable orgy of small-item shopping, without running up a big cab bill.

All of this in one store, mind you, and . . . Excuse me, there's somebody at the door. I think it's the CIA.

How I Died in Greece

Seattle Post-Intelligencer, May 11, 1976

ATHENS, AS IN GREECE — Not since the Golden Age of Pericles has any tourist been quite as sick as I was here in the cradle of Western Civilization. If that statement sounds a bit high-flown, it is meant to be, since I regard sickness as a highly subjective matter. When I set my mind to it, nobody gets as sick as I do.

Without even trying, I managed to get double-lunged, deep-dish, ultra-super pneumonia. Before I was finished, I had ingested enough antibiotics to stop an epidemic in a small, emerging Third World nation. I had two splendid Greek doctors, fretting in attendance, but I was too out of it to record their names. I got the kind of virus that should be put in a museum.

When this thing first hit, Ozzie Bender and I were soaking up sunshine and Greek cuisine on a beach just outside Athens. "I feel fuzzy in the head," I told him. Ozzie didn't exactly say "What else is new?" but he was tempted. "You feel ill?" he said. "No, I feel sick," I said, "I'm probably going to die and you are hereby charged with writing my obituary. Tell my creditors back home that I'm sorry. Put some feeling into it."

What do you do when you get sick in a strange city in a strange country where you can't even read the phone book? It's tough enough getting sick in Portland or Grand Rapids, Mich., where you might luck out finding a good healer. But in Greece? The task is formidable.

"Tell you what," said Ozzie, "we'll check into the biggest hotel in town. I've been reading the travel brochures, and this one has two bars, three restaurants and a swimming pool. I'm sure they have a house doctor, and if all else fails, they probably have a house mortician."

Two hours later I was sitting in the office of the house doctor. "Ah," he said, "you are ill?" "No, I'm sick," I replied. "A semantic quibble," he said pleasantly, writing things down. He thrust a thermometer under my tongue. When he removed the thermometer, his eyes widened. "You have," he said, "the highest temperature this thermometer records. Injections are in order."

From that moment on, I was a walking repository of drugs, pills, vitamins and yogurt. As he worked, I noticed an ancient brass scroll behind the doctor's desk. It was blurred, but reassuring. It was a copy of the Hippocratic Oath. Like almost everything else, it seems, the Greeks invented medical science. "Yes," said the doctor. "The Hippocratic Oath, composed by Hippocrates in 475 B.C." Almost 2,500 years of medical tradition; I felt safer.

Days passed. Sweats. Chills. Coughing. Ozzie, meanwhile, managed to overcome his anxiety by sunbathing at the pool. "You have nothing to worry about," he said, cheerfully. "Morticians are reasonable in Athens. We can even put it on your American Express card."

By now I had two doctors, worrying in relays. The second doctor spoke even better English than the first. "I was educated on the continent," he told me. "On the continent and in England and in Egypt. I think you brought your virus with you."

Then the big day arrived. The doctor came and took my temperature again. "Your friend," he said, pointing to the typewriter, "what is he writing?" "My obituary," I said. "I'm too weak to get up and censor it." Later, he pulled out the thermometer. "Aha," he beamed. "It is broken. No more temperature!" For a moment there, I thought we were going to crack out the champagne, but his bag only produced more pills. "I was very worried for you," he said. "The highest temperature ever recorded in this hotel. It was 104."

I did not, however, qualify for the Guinness Book of World Records. Man named Christopher Legge, in the Hospital for Tropical Diseases in England, 1934, suffered a temperature of 110. "You have," the doctor told me, "a bad case of pneumonia. Rest, eat, and stay out of the sun. In a few days you can tear up your obituary."

So that is the way the trip ended—flat on my back in a Greek hotel. When I found out the room was costing $42 a day, my recovery was miraculous. Nice to be home.

▼

A Day to Remember

Seattle Post-Intelligencer, June 18, 1980

NEW YORK CITY — She came by the hotel, this girl I had a date with. She is tall and has frosted blonde hair, beautiful straight teeth, a radiant smile and eyes that flash with interest and amusement. She still answers a telephone as though every call is an invitation to a party. We met in the lobby of the New York Sheraton, where the Mariners stay when they play the Yankees. It was a warm, sunny day in New York, very low humidity, and I had put on my super-duper Etonic walking shoes because she had said, "In New York we walk a lot. It saves money and you get to see more." She took my arm and we headed east along 56th Street. The sidewalks, on this sunny morning with the sun filtering down through the cavernous buildings, seemed even more crowded than usual.

I asked her if she'd seen a story in the Daily News about how the Transit Authority had borrowed three cops and a woman "decoy" to ride the subways. The woman rode subways until somebody tried to snatch her purse or her necklace, and then the cops moved in and made arrests. In one day the team made 10 arrests, the story said. "I know," she said. "That's all anybody talks about—the crime rate or the price of real estate."

"You learn to survive in this town," she went on. "There was a story recently that one out of every 65 New Yorkers would come to some kind of harm at the hands of a stranger. So you learn. You never, ever ride the subway at night. You stay out of certain neighborhoods. You are always aware, but the idea is not to dwell on it, or you'll go crazy. You just adjust to it and enjoy New York."

She has been enjoying New York for 10 years now. She was raised on Queen Anne Hill, but now she is a confirmed, incurable New Yorker, and her home town of Seattle seems very far away. "I guess I like the excitement," she said. She goes to Carnegie Hall a lot, the museums, and delights in finding small, unpublicized restaurants that aren't on anybody's "in" list; she knows where you can find the best bargains in shoes, what sidewalk markets carry the fresh vegetables. She has gotten to know celebrities such as Gene Shalit and Pete Hamill and Dorothy Collins, the one-time Lucky Strike Hit Parader. She is tall and lovely and good and knows all about it.

We reached 5th Ave. and paid a sort of ceremonial visit to the Steuben store, home of the exquisitely crafted glass sculptures, where we priced one small candlestick that cost $600. Then we went to Cartier's, trying to look nonchalant under the gaze of the armed guard, and after that to a new Gucci store. I fingered a pair of slacks and looked at the price tag. "How would you like to be seen with a man who wears slacks that cost $225?" I asked. "I'd think he was crazy," she laughed. We went on up to St. Patrick's Cathedral, which was built in 1879, watching the people light candles, hearing the echoed sounds on the floor under the enormously high ceiling. "Would it be sacrilegious if I lit a candle for the Mariners?" I asked. "They're playing the Yankees tonight," "Don't do it," she hissed, laughing. "It wouldn't be—well, appropriate."

We kept walking, block upon block, past the fresh-orange-juice carts that have become all the rage in New York, around street barricades, yelling to hear each other above the shattering noise of jackhammers. Song of the city—jackhammers. Narrow streets, a sea of yellow taxis, honking, seemingly mired in the last, ultimate traffic jam. This girl I was with loves it all. She lives on the 31st floor of a building on E. 59th, paying an obscene rent so she can look out over Manhattan, over Central Park, the George Washington Bridge, the World Trade Center, the gardened roof tops. We walked on, block by block, looking and gossiping, and stopped in front of a bay-windowed townhouse at 142 E. 65th. "Richard Nixon lives here," she said. "It's nice," I said, and she laughed. "Enjoy it," she said. "We (taxpayers) are paying for it."

We walked back to the Sheraton and it was time to end our date. She flashed that smile with the bright, even teeth, and I remembered then how long she had worn braces to make them straight. I stood and watched her, walking briskly, moving away through the traffic and thought, "How lovely she is—what a lovely girl." Only yesterday, it seemed, I had walked with her up the steps to John Hay, on Queen Anne Hill, taking her to her first day in school.

▼

Pilgrim's Progress

Seattle Post-Intelligencer, June 20, 1980

BOSTON — If you travel with me, Heaven help you, it's an endless adventure in lost luggage, misplaced laundry, broken plane schedules, changed plans, false starts and catastrophic endings. I can't even get on the right tour bus. But here we are, old Joe Yahoo, the Seattle innocent, schlepping around New England with a fistful of maps, brochures and picture postcards. But somehow that Great Travel Agent in the Sky takes care of people like us, the journeying left-footers of this world. We quaver at the cold stare of a waiter; we cringe before cab drivers; we gawk at celebrities, but somehow we muddle through. Come spend another day with Joe Yahoo, the oracle of 6th and Wall, Seattle, Wa. 98121.

So the other day I approached this nice lady at the Gray Line Tours desk. "I want to go down to that dock where they threw the tea into the harbor," I said. "Threw the what?" she said, politely. "The tea," I said. "Where they threw the tea overboard like it said in my schoolbooks." "Ah, yes," she replied, coolly, "where they had the Boston Tea Party, right?" "I also want to see Faneuil Hall, where they shook the rafters over King George's taxes." She nodded. "And don't forget the Old North Church, where they lit the flame of revolution. One if by land and two if by sea, and I on the opposite shore will . . . " "You want Tour No. 2," interrupted the Gray Line lady. "Three hours. Departures 9:30, 10:00, 10:30, and 1 p.m. Be here 15 minutes before departure. That will be $7.35, please."

Right on schedule, old Joe Yahoo, trying to play Mr. Cool, climbed on the bus and got a seat by the window. The driver turned out to be an amiable old con artist with one of those Boston Irish brogues that seemed a bit cultivated. "Been driving this bus for 23 years," he announced, "and never a dissatisfied customer. I love tourists." He drove past Boston Commons and down to the Copley Plaza, where he picked up some more tourists. Sometime after that I must have dozed off, because when I opened my eyes we were—out in the country! I went up and tapped the driver on the shoulder. "They didn't dump any tea in a hay field," I said. "Where are we? They must have moved the Old North Church." "You got on the wrong bus," he said, "because we are going to America's home town. The Old North Church is on Tour No. 2. You missed that. You are on Tour No. 1. To America's home town."

America's home town—Plymouth, Mass. Where the Pilgrims first landed in 1620. The *Mayflower*. At least the Pilgrims got on the right tour boat. So the *Mayflower II*, sitting there at dockside, took on another load of tourists. The *Mayflower II* is a replica launched in 1957 and sailed over here from Plymouth, England. "Nobody knows what happened to the original *Mayflower*," a guide said. "They sailed it back to England after it came here. It never occurred to them to preserve it, because they didn't think sending 102 people over here was any big deal."

After that we saw Plymouth Rock, or what's left of it. About 100 years after the Pilgrims landed at this rock, some idiot, some Chamber of Commerce type in the 18th century, had it cut in half and hauled up to the commons of the village of Plymouth. Later on, some people with better sense hauled it back down to the beach. What's left of it now sits under a portico, a gift of the Colonial Dames of America. So there it is— America's Pet Rock.

Then we went up to Plimouth Village, an authentic replica of the original Pilgrim headquarters, which was the original town of Plymouth, Mass. Plimouth Village (I don't know why it's spelled differently) has been recreated a ways from town: stockades, thatch-roofed houses, gardens, fireplaces, town square, tools—everything exactly as it was in 1627. The village has its own resident population. These are people who dress as the Pilgrims dressed, who speak a variety of English dialects, who have studied the habits, customs and history of that time. "They live in a fantasy world, as though the 20th century doesn't exist," we were told. "Say nothing to them about anything that happened after 1627."

"Do you miss electric lights?" a lady tourist asked. "Mum?" replied the resident, puzzled. She pretended not to know the word. Soon we were all talking in the present tense. "Do you have any problems with alcohol?" I asked a village leader, who seemed to be Miles Standish. He looked puzzled. The word "alcohol" was unknown in 1627. "Spirits," yes; not alcohol. It became eerie, talking only in the present tense, circa 1627. In various dialects, they explained about Indians, food, cooking, musketry, courtship, marriage and death. I forgot to ask Miles Standish if John Alden was making out with Priscilla.

Back in the city, I took a cab down to the waterfront. I stopped in a cafe, had some coffee, then asked the waitress for a bag of tea. "Here's a dollar," I said, "bring me a bag of tea. I want to go out and throw it in the harbor." She gave me a look that said, "It takes all kinds."

▼

A Walk Through History

Seattle Post-Intelligencer, June 26, 1980

BOSTON— The playwright Ibsen, who probably never saw Boston, said it long ago: "You should never wear your best trousers when you go out to fight for truth and freedom." Good advice for a mere tourist, as well, who starts out on Boston's "Freedom Trail." Taking Ibsen's advice, I put on an old pair of pants and laced up the sturdy old Etonic walking shoes, actually built for jogging, but great for hiking along Boston's brick and cobblestone streets. It was a lovely warm summer day and this city, rich in history, had blown its top with color and good cheer. I rode a cab the three or four miles to Boston Common. The driver was a young black kid with a sunny smile, who seemed delighted that I was doing such a touristy thing as taking the mile-and-half "Freedom Walk," which begins on the Common. "You have yourself a fine time now," he said. "Beautiful day for walking, lots of sun and trees and flowers. Don't forget to stop and smell the flowers." "That's right," I said, "we're only here a short time, so we should stop and smell the flowers while we can." "Right on," he grinned. "You go soak up some of that history."

George was waiting at the entrance to Boston Common. Our George. Big George. Up there, astride his horse, one of Boston's many beautiful statues. The grass was warm and thick, people lying down reading, or flying kites, and I walked up by Flagstaff Hill where the British artillery was stationed during the siege of Boston. Flagstaff Hill. Where they had a gallows in 1683, "for the execution of Indians, Quakers, Pirates and other malefactors." Boston Common, now a lovely city park, where once cattle grazed and people were taken to the whipping post, or put in a cage as "Sabbath Breakers," or in the pillory and stocks, where outdoor smoking in Boston was permitted only on "Smoker's Hill."

On up to the State House in Beacon Hill where the dome was once sheathed in copper by Paul Revere himself. Outside at the entrance are the two statues of Horace Mann and Daniel Webster (now *there* was an orator); on down to Park Street Church, on "brimstone corner," where they made gunpowder for the War of 1812. Red bricks are embedded in the sidewalks to mark the Freedom Trail so tourists like me won't get lost. "America" was first sung in the Park Street Church, and next to it is the "Old Granary" burial ground. Simple gray and red slate marking the graves of such as Samuel Adams, Robert Treat Paine, John Hancock, Mary Goose (who wrote the "Mother Goose" nursery rhymes) and Christopher Snider, a Boston boy killed by British soldiers in the Massacre.

The red brick trail led to the King's Chapel and Burial Ground, where two presidents, John Adams and John Quincy Adams, are interred; the Old South Meeting House, which the British destroyed, using the pews and pulpits for firewood, where Washington, at war's end, came to look down in disgust at the desecration; and where, after meeting there, the Sons of Liberty set out on the Boston Tea Party. After Faneuil Hall, next to Quincy Market, I stopped at the Union Oyster House and had crab cakes for lunch. Louis Philippe, later King of France, lived upstairs during his exile, and one wonders what a Frenchman would say about heavy, deep-fried crab cakes.

Union Oyster House was a mistake, because nearby was Quincy Market, vast rows of food stands, cafes, fruit stands and seafood houses. If John Steinbeck had ever come here, he'd have written a book about Quincy Market called "Calorie Row." After Quincy came Paul Revere's House, with his original kitchen, a walk-in living room fireplace, and a picture of his wife on the wall that caused a guy behind me to say. "No wonder he spent so much time riding the countryside." Then on to Paul's statue, and the Old North Church.

I sank into a pew of the Old North Church (actually Christ Church), and the assistant vicar gave a nice talk to us Freedom Trail walkers; he said the high "box pews" helped worshipers to keep warm in those pre-Revolutionary Days, that the organ, "functional then, functional now," was the first organ built in the U.S. The asst. vicar's name is Benjamin Lentz, and he said that every April 18 they put up the original lanterns ("one if by land, two if by sea") and light them again to commemorate Paul Revere's midnight ride. He said the church clock (1726) still works, and the brass chandeliers date back to 1724, "but our candles," he said, "date back to yesterday."

I walked down the hill toward the *USS Constitution*, the last stop on the Freedom Trail. The crab cakes were sitting in my stomach like a bowling ball, and I felt a little queasy. I decided to pass up a visit to the *Constitution*. "What would people say," I thought, "if a tourist goes aboard and gets seasick on Old Ironsides while she's moored? Some patriot."

The Nickel View

Seattle Post-Intelligencer, July 4, 1980

CHARLOTTESVILLE, VA. — Followers, if any, of this cut-rate, semi-patriotic Eastern odyssey may remember that it started at Plymouth, Mass., with a close-up inspection of America's Pet Rock. Lexington and Concord, a tour of downtown Boston, where our forebears got downright seditious, throwing tea in the harbor, holding shootouts with the Redcoats and generally raising all kinds of hell. The Old North Church, Paul Revere and all such as that. Later came Washington, D.C., with a long walk past the great Grant statue, down to the Washington Monument, and beyond, a great distance to the Lincoln Memorial. So here I am, on July 4, out of money, out of laundry, out of ideas to go further. A trek to Monticello seems a good way to end it. In Charlottesville it is "T.J." country. "So you're going up and visit T.J.," a friend said, and I said "Yes, why do you call him T.J.?" He said a lot of people around Charlottesville call him T.J., but the guides at Monticello, of course, they all call him Mr. Jefferson. It is the beginning of high summer in Charlottesville, the sun warm, a light breeze, but not all that humid yet. Monticello sits up there on a hill that Jefferson loved, a glorious, expansive view of the soft, rolling Virginia countryside.

"Monticello means 'Little Mountain,' " the guide said. "You are standing in the entry where Mr. Jefferson greeted his guests. The trophy heads of elk you see on the wall were brought back to Mr. Jefferson by Lewis and Clark. The counterweight clock over the door was installed by Mr. Jefferson when he finished his presidency in 1809." The guide led us into the library. "Mr. Jefferson could read in five languages," he said. "You will note that there are few books here, but there is his architectural desk, where he designed many buildings. When the British burned the Library of Congress in the War of 1812, Mr. Jefferson sold 6,500 volumes to Congress, thus forming the nucleus of the national library we have today."

He was everywhere in the house. His canopied bed is a room divider in a large bedroom with desk and lounging seat. The dining room: Chippendale furniture, dinnerware brought home from France; and, in the bow of the dining room, busts of Washington, Franklin, Lafayette and John Paul Jones.

He designed the adjoining buildings, the stables, the servants' and slaves' quarters, the octagonal dome, the pond, the walkways; beginning before the Revolutionary War, he was 40 years designing and developing Monticello. As we moved from room to room, I tried to paraphrase what Kennedy said when he invited all those Nobel laureates to dinner at the White House. "Never in one room has there been such a gathering of brilliance, save possibly when Thomas Jefferson dined alone."

He was a statesman, author, scientist, philosopher, architect, apostle of freedom and enlightenment. And just for the record, in case anyone has forgotten, he was a pragmatist who bent the Constitution to pull off the slickest real estate deal in the history of the world. He was an expert in paleontology, ethnology, geography and botany. He introduced French cooking to the United States. He believed passionately in education for all. "Enlighten the people generally." he said, "and tyranny and oppressions of both mind and body will vanish like evil spirits at the dawn of day."

After a while I went out in the gardens, facing the West Front of Monticello. I sat down under a huge, ancient tree, held together by cable and a metal shaft, and took in the "nickel view." The garden, at this beginning of another warm Virginia summer, was ablaze with exotic flowers; they are all kept and replenished as Jefferson first planted them, since he kept meticulous records. The nickel view? Well, take a nickel out of your pocket and you will see T.J.'s profile. Turn it over and there is the West Front of Monticello.

Later I went down to the family graveyard where Jefferson is buried, his place marked by a simple obelisk. The inscription tells everyone that he wanted to be remembered not as a holder of high office, but as one who wrote the Declaration of Independence, helped establish religious freedom in Virginia, and was the founder of the University of Virginia. He said it another way: "I have sworn upon the altar of God eternal hostility against every form of tyranny over the mind of man." Happy Fourth of July.

Part 6
The Editorial Page

In aircraft technology, there is a thing called "the envelope." An airplane's envelope is a set of specifications defining the plane's "structural integrity." It governs maximum speed, the g-forces, altitude, climb capabilities, engine temperatures, and perhaps a zillion other restrictions built in to ensure that the plane, its pilot and its passengers do not bore an expensive hole in the ground. Pilots, particularly test pilots, will occasionally do what they call "pushing the envelope." In other words, they take the plane out to (and sometimes beyond) the limits of its capability to stay intact.

There is a similarity here to the business of writing columns. Columns have their own "envelope," and sometimes the writer, if he is experienced or reckless enough, will "push the envelope" to see what he can get away with. Unlike aircraft specifications, a column's "envelope" is mostly understood, rarely spelled out, but learned by a process of newspapering osmosis—which means "the diffusion of fluids through a membrane or porous partition." In other words, the porous partition is the columnist's brain pan and the fluids that penetrate are the generally accepted limitations of his craft.

Of course, the stakes are much higher if you push the envelope too far in a flying machine. The worst that can happen to an erring columnist is that he or she will be fired or salted away on the copy desk.

For the most part, I think, the good columnists are willing to push the envelope. They have emotions, opinions, causes, ideas; too many are "safe" columnists, never straying far from management's special view of society and the world. Self-censorship has ruined more columnists than free drinks.

Back in the 1950s it was generally assumed, or understood, at The Seattle P-I that you would never write a feature, or column, about Giovanni Costigan, the late, great UW history professor. You could write about him, of course, if you emphasized that he was left-leaning, a rabble-rouser and otherwise something of an intellectual eccentric. Preferably, you ignored him, because in the Hearstian journalism of that time, Costigan was seen as some kind of offal who had survived the glorious, cleansing years of Sen. Joseph R. McCarthy.

So on one bright spring morning I decided to push the envelope. I went out to Costigan's office and talked with him for nearly two hours. He was a gentle man, a kind man, a man of dignity and courtesy, who spoke in what can only be described as wisps of poetry. I found him unrepentant of his McCarthy-era heresies, a fellow of fierce, anti–Cold War convictions, the constant, abiding liberal who so infuriated the downtown establishment, which included the directors of The P-I itself.

I came back and wrote a glowing account of my morning with Dr. Giovanni Costigan. I was a sportswriter then, but I occasionally did pieces for our Sunday magazine section. The editor took my piece and scanned it rapidly.

Then he said, "Oh, shit, we'll never get this in the paper." But we did. With whatever reluctance I wasn't privy to, the story on Costigan ran virtually untouched. I had gone outside the envelope and survived, to write several columns defending Giovanni during the prime of John Birch and his idiotic Society.

Now, pushing the envelope should never be confused with having good sense. But as the years passed, and I got completely away from sports, I found that the envelope was larger than I first had thought. I was very lucky in the matter of editors. In my sports days, Royal Brougham gave me unlimited freedom, including the heresy of putting non-sports pieces on his sports pages. I had come to Mr. Brougham's aviary from a background of The Seattle Star and The Seattle Times. The latter was tightly edited, and one of its injunctions was that you could never use the word "blood" in a sports story. This restriction was put to a severe test on nights when I wanted to write about boxing. As for The Star, we were so short-handed that I often wondered if it was edited at all. But it was generally understood (the envelope, please) that we did not put a black man's picture in the paper.

I worked about 33 years for the old P-I, and they were wonderful times of spontaneity and fun. At least they were for me. I was lucky to test the waters of non-sports because, as I say, Brougham was tolerant. I was also lucky in the fact that Ed Stone, the managing editor, probably never glimpsed the sports section. Royal once said, "If the World Series were being played in the parking lot across the street, he wouldn't look out the window." In some 50 years of whanging away on typewriter and word processor, I probably have had no more than five columns killed. Three of them, as I reflected later, deserved to be killed. They were pompous and nonsensical, and whoever killed them did me a favor.

The first one was only a near-kill, nothing fatal. I wrote a column about the arrival of black power. It was the decade of the 1950s, a wonderful, exciting time, because these were the days when a woman named Rosa Parks refused to take a seat in the back of the bus, and when Chief Justice Earl Warren rallied the Supreme Court to rule that education was for all, regardless of complexion. It was a time when a strange creature named Orval Faubus decreed that black children could not go to school with children of his complexion; Federal troops enforced school integration in Arkansas; and the Rev. Martin Luther King Jr. led his peaceful demonstrators on the long, violence-ridden march from Selma, Alabama, to the state capital of Montgomery. So I wrote this heady, upbeat column which was titled "The Negroes' Summer Has Arrived." An anxious editor took it up to Charley Lindeman, then The P-I's publisher, and Charley killed it. I asked for permission to lobby my masterpiece into the paper.

Charley was a good man and very kind. Like millions of others he had been born in the wrong part of the century. He talked about black people the way a lot of people in those days talked, questioning their character and motivations and morals. Finally, I said, "Charley, maybe if I reworked this thing, it would be okay." He nodded. So I went back downstairs, rearranged a few paragraphs, and brought it back upstairs. "Why, this is fine," Charley said. Except for a little juggling, "The Negroes' Summer Has Arrived" ran as originally written. Once again, I had gone outside the envelope and survived.

Over the years, I found, as I pushed, my envelope expanded. In time, I came to feel free to write about any subject I wanted to, to state any opinion, however unwise, that I held dearly. These opinion columns were, by their very nature, provocative. My mailbox would overflow; most letters would be contrary, often full of the most personal insults. I took, and take, no offense. To a columnist, his mailbox is like a mirror in an emergency ward: a simple device for determining whether the patient is still breathing.

▼

Let Freedom Ring

Seattle Post-Intelligencer, July 4, 1972

IT WAS ACCIDENTALLY FITTING, IT SEEMS TO ME, that Mr. Justice Douglas spoke here almost on the eve of July 4th, the day we celebrate our independence—and all the freedom that this implies. Rarely in our history has any man come down so hard on the side of freedom. A few years ago, I had a long conversation with Justice Douglas, whose low-keyed speaking style, transposed to paper, added up to a ringing cry for freedom for all people everywhere. Time and again, the course of a wide-ranging discussion, he talked of "getting government off the backs of people."

The other night, speaking before the Seattle–King County Bar Association, Justice Douglas used the phrase again, saying that the "need to keep government off our backs is greater than all the B-52s and atomic bombs." At another point he said:

"We all know that power is an obsession that grows and grows. To keep the spark of individual liberty alive is going to require a tremendous effort."

Very little in all the Independence Day rhetoric I have heard or read symbolizes the spirit of July 4th as much as those two sentences. On this day of fireworks and celebration we sometimes forget, I think, the profound implications of the very word "freedom." It is a delicate, fragile and—to many—a very dangerous word. It belongs to nobody. What is one man's freedom can result in another man's oppression.

Too often, the concept of freedom is equated with wars. Certainly, the Revolutionary War was a just conflict for freedom. But tragically few others have had anything to do with freedom. Yet freedom itself is the epicenter of constant battles; the tiny wars for freedom never end—they go on forever, in the courts, in literature, in classrooms, meeting halls and almost any place else one can name.

Freedom, the very thing we celebrate today, is not always a popular issue. In one of his dissents, Justice Douglas, alone among nine justices, found worthy of consideration a plea by three Dallas youths that high school boys have a right to wear long hair. However trivial it seems, the right to wear long hair is an important freedom.

"I suppose," said Justice Douglas, "a nation bent on turning out robots might insist that every male have a crew cut and every female wear pigtails. But the ideas of 'life, liberty and the pursuit of happiness,' expressed in the Declaration of Independence, later found specific definition in the Constitution itself, including, of course, freedom of expression and a wide zone of privacy."

What is freedom? I would never be so arrogant as to try to define it. It is the right to wear long hair or flowing beards. It is the right to dissent, without fear of reprisal. It is the right to demonstrate, the right not to have your phone tapped, the right to watch a pornographic movie, the right to open or close any corner of your mind.

It is indeed true that "power is an obsession that grows and grows." It is never more obsessive than among the righteous. It grows and grows as acceptability is imposed. The fights—the little bloodless wars—to preserve freedom are often lonely, and few medals are passed out.

Sometimes victory for freedom rests with one man. Clarence Darrow, once reviled but now famed as a fighter for lost causes, spoke of the jury system. No matter how hostile the climate he fought in, Darrow said, "always there is one man"—a man on the jury he could reach and make understand. Eugene Debs, a labor leader jailed for his views against a war, once said: "As long as there is a lower class, I am in it. As long as there is a criminal element, I am of it. As long as there is a soul in prison, I am not free."

Many have, as the patriots rightfully tell us, "died for freedom." Less celebrated are those who live for it. Living for it—to truly understand its implications, to want it for others—can invite scorn, ridicule and even worse. Too often the bloodless battles are lost.

Every time the courts are wantonly attacked, freedom loses. Every time a speaker is denied a hall, freedom suffers. Every time an advertiser clubs a publication or an airwave, freedom is lessened. Despite charges of a new "repression" at large in the land, I think we are getting better. The "permissive society," deplored by many, has in reality spawned a whole generation of voices demanding more freedom.

To me, at least, this is what the Fourth of July is all about—the growth of freedom. Carl Sandburg, the chronicler of Lincoln, summed up freedom's pervasive, ever moving spirit, in a few lines from a poem. They are words that should be heard above the noise and the fireworks:

"The free man, willing to pay and struggle and die for freedom for himself and others—this free man is a rare bird and when you meet him, take a good look at him and try to understand him. because when the United States of The Earth gets going and is running smooth and pretty, there will be more of him around than we have now."

▼

Initiative 13, a civic aberration which visited us in the fall of 1978, would have repealed the city's Fair Employment and Open Housing ordinances. It was aimed toward exempting gays and lesbians from prohibitions against discrimination. Bill Russell, the basketball player, writing in The Times, said it was "a witch-hunt being conducted against homosexuals."

The Rights of Man, and Woman
Seattle Post-Intelligencer, October 8, 1978

IF IT WERE NOT FOR THE STENCH OF THE THING, one could shrug off Initiative 13, the anti-homosexual measure, as just another of the periodic aberrations that afflict us. But a stench it is, because it singles out one ill-defined segment of our population (said to be 10 percent) for especially bad treatment. At the risk of repeating what you've read elsewhere, Initiative 13 will do a number of damaging things to our community, two of which are extremely important. The measure would allow employers to lay it on with a license—they could sack, or refuse to take on their payroll, any individual whose "sexual orientation" they didn't like.

This is nasty business. As in the case of restricted housing for blacks and minorities, it will cause festering bitterness. Before we got open housing laws and fair employment measures, landlords, employers, unions, schools and other institutions were allowed to practice bigotry. They did very well at it, because they practiced it so much. Initiative 13 proposes to turn the clock back and permit people to practice yet another form of prejudice. They, too, will get good at it, since practice makes perfect.

Ever since Anita Bryant, the orange-juice hustler from Florida, helped get a similar anti-homosexual measure passed in dim-brained Dade County, the virus has spread. Dade County was followed by such centers of tolerance and enlightenment as St. Paul, Wichita and Eugene. Seattle, a city heretofore noted for its tolerance, is being asked to join such company.

Fortunately, Initiative 13 has soured the taste buds of a number of Seattle people—all willing to go on record against it. In front of me is a four-page list of people who have joined Citizens to Retain Fair Employment. The list includes a broad spectrum of Seattleites—ministers, politicians, businessmen, judges, teachers, counselors; conservatives and liberals alike. An impressive list of organizations have gone on record against Initiative 13. This is mentioned to allay any impression that I like the sound of my own voice crying in the wilderness. Thank God, I'm in good company.

Anyone who lived through the McCarthy era should know what we are up against here. In those glory days of the witch-hunting know-nothings, all rules were suspended. One did not have to be "disloyal" or "soft on communism" to be ostracized or fired from a job. All it took was a whispered "charge," a "suspicion," however false, and you were branded. People's lives and careers were ruined by unfounded charges.

Not enough has been made of this, it seems to me, in the case of Initiative 13. Homosexuals and lesbians come in all sizes, shapes, forms, occupations and stations in life. They are not readily identifiable. In the case of men, most are not the mincing, lisping stereotype; in the case of women, most lesbians are not masculine in demeanor or appearance. Look in a mirror, and you will see what the "average" homosexual or lesbian looks like. What Initiative 13 can do is infect the community with McCarthyism once more. A whispered charge, a rumor, an innuendo can brand anyone; if the landlord or employer thinks your shirt is too bright your hair too long (the stereotype) he can see you as "homo" or "les," therefore different; therefore out with you.

Heaven forbid; we have enough to fear in modern society. Accidents, disease, pollution, terrorists, inflation, hard drugs, joblessness—the gamut. But I think we should refuse to be frightened by the lies of Anita Bryant and her followers, that peculiar fright wing that is ever among us; those spiritual descendants of a know-nothing fundamentalism that made Clarence Darrow famous and Dayton, Tennessee, a laughingstock.

The more one hammers away at this topic, the more unnecessary it seems. All we are saying, really, is that 10 percent of us are "different" from the rest of us. Taking their rights away—by initiative, for God's sale—isn't going to make this society one whit more livable, safe or fulfilling. Let us fret about more important matters and accord people the respect and compassion that one human being owes another.

Time to Speak up

Seattle Post-Intelligencer, November 5, 1978

THREE WEEKS AGO I SOUNDED OFF, perhaps at unconscionable length, about the dangers and pitfalls of Initiative 13, a blatantly bigoted legal contrivance aimed specifically at one minority group—the homosexuals among us. The cascade of mail and phone calls can now be divided, roughly, into three kinds. The first kind was complimentary, often flattering; some of the writers seemed to imply that mine was the lone brave voice speaking out against Initiative 13, some even suggesting that it took "courage" to do so. Well, it's nice to get your back scratched, but that is nonsense. Thousands of people are speaking out against this pernicious bit of mischief, pounding the pavements, ringing doorbells, and sometimes being personally abused for "sticking up for those queers." A taste of what we are in for, if this initiative passes, already is apparent. Straight people who work against Initiative 13 already are being branded as homosexuals.

The second kind of reaction is religious in nature. By not being in favor of denying homosexuals employment rights, I have offended God. Those who know Him well, it is implied, have talked my case over with God, and there is going to be hell to pay. I should be getting a summons any day. God hates homosexuals, just as they do, and anyone who thinks homosexuals deserve an even break, along with the rest of us, speaks blasphemy.

The third kind of letter is beautifully scatological. Allied with the fundamentalists who know God intimately are the people who know every foul word in our language. Of all the letters, these are by far the most fun to read. They even trigger a bit of nostalgia for a childhood many years ago, when I learned the meaning of such words on street corners. If God truly hates homosexuals, as the fundamentalists tell us, then He must be wearing cotton in his ears to march with troops like these.

As anyone above the intellectual level of a Lloyd Cooney should be aware, Initiative 13 belongs in a sewer, not on a ballot. It is conceived in bigotry and intolerance, for it singles out a minority of our citizens and attempts to strip them of their dignity, their rights as equal citizens. It singles them out by emphasizing, through discrimination, their difference from the rest of us.

Let this piece of pernicious mischief pass, and you will not have heard the end of it. Because this will be a victory for those narrow-minded idiots who will use it for their own prejudice, or their own profit, against almost anyone. If you are a person—no matter how "straight" you may be— who happens to have one or two of the same physical or psychological characteristics of a homosexual, or a lesbian, look out. You may have enemies you didn't know existed. This measure leaves anyone vulnerable to scurrilous, side-of-the-mouth gossip, dark whisperings, innuendoes and worse. A jealous co-worker could do you in at your job; a tenant could damage your reputation in the place you live, if his mind runs in these dirty channels. And you will never know who did it to you.

But isn't that overstating the case, you ask? Aren't a lot of "respectable people" in tune with this legislation against homosexuals? Listen, friend. They are no more "respectable" than the people who denied Indians full citizenship, than those who barred Jews from clubs, hotels and schools; no more worthy of respect than those who decreed early on in this city's history, that the Chinese should be run out of town; than those who expropriated Japanese property only 36 years ago, and who, until only recently, decreed toilets for "colored."

Singling people out as "different"—hence deserving of special treatment— is the oldest scam in the world. Unless you are a blob on this earth, then you are different, too. All of us are different in some way, if only in our beliefs, our individuality, our style of life, our personal preferences. A much-quoted passage these days is one by the great German Lutheran pastor Martin Niemoeller. It may seem a bit overblown in these times, but it is worth repeating:

"In Germany they came first for the Communists, and I didn't speak up because I wasn't a Communist. Then they came for the Jews, and I didn't speak up because I wasn't a Jew. Then they came for the trade unionists, and I didn't speak up because I wasn't a trade unionist. Then they came for the Catholics, and I didn't speak up because I was a Protestant. Then they came for me, and by that time no one was left to speak up."

A Vietnam Vigil

Seattle Post-Intelligencer, November 16, 1969

YESTERDAY MORNING, IN A SMALL BUT—to me, at least—important gesture of protest, I stood on the U.S. Courthouse steps on Fifth Avenue and read off several hundred names of the Vietnam war dead. Nothing about it was very dramatic. What excitement there was about the weekend Moratorium had occurred here Friday, and protests of a much larger magnitude were taking place in San Francisco and Washington, D.C. It was just a concerned citizen's work. Along with several dozen other citizens of Seattle, who kept a vigil of name-reading all through the night, mine was only a 15-minute contribution.

A friend had told me his own reaction when he took his turn reading names of the dead on Friday afternoon. He was a World War II veteran of the South Pacific, and he said he found himself pausing on occasion when he read a familiar name.

"There were guys in my outfit then with those same names," he said, "and as I read them, I couldn't help wondering if they were possibly sons of the men I knew in the South Pacific."

The reading of the names, he added, finally took on almost a religious solemnity as he read on and on. I came to share this feeling, reading aloud the names of young, dead soldiers, killed in Vietnam, calling them off in the early November morning with the rain clouds boiling over the city. As I read, it somehow seemed terribly important to say each name right, to pronounce it exactly as it was supposed to be pronounced. This was impossible, of course, because American names are Polish names, Italian names, Swedish, Norwegian, Czech, German, Russian and many others. But even though the courthouse steps were deserted by then, and there was no one to hear my often stumbling pronunciations, it seemed only right and respectful to try and get every dead soldier's name right.

Actually, I guess I'm a charter member of the "Nervous Nellies," as Pres. Johnson called us when he escalated the war in Vietnam. That was almost 30,000 dead ago, approximately eighty billion dollars ago, and I can't remember how many promises of "an early end" to the war. Since then, a new President has called us "bug outs," and lately he has turned his Vice President loose on us. Now we are known as "effete snobs," and "parasites," and "rotten apples" to be disposed of without regret.

Well, as the Vietnam Moratorium goes on, it becomes increasingly difficult not to be alarmed by a Vice President who says such things. The administration which promises to end the war (one more promise) now has taken it over, adding nothing new except more invective against those who oppose it.

Quotation: "Decisions made with maps and oval tables in the conference halls of power are made by men whose own youth has passed. Not privy to the policies that formed their own fate, the young are used to play the games of violence imposed on them by their elders . . . We might question whether the generation that designs or the generation that fights war is the truly violent one."

This was said by Marvin E. Wolfgang. Since he happens to be a professor of sociology at the University of Pennsylvania, I guess he would be classed as a "rotten apple" by our Vice President. Being an intellectual, he is automatically suspect. Forget him, because Bob Hope was in town this weekend to tell everybody, in effect, to shut up in the name of unity. He is funnier than he knows.

Three years ago, I had lunch with Sen. Henry Jackson, a man I respect, and one of the country's foremost hawks on Vietnam. When I expressed doubts about the wisdom, the strategy or the moral good of being in Vietnam, he said it was a matter of "ports, power and petroleum." When we knock out their ports, damage their power and cut off their petroleum, he said, the war would be quickly over. "Remember the three P's," he said. It all sounded so neat. That was three years ago, and we are worse off now than we were then.

More recently, a columnist, Herb Caen, observed: "Here is a war that is slowly destroying the United States by meaningless death, attrition, division, inflation, internal revolt—could any radical, in his wildest dreams, have asked for more?" That is one reason that a lot of us felt called upon to read off the names of the dead on the U.S. Courthouse steps.

From time to time, anyone who speaks out against the war in Vietnam is called down with the question "Who are you to be telling us about Vietnam?" Well, for years I have heard Sen. Jackson, Pres. Johnson, Dean Rusk and dozens of blurred, patriotic faces at cocktail parties tell me about Vietnam. Now a new cast is telling me about it—Nixon, Laird, Agnew, Bob Hope; they are all telling us, in effect, to shut up. To the question of "Who are you to say 'get out of Vietnam?' " there is only one answer. It's Oscar Levant's rejoinder: "Who do you have to be?"

The woman in my office whose anguished anger inspired this column was Barbara Huston, my then helpmate and friend. A very sad morning, indeed.

Kent State

Seattle Post-Intelligencer, May 6, 1970

THE WOMAN IN THE OFFICE WAS STARING out the window when I arrived for work yesterday. On her lap was the front page of the paper. "I find it hard to believe," she said. "Don't you find it hard to believe?" She pointed at the front page of the paper, which showed a dead student of Kent State University, in Ohio, stretched out on the street—one of four killed in a close-order volley of gunfire by the National Guard. Fifteen others were wounded. "I mean I find it hard to believe that our own National Guard deliberately shot down our own kids. They *are* our own kids, aren't they?"

The news was not at all good that morning. The U.S. invasion of Cambodia (about which the Kent students were protesting) had just encountered its first serious resistance. Sen. Allen Ellender spoke of a "big intelligence blunder," as the strange invasion goes on. Telegrams on Cambodia (most against) pour into Washington. Promises of more violence on more campuses, fired by the Kent State University killings, are in sight.

The same morning the telephone had rung at home. "I saw the front page this morning and burst into tears," said the girl's voice. "I don't want to hate this country as much I hate it right now." Out at the UW, some thousands of students massed to protest the war and the Kent State University killings.

"This is different from anything we've ever had before," a student told me. "Before, there might have been 300 or 400 of the hard-core demonstrators. But they're pouring in from sororities and fraternities today. Usually the moderates stay away, but this is different, this has never happened before."

Four students gunned down by National Guard, two of them girls. Fifteen wounded. The four were non-violent, middle-class kids, protesting Cambodia at a middle-class university in a small, middle-class town in Ohio. Spiro Agnew was at his brilliant best. He talked about the "grave dangers which accompany the new politics of violence and confrontation." The Vice President, of course, has done as much as anyone— probably more—to inspire confrontation by his fiery speeches denouncing student dissent. "Impudent snobs" and "effete corps of intellectuals" are now part of our language.

President Nixon was also in rare form. "When dissent turns to violence it invites tragedy," he said. Anyone who composed the Checkers speech should be able to do better than that. Nixon, who always has a dog, or a little girl to assist him, a week ago was calling the students "bums." Not long ago, he was inspired, he said, by a little girl's plea to "bring us together." That was his theme, the soft voice—and bring us together.

Not long ago in another burst of rhetoric that seems to please so many silent majorities, Gov. Reagan spoke loosely of a "bloodbath" in dealing with student dissent. Thankfully, before Kent, Ohio, the governor recanted in part: "I didn't advocate a bloodbath, and as a matter of fact, I think there's something neurotic in someone believing that what was a figure of speech in a lengthy answer to a question should be interpreted literally to mean that anyone would be advocating solving a problem by bathing the students in blood." But when such words as "bloodbath" pop out of a leader's mouth, in any context, one wonders.

The Attorney General and his charming wife, Martha, have not been heard from. Somewhere, Mr. Mitchell is sucking on his pipe, perhaps pondering his influence on Mr. Nixon to invade another country in Asia, yearning perhaps for "preventive detention" and a "no-knock" policy for the nation he polices. The hard line grows harder, but the violence increases.

On yet another page of this sad morning paper, the black journalist Carl Rowan, a moderate by any standards, predicts that the U.S. is on its way to becoming a police state. He is not the first. A friend of mine reports that a middle-class lawyer acquaintance of his, who erroneously thought two Guardsmen had been killed at Kent, Ohio, burst out: "If I were running things back there, I'd string every damned student up from a pole." They didn't do that well—they shot 19, and four are dead. No Guardsmen were killed.

It was hard to think clearly on a morning like this. It is entirely possible (because it already happened in Chicago) that within a few weeks a poll, Harris or Gallup, will report findings that 58 percent or 62 percent, or some other terrifying majority of Americans, approved of what the National Guard did in Ohio. It may well be that the Cassandras are right. If so, then we might as well stop calling ourselves a democracy, and begin calling ourselves something else.

Vietnam Blame Game

Seattle Post-Intelligencer, April 9, 1975

ONE CANNOT HELP BUT BE WARMED, as in grateful, these days by the generosity of our commentators, several of whom have invited us to share the guilt, or blame, for the debacle in Vietnam. Only yesterday, James Reston, firmly astride the middle and speaking with the cool voice of reason, asked us to share. "There is enough blame in this tragedy," he wrote of Vietnam, "to cover us all."

Well, I cannot speak for you and you and you. But I can speak for this kid, and I do not care to accept such largesse. If anyone is passing out blame for Vietnam, don't pass any out on my account. I am one of the world's great collectors of blame—I've goofed a thousand times—but in this case, modesty forbids. I am not worthy. Skip it, Mr. Reston, and anyone else who wants to pass out separate checks for blame, now that the party's over. My share was zilch.

I was a charter member of Lyndon Johnson's "Nervous Nellies." Before that, I had to have my eyes examined, because I could not see the light at the end of the tunnel. In 1953, I voted for LBJ because he said Asian wars were for Asian boys, not ours, and I thought Barry Goldwater was a madman when he said, "Let's turn it over to the military." In those days I was only dimly aware that John F. Kennedy once tried to get David Halberstam kicked out of Vietnam because Halberstam, who won a Pulitzer Prize, was writing the truth about the war.

Later I enlisted (or was drafted) into the disloyal legions of "effete snobs" and "parasites" and "rotten apples," to be disposed of, without regret, by that noted apostle of patriotic rectitude, Spiro Agnew. President Nixon called me a "bug out" because I didn't want the war. Of course, there were millions like me, so it really wasn't all that lonely being called "traitor" by those who believed we had something nifty, and uplifting, going on over there in Vietnam. A lot of good guys died to keep our leaders in patriotic rhetoric.

Back in 1969, I joined some people here on the courthouse steps to read off names of the Vietnam dead. It wasn't much, really; just a gesture. Just a concerned citizen's work. It didn't compare at all with the efforts of 250,000 people who marched on Washington, along with hundreds of thousands of other citizens in other cities who did the same, trying to get the war stopped. I don't think they deserve to share in this abundance of blame being passed around these days.

In 1966, a friend and I had lunch with Sen. Henry Jackson in Washington, D.C. He was a hawk and we were two doves. When I expressed doubts about the wisdom, the strategy, or the moral good of being in Vietnam, he said it was matter of "ports, power and petroleum." It would all work out. We would knock out their ports, bomb their power and cut off their petroleum. He said when we did that the war would be quickly over. "Remember the three Ps," he said. A formula for victory.

It got worse. It always was a racist war, of course, and an American general was quoted as saying he "just loved to kill those Congs." The term "gook" was used often, and I always thought the general's use of "Cong" really meant "gook." In disproportionate numbers, American blacks were sent over to kill Cong. Middle-class whites stayed out of Vietnam by getting good grades in school.

But a lot of kids protested, the "rotten apples" and "bug outs," and many of them left the country. President Nixon said they would be treated with "no pity." At the corner of 4th and Pine, one morning, I saw a young girl passing out anti-war leaflets. A large, heavy-voiced, angry man denounced her, loudly, while a crowd gathered, and she looked flushed and pained. If they're passing out blame for all of us, does she get her share now?

It always was a war of lies. Lies and deceit. Lies and deceit of slogans: "Peace with honor." Later Halberstam would write *The Best and the Brightest*, a book to cry over; how the best of them, Rusk, McNamara, Kennedy, Johnson, Westmoreland, Humphrey, Rostow, McGeorge Bundy, Laird, got us into it. Just a little war that finally cost 55,000 American lives, $108 billion, and tore a small country to shreds. Now the hawks are telling us if we'd really tried—really supported this obscenity—we'd have won. What would that have cost? 110,000 lives? $216 billion! We should have listened to LeMay. Back to the Stone Age.

I can't remember what the commentators, including Reston, were saying all those years. It all seems rather hazy, now, hazy and fence-straddling. It's anybody's privilege to be that way, of course, but I don't want to share any of their goddamned blame.

Nixon as Role Model

Seattle Post-Intelligencer, May 2, 1974

(THIS COLUMN IS A SUMMARY OF 240,000 WORDS, adding up to 1,398 pages of evidence taken from tapes made of conversations between its author and various parties I have bugged on my Sony tape recorder in the past eight hours, minus 18-1/2 minutes, when my secretary stepped on the microphone. The full transcripts are being transported by truck and trailer to a remedial reading school in Pine Bluff, Ark., for which I will accept the usual tax deductions. This summary will prove beyond doubt that I am innocent of anything, including good taste, no matter who gets shafted. The words "inaudible" and "unintelligible" have now replaced "inoperative," so let the subpoenas fall where they may.)

Actually, some of the omissions of the transcripts of tapes released by the White House this week were done to censor language used by President Nixon. Mr. Nixon, it now turns out, is capable of language that would make even the late President Truman blush. Mr. Truman, you know, was famed for his salty language (see Merle Miller's *Plain Speaking:*

An Oral Biography of Harry S. Truman), and back in 1960, this became a subject in the televised debates between then Vice President Nixon and then Sen. John F. Kennedy.

To check on this, I got hold of Bill Shadel, of the UW's School of Communications, a fellow who was pretty close to the scene. I mean he had a good seat for the debates. With ABC at the time, he was moderator of the third one.

During it, correspondent Charles Von Fremd, of CBS, brought up the fact that Mr. Truman had used some blunt language in telling Mr. Nixon and the Republican Party where to go. (He probably said "hell," but we'll use "unintelligible.") Mr. Von Fremd asked Senator Kennedy if he thought he owed Mr. Nixon an apology.

Mr. Kennedy: "Well, I must say that uh—Mr. Truman has uh—his methods of expressing things; he's been in politics for 50 years; he's been president of the United States. They may—are not my style. But I really don't think there's anything that I could say to President Truman that's going to cause him, at the age of 76, to change his particular speaking manner. Perhaps Mrs. Truman can, but I don't think I can . . . "

Mr. Shadel: Any comment, Mr. Vice President?

Mr. Nixon: "Yes, I think so. Of course, both—Senator and I have felt Mr. Truman's ire; and uh—consequently I think he can speak with some feeling on this subject. I just do want to say one thing, however. We all have tempers; I have one; I'm sure Senator Kennedy has one. But when a man's President of the United States, or a former President, he has an obligation not to lose his temper in public. One thing I've noted as I've traveled around the country are the tremendous numbers of children who come out to see the presidential candidates. I see mothers holding their babies up so that they can see a man who might be President of the United States. I know Senator Kennedy sees them, too.

"It makes you realize that whoever is President is going to be a man that all the children of America will either look up to, or will look down to. And I can only say that I'm proud that President Eisenhower restored dignity and decency and, frankly, good language, to the conduct of the presidency of the United States. And I only hope that, should I win this election, that I could approach President Eisenhower in maintaining the dignity of the office; in seeing to it that whenever any mother or father talks to his child he can look at the man in the White House and, whatever he may think of his policies, he will say: 'Well, there is a man who maintains the kind of standards personally that I would want my child to follow.' "

This was long before we discovered that Mr. Nixon practices a different language than he preaches. Shadel recalls that, after this debate ended, Mr. Nixon was furious at him. Nixon suspected Kennedy of using notes (against the rules), and as Shadel recalls it, "The air was blue. He really tore into me." Before Mr. Nixon's noble thoughts on strong language reduced me to tears, however, I turned to Arthur Schlesinger's article on impeachment and Mr. Nixon in this month's Harper's.

"The President of the United States occupies a peculiar but recognized place in the moral organization of American society," Schlesinger writes. ". . . Parents used to hope their children would grow up to be President. Children like to see the President, whoever he is, as benign and wise, the national father to whom they can safely entrust their lives and their destinies. What happens to this bond when a President no longer sets a particularly edifying example? No doubt it is healthy not to see a President as a superhuman figure. Yet it troubles the whole society when he can no longer be seen as any sort of example at all. Few among us can hate our children enough to urge them to model themselves on Mr. Nixon . . . "

Nixon, The Last Goodbye
Seattle Post-Intelligencer, August 9, 1974

AND NOW, AT LAST, HE IS LEAVING.

It began, I remember—this malignant revulsion toward Richard Nixon—a very long time ago, when I was young and the world seemed bright and full of promise. It was a time of life when my head was full of inspiring words from textbooks, the words of Jefferson, the poetry of Sandburg, the journalism of Lincoln Steffens, the soaring summations of Clarence Darrow, the great defender, and a President who told us, in another time of crisis, that we had nothing to fear but fear itself.

We are what we are shaped to be, and each of us is a part of all we have met.

There were writers of books and there were teachers. They were the ones who shaped the mind, who developed the process of thinking, gave skepticism to shoddy values and opened new horizons of awareness. Thus I was educated, like many millions of other Americans in the fragile process of democracy, believing that, whatever its faults, it was the most beautiful experiment in human history.

It was a game you played by the rules. Life in America was a contest of ideas, often of profound disagreements, but it was a game that depended for its survival on the goodwill of the contestants. No man should be called "traitor" for his beliefs, and each man should be inviolate in what Adlai Stevenson called "the sacred privacy of the mind." History, of course, abounds with scoundrels, fools and knaves. But somehow it worked, this fragile process, and all this I believed as a very young man.

He broke the rules. From the very beginning, when he tarnished Jerry Voorhis and Helen Gahagan Douglas with a communist label, he broke the rules. When he ran for the House, then the Senate, he smeared and lied to get there. He came to be a skilled practitioner of middle-of-the-gutter politics, putting down people of other beliefs as "disloyal," libeling President Truman as a coddler of traitors.

He made headlines as the man who exposed Alger Hiss, the alleged communist spy, in a time when Red-hunting was in vogue. He ran with the hounds, cheered on by newspapers who found him exciting, and A. J. Liebling was later to write of him: "He bet his new political fortune on General Eisenhower . . . into the vice-presidency of the United States. That first two-dollar bet, in fact, landed him within a heartbeat, a yard of intestine and 112,000 votes of the White House, on three separate occasions, and in that order. Nixon, however, was never of more than almost–importance, since he was running too fast to leave footprints on the sands of time. He just skimmed them, like a coot taking off."

He played the hatchet role for Eisenhower. He slandered Adlai Stevenson, whose eloquent integrity set a standard for excellence in public debate for this century. He tried to link Stevenson with Alger Hiss, lying in the attempt, and for eight years as Vice President he was known as the "gut fighter" of the administration. Later, when he sent Agnew on similar missions, Agnew became known as "Nixon's Nixon."

He might have been President in 1960, but by then even Eisenhower couldn't stand him. He got no support from the general. There was one, final gutter campaign for governor of California, and then even he thought he was finished.

But Liebling's summation was wrong. We elected him again, and for 2,026 days he ruled this nation. He was the "new Nixon." There were some of us who hoped—even believed—that the presidency itself, by some alchemy of morality and spirit, elevated the man who held it. But now we know it does not, and our anguish is best expressed in the question "Who would have thought that Richard Nixon would turn out to be Richard Nixon?"

A nightmare of horrors was the legacy of this base, banal, unctuous man. He obstructed justice, he lied not only to the nation, time after time, in televised speeches, but even to his lawyers, his intimates, and perhaps his own family. As the horrors unfolded, it became clear he was out to dismantle social progress, punish dissent, defile the courts and make a mockery of the Constitution. He damn near wrecked the nation.

Pity the poor bastard? There isn't time for that. We got what we deserved, and we must strive to deserve better. What do we have to work with? We have some words, and they are these:

"The task is yours. Yours is a democracy. Its government cannot be stronger or more tough-minded than its people. It cannot be more inflexibly committed to the task then they. It cannot be wiser than the people.

"As citizens of this democracy, you are the rulers and the ruled, the lawgivers and the law-abiding, the beginning and the end. Democracy is a high privilege, but it is also a heavy responsibility whose shadow stalks, although you may never walk in the sun.

"I say these things to you, not only because I believe them to be true, but also because, as you love your country, I love my country, and I would see it endure and grow in light and become a living testament to all mankind of goodness and of mercy and of wisdom."

They are the words of a man whom Nixon once defiled: Adlai Stevenson.

Righteous Christians, in the robes of the Moral Majority, were riding high in 1980. Since the Moral Majority would not let me speak to God, as they did, I decided to call up the Devil instead. It was a device I employed fairly often while the Moral Majority (such a pompous title!) was in business, and I probably overdid it. But even a columnist has to have some fun.

Speak to the Devil

Seattle Post-Intelligencer, October 5, 1980

WELL, I HAD A LONG TALK WITH THE DEVIL the other day, but before you accuse me of name-dropping, or social climbing, an explanation is in order. You see, before calling the Devil, I tried to get wired into the Moral Majority, which has become a force in this political season. The Moral Majority, as you know, is very much in news (radio, TV, print media) because they are influential in the presidential race, particularly in the campaign of Ronald Reagan. They advise Mr. Reagan (Carter, too) on such matters as nuclear superiority, welfare bums, gun control, and matters pertaining to abortion and the Trilateral Commission. Well, sir, some people are born Moral, some achieve it, and some have Morality thrust upon them. Falling into the latter category, I tried to cleanse my soul and find what my position should be on the MX Missile. It was no use. The Moral Majority would have none of me. "You are almost beyond redemption, Watkins," one of them said. "We know for a fact that your father was on the dole in 1935. You once wrote nice things about Harry Truman. Your stand in favor of hot school lunches is almost communistic. You consider abortion to be a private matter. Before you can join us, the Moral Majority, you must get yourself born again. There isn't much time—the election is Nov. 4."

This Moral Majoritarian said it was no use trying to go over his head on this matter. "Don't try to call God on this," he said. "He knows, for a fact, that you are soft on welfare bums and sending troops into the Persian Gulf. I have already told Him." "What did He say?" I asked, tremulously. "He was speechless," came the reply. "No, Watkins, you are not of Moral Majority caliber," he added. "We of the Christian Moral Majority, the nuke-ready neo-conservatives, have no need of your ilk. God has told us so." "I thought you said He was speechless," I said. "His speechlessness is a figure of speech," came the reply. "He tells us what to do, never fear."

No question about it, he had me. Friends and critics alike say my credentials for the Immoral Minority are impeccable. That is how I came to be talking to the Devil the other day. If the Moral Majority is guided by God, then the rest have but one choice. I dialed 1-555-1212. "What city, please?" came the voice. "I want to talk to the Devil," I said. "Oh," said Directory Assistance, "that's any city you can name." I was astounded to learn that the Devil has a toll-free number, 1-800-277-0010. "Does God have a toll-free number, too?" I asked. The reply was firm. "God has an unlisted number," said Directory Assistance, "unless you belong to the Moral Majority. They talk to Him all the time."

The Devil's toll-free number answered on the first ring. "This is Everett Watkins," I said, "of the Immoral Minority. I have a problem." "The Heaven you say!" exclaimed the Devil, chuckling. "You can't get into the Moral Majority, right? No wonder. You didn't go along with Impeach Earl Warren, you believe in fluoridation of water, you are soft on Trident, you believe in public health care, you make fun of Lloyd Cooney, you have not stood up for prayer in classrooms, and you have been seen in the company of known Democrats, like Warren Magnuson. Man, you are a moral mess," chuckled the Devil, "welcome to our flock."

"Look, I'm not so keen on you," I said, "I can find another political adviser." "Where?" he cackled. "The Moral Majority has not only drummed you out, but more of your candidates, too. They rate candidates. Yours are mostly zero. So are you. If you can't be moral enough to suit them, you must be immoral. By definition, you have nowhere else to turn but to me." "But for Heaven's sake!" I cried. "Don't use that language to me," he snapped, "I don't tolerate rough language. Now, about your problem . . . "

I said that several things trouble me about the election. The Moral Majority is exhorting both candidates to cut taxes. "Thirty percent, forty percent. The Moral Majority doesn't want abortions, but we're up to our ears in people right now. They want to protect the unborn. They've got Reagan and Carter promising more missiles, more subs, more troops, more ding-dong doomsday bombs, invisible airplanes, fail-safe delivery systems, more military bases. Is God telling them all this?"

I heard a devilish cackle on the line. "It is my policy," the Devil finally said, "never to mention my opponent by name during a campaign. But the answer is no, my opponent is not telling them all this. Even my opponent is smart enough to know that you can't cut taxes and build zillions worth of lethal hardware. Even he knows the irony of their position. If you are going to protect the unborn, well and good. But if you protect a few million unborn and end up killing 100 million of the already born, it's a travesty in arithmetic. How delightful!" he snickered.

After a long pause, he came back on the line. "Excuse me," said the Devil, "but I had to handle another call. Things are going beautifully in our ghettos. A fine, fine war in Iran. Marvelous reports from Cambodia and Bangladesh. Now, go back to your piddling problems and stop bothering me. By the way, did they ever impeach Earl Warren?"

This is probably the dumbest column I ever wrote. (From this distance, two decades later, it is even more appalling.) But, having publicly displayed my ignorance, my awareness of the status of women in society was to be heightened suddenly and swiftly. A landslide of justified anger engulfed me. The response drove me to seek shelter in the company of writer Jane Adams, who undertook to continue my education. I had much to learn.

Female Orgasm, Ho Hum

Seattle Post-Intelligencer, November 11, 1976

I AM SORRY, FRIEND, BUT IF I READ, or even hear about, one more book on female sexuality (orgasm div.), I think I will propose Gloria Steinem as a cover girl for the next issue of the Smithsonian magazine. That statement alone will get me a half-dozen letters from NOW, accusing me of anti-feminism, when I'm not too busy performing arson on orphanages. Lately, it develops, a woman interviewed 3,019 other women and came out with something called *The Hite Report*, after the author, one Shere Hite.

This one went strong on self-stimulation and left the impression that women could still reach the outer perimeters of sexual ecstasy if all men were thoughtful enough to quit the planet. The whole thing, I gather, adds up to one fat masturbation manual, selling for $12.95, and no, I have not read it. I don't intend to see the movie, either, if it gets to that. This paper's Paul O'Connor, who did read the book, called her a "sexist charlatan," and I'm willing to leave it at that.

It is not anti-feminism, with me, but apathy. For years—it seems like hundreds—magazines, books, newspapers, radio and TV have concerned themselves with whether women "achieve" orgasm, or a reasonable facsimile thereof. Most of it is based on "samplings," or "in-depth" research, ad infinitum, ad nauseam, add another sampling, add another book. Maybe they get some kind of orgasm just by reading about themselves.

As I say, this is nothing new. More than a dozen years ago, a friend of mine, Barry Farrell, then working for Life magazine, went out to Kansas to interview Dr. Karl Menninger, the famed psychiatrist at the Menninger Clinic. Then, as now, everybody was in a frenzy about what percentage of women, if any, got to that heavenly state known as female orgasm. Dr. Menninger, as Farrell recalls it, was either in a foul mood or fed up with the subject. Perhaps the latter brought on the former.

"Orgasm," he raged. "Everybody's talking about women's orgasms. Why do they talk so much about it? What's so important about it?"

Later, on his way home, Barry rented a small plane to get him to a main airport. As they flew, at a height of about 600 feet over the Kansas meadows, Barry reflected on the cattle grazing below. "Do cows have orgasms?" he suddenly asked the pilot, a handsome, corn-fed country boy. The boy looked stunned. He reached down and pulled back the throttle. "What did you say?" he gasped. "I said, do cows have orgasms?"

said Barry in the frightening silence of the cockpit, as the plane nosed down. "Never mind, never mind," he added, "but get this thing back in the air!"

The feminist movement, in many ways, is the greatest thing to happen in this nation since Lincoln started writing on his shovel. But women interviewing women about their orgasms is not one of them. In fact, when women write about women, and their problems, a strange effect takes place. By implication, at least, one half of the world's population, women, are somehow pictured as having the combined qualities of Madame Curie and St. Joan.

Such is not the case. Anyone who ever has read *Generation of Vipers*, by Philip Wylie, or uses eyes and ears, knows this. A large number of women, like men, are vain, dumb, dishonest, conniving, mean, incompetent, selfish, dirty, and altogether without redeeming qualities. They don't deserve to have orgasms.

But don't get me wrong, some of my best friends are women—or at least they were until today. Meanwhile, if a new statistical study shows that cows have orgasms, lead me to it. One of the burning topics of our time.

Female Orgasm, New Thinking
Seattle Post-Intelligencer, November 14, 1976

"TURN OUT YOUR OWN COLUMN TODAY, YOU SEXIST," read the interoffice memo, signed, "Your Liberated Clerk." Thus began the brickbats over Thursday's epic on female sexuality writing, and the numbing effect thereof. Clad in football helmet and riot gear, I then sought out one of the leading female authorities on sex in this city (one of its best writers, too) and confessed my sexist sins. She laughed uproariously at the whole thing, and expressed some reservations herself about *The Hite Report*, the book that got me fulminating in the first place.

And wouldn't you know it? She's writing a book on sex herself. Step forward, you nervous males, and meet Jane Adams, as cheerful a revolutionary as you will ever find. You've got hangups? You feel threatened by the growing, if not incessant, preoccupation by women with liberated sex? Jane is your person. She'll listen to your problems and give it to you straight.

Jane Adams' book on sex and the single parent, for Coward-McCann publishers, is due out next year. It involves, of course, divorced parents, both men and women, who end up trying to carry on active sex lives while raising small kids. In the course of this, and other related research, Jane has come to one conclusion—the old male machismo, as so many studs have known it, is going out the window.

Jane Adams whose work appears regularly in The Weekly, has interviewed dozens of men, all of whom, she asserts, feel threatened by sexual equality, as well as by every other phase of women's rights. "Men can keep them out of their boardrooms," she said of job discrimination, "but if men want them in the bedroom, it has to be on equal terms." Meanwhile, the threatened men are saying, "I may have to give her what she wants in the boardroom, but not in the bedroom."

What she finds, she says, are a lot of men "whose egos are on the line," who are all strung up by women's demands for complete—emphasize "complete"—sexual fulfillment. "Men say they want women who are 'secure' and 'together,' but they really don't," she said. "Equality, as men see it, stops at the bedroom door."

The spate of books, stories and interviews on women's orgasms, which I decried last week, is a logical result of the female drive for a square deal in life. Thus, women who never knew true sexual fulfillment are reading about it, learning, going to "pre-orgasmic classes," and the whole process is burning down the old machismo. One man she interviewed "found himself sexually inadequate with the kind of woman he admired—independent, bright, economically free. He can't accept an independent woman, because he won't give her the commitment it takes. So he picks up some bubblehead in a bar. She doesn't make demands, she's safe."

Another fellow, a professional man, was "rendered completely impotent" when he learned his wife attended pre-orgasmic classes. The marriage broke up, and now he's bisexual. One man told her, in speaking of the female drive for equality: "It's a tide and it's engulfing me. At work, on the streets, and now in the bedroom. I feel like I'm hearing jackboots in the distance."

All of these interviews and many more, both men and women, come out in yet another book. "Even the bubbleheads are dying out," she said. "They're reading those magazines under the hair dryer." In short, she says we men are scared, insecure and threatened. "Always the men were permitted to lust, but now it's lust for women, too, it's available to them, on their terms. This is the age of the one-night stands for women."

It went on like this, example after example, until I began to feel like an endangered species. When we parted, I noticed she was wearing a divided skirt, with fashionable high boots. "Remember," she laughed, "jackboots in the distance!"

Like many in Seattle who thought of the Space Needle as "our symbol," when the Needle's owners decided to gussy it up with a second, lower level, restaurant, I was annoyed. I still think the owners should be ashamed.

Save the Space Needle

Seattle Post-Intelligencer, September 13, 1978

I USED TO KNOW A GUY IN NEW YORK named Tommy Brophy who was raised on the streets and talked like it. He sounded exactly like his brother, Eddie Brophy, a well-known character actor in movies of the 1930s and 1940s. Eddie Brophy was short, stout, round-faced and funny; he often played gangster roles, frequently in period pieces wearing a derby hat. His jowls were a delight to behold and his accent was thick with the Bronx. Now you know how my friend, Tommy, looked and sounded, because he was a dead ringer for his brother, the movie player. Not to make this an interminable introduction, but I used to meet Tommy Brophy at Bleeck's, the old Artists and Writers saloon, where they served magnificent pig's knuckles and sauerkraut. Tommy was full of New York lore, and the more beer he drank, the more lore he was full of.

One evening, after a day of column-hunting along 5th Ave., I found Tommy at Bleeck's bar. Over dinner, I rambled on about the buildings, the fine old recessed penthouses, the stone masonry, the terra cotta flourishes, the dimensions and the dignity of the architecture. Tommy nodded, probably amused by this outburst of yokelism. "Glass and aluminum," I said, "that's all we get today. Why do you think those old buildings are so much better?"

Tommy probably was bored by the whole subject. But he gave the question some grave thought, then replied: "I guess it's because the guys who built those old buildings weren't the kind of guys who would put clocks in the bellies of statues."

Tommy Brophy comes to mind quite forcefully now, since we have some people in Seattle who are determined to put a clock in the belly of a statue. That's a loose analogy, of course. What they are determined to do is put a restaurant in the belly of the Space Needle. Now, the Needle isn't a statue, but it is a city emblem. In its comparatively short life, the Space Needle has become a symbol of the city, a remembrance of the World's Fair, a towering, elegant structure, precise as to form, detail and proportion. By accident or design, it has come to represent one of America's loveliest cities. Millions of pictures, spread all over the world, identify the Space Needle with Seattle. So in a sense, the Needle has become a statue. It doesn't need a clock in its belly.

The Space Needle's owners, known as the Pentagram Corp., are determined to stick a restaurant up there. It will cost $1 million, they say. To hear them tell it, they are building an invisible restaurant. "You won't even see it," they keep saying. To convince us that $1 million will build an invisible restaurant on the Space Needle, they have produced side-by-side drawings, one with a restaurant on the Needle, another with a hamburger. Given a choice, some people would prefer the hamburger.

By accepted estimates, some 1.5 million people a year use the Space Needle. Adults shell out $1.50 a piece to ride the elevator, kids go for 75 cents—the tariff to reach the Needle's splendid height. At an average price of more than $1 per ride, that adds up to income in excess of $1.5 million per year, not counting lease income for the present restaurant. The height of sophistry comes cheaper. These are the words of John Graham, one of the Needle's partners: "If the new facility does not become a reality at the Space Needle, we will have no choice but to increase elevator fares to meet our increasing costs."

That is the kind of pablum even babies can't swallow. It will take one hell of a restaurant—or a sweet lease deal from Western International Hotels, the food concessionaire—if it will prevent a price rise to, say, $1.75 or $2 per elevator ride.

But a point is better made by staying with Tommy Brophy's aesthetic judgment. To become actively disliked in a community takes a lot of planning and hard work. The Pentagram people are succeeding, through a high-powered ad campaign, by insisting on a clock in the belly of this statue. Rightly or wrongly, hundreds of thousands of us think of the thing as "our" Space Needle. Tamper with a civic symbol at your peril.

No, I don't think Seattle will float off into Puget Sound to drown its shame if the Pentagram people get their way. But if they're dying to spend $1 million on a restaurant, why don't they find another place for it? Tommy Brophy never saw the Space Needle, but I think he'd like it just the way it is.

The Case for Sloth

Seattle Times, July 1, 1984

THE CASE FOR SLOTH HAS NEVER BEEN PROPERLY MADE, and I count myself among the laggard trumpeters of this noble condition. Summer is the time for sloth. It is that splendid, suspended condition during which you stare out of windows, twist paper clips, make a halfhearted pass at the crossword puzzle and view the world with a dreamy indifference.

Some great men have endorsed sloth in the past. For example, the brilliant Bertrand Russell believed that four hours of work a day was enough for anyone. And here is William Faulkner, that superb master of prose, bemoaning a society that rivets itself to the work ethic: "One of the saddest things is that the only thing a man can do for eight hours a day is work. You can't eat eight hours a day, nor drink eight hours a day, nor make love eight hours a day—all you can do is work."

A case can be made, I think, that our do-nothings in high office make for better government. Lyndon Johnson, for example, was a hyperactive workaholic. It is instructive to reflect how much better a President he'd have been if he had been prone to cat-nap and daydream. He might never have overworked himself (and us) into Vietnam.

The more I participate in its delights, the more I think that sloth should be a man's right, protected by law, under some Affirmative Non-Action program. One can almost hear howls of indignation from the productivity boys, the Gross National Product prophets, the disciples of Calvin. Ignore them. In a long-ago article I treasure, the author made what I regard as a definitive point:

"Most great hunches and major breakthroughs seem to have popped into people's heads when they weren't working—when they were staring into space, goofing off or even sleeping. Stanislaw Ulam, the Polish expatriate physicist who, with Edward Teller, hit on the design for the hydrogen bomb in 1951, was considered spectacularly lazy by his colleagues at Los Alamos. While everyone else worked around the clock to win the Cold War, he never appeared at the lab before 10 and was gone by 4."

But you say, "If a slothful person helped develop the weapon that can destroy the world, what is the case for sloth?" Easy. Without hyperactive, supermotivated warlords in Japan and Germany, we would not have tried to develop such bombs at all. Moreover, with lazy, slothful leaders in

Washington and Moscow, there might not have been the subsequent national frenzy to build more and deadlier weapons.

In order to steal the Indians' lands, in order to colonize much of Africa and Asia, in order to invade peaceful countries, in order to capture slaves, exploit whole populations, expropriate the earth's resources, embark on religious crusades—to accomplish such things—man, you have to work at it.

A little well-placed sloth could save us a lot of trouble. But the nature of sloth is also its problem. That is, slothfulness is a natural, wonderful, peaceful condition that comes over us spontaneously. It can't be programmed. You cannot turn on the beautiful, semicomatose state of blissful sloth the way you can a production line. We must work on this problem—but not too hard. My guess is that a solution will come during those treasured moments when one of us is enjoying sloth. Perhaps unions and managements, coordinating their periods of creative sloth, can work it into collective bargaining contracts.

"But my workers goof off enough already," a tycoon might say. And what is the answer to that? Well, thousands and thousands of auto workers keep production lines humming—in order to produce what a hard-working, hard-driving, ulcer-prone management ordered them to produce—the Edsel. And don't kid yourself, a lot of folks worked hard night and day in order to produce WPPSS.

Perhaps the first step to be made in promoting more and better sloth is to take the guilt out of it. Too many of us fail to enjoy our sloth because that tiny voice in the background is always saying, "Leisure is self-indulgence, laziness is the work of Satan, sloth is sinful."

One way to get around this guilty feeling is to counterattack. When you are lolled back in your chair, feet on a desk, shooting two-pointers at the wastebasket—when you are in this somnolent state, and then you hear the voice of Calvinist conscience, don't quit being slothful. Come out roaring. Shout, "Remember the Edsel!" "Don't forget WPPSS!" "Down with workaholics!" This will get you a lot of attention around the office, to be sure, but yours is the cry of spiritual contentment and freedom.

So now it is time to stare out the window again. It is time to relax and turn paper clips into figure-8s, to sail paper airplanes out the window and just dream about things. That's all I seem to be able to accomplish right now, but I'd better get cracking or we won't have a column today.

▼

A Christmas Card

Seattle Post-Intelligencer, December 25, 1960

THESE THINGS I WISH FOR ALL OF US do not come gaily wrapped and tinsel sprayed, nor will they fit in Santa's bag or in a child's stocking. And they cannot be placed under a tree and admired among the packages and ribbons. Neither cash nor charg-a-plate will affect their possession. They are just some of the things I wish for all of us and all of you . . .

Given the storied gentle magic of Father Christmas, I would bestow the chance to relive, and perhaps correct, those days in all our lives when everything came up knotted shoelaces and burnt toast . . . I would bestow the Second Effort to every man, giving him a chance to redress past rudeness, to remember overlooked birthdays and anniversaries, to strike from the record the bon mot that fell flat, the unseemly insult and the careless slight . . . Given this mythical power to give, I would dispense the largesse of self-respect to all the outcasts stumbling aimlessly on Skid Road, having missed their chance at life. And always, too, an ounce of humility to those on the brighter side of the tracks, enabling them to ponder the thin line which divides us from less fortunate fellow men.

The gift of resiliency would go to those tight, tidy contented thinkers among us—a glimmer, perhaps just a spark, to make them hazily aware that man's slow journey to "broad, sunlit uplands" is marked by the milestones of the people who Doubt . . . To all adults, however well endowed, would go the occasional use of the wonderfully wild, uninhibited imagination of a child who knows nothing of conformity, who thrives and grows within his own personal world, a world where fine, logical relationships exist between cows and peanut-butter sandwiches . . . And with it would come a gift of inspiration to the human spirit—to bring alive the books unwritten and unread, the plays never finished, the composition uncompleted, the half-done or never-started painting and yes, of course, the letter to a loved one that somehow never gets written.

To the terribly forgetful legions among us, that not-so-exclusive order, The Casters of First Stones—to these would go a moment of hesitation before the arm snaps forward and the self-righteous follow-through is completed . . . A stark revelation, bare of bright paper and ribbons, is my bequest to the tormented souls who see The Enemy everywhere, and nowhere more frightful than in the puzzled eyes of a Negro child being led to a new school . . . To all men, everywhere, would go the power to endure loneliness, and soon, perhaps, to learn its virtues—a special gift to the "group-minded" people to enjoy their own company on occasional strolls through the woods, or over a deserted beach at night.

The spirit of Christmas-wished-for embodies the gift of smooth speech to the stammerers, a light under the bed for the timid, and a pat on the back (or many broad smiles of welcome) for the people who can't enter a crowded room without trembling a little . . . To all the left-footers of this universe would go a little adjustment in the psyche, a slight turn of the screw, giving them at least a chance to get things right, to say the bright lines at parties and wipe away forever the desperate look of hope in their eyes—eyes pleading for more than polite laughter at their favorite joke . . . And another gift, as well, to the defiantly "well-adjusted" individual—perhaps a medium-sized problem to make a man of him.

For those who live their lives as watchers in the wings, I would take away their fantasies—if only for a little while. So the man who cheers the halfback will get his chance to run with the ball, and the fat girl in the movie house would have her time, however brief, to be what she sees on the screen—lovely and sought-after and adored . . . But to each of us, crippled by illusions, would come a further gift—the rare perception to look beyond the pompous pretensions and see the King naked.

Given the place of Father Christmas, I would want us all to have a magic mirror which reflects not mere beauty or tired lines on aging faces, but a mirror which shows us how we really look. A magic mirror with the power to make us laugh at what we see . . . Not for one day, but for every day, I would like to see the tender compassions of this season at work among the people, to look everywhere and see always the light of hope that sparkles as in a child's eyes at the thought of Christmas . . . And what else is left? Perhaps a warm wink of fellowship, or a pat on the hand to the people who guessed wrong when the time was right, the ones who zigged when they should have zagged, the souls who faltered when only strength would do . . . To the lovers who lost—what for them? A fond wave of the hand, a touch on the shoulder; a toast of cheer to all the brave lovers, past and present, the gift of long moments of reflection on the sweet quiet hours behind.

The spirit of Christmas wished-for, like the wishes themselves, leads along a road of daydreams, unmarked by signposts of logic . . . There is an Irishman I know who once stated, with no solemn predictions of success, that he is involved in a crusade "to give Christmas back to the amateurs" . . . I don't think he is going to make it, but it's worth a try . . . He has a delightfully nutty way with words, twisting them around, transposing syllables and slap-dashing phrases together, but always they seem to come out exquisitely sensible . . . So as the end of a long, long column of wistful wishes, I offer you Walt Kelly's poem, which might not explain everything, but it certainly won't do you any harm.

A song not for now you need not put stay . . .
A tune for the was can be sung for today . . .
The notes for the does-not will sound as the does . . .
Today you can sing for the will-be that was.

Part 7
The Sports Pages

For a long time I was typecast as a sportswriter and this was not all bad. I liked sports but came to be bored with the grind of covering games, putting dots into baseball scorebooks, running down every choice morsel of cliché some player or coach would say in a football locker room. The pursuit of happiness and fulfillment, I submit, should never rely on success of athletes.

The part about sports I liked best were the people in it, the interesting ones, and I wrote a lot of magazine pieces about them. I was for many years the Northwest correspondent for Sports Illustrated, beginning with its first issue in 1954 and carrying on through the 1970s. Through Sports Illustrated I met and was able to deal with some outstanding editors and writers. These included Dick Johnston, the magazine's assistant managing editor, who gave me several choice assignments. They also included Robert Cantwell, a man of unbounding generosity. It was Cantwell who sent me to Glacier Park to investigate the story of two grizzly bears that had killed two girls in widely separated areas of the park on the same night.

I worked my tail off on this one, for it was the height of the tourist influx and the season of forest fires in Glacier Park. One of the boys who witnessed one of the killings threatened to brain me with a tire iron he was using in a gas station. He would not talk about the horrible event, and in retrospect, I don't blame him. I filed a very long story and it was Cantwell who checked out my facts and put the story together. He put my name on it and even wrote a "publisher's letter" about me.

Another I got to know well was Jack Olsen, then a lead writer at Sports Illustrated. Jack now lives on Bainbridge Island and turns out best-selling "true crime" books. In the 1960s, the nation's black athletes "revolted," in a sense—that is, they were tired of getting the dirty end of the stick from college administrators and coaches. Olsen wrote a five-part series that deserved a Pulitzer Prize. Anyway, I worked with and for Jack, sending in long files about the University of Washington. These files needed help from Hilda Bryant, an investigative reporter at The P-I, and Joe Jones, a black fullback on the earlier Husky Rose Bowl teams. The labor was one of love, and it was educational, not only for readers, but for me.

In all, I wrote 22 bylined stories for Sports Illustrated, thanks principally to Dick Johnston, as well as Earl Burton and his successor as chief of correspondents, Eleanor Milosovic. But the man who really gave me a start in national magazine writing was Ed Fitzgerald, who went on to become president of the Book of the Month Club, among other publishing achievements. In those days, the 1950s, he fashioned a miracle in publishing on a low budget. In addition to putting Sport Magazine in the forefront of quality publications, Ed ran another magazine, one of those men's Americana adventure magazines. With this latter publication, the name of which I have forgotten, Ed got me out of strictly sports writing when he assigned me to write a long profile of Leonard Seppala. For those who wonder, Leonard Seppala was a national hero when he was mushing dog teams back in the 1920s. He became a

genuine national hero when, in the winter of 1924, he drove his dog team out from Nome to meet a relay of other dog teams carrying diphtheria antitoxin; Seppala then drove his team to record speeds in order to get the medicine back to Nome, which was gripped by an epidemic.

As I say, Ed worked from a tough budget at Sport Magazine. He had no money to send writers away on stories. In my case, he would study the Pacific Coast League baseball schedule (I covered baseball then) to see what weeks I could be in what town where he wanted a story done. This way, the newspaper, or the old Seattle Rainiers, paid my way. I would research stories during the day and cover the games at night. Out of this came my first really long story. Most Sport assignments called for 3,000 words and a standard fee of $250. This one was a 10,000-word cover piece on the Washington Redskins and their new quarterback, a short but magical guy named Eddie LeBaron, a story called "New Chief of The Redskins."

So I was very lucky because I had a chance to learn from the best. I became friends with Roger Kahn, then sports editor at Newsweek, who later would produce perhaps the best baseball book ever written, *The Boys of Summer.* There were also Tim Cohane, sports editor of the old picture magazine Look and the great Pogo cartoonist Walt Kelly, a gifted essayist and poet himself, who was of immense help. And most important of all was my true hero in the craft of writing, John Lardner, son of Ring. I always thought John Lardner was better than his father, and I will also say, without equivocation, that John Lardner was the greatest sports writer who ever lived. His focus was mostly sports (he wrote many other things, including TV and theatre criticism for The New Yorker), but his abiding interest was the fusion of words and sentences into classic essay form.

He first became my hero when I was still at the UW, when the Times occasionally carried his daily humor column. He was then twenty-three. The greatest luck of my life was being taken into the confidence of this tall, elegant, very quiet and private man, whose wit could strike sparks. As Kelly once wrote of Lardner in the preface to a collection of his work, *The World of John Lardner,* much of what John wrote was written in the midst of "internal tragedies that would have slowed, in fact, stopped, other men." And Kelly, who knew John well, added: "Much of what is here was written against a background of tuberculosis, the pain of heart disease, multiple sclerosis, personal troubles too private for anyone else to reveal, and a gnawing, understandable premonition that he would not live to be forty-eight years of age." He almost made it. He had just about a month to go.

Memories of Baseball in Seattle
Seattle Times (Pacific Magazine), April 7, 1985

IN MY GRASP AT THE MOMENT IS A BASEBALL. It is an object I long ago gave up throwing for any useful purpose and it sits on a shelf in my bedroom, a neglected artifact of my past, faded and inoperative, something that will never again be thrown in joy or anger.

The inked-on signatures are faded, too. But they can still be deciphered: Seattle Rainiers, 1942 . . . Bill Lawrence . . . Len Gabrielson . . . Eddie Carnett . . . Hal Turpin . . . Lynn King . . . Sylvester Johnson . . .

Pete Jonas . . . Hal Patchet . . . Bill Matheson . . . Hal Sueme . . . Bill Skiff. Once I played on this team.

As I contemplate this baseball in my hand it is interesting to examine its character. The ball is very hard, covered with cowhide (not horsehide, as legend has it) and it is held together with exactly 216 raised red stitches. It is just over 5 ounces in weight and measures anywhere from 2.86 to 2.94 inches in diameter. Inside it are wrappings of wool yarn, and a coat of rubber cement, and a small composition cork center, around which the wool yarn is wrapped.

This ball probably was made in Chicopee, Mass., since it was manufactured in 1942. It has the official stamp on it, "Pacific Coast League," and the official signature of that era, "Clarence Rowland, Pres."

When the Seattle Mariners arrive home for the official opening of the 1985 season on Tuesday in the Kingdome, they will be throwing, catching and hitting a ball that is exactly the same as the one I hold in my hand. The only differences are that the cover will be stamped "American League," not "Pacific Coast League," and the ball was manufactured not in Chicopee, Mass., but in Taiwan. Thus, the hundreds of thousands of baseballs used in America's "national game" now contribute, in some measure, to our massive foreign trade deficit.

But what difference does that make? To understand the hold that baseball has on us, you must go and see Robert Redford in *The Natural*, and you must listen to the character he plays. You must listen to Redford, playing Roy Hobbs as a young man, carrying his magic bat, like Excalibur, and enunciating the dream of all American boys: "When I walk down the street, I want people to turn and say, 'There goes Roy Hobbs, the best there ever was.' "

To understand baseball, you must read Mark Twain and Ernest Hemingway and Ring Lardner and Roger Angell and George Plimpton and James Thurber and Robert Frost and Thomas Wolfe and Sherwood Anderson and James T. Farrell and Ogden Nash and John Updike and P.G. Wodehouse. Jacques Barzun, the distinguished French-born historian, once said: "Whoever wants to know the heart and mind of America had better learn baseball."

Can you imagine any of those people, celebrated writers and poets, wasting their talents on basketball or even football?

George Plimpton once said that he thought the amount of good writing on American games has been produced in an inverse ratio to the size of the ball. "There have been many great books written on baseball," he said. "A handful of good things have been written about football and very little on basketball. There are no books on beach ball."

To truly understand baseball, you must have lived in Seattle (or any town in America, for that matter) in the 1930s. There would have been no professional basketball except for the Harlem Globetrotters; no professional football to speak of; no hydroplane racing on Lake Washington; and certainly no television, no VCRs, no home computers, or any other technological distraction.

And by understanding baseball, you would also understand Seattle a bit more than you do now.

Every city and town in America, from the smallest hamlet to the largest metropolis, has its tradition of boys playing baseball. We played it in streets and cow pastures, on vacant lots and community playgrounds. To play a game, you needed little more than a single bat and a ball (sometimes wrapped with bicycle tape when the cover wore off); beyond that, all you needed were space enough and time. You roamed neighborhoods, challenging other teams, and in Seattle, for sure, sometimes played in the mud.

When I was growing up, the town team, the real professional club, was called the Seattle Indians. They played on the old grassless, dirt surface at Civic Field (where High School Memorial Stadium now stands). It was a terrible field, surrounded by heavy wire-mesh fences with barbed wire on top and sheet metal all around it to foil the freeloaders from watching from the street.

Opening day was a license to skip school. Civic Field was a piece of cake when it came to sneaking in because you could dig the toes of your Keds into the wire mesh and climb the fence like a monkey, which is what we were, a bunch of unruly monkeys who outsmarted the guards. We worked in relays. One ruse was to set up a horrible clatter by hammering on the fence and shouting obscenities at the guards, who would rush to quell what seemed like a riot; this was a signal for other boys in the unpoliced areas 200 feet away to vault the fence, leap down inside and disappear into the crowd.

Another way was to wait, poised, near the top of the fence and listen for a home run. The old Indians had some great homerun hitters like big Art Hunt and "Scrap Iron" Freddy Muller, and when they unloaded a drive against the balcony of the old Civic Ice Arena beyond left field, all eyes were on the ball and you could drop inside unnoticed. Oh, the old Civic Field was a glorious sieve!

Inside the relatively small park, every seat was a good one. Peanuts were a nickel a bag. One of the more enterprising peanut salesmen was a quite large young boy, age 15, named Dewey Soriano. By day Dewey was a student at Franklin High School, and he worked by night, selling peanuts to help out his family. In his school days, Dewey was a strong, sturdy young pitcher who dreamed of one day playing for the Indian team. Dewey's dream was shared by another young Franklin student, Fred Hutchinson. They were close friends, and working separately, but sometimes together, they would revolutionize the sport of baseball in Seattle.

Also present at every Civic Field game the Indians played was a compact, loquacious Italian kid who grew up in Black Diamond but later was a star athlete at Queen Anne High School. His name was Edo Vanni, and he had a very large nose and a very large voice, and his feet were so mercurial that he dazzled people with his speed on high school base paths.

There were others, as well. There was Jeff Heath, a broad, heavy-muscled slugger from Garfield High School; Hunk Anderson, a large pitcher from Ballard; Ira Scribner, from West Seattle; Earl and Chet Johnson, from Ballard; and a huge, strapping pitcher from Queen Anne named Mike Budnick.

All of them shared the American dream of millions of boys across America. Like Roy Hobbs in *The Natural*, they wanted to walk down the street and hear people say, "There goes the best there ever was."

This was the Depression era of 1933 to 1937. We had no money then, so we ritualistically banged on the old tin fence and taunted the guards, dropping safely inside to cheer on our heroes—Bill Lawrence, Joe Coscarart, "Scrap Iron" Muller, big Art Hunt, Johnny Bassler, Chick Ellsworth, Alan Strange, Dick Gyselman, Kewpie Dick Barrett, Farmer Hal Turpin, Clarence (Snake Eyes) Pickerel. We were drawn to them by our own fantasies, but also by a shrill, siren voice of excitement that beamed out of a cramped little wooden broadcasting booth onto the airways:

"Good evening, ladies and gentlemen, this is Leo Lassen speaking. And now, another exciting game of baseball, brought to you by crispy, crunchy Wheaties, the Breakfast of Champions!"

There were usually parades on opening day. A man named "Baldy" Baldwin was usually the general chairman, and there were prizes for the player who got the first hit, stole the first base, or scored the first run on opening day. Always on hand for these openers was a tough, rotund labor leader, whose offices were not far from Civic Field on Denny Way. His name was Dave Beck, and he was the powerful head of the local Teamsters. He, too, would do much to change the game of baseball in Seattle.

The old Indians were an impoverished franchise, owned more or less jointly by a bland, clever fellow named "Bald Bill" Klepper and George

Vanderveer, the famed criminal attorney who was already a legend in Seattle courtrooms.

The Indians were so impoverished by 1936 that county and city officials appeared regularly to collect back taxes out of the gate receipts. So the manager, a man named Dutch Reuther, would coach at third base with his baggy baseball knickers filled with paper money. This was the evening's receipts, collected at the gate, which Klepper was forced to hide from the impatient city tax collectors.

As for George Vanderveer, he found that you could not support a baseball team on revenue earned by defending prostitutes and criminals. So one day in the winter of 1937, Vanderveer walked into Dave Beck's office on Denny Way and said, "Sign this piece of paper and you will own the Seattle Indians. They won't cost you a dime."

"Are you crazy?" said Beck. "I don't have enough money to pay the first-baseman's salary. But I know somebody who does."

Within a matter of days Beck persuaded Emil Sick, a wealthy brewery owner, that it was his bounden duty to buy the Indians and rescue them from possible bankruptcy. "You will be a big man in this city and you will sell lots of beer," Beck said.

So for little more than $100,000, and some back debts, Emil Sick acquired the Seattle Indians. The old Indians quickly became the new Rainiers, named after Mr. Sick's Rainier beer, and that is how, in 1938, Seattle had two opening days of baseball.

The first one was at the Civic Field and the place was crawling with dignitaries, including Gov. Clarence D. Martin and Mayor Arthur Langlie, and of course the league president, Mr. Wilbur (Two Gun) Tuttle, who got his nickname because he made his living by writing cowboy-story shoot-'em-ups for pulp magazines.

There were 11,000 fans there, too, because they now knew that Mr. Sick and his money had given them hope, that they would not need to watch players whose skills, in a figurative sense, were scarcely good enough to keep them off a WPA project. For one thing, Mr. Sick had signed Fred Hutchinson, the Franklin High school kid, for a lusty bonus, and he had also signed Edo Vanni and Mike Budnick. To put it bluntly, the whole town went crazy over the new Rainiers.

They were even crazier when the Rainiers had their second opening day on June 15, 1938—that is, the official opening of Sicks' Seattle Stadium, out in Rainier Valley. This spanking new temple of baseball worship was built at a cost of $350,000 and was judged to be the finest minor league park in America.

On that opening night, the place was jammed because by now, the Rainiers were up there fighting in first division. Hutchinson, the 18-year-old schoolboy, was stringing together a remarkable number of victories, and the papers were full of his deeds. And Edo Vanni, also 18, was batting a merry clip and running wild on the base paths. On opening night, in fact, Edo got the first hit, stole the first base and scored the first run ever recorded in Sicks' Stadium.

That year, the Rainiers broke all attendance records and when the season ended, Hutchinson had won 25 games and Mr. Sick sold him to the Detroit Tigers for the then unheard-of sum of $50,000 and four players. Even the great Joe DiMaggio fetched only $25,000 when the New York Yankees brought him from San Francisco two years before. Edo Vanni had batted .332.

Then came the glory years. The rollicking Rainiers won the pennant three seasons in a row. Flushed with money and success, they featured a colorful cast consisting of Jo Jo White, Gilly Campbell, George Archie, Barrett, Turpin, Paul Gregory, Dick (The Darning Needle) Gyselman, and Bill Schuster, otherwise known as Schuster the Rooster, after his penchant for climbing the grandstand screen and crowing at the fans.

Oh, yes, they were a rollicking crew of winners. Barrett sold insurance on the side, and he would arrive at the ballpark, nattily dressed in a business suit, carrying his briefcase. Fortunately, the youth of Seattle did not know what was inside that briefcase. It contained a few papers, perhaps one pencil and two pints of Seagram's VO. "Do you ever drink that stuff during a game?" somebody once asked Dick. "It depends on how long the game is," Barrett said. Well, Barrett's games were always long because he usually ran the count to 3-and-2 before either walking or striking out the batter. This made for 3-1/2-hour games, and connoisseurs of baseball quickly noted that Barrett usually pitched on Saturday nights, a busy night for concessions. He was known as a "concessions pitcher," because fans had time to drink lots of Mr. Sick's beer when Barrett pitched.

Vanni continued as a hometown star, and there was much sentimental nonsense written about how Jo Jo White and Gilly Campbell nurtured the boy along with their sage advice. "Yes, they taught me a lot," Vanni would concede. It was years later before Edo amplified that tribute. He observed that they had taught him where to find the best nightclubs and how to sneak in after curfew at various hotels in the other seven cities of the Pacific Coast League.

One guy Vanni learned a lot from was Pepper Martin, who was the playing manager for Sacramento. Pepper came here for the opening day of 1942 season at Sicks' Stadium, and fans flocked out in droves to see "The Wild Horse of the Osage," as Grantland Rice had dubbed him when he played for the St. Louis Cardinals' famous "Gashouse Gang." Pepper was in the autumn of his great career, but he could still show kids like Vanni a thing or two about base-running and hitting. Pepper was immensely strong, built like a brick outhouse, and he was one of the few players in those days who took his Christianity seriously enough to go public with it, the way so many athletes do today.

The end of the glory years came in 1943. World War II and the military draft and defense plants took away so much of the talent that even I could make a team. Or so I thought. On that lovely April day at Sicks' Stadium I was in a vanguard of 4-F's who began the 1943 season. We played the San Francisco Seals, whom the legendary manager, Lefty O'Doul, had wisely stocked with players too old to be drafted.

I had a good seat for that one. I adorned the Rainiers' bench wearing No. 9, which was Edo Vanni's old number—but none of Edo's mercurial base-running talents rubbed off on me. Sent in as a pitcher-runner at second base, I was waved home ahead of a run-scoring single by Bill Lawrence, my boyhood idol of the old Indian days. Rounding third, I fell down. In front of 9,000 witnesses, I landed in a sprawling heap and crawled back to third base like a sand crab exposed to danger by a receding tide. Oh, the ignominy of it all! I was promptly fired the next day.

But the glory days returned to Sicks' Stadium not long after the Potsdam Conference. Once again the kids of Seattle had true heroes to worship. Charles Dillon "Casey" Stengel brought his Oakland Acorns to town; it was in 1948 that Stengel won the pennant with Oakland, after which he moved on to fame and eventual fortune as manager of the New York Yankees. But Casey was ours for one season, and it was Casey who defined, as well as anyone ever did, the art of managing a baseball team.

"The trick to running a baseball club," he said, "is to keep the five guys who hate you separated from the five who are undecided."

In those postwar years we thrilled to the playing of hometown luminaries like "Jungle Jim" Rivera, "Skinny" Brown, big Walter Judnich and such colorful opponents as Ferris "Cocky" Fain, Calvin Coolidge McLish, Minnie Minoso and Cletus Eldwood (Baron Boots) Poffenberger.

Then Fred Hutchinson returned to Seattle in 1955, after a long career in the major leagues. He was brought here by his old Franklin High School teammate, Dewey Soriano, who was by then the general manager of the Seattle Rainiers. Together they fashioned Seattle's last real Pacific Coast League pennant winner—a team solely owned by Emil Sick. But after that, attendance dwindled to crowds of 600 and 800; soon they were (alas) the Seattle Angels, owned outright by the California Angels.

The major league Pilots arrived in 1969, and there was much rejoicing among the populace. Parades of welcome were formed on opening day, and for one brief, exciting season, the Pilots performed in the American League. Major league at last! The Pilots were managed by genial Joe Schultz, who declared on opening day: "All right, gang, it's played with a round ball and a round bat and we gotta hit it square."

The Pilots, though they lasted here only one year before bankruptcy set in, were a colorful lot. It was the year that Mike Hegan, a young first baseman, told an interviewer after a road trip that "the toughest thing about baseball is trying to explain your wife why she needs a penicillin shot for your infected kidney."

Eight long years passed before another opening day came to Seattle. Not until 1977, when the Mariners arrived in the new Kingdome, had real baseball been part of the city. Since then it has been a checkered nine years of quarreling owners, pointing fingers, litigation and great public wailing about whether Seattle can support a major league team.

Salaries have now skyrocketed into the stratosphere. Where once our great stars, like Kewpie Dick Barrett and Jo Jo White, pleaded to get as much as $1,000 a month, new players, fresh young faces, are represented by agents who get them contracts of $300,000 or $400,000, and even higher.

But the strength of baseball is that no matter how they mismanage it, no matter how callous its owners seem, no matter how fan loyalty is used and abused, nothing ever destroys the game itself. Each spring brings a renewal of spirit, another season of hope, a rebirth of optimism and room for new heroes. The Mariners of this season are filled with young players and strong arms, kids with the blast and drive of youth in their legs, and within all of them, unspoken but alive, is the dream of Roy Hobbs: "I want people to say, 'There goes the best there ever was.' "

Something else has to be said about this enduring hold that baseball has on the people of America. It is, in large part, a loser's game. Most of major league baseball's 26 teams will, inevitably, lose more games than they win, and some will lose horrendously more than others. It has always been so. Yet it's a curious fact that some of the most popular teams, the ones remembered in song and story, were chronic losers like the Seattle Pilots and the Mariners, the old St. Louis Browns, the Brooklyn Dodgers of generations past, Connie Mack's hapless Philadelphia Athletics, and the early New York Mets.

The Mets of 1962 were loved far more than their cross-town rivals, the Yankees, but this was the most inept team of all time. The Mets lost 120 games in a single season! Jimmy Breslin tried to explain, via the Mets, America's affection for losing baseball teams.

"You see, the Mets are losers, just like everybody else in life," he wrote. "This is a team for the cab driver who gets held up and the guy who loses out on a promotion because he didn't maneuver himself to lunch with the boss enough.

"It is a team for every guy who has to get out of bed in the morning and go to work for short money on a job he does not like. And it is the team for every woman who looks up 10 years later and sees her husband eating dinner in a T-shirt and wonders how the hell she ever let this guy talk her into getting married. The Yankees? Who does well enough to root for them, Laurence Rockefeller?"

More than any other sport, baseball is a game of vivid, stop-action memory, which, because of its open expanse, freezes the action forever in one's mind. Football is a mass collision of bodies, and basketball's action has a sameness that dulls the senses. Not baseball.

Even as I look at this 42-year-old ball I hold in my hand, many scenes of that 1942 season are still fresh. Looking at the faded signatures, I can still envision Bill Lawrence, tall and graceful and swift, going back . . . back, back . . . taking in a long drive against the fence; I still see the flash of Eddie Carnett's yellow bat and Eddie rounding first base with that peculiar ducklike run he had, and Hal Suerne uncoiling out of his catcher's crouch to pick off a runner at first. Each of us has what Roger Angell calls our "interior stadium" in which lovely scenes are played over in our memories, ready to be called up again and again by nature's own videotape recorder.

And finally, there is the dimension of time. "This is the unique, unchangeable feature of baseball," says Angell, "and perhaps explains why this sport, for all the enormous changes it has undergone . . . remains somehow rustic, unviolent and introspective.

"Baseball's time is seamless and invisible, a bubble within which players move at exactly the same pace and rhythm as all their predecessors. This is the way the game was played in our youth and in our fathers' youth, and even back then—back in the country days—there must have been the same feeling that time could be stopped.

"Since baseball time is measured only in outs, all you have to do is succeed utterly; keep hitting, keep the rally alive, and you have defeated time. You remain forever young."

I first knew Fred Hutchinson when we were 15-year-old schoolboys together at Franklin High School. I was his catcher and he was the city's most prized pitching prospect. I don't know who got the idea at Sports Illustrated to send me to St. Louis to do a long profile on Hutch because I was "his onetime high school battery mate." I spent three weeks traveling and living with the St. Louis Cardinals, the team he managed, and while the result was passable, it firmed up my private resolution that I would never again go back to covering sports on a full-time basis.

Hutch was not easy. He was not eloquent. But when you had known him since boyhood you learned to interpret his long silences, to ask the right questions in the right way, to just "be" with him. He was always a leader, and at Franklin High there was a sort of "Hutch cult," kids who liked to hang out with him. The story on Hutch also illustrated the danger of knowing your subject too well: it's tough to write dispassionately, to maintain balance. No writer should ever attempt a long profile about someone he so admired and loved.

Fred Hutchinson

Sports Illustrated, August 26, 1957

FOUR MEN GATHERED LAST MONTH in Gussie Busch's plush office beneath the bright, clean, richly decorated grandstand of Busch Stadium, home of the St. Louis Cardinals. Three of the men were looking intently at the rock-hard face of Fred Hutchinson, a face that might have been hacked out by an angry sculptor with a dull chisel. Hutchinson, manager of the Cardinals, had called the three together. He spoke softly, so low that at times his words were almost inaudible.

The men who listened were August Anheuser Busch Jr., the baronial-born president of the Cardinals; and Richard A. Meyer, the team's executive vice-president and a ranking lieutenant in Busch's beer and baseball combine. Finally, there was General Manager Frank Lane, the stormy extrovert, a man of constant opinions, who seldom lowers his voice below a shout. These men are not accustomed to listening, but now they heard the manager out.

Hutchinson was quietly calling his bosses down on Gussie Busch's thick carpet. This was a month before the National League pennant race fell apart under the sudden weight of the Milwaukee Braves' ten-game winning streak, and the Cardinals were still eagerly fighting for the league lead. "You all want a pennant, and we can have it," he was saying. "We've got an outside chance. But I've got to be left alone to do my job. It's hard enough to fight the opposition on the field every day without answering to my own front office in the newspapers. Criticize me all you want. Second-guess me in private. I get paid to take that. But when your criticism hits every newspaper in the country, it can wreck the morale of this ball club. That's one thing we can't stand."

The meeting in Busch's office was the breaking point in a curious, panicky sort of pennant fever that gripped St. Louis in mid-July. Off to a slow start, the Cardinals abruptly burst three games in front of the five-team National League dogfight for first place. But, just as quickly, the lead disappeared. Four straight losses on an eastern road trip dropped the Cards into second place. Then the blowup came. In a final series game at Brooklyn on July 18, the Cardinals rallied for seven runs in the ninth inning to take a 9-4 lead. With one run across and the bases full of Dodgers, Hutchinson grimly ignored accepted baseball practice when he left Wilmer (Vinegar Bend) Mizell, a left-hander, in the game against Gil Hodges, Brooklyn's right-handed power hitter. Hodges slammed a bases-loaded home run to tie up the game 9-9, and Brooklyn went on to win 10-9 in 11 innings.

St. Louis fans exploded with outrage. Irate calls flooded newspapers, radio stations and the Cardinal office. Many demanded a change "while there's still time." Hutchinson made his own plight worse by barring the clubhouse door to St. Louis writers. Frank Lane, a volatile critic and enthusiastic second-guesser, openly raged at his manager's judgment. Meyer, the vice-president, publicly called the game "pitiful, tragic and disastrous." He also scorched Hutchinson for resting Alvin Dark in the ninth inning "when you know that Dark is the glue that holds the infield together and keeps the pitchers on their toes." Wire services carried stories quoting Lane and Meyer, hinting club dissension, a Cardinal collapse and the finish of Hutchinson.

None of this bothered Hutch except the public blasting he took from Meyer and Lane. A column by Al Abrams of the Pittsburgh Post-Gazette, which discussed the executive criticism of the Cardinal manager, triggered one of baseball's most violent tempers. Hutchinson searched out Al Fleishman of the Fleishman-Hillard public relations firm, which handles the Anheuser-Busch account. "How much of this can a man stand!" roared Hutchinson, hands raised and fists clenched in controlled fury. "Get 'em all together before they wreck us!" Fleishman paled, then helped arrange the meeting in St. Louis. It lasted only 20 minutes. And Hutchinson, a man whose tantrums have shattered the furniture in a dozen clubhouses, was calm and forceful in the way he made his point: "Let me alone to do my job." Then he walked out of Gussie Busch's office and continued doing his job, which, despite an inexplicable midseason hitting slump that plunged his team into a nine-game losing streak, had kept the Cardinals, 10-1 outsiders in spring handicaps, a persistent second in the wildest National League pennant race in decades.

Of all the 16 major league baseball managers, Hutchinson is perhaps the least known, the least understood. American Leaguers remember him as a plate-shaving control pitcher, a murderously grim and intelligent competitor; or they remember him as a firm, diplomatic player representative, who helped gain or preserve such benefits as minimum salaries, training-camp expenses and pension funds. And in Detroit they remember him as a young and successful manager, who turned his back on a $40,000 contract to go back and manage in his home town of Seattle.

But St. Louis doesn't know him well. For two years Hutchinson has worked quietly under the publicized, player-swapping Frank Lane and wealthy, flamboyant Gussie Busch. Unlike either Lane or Busch, Hutchinson rarely indulges the private luxury of merely listening to his own voice. Off the field, he is gentle, affable, even courtly. But on his own professional grounds, where success is determined by an uncompromising scoreboard, he shows little except a monumental rage to win.

Hutchinson looks at the world through an angry scowl, but this is partly a facade. "He's really kind of a happy guy inside," says Joe Garagiola, former Cardinal catcher, now a St. Louis television commentator, "only his face doesn't know it." Some of baseball's best quips have bounced off the stony Hutchinson exterior. He can't find it in himself to laugh when he doesn't feel the joke. Nor can his thin, compressed lips form the safe, comfortable "yes" if what he really thinks is "no." Some time ago, Owner Busch developed a fondness for a certain player on the Cardinal roster. His fondness bordered on an outright order to play him in the Cardinal lineup.

Hutchinson studied his boss, who rarely hears a "no" from a subordinate. "Mr. Busch," he said, "do you want me to say what I really think, or what you want to hear? If I wanted to play a clown, I'd go hire Emmett Kelly." With that, he stalked out of the room.

After a moment of silence, Frank Lane turned to the Cardinal owner. "Mr. Busch," he said, "that man is worth a million dollars to you, because he always tells you the truth."

Such nicknames as "Sphinx-Face," "The Moose" and "The Bear" have been applied to Hutchinson, but none have quite stuck. "The Bear" is currently popular in St. Louis, and curiously fitting. During games, Hutchinson, a square-set man of 6 feet 2, weighing 200 pounds, paces restlessly in the pine-green dugout of Busch Stadium, hunched slightly forward, his huge hands nervously rattling a few of the white pebbles that line the outer rim of the field.

Frequently, the frustration of losing a close game touches off wild, demonstrative rages. He has broken water coolers, stools, light bulbs, and once—last year in Cincinnati—he hammered his own fists against a board-covered concrete wall until his knuckles were bloody and swollen. But his rages are rarely directed at an individual player; knowing his own temper, Hutchinson makes it a private rule to wait until the next day to chew out a player for his mistake. Sarcasm, the goading tool of many baseball managers, is not part of Hutchinson's nature. His bluntness is deceptively simple.

"When I first came here," he once said, "I kept hearing about how this pitcher couldn't pitch in Brooklyn, that pitcher couldn't pitch in Philadelphia and how somebody else was effective at home. One guy couldn't hit against a certain background and somebody else got a bellyache in Chicago. The hell with that. I want men. I want big leaguers, guys who grind and fight until somebody gives in, guys who can play every day under all kinds of conditions."

One of the arts in managing a modern major league baseball team over a long, crisis-ridden season is the art of patience—and patience is Hutchinson's paradox. The man of a short-fused temper has an amazing reservoir of restraint with young players and a deep compassion for ballplayers as a group. The answer may be that Hutchinson, who brought to baseball pitching no blazing natural equipment, understands the degree of difficulty baseball presents. For the loud-talking grandstand critics, he has only contempt. "They've never been there," he says. "Never crossed those white lines. What do they know? Do they know what it's like to hit against Newcombe, or bunt against him with Hodges coming down your throat? Hell, anybody can play ball in a saloon!"

If you will examine the esprit de corps of the Cardinals, it must be done among the men who play for Hutchinson. They dress a few yards away from the Busch Stadium executive offices, in a long, immaculate, blue-tiled dressing room, complete with a hi-fi record player. Musial sits in front of locker No. 6, sorting his usual large stack of mail. Dressing next to Musial is Del Ennis, a broad, heavy man who is built for all the world like one of Anheuser-Busch's famed Clydesdales. At one end of the narrow room a group of the younger players listen to some hillbilly songs (the words composed by Catcher Hal Smith). At the other end is Doc Bauman's glistening white training room, where Sam Jones, the resurrected curve-ball artist, is getting a shoulder rub.

Musial, holding his box of mail across his bare legs, talks slowly, choosing his words carefully. "Essentially," he says, "this team will stand or fall on its young players. Hutchinson is patient with them, knows how to use them. You'll never hear him taking credit.. He never does that. But he brings out the best in us, because everything's out on the table with him."

Musial pauses, shuffles through his stack of mail for perhaps 30 seconds, then adds: "Let's put in this way: If I ever hear a player say he can't play for Hutch, then I'll know he can't play for anybody."

Doc Bauman, who has trained both the Browns and the Cardinals, working under all types of managers, sits on the black-surfaced rubbing table. A sensitive, intelligent man, Bauman speaks with emotion.

"I'd have to go far back in my memory to recall a finer man. I've seen him leave the clubhouse for a few minutes and stop to ask the clubhouse boy if he could bring him back a sandwich. He's got real humility.

"Some of these guys—and I've seen them—they get to be a manager and right away they have to prove they're big men. They're quick to take credit for anything good a ballplayer does. But Hutch never does that, and these players respect him for it. He goes right on being himself, same to everybody, because he is a big man. I don't know how to say it"—Bauman shakes his head—"he's humble, he's kind, he's strict and he's tough. He's all these things in one man."

Out on the bench Alvin Dark, 34 years old, sits slouched, staring out across the diamond at the socko-red-and-green grandstand of Busch Stadium, and speaks with his soft Louisiana drawl.

"I saw where the front office blasted him for taking me out of that game in Brooklyn," Dark says. He holds up the forefinger of his throwing hand, which had a piece of tape glued over the nail. "I had this bad finger. It was the only time I ever asked to be taken out of a game in my life. So he got blasted for taking me out. But he never once opened his mouth to explain. That's the kind of a man he is."

Hutch looks deep into a player to decide those who deserve his patience. "There's no secret to it," he once said. "A man is what he is, way back. I don't mean when he's 18 or 19, but long before that. It's deep in his makeup and nobody is going do to much about changing it."

Fred Hutchinson, 38, is his own best example. His high school coach, Ralph (Pop) Reed, remembers the way he stood on the Emerson grade school playfield, in Seattle, his catcher's mask pushed back over a shock of curly red hair, his face twisted in thin-lipped anger, eyes narrowed, arguing with an umpire. He was only 10 years old. "When I saw him stand up and have it out with an adult umpire," says Pop Reed, "I knew that here was a real competitor. The thing that impressed me was that he wasn't just shooting off his mouth. He was right and he knew it, and he had courage enough to say what he thought. He was already a tough, thinking ballplayer."

Hutchinson is the youngest son of a prominent Seattle family which settled in the Rainier Beach district near Lake Washington. His father, Dr. J. L. Hutchinson, who died a few years ago, was a prominent physician and surgeon. His oldest brother, Dr. William B. Hutchinson, is one of Seattle's leading chest and abdominal surgeons. Middle brother John is a full professor of physical education at Columbia University. Both of Fred's older brothers had a brief fling at professional baseball and they decided, even when Fred was tiny, that he would be the best athlete in the Hutchinson family.

Together they would stand Fred up against a garage door and fire tennis balls at him, taught him how to hit left-handed with a broomstick. They worked on him by the hour, coached him incessantly and, by his freshman year at Franklin High School, when he first reported to Pop Reed, he had the poise of a veteran. In his sophomore year, Hutch turned to pitching. Immensely strong as a youngster, Fred could almost lose a baseball in his huge hand, yet he never became an overpowering pitcher. His chief weapons were amazing control, a natural sinker, a short, choppy curve and a thoroughly domesticated change-of-pace. Those were his weapons, plus fine baseball instinct and a consuming desire to win.

Pop Reed, an acutely perceptive man, who now lives in semi-retirement in Long Beach, Calif., still keeps in close touch with professional baseball. Says Reed: "If baseball wasn't a competitive sport—if it was just something you did for exercise—I don't think Fred would be interested in it. Looking back on it, I think he may very well be the greatest competitor baseball has ever produced."

In three years as a schoolboy pitcher, Hutchinson won 60 games, lost only two, yet major league scouts, almost to a man, shied away from his mediocre fast ball and wrinkly curve. The Seattle Rainiers, newly renovated under wealthy brewer Emil Sick, signed Hutchinson for $2,500 and 20% of any sales price that might result with a big league club.

It developed into one of baseball's most celebrated deals. As an 18-year-old in 1938, Hutch won 25 games for Seattle. Ball parks were jammed with fans, curious to watch this calm, dead-faced youngster deftly handle the league's best hitters with his uncanny control. The inevitable club-house lawyers, attuned to the big crowds, urged Hutch to demand an increase over his $250-a-month salary. But Fred's father, the distinguished, goateed Dr. Hutchinson, got wind of the move. "By the Lord, you're a Hutchinson!" he thundered. "You made a bargain and you'll stick to it—or you can pack up and move out right now." Hutch stuck with the bargain, and when the season was over he was named the league's Most Valuable Player by the St. Louis Sporting News.

That winter Hutch was sold to Detroit in a deal worth $100,000 to the Rainiers ($20,000 to Hutch). Hutch's entry into the major leagues was no instant success.

Big league hitters gleefully hammered his limited pitching stuff. Almost instantly, he was branded a "$100,000 lemon." Indeed, Hutch spent two more seasons in the minors, at Toledo, then Buffalo (where he won 26 games in 1941), with only brief periods at Detroit before entering the Navy for a four-year term in 1941. It was only in the postwar baseball years that he became established as a big league pitcher. He became a steady winner, but worked in the elegant shadow of such Detroit greats as Hal Newhouser and Dizzy Trout. But Hutch's intense combativeness and accomplished pinch-hitting made him a favorite among Detroit fans. His displays of temper became legendary in the American league. "I always know how Hutch did when we follow Detroit into a town." cracked Yankee Catcher Yogi Berra. "If we got stools in the dressing room, I know he won. If we got kindling, he lost."

His clashes with umpires were frequent. Once, after he was tossed out of a game by Umpire Bill McKinley, reporters sought him out in the Briggs Stadium dressing room. "You can say for me," Hutch growled, "that they shot the wrong McKinley." His manager for several years was Steve O'Neill, a man he still worships, and from whom, one gathers, he learned the virtue of patience with young players. "If I needed one game on which my whole season was based," O'Neill used to say, "if my career depended on that single victory, I'd pick Hutch to pitch it for me."

Detroit players elected Hutchinson player representative in 1947; a year later he became the American League representative, a post he held until midseason of 1952, when Walter O. (Spike) Briggs, the Detroit president, picked him out of the ranks to succeed Red Rolfe as manager. In 2-1/2 years as boss of the Tigers he moved the club from last to sixth to a single game out of first division. Then, in a typically stubborn Hutchinson gesture, he quit his $40,000-a-year job. Long aware that he wasn't being consulted on player deals or inner council planning, Hutchinson demanded a two-year contract.

A few days later, after a meeting of the Detroit board of directors, Briggs telephoned Hutchinson at his home. "It's a club policy," he said. "One year is all we can do."

"Then I'm turning it down," Hutch replied.

At less than half his Detroit salary, Hutchinson went back to Seattle, where he signed a three-year contract to manage Emil Sick's Rainiers. His old high school teammate and close friend, Dewey Soriano, by now was general manager of the Rainiers. Together, they ripped apart a fifth-place roster, made 67 separate player deals and turned out a winner. Without a regular .300 hitter or a 20-game-winning pitcher, Hutchinson juggled his lineup almost daily (he used eight second basemen during the season) and finished in front of second-place San Diego by three games. Pacific Coast League baseball writers elected him Manager of the Year.

One of Hutch's spot-winners on the Rainiers, Old Pro Larry Jansen, paid his manager a pitcher's definitive baseball tribute: "I never saw a better man with pitchers. Hutch saved half a dozen games by moving his pitchers at the right time. He was almost psychic."

Frank Lane, meanwhile, had taken over as general manager of the Cardinals, who had steadily declined from third to sixth to seventh in three years of Gussie Busch's ownership. "I knew we were going to have to build with young players," Lane says now, "and I needed a manager who could handle them." When Lane proposed Fred Hutchinson as manager of the Cardinals, Gussie Busch's reaction was typical of a relative newcomer in baseball. "Who's Hutchinson?" he wanted to know.

Even today, Gussie Busch sounds vaguely bewildered when he discusses his manager. "He doesn't say much," says Busch, "and he's the kind of man who won't say anything he doesn't believe. I've found that out. Sometimes I think he's made mistakes in strategy, and I think the press rode him kind of hard about that Mizell incident in Brooklyn. Certainly, I disagreed with him. But Hutch has the courage of his convictions. We all admire that."

To Frank Lane, the selection of Hutchinson to boss the Cardinals was obvious. "Did you notice his conduct at Detroit?" Lane asks. "He left because he couldn't be a puppet. But even when they treated him like one, he was never disloyal. Never tried to justify himself, and he didn't sound off about his troubles. And even when they wanted him back, he walked out. He never carped or complained or criticized. He's all man."

Lane thought a moment and continued: "Hutch has a rough, tough demeanor, but he has that damnable patience. I've even accused him of being a character-builder. I cuss him out from the stands because I'm that way—when I've got anything to say, I tell the world about it. I don't think Hutch has ever experienced fear in his life. In a way, that's a minus factor in his makeup. He applies it as a yardstick to his players.

"As a strategist," concluded Lane, "I think he's unimaginative, but he goes right on getting results. Hutch just won't 'yes' anybody."

Bob Broeg, veteran St. Louis Post-Dispatch baseball writer, summed up Hutchinson in part when he wrote that he is "a man who has a way with men . . . who makes no pretense of maneuvering or manipulating with the winking wisdom of Casey Stengel, the mysticism of a Paul Richards, the daring of a Leo Durocher or the bravado of a Charley Dressen.

"If, as a tactician, Hutchinson is uninspired, he has the rich quality of holding the confidence and loyalty of his players, a combination that has produced a team spirit the club knew under neither of his immediate predecessors, Harry Walker and Eddie Stanky. The Cardinals like their rugged manager . . . he has the players believing they can win."

To all of it—the bombast, the criticism, the tributes and the vague half-truths he hears and reads about himself—Hutchinson is stoically realistic. He knows that each day, as the National League battle for supremacy approaches its September climax, that each day will bring the pleasant, temporary pleasure in winning, or the boiling, inner sickness of defeat. "You have to love misery to do this," he once said. In the few hours of respite between games, Hutchinson is relaxed and sometimes warmly communicative. Now he was sitting in a cool, near-empty St. Louis cafe, late after a night game the Cardinals had won.

He was scowling, and the four heavy lines across his forehead deepened. He cracked ice hard with his teeth, a faintly disturbing habit, and his long jaw muscles bulged. His once-red hair is now a dark brown, peppered with gray, and the sharp lines down each side of his face, the strong, prominent chin and the thin, pulled-down mouth give him a look of perpetual, sad toughness. Then he began to talk, in the heavy deep voice that makes a listener strain to hear.

"The important thing is not to panic," he said, staring into his half-empty glass. "You have to grind, day after day, and forget about yesterday. The easiest thing to do is second-guess, but the worst thing to do is to second-guess yourself. Then you panic.

"Lane gets excited. They all get excited. I don't mind it from Lane, because he's always been that way. He dies on every pitch. Funny thing about Lane, the way he cusses the ballplayers out and jumps on me from the stands. If anybody else did that to us, I think he'd fight."

Hutchinson turned his glass, spilled another piece of ice in his mouth and cracked down hard with his teeth. Then he talked again: "The big guy with us is Dark. He's making a winner out of Blasingame. You don't see those things from the stands, but every day I see Blasingame get better because Dark is showing him how to win. Musial you don't have to manage. What can a manager do for him?

"The pitching—maybe I could take credit for that. That thing with Mizell in Brooklyn, I just wanted to get him over a hump. Sometimes that's all it takes—a man gets over a rough time and he goes on from there." Hutchinson gave a short laugh. "Guys ask me about Von McDaniel. What did I do for him? I just put him in there and he came through. Could I take credit for that?

"I try to make a ballplayer believe in himself, and the only way you can do that is to give him a chance. If he plays his way out of the lineup, then you try somebody else. And if you haven't got 'em, you're dead. I seldom read the newspapers. If we won, I know how. If we lost, reading about it won't get the game back."

A man and woman stopped by the table and spoke to Hutchinson about the Cardinals. They wished him luck and went away. "People like that are the ones I like," he said. "They didn't ask for anything, or tell me how to run things. There are thousands like that." There was one piece of ice left in the glass and Hutchinson put it in his mouth. He cracked it, then spoke again.

"You know, I didn't always agree with Harry Truman," he said. "But when they were firing at him, you never saw him pull back. The little man from Missouri never put his foot in the bucket. They wrote him off in 1948, and he was the only one who believed in himself. He went out among the people and scratched for it. He didn't flinch or run to hide. He knew how to win."

There was a long period of silence. Hutchinson scowled into his empty glass. The light strains of the French melody *La Seine* came through on the piped-in music, disturbed slightly by a rattle of glasses, making the scene of the realistic, intense man, speaking out his thoughts, seem incongruous.

"We haven't got the best club," he was saying, "but they believe in themselves. They go out every day and grind. Baseball doesn't have many naturals, a lot less than you might imagine.

"The ones who work hardest are the ones who make it, the ones who win. Sometimes that's the only difference. If you don't work hard at this game, you might as well hang them up. Sweat is your only salvation."

▼

To a writer, someone who is "wonderful" is the person who can produce great material; writers love scoundrels. Jack Hurley was wonderful only in the sense of his publicity gall, and he was the kind of scoundrel who would never land in jail but would not be permitted entry to any private club.

Hurley was a fight manager of the old school, the kind that flourished in the early part of this century and throughout the 1920s and 1930s. We used to call him "reasonably honest Jack," or "the Deacon." He was a propagandist on behalf of his fighters but mostly for himself. I owe a lot to this cantankerous, dyspeptic, colorful, conniving semi-scoundrel.

I wrote a lot about him because he practically got me syndicated. Each time a column of mine appeared on his behalf, or his fighter's, he would buy hundreds of newspapers and mail them to editors and writers across the country. Because of this, and for no other reason, I became kind of a Northwest celebrity. In addition, I sold numerous magazine stories on the Deacon and his doings, which added up to enough dough to get my oldest daughter through college.

Jack Hurley

Seattle Post-Intelligencer, September 6, 1963

WITH NOTHING MUCH ELSE TO DO THE OTHER DAY, I wandered over to the Olympic Hotel and split a rheumatism pill with Jack Hurley. Things have not been going so well, either with Hurley or Seattle, the difference being that Hurley knows why. The town's ball club can't draw, promoters are thinking of dropping the summer pro football game and the restaurant and night club owners are wringing their hands over empty tablecloths. Even since Von's closed, Hurley has been a man without roots, so to speak. "No night people anymore," he moaned. "They've closed down the cardrooms and the pinball games and now you don't see any night people around. I eat my main meal at midnight. Have you ever tried to eat a good dinner at midnight? There's one Chinese joint up here that stays open, but I got Chinese food running out of my ears."

The city's most determined hypochondriac admitted (somewhat sheepishly) that he has given up drinking and smoking. "Woke up one morning and one hand wouldn't work and the doctor said that was from drinking," he said. "Well, the other day I was watching 'em dig that hole for the Olympic parking garage and I got dizzy and nearly fell in. Hell of a way to go. I went back to the doctor and said, 'Look, I guess I just had a heart attack.' He said, 'No, no, you got inflammation of the middle ear.' So now, when I get dizzy I just go lean up against the side of a building for a while. Let a new disease spring up and I guarantee I'll have it in 24 hours."

Hurley's business, which is boxing, is dead, killed off by television. The game, he says, is infested with amateurs and former streetcar conductors. "That's the real reason for all our troubles," he said. "Free TV. That **&&!; free TV. It's broken boxing, it's breaking the theatres, ruined the nightclubs and loused up the restaurants. It's even bankrupted the transit system." This was news to me—that the transit system is bankrupt—but Hurley says it's true, so I assume Lloyd Graber is looking for a job.

"TV is the most terrible thing that's happened to the human race," he said. "People don't go no place, they don't spend no money. They see so much for nothing for so long, now they don't want to pay for anything. No money left in this town, anyway. I was talking to Tom Gildersleve the other day and he said things were slow. I said, sure they're slow. This town just had a World's Fair and it's the history of World's Fairs that a town goes to pot for two years after you have 'em.

"Why, that World's Fair was the biggest swindle ever put over. They lied about the attendance and then they said it broke even. What a laugh. Outside money put up a lot of those things, and those guys got their money out and left. It's a terrible thing!"

The man they call the Deacon polished off the last of two soft-boiled eggs (it was 1 o'clock, first meal of the day) and we went out past the Grand Ballroom, where the Rotarians, or somebody, were having a meeting. "Look at that," Hurley said, pointing at a man's hat in the corner. "I'll tell you about that hat later. Let's go outside where I can have a chew of Mail Pouch." We stood on the corner of 5th and University, second-guessed the engineers of the new IBM Building, and went on talking about the town.

"You want to know what's the matter with this place?" he said, peering over his glasses indignantly. When Hurley gets indignant, his face takes on a prissy, disapproving look, like a minister who has just caught a choir boy with a copy of Confidential. "The trouble with this town is that it's run by amateurs. I tell you, we are in the hands of the Philistines. This town gets nervous with professionals around. It don't want to pay good people for guidance, so the amateurs run it."

Seattle, according to Hurley, is a town full of dreamers. The trouble is, he says, they're the wrong kind of dreamers. "They dream of big things, always talking about big things," he declared, "but they won't put their money where their mouths are. A bunch of &**!%!! freeloaders."

Hurley shifted position and changed the subject. "Lookit that," he said, gazing at the beginnings of the IBM Building. "No structural steel. That thing's going to be 20 stories high, and no structural steel. Maybe they know what they're doing, but I don't trust 'em. First earthquake, and over it goes.

"No place," he continued, "is worth a damn without a little larceny. You gotta have larceny to make things go. Ever stop to think that nothing would ever be accomplished in the whole world if there wasn't something for somebody to steal? It takes larceny to make a town go, but this town is full of amateurs. It'd be a terrible drab world if we didn't need police departments. I don't know, maybe I'll have to get out of this town. I got a call from my brother in Fargo and he wants me to come back and help him run a religious bookstore. The trouble is, Fargo doesn't have any restaurants open after midnight either. I guess things are bad all over."

Hurley sprayed the curb with Mail Pouch, looked up at the IBM Building with a look that made you expect it to collapse in a heap, and shrugged sadly. "Oh, I forget to tell you about that hat, that one we saw sitting on the floor in the corner. That guy, that Rotarian, he put that hat in the corner so he wouldn't have to check it. If he went up and checked it, he might be shamed into giving the girl a dime. That's what's wrong with this town. Good day."

In many ways, Harry (Kid) Matthews, a blown-up middleweight fighter, was Deacon Jack Hurley's finest creation. Because they were good and colorful, they got me into The Saturday Evening Post. Again, I acknowledge my literary (and financial) debt to Jack Hurley, the old con-artist. As for Matthews, who now lives and works in Everett, he was one of the nicest athletes I ever knew.

Harry (Kid) Matthews

Saturday Evening Post, March 22, 1952

EXCEPT FOR ONE CIRCUMSTANCE, Harry Matthews, a twenty-nine-year-old resident of Seattle, Washington, would be a thoroughly commonplace man. He lives a quiet middle-class life in a quiet middle-class neighborhood. He has a modest five-room brick bungalow and a modest two-year-old car. The only women in his life are his wife and two daughters. The only parties he attends are banquets in his honor, and the last time he took a drink was in New Guinea on V-E Day, when the boys celebrated by brewing up an explosive potion called "jungle juice." It made Harry very sick.

The one unusual thing about Harry Matthews is that he is a prize-fighter, and a good one. In fact, he is one of the hottest items in the fight game today. Many authorities think that all he has to do to become light-heavyweight champion is to get into the ring with Joey Maxim, and some feel that he could take Jersey Joe Walcott's heavyweight crown.

Under the shrewd handling of Jack Hurley, the salty old-timer who now manages him, Harry (Kid) Matthews has become a sports hero in the Pacific Northwest, and a rising gate attraction in other parts of the country. Operating mostly without benefit of New York City, the International Boxing Club or the television cables, and campaigning in places like Omaha, San Francisco, Boise, Portland, Seattle, St. Paul and Cleveland, he grossed more than $150,000 last year. With the probable exceptions of Sugar Ray Robinson, Ezzard Charles and Joe Louis, no other fighter drew so much money in 1951.

Matthews also drew such kudos as an award from the West Seattle Commercial Club for "outstanding citizenship," and a statement by a Presbyterian minister that "If I had a son, I would want him to grow up and be like Harry Matthews." A character rating like this, while admirable, is not ordinarily the sort to inflame the imagination of the fight public. Harry Matthews is in no way colorful. But he has one important quality, skillfully developed and exploited by manager Hurley, which makes him a standout among today's crop of boxers. He really knows how to fight.

Yet less than three years ago, nearing the age of twenty-seven, he was getting nowhere, and just about ready to hang up the gloves. He had been winning, but seldom in a manner to excite the customers. He was making so little money that he had to work as a mechanic between fights to support his family properly. You may wonder why he stayed at it. You may wonder how a fellow like this ever got into the fight game in the first place.

The answer is simple. Harry Matthews is a prize-fighter because his blacksmith father raised him to be one. From Harry's childhood, the father kept telling people around Ola, Idaho, that the boy was going to be a champion. Older boys baited Harry cruelly. "So you're the great fighter!" they would say. "You wanna fight me?"

More often than not, Harry would run away. But his father persisted. Today Harry Matthews doesn't run away from anybody.

For quite a while he was one of those spoilers the big-name fighters avoid, on the theory that they might lose and wouldn't get enough money to make the risk worth while. Now that Matthews is an established gate attraction, top men are eager to split big purses with him—although not, as yet, on terms satisfactory to manager Hurley. Hurley has been holding out for a bigger cut than he has been offered to send Matthews against Joey Maxim. As for Jersey Joe Walcott, that venerable champion would gladly have signed for a title defense against Matthews if he had not been stymied by contract commitments to give Ezzard Charles first whack.

Why did it take Harry so long to reach the top? He was almost there as long ago as 1940, when he was not yet eighteen. Tony Zale, who had recently won National Boxing Association recognition as middleweight champion by defeating Al Hostak, was out in Seattle to give Hostak a return match. Harry Matthews was then a promising young middle-weight, strong and aggressive, with a record of sixteen straight wins—ten of them knockouts.

Nate Druxman, promoter of the Zale-Hostak fight, suggested Matthews as a sparring partner for Zale. "For two bucks a round you can work with a champion," Nate told young Harry. "Be careful in there, and the experience will do you good."

Two rounds and four dollars later, Sam Pian, Zale's manager, stormed into Druxman's office.

"What the thus-and-such are you trying to pull?" he demanded. "You want to wreck the fight? Why, that punk, that —"

"Matthews?" Druxman inquired, looking hurt.

"Get him out of here!" snapped Pian.

Druxman found Matthews—already detached from the Zale camp and counting his severance pay—and explained that it was considered neither good diplomacy nor good business to rough up a champion three days before a sell-out fight. The lecture lasted several minutes.

"I just messed him around a little," Matthews said sheepishly. "He's not hurt."

Druxman mumbled a final warning to his protégé and turned to leave.

"Nate," Harry called.

"Yeah?"

"Get him for me, Nate. I could kill him."

This statement—which Harry never got a chance to prove—was one of the few he has ever made which fell short of complete modesty. Outside the ring, although not inside it, he is the humblest and mildest of men. "Harry Matthews could demand $30,000 today just for fighting temptation," Seattle promoter Jimmy Fitten has said, "except that he hasn't got enough bad habits to make it a contest."

To judge by Harry's handsome, unmarked face, he has never fought anything more punishing than temptation. The terrain around his sharp chin, deep-set, narrow eyes and fairly prominent ears is completely free of battle scars. A slight deviation at the bridge of his nose is his only souvenir from 101 professional bouts. He has lost only three fights in his entire lifetime. Sixty of his victories ended in knockouts. At a recent count, he had gone sixty-seven straight fights without a defeat.

However, he started off under the managership of his father, Lou Matthews, who died shortly before the Zale episode. Then Harry drifted into a long period of mediocrity, under a succession of managers and advisers whose chief contribution was too turn a hard-punching, crowd-pleasing fighter into the type that inspires yawns.

Another answer to Matthews' mysterious decline may be that the characteristics which make him a good friend, neighbor, father and husband were the very things that betrayed him as a boxer. "Harry is always afraid of hurting somebody's feelings," says his wife. During the lengthy doldrums of his career he absorbed all shades of opinion. He would take advice on fighting from a carhop.

What snapped him out of it? A psychiatrist might reason that the whole cycle stems from Harry's boyhood under his strong, domineering father. The father demanded strict obedience, constantly prodded Harry into boxing. To please his father, Harry became an adept fighter. Then his father died. Without really knowing why, Harry slid back as a boxer.

Later in life, when he came under the guidance of a man with character traits similar to those of his parent, Harry reacted toward that man as he had toward his father. Once more he was trying to please father, and again he became a good fighter.

Take that explanation or leave it, but there is no denying that a second "father" in Harry's boxing life has come along in the person of manager John Cornelius (Jack) Hurley, a master politician of the fight business, who once managed Billy Petrolle, the old Fargo Express, to boxing immortality and a $247,000 bank account. Tall, lean and distinguished-looking, Hurley might be taken for a professor or a deacon until he opens his mouth, which is frequently. Jack was recovering from the effects of managing the late Vince Foster, a welterweight with the social tendencies of a headhunter, when the quiet, easy-to-handle Matthews came along.

"Jack is known as a great teacher and press agent," said an Eastern boxing writer recently, "and that kind is scarce today. He's the last of a colorful gang of independent fight managers who really work at their trade. But there's one other unique thing about Jack—he's honest."

By the time Matthews met Hurley, Harry had deteriorated into what Jack describes as "the stab-grab-and-apologize type." In solemn truth, the average promoter could assure himself an evening of virtual solitude by booking a Matthews main event. On April 28, 1949, Harry broke a hand while beating Henry Lee before a small, apathetic audience in Seattle. A few days later his contract with his manager, Bert Forbes, expired, and Harry was considered through.

"I was sick of the fight game and sick of myself," Matthews testifies today. "I was tired of small-time purses and managers who couldn't help me. But I still had that urge, that ambition to be a good fighter. Maybe it was pride, or just dumbness, I don't know. Two people—my wife Jo and Sammy Casmir, a tailor here in Seattle—urged me to go see Hurley. Sammy knows Hurley from years back, and Josie knew I'd never by happy as long as I was a failure as a fighter."

Matthews and Casmir, piloting Harry's old car, drove to Chicago and looked up Hurley. Matthews now admits he took an active dislike to the manager, whose opening gibes were hard on the one thing he had left—his pride. Hurley arranged an "audition" at Chicago's Marigold Gardens, booking Harry in a main event with one George Sherman, whom he decisioned in ten rounds. Afterward Matthews asked Hurley what he thought of the fight.

"Fight?" Hurley rasped. "Hell, you can't even spell fight. You call that a fight? Why, you couldn't get arrested for doing that in the street. In a few weeks maybe. I can help you. In three months I can make a fair fighter out of you. In six months, maybe a good one. I'll pay all expenses, but you do what I tell you."

Matthews swallowed his pride and put himself in Hurley's hands. He had been on a two-meal-a-day diet, designed to keep him among the middleweights. Hurley ordered him to start eating with both hands, if necessary, to put on weight. Harry shot up to 175 pounds.

He embarked on a difficult schooling program. "I had to unlearn him everything," Hurley says.

Hurley had a harness constructed which would tie either hand to Harry's side, allowing him only to hook. Matthews often went in against sparring partners with a glove on one hand and the other strapped down. Gradually he learned to slip punches and be in position to throw one back. He became a counterpuncher.

Matthews now discusses "leverage and balance" in a clinical manner. The turning point in his re-education occurred on December 7, 1949, two months after the apprenticeship began. Harry was fighting a light-heavyweight named Bill Davis in Omaha. Davis came out jabbing in the classic manner. Matthews traded jabs for a minute, slowing the pace down. Davis suddenly darted in with a good left. Harry leaned a fraction inside the punch and whistled a murderous left hook to Davis's jaw. Billy stiffened and toppled to the floor for the count.

Harry returned to his corner, white as the canvas. "Is that all there is to it?" he asked.

This episode rated no more than an agate line of type under Fights Last Night in most of the country's newspapers, but it was the key phase in the remarkable transformation of Harry Matthews. He began to feel power and confidence. In a little more than two years Matthews registered thirty-one straight victories, twenty-six of which got the fans home early. He averaged only 4.3 rounds of work per opponent.

Matthews seldom talks about his fighting, but he once made a revealing observation to a friend, Ruel Vann, about his newly developed "killer instinct."

"I never dreamed money could come as easy as it's coming now." he said. "I mean, no more seven o'clock in the morning and lunch pails. When I see a man across the ring, he represents a sort of danger to the way I'm living, and I want him on the floor."

The hotter Matthews got, the hotter the fire Jack Hurley was able to build under the dominant promotional power in the fight game, the International Boxing Club. The Matthews-Hurley crusade against the IBC has been one part financial and one part moral, with emphasis on the financial. Actually, the big reason Matthews hasn't fought under IBC auspices is Hurley's insistence on a greater share of television and gate receipts. Hurley says he fell from grace with the IBC when it was first formed in 1949, and he refused a post he had previously filled for the better part of twelve years—matchmaker at Chicago Stadium.

A few months later, after the Billy Davis fight in Omaha, Hurley took Matthews to New York in search of a Madison Square Garden fight.

"We needed the work bad," relates Hurley. "I went to Al Weill, the IBC matchmaker, and asked for a semifinal bout on the Garden's regular card. The standard purse was $1500. Weill turned me down, said he was booked solid for weeks."

Hurley then tried his luck with Harry Markson, managing director of the IBC, with no success. Finally he talked to Jim Norris, the IBC president. Norris also turned him down.

Hurley, a matchmaker himself for years, says, "I knew I was getting the freeze. I told Norris, 'Forget I asked you. Forget I came here. But you'll be asking for Harry Matthews someday. You'll get Harry Matthews in your hair from this day on. You'll have to have him, because I'm going to take Harry Matthews out in the sticks and build him up the hard way. And when you want him, Jim, you're going to have to pay—right through the nose. This guy is going to cost you.'"

In the tactical war that ensued, Matthews campaigned vigorously around the Northwest. He beat nobody of championship stature, but Hurley made the most of the victories. After each knockout, Hurley would buy as many as 200 copies of the local papers, clip mentions of Matthews, and mail them to sportswriters, broadcasters and other people of influence.

It became common talk on the sports pages, especially those west of the Rockies, that Hurley couldn't get a fight in Madison Square Garden because he wouldn't give any of the IBC crowd a cut of Matthews. At last, early in 1951, Matthews got a Garden fight with Irish Bob Murphy, one of the prize tigers on the IBC leash. Murphy had a string of fifty-eight consecutive victories, fifty by knockouts.

It was said that matchmaker Weill wanted to get Matthews knocked off, and also that Weill had run out of box-office opponents for Murphy. The fight was one of the most satisfying brawls in recent history. Matthews punished the San Diego sailor with a terrifying body attack, played "Chopsticks" on his chin, and left him weaving back to port at the end of ten rounds. The crowd stood and cheered both men after the final bell. Murphy, who that night replaced Yogi Berra as New York's best catcher, mumbled a tribute to his conqueror.

"I told you he's terrific," Murphy said. "It's like being hit with a freight train."

New York newspapers hit the IBC even harder. "Who threw the overhands in Mr. Murphy's chowder?" read a picture caption in the Daily News. Jesse Abramson, of the Herald Tribune, spiced his fight story with the comment "The IBC ought to be investigated for keeping Matthews out of the Garden so long." The Mirror's tough Dan Parker snorted, "Jim Norris not only knows what is gong on but approves of it. Otherwise he'd have kicked matchmaker Al Weill out into 49th St. months ago. The case of Harry Matthews is the latest example of Weill's misuse of his powers."

Weill offered Matthews a return fight with Murphy—on the same terms, Manager Hurley refused, saying, "My guy is the draw now, and we want to get paid for it. Remember, I told you you'd want Matthews back, and you'd have to pay for him."

The full storm of resentment against the IBC materialized some weeks later when the loser, Murphy, was given first a lucrative bout with Jake LaMotta at Yankee Stadium, and then a light-heavyweight championship match with Joey Maxim. Newspaper columnists, fortified by a sense of fair play and clippings from Hurley's private service, teed off in earnest. On August 3, Washington state's attorney general asked J. Howard McGrath, United States Attorney General, visiting in Seattle, for a Federal probe of the IBC. McGrath said he would think about it, and maybe he did.

On August 6, Sen. Warren G. Magnuson, Washington Democrat, introduced a measure in the United States Senate calling for an investigation of boxing and wrestling. On August 13, Senators Harry Cain, of Washington, and Herman Welker, of Idaho, running as a Republican entry, also asked for a congressional probe. Representative Clemente, New York Democrat, introduced a resolution in the Lower House aimed at investigation of the IBC. A few days later, a Federal grand jury went into the matter, but at last report hadn't come out with anything.

Meanwhile Matthews was cashing in out West. After Murphy came a succession of people such as Ron Whittle (KO–2), Frank Buford (KO–3), Freddy Beshore (TKO–7), Bill Peterson (KO–4), Baby Dutch Culbertson (KO–4).

The Murphy fight in New York had pulled only $23,970. In Seattle, Matthews drew $31,138 for two minutes' work on Lloyd Marshall. In Boise, his birthplace, he set an all-time record for fight receipts, $31,720, for stretching Dave Whitlock in the sixth. In a rough ten-rounder in Cleveland with Danny Nardico, there was $73,870 worth of house guests. Harry now was fighting for as high as 45 percent of each gate he drew, and getting more invitations than a convention of Elks.

Harry has hardly been flinging around his share of these proceeds. "I guarantee you one thing about The Athlete," says manager Hurley, using his favorite nickname for Matthews. "He might not have the first dollar he ever made, but he can tell you where it went. One time we fly to Boise for a fight—he don't like to fly—and he's giving me a bad time about one of the motors. He's a mechanic, and he thinks he can tell the health of a motor by its sound. By the time we get to Boise, he's got me nervous as a bride. Anyway, we land, and The Athlete leans back in his seat and signs, 'Well, another quarter shot.' I don't get what he means until I remember he bought one of those two-bit insurance policies at the airport. Don't worry about that boy—he'll do all right."

Harry's neighbors in the White Center district of West Seattle have grown used to a pair of panel trucks, prewar vintage, parked outside the Matthews house. He uses the trucks for frequent fishing trips into the more inaccessible regions of the Cascades, and they also serve as laboratories for mechanical tinkering.

Said his wife recently, "Harry goes out and buys a truck for $100 and comes home with wild tales about fixing it up and selling it for $500. But he never gets it fixed quite right, and I suppose we'll eventually fill the whole block with old trucks."

Harry Matthews' career as a fighter began back in the little Idaho village of Ola. His father, the town blacksmith, rigged up a treacherous contraption in the living room of the Matthews home—a punching bag suspended from the ceiling and anchored to the floor. Lou Matthews would sit on the sofa and bark orders, "Now the right! Throw that right! Hook with the left! Harder!"

The house shook. Lou Matthews roared. Mrs. Frances Matthews, Harry's mother, a woman of rare patience, frowned and sewed. Harry socked. Not infrequently, the punching bag socked back, knocking Harry to the floor. He was nine years old, and virtually an only child, since his one brother was twenty years old.

For years, the punching bag hung like a grotesque chandelier in the Matthews living room, while Lou Matthews regaled the farmers who came into his blacksmith shop with tales of the championships to be won by "the kid."

Such talk made Harry squirm. "I was a timid kid," Matthews explains. "I remember begging my dad to stop bragging me up as a fighter, and I can even remember other people asking him to quit talking about me. But I was stuck with it. He used to go around saying, 'The kid will be a champion someday.' I can feel the embarrassment all over again, thinking about it.

"I wanted to play basketball and baseball in high school, but I couldn't, because I was a professional boxer at fifteen. I wound up going three months to high school. If I ever have a son, he's never going to be a fighter. Don't get me wrong, I loved my dad, but fighting's no business for any kid. If my son could have Jack Hurley for a manager, I'd say all right. But Hurley will be dead by then, and there's only one Hurley."

Harry can't even recall his first fight—a one-round knockout victory in Ontario, Oregon, in 1937—only that his father passed him off as eighteen. In between those early fights he worked as a blacksmith, cowboy, logger, mail driver and mining hand. By 1940 he was, as has been noted, a promising middleweight, but when his father died, Harry's style changed for the worse. After a disappointing draw with Al Hostak in 1942, Matthews quit the ring and went to work in the booming shipyards of Seattle. He became a skilled welder and mechanic; he still holds cards in the International Association of Bridge, Structural, and Ornamental Ironworkers, AFL, and in the powerful Teamsters Union.

One factor in Harry's backslide was an unfortunate marriage to a girl still in her mid-teens. His older daughter, nine-year-old Patsy, is a product of the marriage. Following a divorce, Matthews retained custody of the child, raising her with the aid of his mother, who still lives in Idaho.

Shortly before going into the Army, Harry met a settling influence in the person of Josephine Cintori, a nineteen-year-old Sunday-school teacher. Jo is a girl of sensitiveness and intelligence who balked, at first, at the very thought of meeting a fighter.

"To me, all boxers were gorillas with bashed-in noses and funny-looking ears," she says. "I guess I expected Harry to come into the room skipping rope. He turned out to be beautiful! He was gracious and kind and considerate—like a good-looking college kid, only with better manners."

Harry and Jo were married during his induction furlough. In hopes of getting a quick stake, Matthews wired his manager of the period, George Blake, to get him a fight in Los Angeles. He was eight months away from the ring when he fought Jack Chase, a ranking middleweight, in July 1943 in Hollywood. He lost a decision and suffered a broken nose. Two weeks later, still fighting with a broken nose, Harry took a savage beating from one Eddie Booker, losing the only knockout of his career, a TKO in the fifth round. He returned home with $800 and a face that only Jo could love.

Matthews trained for the amphibious forces in New Orleans, near Lake Pontchartrain, and was cited for bravery in saving four lives during a tragic training accident, when one of the boats capsized in a storm. Later Harry was assigned, as a mechanic and welder, to the 465th Amphibian Truck Company. He made one landing—on Luzon Island, in the Philippines—and eventually was discharged as a corporal in 1946.

It was in New Orleans during basic training that Matthews struck the only ring blow he ever has thrown in anger. Harry went to his commanding officer and asked for a little time off to fight for a local promoter, Lew Raymond. "I could get maybe $300 to send home to the family," he told the CO.

The commanding officer, no follower of boxing, looked at Harry's unmarked, unpugnacious face, and smiled. "You're no fighter, son," he said. Matthews patiently explained his background, but the CO shook his head. A few days later he called Matthews into his office to fight in a USO smoker—three rounds against a heavyweight.

"But that's amateur," explained Matthews. "I'm a professional fighter."

Something about the contemptuous look on the CO's face enraged him, Harry recalls, and he agreed to what he considered a waste of time. The night of the fight he was still angry, and when the bell rang he forgot all the safety-first mottoes he had learned and reverted to his old style as a kid. Instead of dancing and jabbing, Matthews walked across the canvas, threw one savage right hand, and the heavyweight toppled in an unconscious heap. Still too angry to talk, Matthews climbed out of the ring and went back to his dressing room, to brood over the $300 he didn't have.

"The CO never called me in after that," grins Harry. "I guess he thought it was a fluke."

Following his discharge, Matthews went back to fighting, for reasons he has difficulty explaining today. He found himself carrying the lunch pail more frequently than ever, because he was still a safety-first fighter, deadly to watch, and his manager of the 1946–49 period, Bert Forbes, did nothing to change this.

"I did a little of everything between fights," Matthews said recently, reflecting on his postwar existence. "Welding for an ornamental-furniture outfit, garage work, truck driving and banging away in a foundry. We did all right. I sent money home when I was in the Army, and Jo worked in a department store, and we had the house. But it's like this"—he felt for words cautiously—"when you're nine years old and you punch a bag in the living room, and your old man gets laughed at around town for saying you're a fighter—well, I guess it's like being raised in the ministry. Sooner or later, you go back to church."

Harry's late rise to success under Jack Hurley almost never came off. The partnership threatened to dissolve before the papers were even signed, over an issue dear to the hearts of all managers and fighters—money. During their first meeting, Matthews asked Hurley what he expected in the way of percentage.

"Fifty percent," Hurley replied.

"Most managers only take a third," Matthews said.

"Most managers couldn't book a flea circus with a dog," snorted Hurley. "I'm a fifty percent manager,"

"But," protested Harry, "you'd be taking half of what I make!"

"How much you makin' now?"

Harry reddened. "Nothin'."

"Well, fifty percent of nothin' ain't much, is it?" Hurley replied. "Listen, it costs me $10,000 a year just to live. You'll be my only fighter, and in order to get that, I've got to make $20,000 for the two of us. You might look at it this way—you're getting fifty percent of me."

The fifty-fifty arrangement provides that Hurley pay all expenses of promotion, travel and training. The split also applies to any other enterprises Matthews and Hurley undertake. Recently the two have acted extremely secretive about an invention, an idea of Hurley's for greater safety and efficiency in automobiles, which Matthews built in his combination machine shop–garage. Matthews himself has a patent pending on a new type of coffee table, a strikingly modernistic creation of glass and spot-welded chains.

Harry's attitude toward Hurley, once a state of animosity, gradually changed to hero worship. "He's like my old man in so many ways—convincing talker, tall, stoop-shouldered, glasses—and bossy as the dickens." Hurley "quarterbacks" all of Matthews' fights from the corner, with a set of hand signals which Harry looks for from the safety of a clinch.

Matthews' personal loyalty to Hurley was put to a severe test last November, when his original contract with the manager had expired. Neither had bothered to go through the formality of a renewal. A group of boxing people, sensing an opening between guard and tackle, offered the fighter "more money than I ever hoped to have" to leave Hurley and go with them. The men—Matthews actually seems afraid to discuss the incident—claimed connections with the IBC and offered Harry a more attractive cut of purses. Matthews went straight to Hurley with the story, swore him to secrecy regarding identities and demanded a new contract for five years.

"I just don't ever want to be tempted like that again," he said. Harry gave the poachers what he believes was the convincing answer. "I told them that without Hurley I wouldn't be any good to them anyway."

A peculiar manifestation of Matthews' effect on people is that close friends seldom go to his fights. "I couldn't stand to see that guy get hurt," said one. Jo Matthews takes an understandably avid interest in boxing, but never has attended one of Harry's bouts. Harry's mother, Frances Matthews, a Seventh Day Adventist, knows little of boxing—only that it must be a wonderful business if her son is in it.

Matthews in the ring is a dead-pan, impassive figure whose masterful poise and tactics have inspired all sorts of extravagant comparisons. Hurley, the man who knows him best, says, "The Athlete isn't what you'd call a great fighter, but he's the best we have around today. He hasn't got that animal in him, like Dempsey had. He's got a little of Tunney, and a hell of a lot of pride."

About a year ago Hurley, through Tex Hager, Boise promoter, made an offer to Jack Kearns, Maxim's manager, to put his light-heavyweight title on the line. The offer was $60,000, and according to Hurley, still stands. Kearns never accepted the match. Much later, Hurley announced that Matthews would campaign as a heavyweight—Harry can scale about 178 pounds.

Since then, the IBC has offered Matthews 20 per cent of gate and television receipts to fight Maxim, an offer Hurley refused, causing much second guessing among Matthews' followers. Some of the people who had campaigned most ardently for Matthews declared themselves disillusioned. As matters stand now, Harry's acknowledged goal is Joe Walcott, or failing that, anybody who dethrones Jersey Joe.

"I'm no kid—forget that nickname," Matthews says. "A year or two, then out. Jack and I have hopes of quitting together. Josie and I are laying blueprints. If I quit with big money, we'd like to have our own automobile agency. If I quit with $75,000 or so, I want a machine shop of my own. Less than that, maybe a welding shop. I've still got that coffee-table invention to think about, and who knows? Jack and I might hit it rich on our car gadget."

Meanwhile, things go along evenly in the Matthews family. Daughter Patsy now has a three-year-old sister, Connie, and Jo Matthews is expecting another child. Harry walks the avenue in West Seattle and passes the time with friends he knew ten years ago. Then there are the pictures to autograph and the fan mail to answer. One letter stays apart from the others.

"Dear Harry," it begins. "You won't remember me, but I knew your dad. He used to brag about you being a champion, and I thought it was funny at the time. I'm sorry about that, because I was wrong and he was right."

Don Heinrich

Sport Magazine, October, 1952

DON HEINRICH, WASHINGTON'S HOME-GROWN, All-America quarterback (vintage 1950), is probably the only player in college football history who ever plunged over a 180-foot embankment in a runaway car and lived to get hurt in a more spectacular way.

For that matter, he probably is the only quarterback in America who ever had his leg broken by a radio announcer on the eve of a big game.

Until the record books are brought up to date, it is safe to assume he is the only player ever to exhort his teammates to greater valor by beating on a bass drum.

He may be the only player ever to quarterback his team for 29 minutes in a comfortable state of unconsciousness.

And if these achievements are tied or beaten, Heinrich adherents can point out that Don is the only quarterback ever to be compared to Nijinsky, Rembrandt and Michelangelo. One long-shadowed afternoon, in the Los Angeles Coliseum, James M. Phelan, the celebrated college and professional coach, watched Heinrich riddle a USC defense with his sharp passing and astute play-calling. Mr. Phelan lifted his eyes to heaven and spoke: "Don Heinrich is the greatest quarterback in college football today. Not only that, he is a lot better than most of the pros. He can dance, he can paint and he can build . . . he's Nijinsky, Rembrandt and Michelangelo all rolled into one."

This is rather heady stuff. All of it—and considerably more—developed since 1948, when Heinrich consented to let the University of Washington refine his intellect in exchange for a few touchdown passes in the clutch. The reciprocal trade agreement suffered a severe jolt last fall, but both sides are earnestly trying to complete the bargain in this, Don's senior year.

Following a serious shoulder injury last year, which kept him out of action completely, Heinrich is back at the same old stand—hunched under the center's rear end, in the classic posture of T-formation quarterbacks. All hands, including Howie Odell, the Washington coach, are certain he will be as good as he was in 1950, i.e., spectacular.

"I wouldn't be surprised," rumbled California's Pappy Waldorf, "to see Washington have its best season ever, now that Heinrich is back."

Pappy's suspicion has support in the raw won-lost statistics by which college teams are judged. Two years ago, during a Heinrich administration, the Huskies won eight and lost two, barely missing Rose Bowl selection; last year with a better team but without Heinrich, the Huskies won three, lost six and tied one.

After breaking almost every known passing record in the annals of undergraduate football in 1950, Heinrich broke the hearts of his loyal clientele on September 8, 1951. Recollection of the exact date is no accident. It sears the memory of many a University of Washington rooter who tearfully canceled reservations to Pasadena. It recalls a livid era in Washington football when chuckle-headedness got out of hand.

Friend and foe acknowledged that the Huskies were loaded last fall— and not just with overconfidence. They had a good line, they had a couple of near-great backs, they had a genuinely great back in Hugh McElhenny, and they had Heinrich. It was favorable weather for pink clouds, which hovered over the practice field. Then the weather suddenly changed.

In justice to Donald, it must be said he does things with a fine sense of timing. He chose to get wounded on a Saturday morning, which gave the Sunday papers plenty of time to prepare pictures, lead stories and tearful obituaries on the death of Washington's Rose Bowl hopes. On a routine scrimmage play, Heinrich was trapped along the sidelines, where some ambitious freshman tipped him over. He landed on his right, or throwing, elbow. Things in his shoulder became separated. Doctors later said they were ligaments.

Everything got pretty irrational after the accident. Newspapers blossomed with pictures of the tragic event; both The Seattle Times and Post-Intelligencer gave almost entire page displays to Heinrich's injury. Doctors were quoted on the probable effects of a shoulder separation. Coach Odell was rushed into a special radio broadcast to analyze the crisis. The climax of hysteria was reached on Monday when The Times, a newspaper of almost timid editorial persuasion, ran a blown-up X-ray picture of Don's shoulder. It still remains a source of wonder that nobody suggested hanging the poor freshman who tackled him.

Heinrich himself uttered one of the few sensible statements surrounding his misfortune. "Isn't is possible," he asked, during the height of the fanfare, "that a couple of guys in Korea might have shoulder separations?"

Needless to say, Don now is being handled like a piece of fine Steuben glassware. Orders were given last spring that he was strictly "off limits" to tacklers, and even this fall, when he fades back to pass in practice, he does so with the utmost peace and security. Once, during a spring session, Donald absentmindedly pulled a quarterback sneak, which calls for a quick dive into a maze of 200-pound intellectuals.

"Don didn't get hurt, but Odell had to go lie down for a while," reported a student manager.

The tenderness with which the coach now regards his quarterback represents a point of view that comes only after a man studies his piece of bread and discovers which side it is buttered on. Heinrich is above all an individual; Odell, a coach who approaches football in a clinical, statistical manner, is upset by the presence of free-thinkers on his squad. Not since the colorful Frankie Albert kept solemn Clark Shaughnessy on the verge of apoplexy with his antics at Stanford have two such divergent personalities been forced to exist together in mutual dependence.

The relationship has been strained numerous times, but never, perhaps, as much as during the Washington-UCLA game in Seattle two years ago. The Huskies had just recovered a Bruin fumble deep in their own bailiwick, with a matter of minutes left to play in the first half.

"Punch it out of there," Odell ordered his quarterback. "Eat up the clock as long as you can."

Seconds later, Odell raised up off the bench in sheer terror as he sighted his baby-faced field general fading back to pass on first down, a bobbing figure among great clusters of linemen. The ball squirted free in a most catastrophic fumble, recovered by UCLA only feet short of the Husky end zone. In went the defensive platoon and out came Heinrich, who treated the entire matter philosophically.

"Tough luck, coach," he announced. "Some guy bumped my arm."

It is a tribute to his teammates' regard for Heinrich that they covered up his monumental disobedience with the most stirring goal-line stand since Horatio denied those people access to a bridge.

Heinrich's effect on the public ranks with his effect on established records. In 1950, he set two national passing marks—one for completions in a single season, 134 (since broken by Loyola's Don Klosterman), and another for percentage of completions (60.7 percent).

He rewrote Pacific Coast Conference passing standards pretty much to suit himself, compiling a two-year total of 198 completions, for a .582 average. In addition to having absolutely no passes intercepted in one string of 70 straight tosses, he acquired the incredible amount of 2,745 yards of enemy real estate from throwing alone.

A comparison of his 1950 passing record with those of Kentucky's Babe Parill and Notre Dame's Bob Williams, both of whom also won All-America recognition, shows that his passing yardage eclipsed that of Parilli by some 200 yards and that of Williams by 300. He had the edge on both in all the statistics except touchdown passes. Parilli beat him there.

Such cold figures gave birth to warm tributes, and one of the warmest came from Ray Eliot, the Illinois coach, who said: "I wouldn't lose a game if I had Heinrich playing for me."

"But Eliot would lose his temper once in a while," said a Washington coach.

Heinrich is in no hurry to get any place unless the place happens to be guarded by enemy football players. He is the despair of student managers, trainers, bus drivers, classroom professors or anybody else with the quaint notion that things ought to get started on time. Actually, Heinrich is a devoted student of football (if not of the more academic pursuits), although you'd never guess it from his offhand approach to high policy.

Several nicknames are attached to Don, notably "The Arm" and "The Q.B." Raised in Bremerton, a town across the bay from Seattle, Heinrich started playing football almost from the time he could lift one, being a product of Bremerton's "Pee-Wee" athletic program. Heinrich's cousin, Myron Stangler, a great natural athlete whose career was ended by severe wounds received in World War II, had a great influence on his development. As a youngster Donald used to hero-worship his cousin, imitating each of his moves which, according to Heinrich, were terrific. His high school coach, Dwight Shear, drafted Donald for the quarterback job in his sophomore year. "Right from the start, he was a leader," reports Shear. "I've never seen anybody with his ability to stand around and look with big men pouring in on him the way Don can. He has ice water in his veins."

Heinrich first came to Seattle with the Bremerton High School team to play Ballard High for the state championship. Before a crowd of 12,000, he calmly completed 11 out of 12 passes to make a complete rout of the game, starting a stampede of college scouts to the Bremerton dressing room. The Huskies got him, and from that time forward very few Seattle citizens took a rational view of the 22-year-old team leader, whose photogenic face has moved thousands to hysteria.

Two days before the California game of 1950—which was to decide the Rose Bowl invitation—Ted Bell, a Seattle radio announcer, was breathing news to his loyal followers through a microphone. At that moment, somebody called to report that Heinrich had broken his leg in practice. Mr. Bell, without stopping to consider that all people with access to telephones are not equally reliable, let fly with a bulletin. "All is lost," he announced, in effect. "Don Heinrich has broken his leg!" It turned out to be a false alarm.

Residents of Seattle, who ought to be immune to accident reports on Heinrich by now, still respond emotionally every time his carcass is endangered, as it was a year ago last winter. Riding in a swift automobile outside Bremerton, Don and his driver-companion plunged over a steep bank. They rattled around inside the car like cubes in a chuck-a-luck cage, but by some miracle both boys escaped death. Don emerged with what somebody described as "only a broken hand."

"Only a broken hand!" screamed an admirer. "That was his passing hand!"

It was, indeed. Heinrich missed the entire 1951 spring practice while a new high in medical bulletins (later topped by the shoulder injury) kept the public informed of his welfare. A friend asked Heinrich about his reaction when the runaway car took wings over the bank.

"It's a funny thing," replied Donald, with a straight face, "but all I could think of was, 'He isn't going to get much of a trade-in on this car.' "

When he isn't figuring out new ways to get hurt, Heinrich develops new ways to annoy opposing teams. One of these, a classic example of inventive genius under fire, occurred against Stanford. Trapped and swarmed under by tacklers, Heinrich spotted teammate Mel Davis standing off to one side. As he was going down, Don flipped a back-handed pass out to the startled Davis, who fortunately ran in the right direction for a ten-yard gain.

This was the same game in which Heinrich quarterbacked a brilliant, if erratic, first half from the sunny side of Queer Street. On the third play of the game he took a rap on the head which cluttered up his wits for the next 29 minutes. Sticking his head in the huddle, Donald would mutter, "I'm a little woozy . . . tell me, how does Left 22 sound?"

It is axiomatic among his fellow Huskies that Heinrich can do no wrong, and they set out to prove it. Not only did they run Left 22, but they ran several other questionable calls at his blacked-out behest. The score was 0-0 at the half; Washington eventually won, 21-7, after smelling salts saved the day.

If Heinrich has a philosophy of life, it must be that people are divided into two classes—those who have fun and those who coach football. Before the Oregon game in 1950, he walked down the Edmundson Pavilion steps toward the dressing room only to discover that the UW band had left its artillery unguarded. Picking out an instrument to suit his personality (the bass drum), Heinrich started a one-man concert. Before long, other Huskies, notably Hugh McElhenny, Jim Mangan, Bryan Zurek and Ted Holzknecht, joined the assault on pure harmony.

The art of T-quarterback faking appeals to Heinrich, and he is extremely adept at this practical-joke aspect of the game. Not since Frankie Albert's time at Stanford has Coast football seen a quarterback so skilled at making a hunk of leather disappear so completely. Donald is quick and shifty when trapped but, unfortunately, he has a serious weakness which probably keeps him out of the select clan of all-time greats. The weakness is, namely, that he cannot run much faster than the average kitchen table.

Heinrich's gift for horseplay and wisecracking might give rise to a suspicion that he is endowed with an excess of suet between the ears. Actually, he has the proper amount of humility and a keen sense of values. In short, horseplay and wisecracking end when the game starts. Don is a cool, calculating customer under pressure. Drollery rather than conceit marks his off-field adventures. Before a trip to Los Angeles to play USC, he was studying a picture of Doris Day, the movie actress. "You know," he announced, "if that girl plays her cards right, she can have a date with me."

Nobody, including halfback Bill Earley, his companion of the moment, was surprised when Heinrich picked up the telephone and called Miss Day long-distance. He actually got her on the line, introduced himself, chatted at some length and received an invitation to visit her at the studio.

The fact that Heinrich went—as a visitor—to watch Stanford, rather than Washington, play for the West at Pasadena last New Year's Day is explained by Earley. "Without Don we had no leader," the Husky back says. "He did things for us besides pass. He pulled us out of jams and kept us on our toes. Without him, we folded up."

Similar testimony from other players confirms Earley's statement. In fact, when the Huskies were wallowing in a state of total collapse last fall, The Seattle Times sent out two reporters to make an "investigation." Most of the players, and coach Odell, conceded that Heinrich's injury was the key to their disaster.

In Odell's case, it was a triumph for Heinrich. Before the season started, the Husky coach made no particular emphasis of the fact that the nation's No. 1 quarterback would be missed. Not a few students of tailor-made, advance-notice alibis were surprised when Odell remained rosily optimistic, even after Don was hospitalized. If Odell didn't miss Heinrich, Don certainly missed Odell. The Times' research brought out the fact that the Washington coach never once went to visit his injured star during the six weeks Heinrich spent in the hospital. This oversight, almost as much as the losing season, caused an undercurrent of bitterness toward Odell that nearly cost Howie his job.

However, to quote mutual friends of Heinrich and Odell, "things are just peachy now." The two are friendly and look on the new season with hopeful rather than rosy optimism. Now that the Huskies have their arm back, things look more rugged for Cal, Illinois, USC, Washington State, etc.

Heinrich has his sights set on professional football—he is a draft choice of the New York Giants—and he was married July 19 to Barbara Wartman, his childhood sweetheart. Miss Wartman ("she sure seethes when I tell her about Doris Day") dropped out of the University after one year to work in the Puget Sound Naval Shipyard at Bremerton.

Because of his marriage, and the ripe wisdom that comes to delayed seniors, it is believed that Heinrich returns for his final year at Washington with a more serious point of view. You want an example? Very well.

During spring practice, Don was running a play which called for a pitch-out pass to the halfback, who was running wide. Noting that Odell's watchful eye was directed elsewhere, Donald flipped the pass behind his back for a completion.

"Lucky the coach didn't see that one," he said, grinning.

But Don didn't know that the entire sequence was being recorded on film for future study by the coaching staff. All was serene until Heinrich's little byplay was flashed on the screen.

"What was that?" Odell snapped. "What's that boy up to now?"

It just goes to show the influence of maturity on the happy quarterback. Two years ago Don would have flipped that pass between his legs.

It is hard for present-day fans to imagine how vividly the O'Brien twins, Johnny and Ed, so captivated Seattle's and the nation's sporting public. When you say they were each 5-feet, 9-inches tall you have said about all of it. When they flourished at Seattle University in the early 1950s, they were thought of as small. In today's world of basket-ball giantism, they would be mere curiosities; nobody would give them a chance. But they were authentic, big-time college basketball stars, and each played baseball at the major league level. They came from South Amboy, N.J., and were raised by their father, whom they called "The Chief," in a strict Catholic upbringing. Johnny, the All-American basketball record-breaker, eventually served as County Commissioner and assistant manager of the Kingdome. He is now retired. Eddie worked as an athletic director at Seattle U. and is today a successful businessman.

The O'Brien Twins

Sport Magazine, February, 1956

WHEN THE O'BRIEN TWINS, JOHN AND ED, were still stuffing baskets for Seattle University back in 1953, they were paid a visit by Bing Crosby, a well-known father, who still had a losing stable going for him as part-owner of the Pittsburgh Pirates. The last Crosby purpose in this visit was to trade witticisms with these brash, good-humored young athletes. He wanted them to sign with Pittsburgh.

"I hear," said the man whose voice was thrilling adolescents when the twins were mere specks on the scenery of South Amboy, New Jersey, "that you fellows also go in for baseball."

John looked at Ed, then at Crosby. "Baseball?" he said. "Tennis is our racket."

Crosby uttered a great sigh. "Kid," he said, "I got thrown out of your home town 30 years ago for using better gags than that."

The conversation took a more serious turn when Crosby suggested that John and Ed might like to play baseball for Pittsburgh after gradua-tion. Onlookers claim it was a sign of their approaching adulthood when the twins didn't suggest to Crosby that they team up as a singing trio.

Since that time, Johnny and Ed have matured. Maybe the responsi-bility of family life has something to do with it. Perhaps it was a sobering spell in the Army, or it may have been the preoccupation with big-league baseball. One can well imagine that hitting against Robin Roberts could emphasize to young men that this is a pretty grim world.

At any rate, the O'Brien humor has a certain thread of realism in it. Branch Rickey's dream of having a double-play combination made up of equal parts of O'Brien still is in abeyance. The Pirates, after establishing John at second base, tried vainly to make a shortstop out of Ed, whose principal fault seemed to be that he executed even short, double-play tosses like long throws from center field. On one such play, he drilled the ball right through John's glove and into his chest.

"I'll say one thing for Mr. Rickey," said John, when he got his breath back. "He's going to make a shortstop out of you if it kills me."

If not grim, life for the O'Briens has indeed become more serious. Both are family men, Ed the father of a son, John expecting his first child in a few weeks. Eddie, the captain and playmaker of Seattle University's basketball team three years ago, recently was made coach of the freshmen. John coaches an independent amateur team.

In addition, the O'Brien twins have taken on what burden there is in seeing that two younger brothers, Jim and Billy, and a sister, Teresa, get through high school and Seattle University. At the age of 24, John and Ed shouldered responsibility for the care of the entire family, following the death of their father last January.

Four of the O'Briens are on the Seattle U. campus right now, only three years after Johnny, a wise-cracking midget five feet nine inches tall, was shattering a sizable group of national basketball scoring records. Captain Eddie got most of the assists. To refresh your memory, Johnny O'Brien became the first big-time college player to score 1,000 points in a single season. Those were the days when a Seattle U. team, led by John and Ed, dazzled Madison Square Garden with a 102-101 victory over NYU. It was a time when their school put a straight-faced ad in the papers: "O'Brien vs. College of Puget Sound Tonight."

It was a time of light-hearted hook shots that earned both of them All-America recognition. They were idolized and courted by captivated fans; they were hot stuff. They dressed alike, studied alike, thought alike, ate alike, and the only shadows on their futures were cast by the draft board and Bevo Francis.

Yet through all this, their quips never quite crossed the line to rudeness; they never lost their heads. No matter what came easiest to them, they practiced what came hardest. And they studied for a mutual, B-plus average.

There was a reason for this, too, and his name was Edward James O'Brien. If you would measure a man by what kind of a father he is, then Edward J. O'Brien was a great man. He was a big man, of enormous strength, with a great, booming voice, a man of friendly sternness and devout principles. The twins called him "The Chief." During most of his life, O'Brien was a marine foreman for the Pennsylvania Railroad in South Amboy, where tugs and barges came to load coal for the industrial centers of the East.

"Don't come to me bragging about your base hits," he would warn the twins. "They've got an error column in the bottom of those box-scores. I look at that."

The twins' mother passed away in 1950, leaving "The Chief" to care for the family of five. He was always the dominant figure in their lives. John and Ed now recall crises of discipline with affectionate amusement, which, at the time they occurred, took on enormous, almost tragic proportions. They always do when you're 12 years old.

"You didn't take out the garbage today," the Chief would pronounce solemnly. "So I burned your gloves and bats. You'll do your share around this house, or you don't play baseball."

Rampant despair would last most of the next day, until about an hour before a neighborhood game was scheduled. Then the telephone would ring with the Chief calling from work. "Tell them the baseball stuff is in the trash barrel behind the furnace," he would say to Mrs. O'Brien. "And tell 'em next time I *will* burn it."

Times must have been desperately hard during the Depression years, if you would gauge them by the sight of identical figures walking along the railroad tracks at night in South Amboy, picking up pieces of coal that dropped from cars. But the stress on family virtue never relaxed. Once, when Johnny flipped a piece of bread across the table to brother Jim, the Chief arose quietly from the table and took out two books from his rather large collection.

"These," he announced heavily, "are books on etiquette. You will read them one hour a day. Keep reading until you learn something of manners."

It was a mandate that didn't bounce. Its effects are seen to this day in the twins' attention to protocol among elders.

If the Pirates ever capitalize on their investment in John and Ed (an investment said to be twin bonuses of $25,000 each), then the patience of the O'Briens' neighbors, Mr. and Mrs. Steve and Molly Krockmolly, must be taken into account. From the time they were tiny, the twins practiced batting and basketball shooting in their living room and kitchen—until they heard the heavy step of the Chief coming down the hall. A tightly-wound bread wrapper made a good indoor baseball, which crashed frequently against the wall of their neighbors' flat.

"Jiggers, the Chief!" was a warning cry heard frequently in the O'Brien home.

The elder O'Brien was known to pop his head into the kitchen, where two forms were ostensibly preoccupied with school books—although such quiet study was not calculated to soak shirts wet with sweat. "Who do you think you're foolin'?" the Chief would growl.

By some special intelligence that children have in their skirmishes with parents, the twins knew that much of the Chief's bluster was bluff. The saving grace was his sense of humor. The O'Briens say it was taxed most heavily the time John launched a real basketball in the kitchen. The hook shot that would one day score a thousand points described a clean arc, banked off the wall, and spun down into a bowl of spaghetti.

"If I didn't like the Krockmollys so well," stormed the Chief, when he discovered the carnage, "I'd push you right through that wall."

"Thank heaven for the Krockmollys," sighed John. The Chief turned away and stalked out of the room—the better, according to memory, to hide a grin.

When Mrs. O'Brien died, the task of cooking and washing fell on Teresa, a pretty, dark-eyed girl, then only a freshman in high school. Billy was only 10, and Jim, nicknamed "Troubles" by the twins because he got them all fired from a job in the same grocery store, was 18. This was the family the Chief raised.

One of the reasons the twins left home for Seattle University was to release the pressure on family finances. The Chief wrote regularly, long four-page letters, full of news about the family. The SU president, Father A. A. Lemieux, has a number of letters the Chief wrote to him. "I had offers to sign the boys with several major league baseball clubs," said an excerpt from one letter, "but I explained to the boys the kind of world we are living in, and how an education was more essential."

This was literally true. One American League team saw the O'Briens' possible box-office value long before Rickey heard of them. The offer was made to pay the twins' way through three years of college, an offer the Chief turned down.

"A college education takes four years," the Chief said. "We'll do it another way."

There are other excerpts that reflect the Chief's affection for his family: "Sometimes if you are talking to the boys, Father," he wrote, "say to them, 'I'll bet your dad is an awful crank.' Just for the fun of it. As you know, I never made a habit of patting them on the back, no matter what honors they gathered for whomever they played with." And further: "I am the happiest father in this part of the country, but still I would not let them know."

Johnny O'Brien was scoring 30–35 points a night. His fantastic ability was bringing national recognition to a school few people outside Seattle had ever heard of; fans jammed the small SU gym to a point where all home games had to be transferred to the Civic Auditorium, and big Goose Tatum, of the Harlem Globetrotters, was saying, "That Johnny O, he ain't no little man. He's a giant." But while the twins were driving SU into its third straight national tournament, the Chief had other duties.

"Tell the two lads," he wrote Father Lemieux, "to keep up the good work on the team and not to let it go to their heads because they won a few games. Tell them they haven't shown anything yet. Billy and Teresa just finished the dishes. Now for home work."

The O'Briens' antics on the basketball floor obscured what ability they had on a baseball diamond—except to a small, sharp-eyed group of men who considered basketball a child's pleasure. They were not at all interested in O'Brien clippings, or how John's hook shot was working; they were baseball scouts, and they were there to put a dollar sign on the muscle.

"Take us as a package or we don't go," said Eddie, who acted as the spokesman in all serious matters, such as baseball and money. "We have to go together."

Several clubs backed off. It is difficult enough to guess right on one baseball prospect, but guessing right on two is twice as hard—with twice as much money involved. Probably only Rickey, and a club like Pittsburgh, could take the gamble of making the O'Brien bonus players. Certainly no club like the Yankees could stand the luxury of a matched set of identical, but untried, twins sitting on their bench. Casey Stengel's taste for knick-knacks runs to pennants.

At any rate, Ed McCarrick, scout for the Pirates, signed the O'Briens in the spring of 1953 to identical contracts. The figure was said to be in the neighborhood of $25,000 apiece, apportioned in bonus and salary over three years. Give or take a thousand, it was a pretty good neighborhood. The National League managed to survive the O'Briens' first visit. Possibly because he had enough worries without wanting to see double, Fred Haney, the Pirate manager, broke the twins into his lineup one at a time. Ed and John hit .239 and .247, respectively, and it might be added, "respectably," for two kids who had never played higher than good semipro baseball. With 20 days left in the season, they joined a bigger outfit with a better draft system. Basic Army training was at Aberdeen, Maryland.

That winter, the twins pooled their bonus money and bought the Chief a house, four blocks from where they were raised. The Army—following its usual practice in the case of identical twins—kept John and Ed together. They divided their free time between picking up $50 to a

$100 a night playing pro basketball for Lancaster, Pennsylvania, of the Eastern League, and visits to the family in South Amboy. In all their lives, John and Ed had never been apart more than 24 hours at a stretch, but something happened in the summer of 1954 that separated them in a highly logical way. Ed got married.

The bride was a pretty, dark-eyed girl named Patricia McGough, of Seattle. They now have a son, James, whose hook shot is still confined to throwing pablum. John was married the same year, three months later, to the former Jean Kumhera, a tall, sparkling blonde. They are expecting a baby in January. Eddie has an apartment close to the SU campus; John lives in a basement apartment on Seattle's Capitol Hill.

"Since we joined the Pirates," said Ed one time, "John can't get out of the cellar."

After slightly less than a year in his new home, the Chief passed away last January, following a long illness that wasted his great frame to a gaunt shadow. He was tough to the end.

"We spent most of our leave time from Aberdeen coming home to see the Chief," recalls John. "It was like a game, sort of, a sad game we played. The Chief knew he was dying, but he never spoke about it. We knew it was true, but pretended we didn't. We would talk for long periods in the hospital, about baseball and about Pittsburgh and the Giants. The Chief was a great Giant fan. 'Get your hits,' he used to say, 'but don't beat the Giants.' "

Obliquely, as he lay in the hospital, the Chief was delivering another mandate. "He never said it directly," remembers Ed, "because he didn't want any of us to admit he was going. But it was spoken in little things he said. We were being told to take care of Jim, Teresa and Billy, to see that they got through school and had a good start.

"But he didn't have to say it, and I think he knew that, too."

Last summer, the twins got out of the Army and rejoined Pittsburgh. Teresa came to Pittsburgh to live with Ed, while Billy lived with John. Brother "Troubles," now 23, also lived with Ed for a short time, commuting on weekends from South Amboy when the Pirates were home.

The Chief lived long enough to know a fact remarkable in the history of collegiate athletics. The Seattle University committee on scholarships approved a plan that gives "Troubles" and Teresa and Billy a four-year grant-in-aid for tuition to the Seattle school. This ex-post-facto "ride" for the O'Brien family was quite frankly described by the scholarship committee as a grateful gesture for the twins' contribution to the development of SU's athletic program. Teresa, now 20, is a freshman, and enjoying some of the fun of school life she missed in high school. Billy, 15, attends nearby Seattle Prep and lives with Ed's wife's parents.

Financially, Ed is caring for Teresa, while John sees to it that Billy has what he needs. John was appointed executor of the O'Brien "estate" by virtue of the fact he is four hours older than his twin. "In matters like this," he said gravely, "there's no substitute for age."

Teresa will receive the money which comes from selling the Chief's house.

"Troubles?" said Ed. "He's no trouble at all. He's the kind of guy who might wind up owning the City Hall."

Billy presented a certain problem. "I suggested to the boys that Billy be left in South Amboy with his aunt—at least until he reaches college age," says Father Lemieux. "My reasoning was only that he should be around boys his own age."

The suggestion was made to Ed, who replied: "No, this is a family thing. It's what the Chief meant. The family stays together."

And that's the way it is. The twins' future at Pittsburgh, while not assured, is at least encouraged by the averages—John hit .299 last summer, while Ed hit .239, despite playing with a broken finger much of the time. "One thing about them," says Bob Scheffing, former coach with the Cubs, "they hustle so hard they practically shame everybody else into playing the same way."

The Seattle University campus is busier now, and much changed since a pair of gay-witted twins walked in six years ago. They are still there, packing books through the final quarter to a degree. Behind is an incredible record of achievement, in which a school's whole athletic program was transformed from obscurity to national attention. Something more than a light legacy of wisecracks and broken records was left along the way, and something was gained from etiquette books long ago. Something truly valid paid off for an old Irishman who couldn't hide a smile on the day a basketball hit the spaghetti.

And deep in the glass-topped desk of a university president is a part of the reason: "I never made a habit of patting them on the back, no matter what honors they gathered for whomever they played with. I think the method worked out very good."

Part 8
The Food Pages

My mom and dad were both from New England, near Portland, Maine, and they were working class and farmers, and my dad, needing fuel, could eat enough to feed a small elementary school. Sometimes he would get up in the middle of the night and make a thick sandwich of raw onions. So I have always thought of Mom as a durable and patient woman. By nature, I guess, I could out-eat almost any kid of my age. I had no taste, but I had capacity. Mom used to make wonderful bread, but I, in my ignorance, preferred Wonder Bread. She made gorgeous doughnuts, deep fried in lard, but I got more fun out of the "store boughten" doughnuts.

The point I'm making is that there always was a lot of food around. For a while we lived on a farm, near Carnation, and I helped my mother churn butter. After churning, you always beat hell out of the new butter in a wooden cradle, and I would eat this stuff by the spoonful. Early, I had been sickly and frail as a child and the doctor said, "He survived because he has a strong stomach." As a kid, I even liked pickled pig's feet. I developed a fetish of mashing boiled potatoes with milk and vinegar. What I got, in effect, was potatoes drenched in sour milk, but it was wonderful.

Potatoes were always my favorite. On my dad's farm we kept a fair litter of pigs, big and little. To feed the pigs my dad would take bushels of potatoes out of our fields and he would boil these potatoes in an old oil drum over an open fire. The aroma was like the siren song in Ulysses. So I would eat these potatoes before the pigs got them all. Every meal in our house featured potatoes. My mother fried pork chops, she baked hams my dad had cured; she made stews and dumplings; corn went from our stalks straight into the boiling water. At an early age I learned to sear beefsteak over an open fire. No kid could have had a better upbringing.

It was only later—many years later—that I developed an interest in cooking. Try as I might, I never mastered my mother's version of

Saturday night baked beans. But I kept trying new things, different things, and then, in the mid-1960s, I fell under the spell of Julia Child. I began watching her cooking shows and avidly read her seminal book, the one that changed America's eating habits forever, *Mastering the Art of French Cooking*. She used to be on Channel 9 on Saturday nights, and so that's where I was on Saturday nights. (I have always been a bit dingy about food.)

One Saturday, after a day of skiing with Rosemary and Jerry Hoeck, I realized we had to hurry or I would miss Julia's cooking show. We were speeding down the highway from Snoqualmie Pass. Rosemary laughed uproariously.

"Never in my wildest dreams," she said, "did I ever think I'd be racing through a snowstorm on an icy road just to watch a cooking show."

Columnists are a miserable breed, as you may have suspected. We fasten onto every activity, every acquaintance, every happenstance and try to turn the fodder into something printable. That is how I began to write about cooking. This combination, the love for food and the need for columns, made a shameless stalker out of me. I sought out and befriended François Kissel, one of the first to bring French cooking to Seattle.

Along with François there was Jean Branaa, who had the Henri de Navarre restaurant in Edmonds. Early on there was John Poghetti, at Victor Rosellini's place at 610 Pine. I befriended people like Kathy Casey and Gretchen Mathers, two of Seattle's great cooks and teachers. Of late I have cultivated young Tim Clancy at Il Terrazzo Carmine in Pioneer Square, and before that Jacques Boiroux, the chef-owner of Le Tastevin, one of the city's finest restaurants. One of my good friends and some-times hint-giver was Tina Bell, who co-wrote two best-selling cookbooks on Northwest cuisine.

I got tips from Nick Athans, who runs two Greek-American cafes in Seattle. And I befriended Joe Ching, who made Canlis one of the city's most popular places. Two long-time acquaintances in the food-refining industry are Jeff Smith, The Frugal Gourmet, and Craig Wollam, his young, gifted assistant. The Frug will talk cooking by the hour, and Craig once came to my kitchen, where we fashioned a genuine "tide flat" clam chowder.

Having said all this, I got an ill-deserved reputation for being a good cook. That is false. I am all thumbs and forgetfulness in a kitchen. But I still love to hammer away at it; there is no joy quite like it. And writing about it.

In Love with Julia Child

Seattle Magazine, May, 1966

MY LOVE AFFAIR WITH A TALL, HANDSOME WOMAN named Julia Child began in the early evening of November 2, 1965. I sat up with her until 2 a.m. our first night together, quivering with joy. I resolved then to be worthy of her. My love for Julia Child, enduring the separation of a continent, has deepened and matured. It does not matter that she is married and so am I. Nor does it matter that she is rich and famous, while I am not. Such a love transcends convention, and I know that she loves me in return.

Who is Julia Child? Months passed before I first heard her voice. This happened at exactly 8 p.m. on February 3, 1966. She stood there, smiling among her pans, whisks, spatulas and wooden spoons, and said, "Welcome to *The French Chef*. I'm Julia Child." We baked a cake together. It was her initial cooking show on Channel 9, and for 30 minutes (uninterrupted by commercials) she carried on in a pleasant, addlepated way, slopping about, separating eggs, folding whites into chocolate, clattering among the pans and racks—while I frantically kept marginal notes in her now-famous book, *Mastering the Art of French Cooking*.

That same night my kitchen was a howling shambles. My children, who had rolled on the floor laughing at Julia Child, were shouted off the premises. Eggs spilled in the sink, flour dusted the stove, spoons, spatulas and saucepans never seemed within reach, and my shirt front was smeared with melted chocolate. But the cake, *Le Marquis* (chocolate spongecake), was finished at 3 a.m. It was the damnedest, loveliest cake I've ever tasted.

Since my life with Julia began last November—the night I sat up late, devouring her masterful book—we have had our triumphs and disasters. A session with *Mousse de jambon* (ham mousse) turned up a strange gelatinous creation that should have greased the ways for Todd Shipyards, while several of my omelettes could easily have been included in the U.S. Senate's tire-labeling proposals. And the grocery budget turned into an inflationary typhoon.

There have been triumphs, great triumphs. I say this with sneaky immodesty, adding that without Julia I would not be what I am today—the toast of several butcher shops and a bulwark for the California wine industry. Have you ever eaten *pot-au-feu*? This massive boiled dinner (beef, pork, chicken, sausage, vegetables), served with three sauces and its own cooking stock, is worth the time (two days) and trouble. Guys go crazy. One of my guests wound up rolling ecstatically on the living room floor crying, "That's the sexiest meal I've ever eaten!"

Filets de poisson pochés au vin blanc (fish filets poached in white wine) elevates the white fish, so traditionally humiliated in America by deep fat and egg batter, to its rightful position of honor. *Gigot à la moutarde* (roast lamb with herbal mustard coating) is an easy victory on the schedule, like building up your status in Ring Record. A much tougher one is *Filet de boeuf braisé Prince Albert* (filet of beef stuffed with foie gras and truffles). Its long list of instructions looks, at first glance, like the preliminary specifications for the Boeing 707. But like the 707, it is a soaring triumph.

Who is Julia Child? This woman I love is an American, born in Pasadena, who found herself with idle time in Paris while her husband worked there shortly after World War II. She enrolled in the Cordon Bleu, studied under a disciple of Escoffier, then joined forces with two Frenchwomen and produced *Mastering the Art of French Cooking*. In the publishing business, where any $4.95 book that sells 15,000 copies is considered a triumph, her book (which costs $10) has sold more than 200,000 copies!

Her television show, *The French Chef*, which originates in Boston, now appears on educational TV channels in 80 cities. Since Julia began appearing in Seattle in February, Frederick & Nelson reports a big rush on her book; the University Bookstore, which sold only a handful before that, has sold dozens in the past two months. The UW's KCTS-TV has booked Julia for another year of weekly shows, responding to such fan mail comments as this: "Keep it up! Julia Child is funnier than Batman. P.S. Our teen-age boys like her, too."

Funny she is, for Julia is a natural, unpretentious comedian. Chatting amiably, almost like a kitchen gossip, she drops things, mislays pans and utters an occasional "eek!" She slams things about, leaves sentences trailing in mid-air, and through all of this, she seems to be saying, "Look, if I can cook, so can you."

Her voice on the telephone (I finally got up enough courage to call her) was clear and familiar; she seemed delightfully astonished that anyone in Seattle had even heard of her. "It's fun, though, isn't it?" she trilled after I complained about the food budget. "And how's your weight? Just eat less, develop good habits. Learn to cook with your head—read the recipes carefully, take notes as you go along, don't be afraid to try things. If you spoil something, throw it away—consider it all part of your training. Keep trying. The quicker you can divorce yourself from recipes, the better off you'll be."

That night I tried *Fricasée de poulet à l'ancienne*. Not great, but worthy of her. I shall try again to make Julia happy.

Bar Tomatoes from Chowder

Seattle Times, February 6, 1990

FOR WONDERFUL ANTI-CALIFORNIAN LESSER SEATTLE WEATHER, you can't beat the miserable stuff that nature has bestowed on us these past few weeks. Rain, wind, slop, and penetrating, bone-chilling dampness.

Heavenly.

As any native knows, our baleful January-February climate demands stout, warming food. Not flaky little salads, not tofu, bean sprouts, vegetable dips and char-burned whitefish. Ladies and gentlemen of Puget Sound, I am talking about real food. Such pneumonia-inducing weather calls for rib-sticking stews, corned beef and cabbage, boiled dinners and (if you are prosperous) a thick slab of prime rib.

And clams, as in chowder.

Consider the clam. When the first Pilgrims arrived, the clam was there to greet them. Zillions of clams on pristine beaches could be had for digging. Out of this bounty came a dish to ward off the harsh cold of New England winters. Thus was born New England chowder.

This gave the first European settlers the strength to go on. As generations passed they got down to some serious plundering, looting and land-grabbing, killing off Indians as they moved westward. There was arrogance in this. In their insatiable greed, these tourists scarcely noticed local culture. The Indians had life figured out—the women did all the work, the men went hunting and fishing, yet the white man had the effrontery to think he could improve on this system.

And so it was that our land-grabbing forefathers finally arrived on Puget Sound. These beaches—indeed, all the West Coast beaches—were alive with clams. Free for the taking. Energy-giving grub. It was inevitable, then, that our Puget Sound forebears would put class in clam chowder. New England chowder came West, but there were setbacks. One setback involved the first idiot who put tomatoes in chowder. He was obviously a transplanted New Yorker because the term "Manhattan clam chowder" describes this awful marriage of clams and tomatoes.

It was then advertised here as "Puget Sound clam chowder." What a travesty!

Let us be blunt. The kind of person who would put tomatoes in clam chowder is the kind of person who would slurp champagne from a spoon. Even the late, great Ivar Haglund used some tomato-flavoring in his chowder. The result was a concoction that looked like it had already been eaten. Ivar was unrepentant to the end, possibly because he got rich off the stuff.

I once spent some time with Pierre Berton, the famed Canadian author and cook. We talked about Canadian history, his recipe for corned beef hash, and ultimately, his recipe for New England clam chowder. In his long-ago book *Just Add Water and Stir* Berton tells about ordering "New England clam chowder" in the Connaught-Sheraton Hotel in Hamilton, Ontario. It came with tomatoes in it, a blatant fraud. It was really "Manhattan clam chowder," or, as it's sometimes called, "Coney Island clam chowder."

Berton charged into the kitchen and confronted the chef. When the chef admitted that, yes, he had used tomatoes, Berton stabbed him to death with an olive spear.

Hauled into court on a charge of murder, Mr. Berton was asked why he killed the cook. "Because he made clam chowder with tomatoes," Berton replied.

"Naturally," he added, "they set me free."

Now, this is not a treatise on how to make New England chowder. Any cookbook worthy of your attention has a chowder recipe. But don't use tomatoes, otherwise you'll be consigned straight to hell, which is just where you would belong.

There are as many subtle variations on making New England clam chowder as there are techniques for romance. In both endeavors, you are encouraged to experiment. Clam chowder can retain its virtue if you favor any of the following ingredients: light curry, onion, bacon, thyme, celery salt, paprika, even evaporated milk. It's up to you.

New England clam chowder is the perfect antidote for our miserable Lesser Seattle weather. There is promise in each spoonful—that the sun will shine again.

Honest Clam Chowder

Seattle Times, March 4, 1990

IF YOU WERE SKULKING AROUND THE EDGES of this column recently, no doubt wishing you were somewhere else, we've laid some heavy stuff on you. All about corned beef hash and clam chowder.

The hashers responded happily. The chowderheads, about half of them, were outraged. That's because I declared there is no civilized justification for using tomatoes in clam chowder. Clams joined with tomatoes—a sinister alchemy, I said, and one that should be abolished forthwith.

Anyway, I promised you a true, honest, upright recipe for clam chowder. It is tomato-less. It is noble. A bowl of this heavenly concoction comes with a guarantee. That is, I guarantee that a bowl of the stuff, created by your own hand, will make you a physically and morally better person.

To achieve this near-perfection, I enlisted the expertise of Craig Wollam, a young cook of outstanding ability. Wollam is the first assistant, right hand, so to speak, of Jeff Smith, the world-famous Frugal Gourmet. It so happens we are neighbors at the Pike Place Market. Instead of The Frugal Gourmet's kitchen, we used mine—a lint-free laboratory with many delicate scientific instruments like pots, pans, steamers and spoons. Craig Wollam can handle these instruments like a brain surgeon.

What we were after can best be called Tide Flat Clam Chowder. This is a chowder with salt air in it, a hint of seaweed, perhaps with a bit of sea water mixed in. The essence of Puget Sound is its trademark. With Craig Wollam as chef, me as gofer, here is true clam chowder, one that will shame 90 per cent of the city's restaurants:

Acquire some clams, by thievery if necessary. About 4 pounds will do, the fresher the better. For one hour, soak the clams in fresh water. They will eject enough sand to repave the Alaskan Way Viaduct. Then drain.

Heat an 8-quart, heavy-bottomed pot. Add a half pound of salt pork. Not bacon, salt pork. Cut salt pork into about half-inch cubes. Cook until browned, but not crispy. Drain off two tablespoons of the salt-pork fat into a separate 6-quart pot. Set aside.

Into the larger pot with the browned salt pork, put one onion and two stalks of celery, each chopped. How fine? Use your own judgment. Sauté for 10 minutes. Then add two large potatoes, peeled and coarsely chopped. Throw some thyme in the pot and sauté 10 minutes more.

Now take the 6-quart pot with the pork fat in it, add two chopped cloves of garlic and sauté gently. Now you are on the brink of greatness. Don't be nervous.

Throw in the clams and about half a cup of wine. White wine, dammit! Don't be precious. Anything fit to drink will do.

Turn heat to high. Bring to a boil covered—simmer for 7 to 10 minutes, until clams open. Those clams that don't open should be cast aside with the same contempt you should use on tomatoes in chowder.

Strain nectar and return to the pot. Remove meat from the clams, set aside on a covered plate. Now throw the clam shells into the pot. Now add some bottled clam juice to go with your own nectar. Use some black pepper here.

Cover and simmer for 30 minutes. Use a stopwatch.

Now strain your finished nectar into the pot with potatoes, celery and onion. Control yourself. You are creating ambrosia.

Add a little more wine, cover and simmer until celery, potatoes and onions are done. The potatoes should be tender and rounded on the edges. This is your thickener; you will need no flour.

Now, at the very last, throw in your clams. Cook only long enough, one minute, maybe, to rewarm the clams. An overcooked clam, I must warn you, takes on the character of a cork-and-rubber center of the official American League baseball.

You are almost finished. Add some Tabasco sauce, perhaps, or some red pepper flakes. Garnish with parsley if you have nothing better to do.

Now, true Tide Flat Chowder is somewhat gray in color. If you insist, add a smidgen of milk for whiteness—but remember, too much milk will violate the intense richness, the very integrity, of this chowder.

There. I hope we have conquered this business of decent clam chowder. The enemy was stubborn, but to paraphrase General MacArthur when he accepted the surrender aboard the battleship *Missouri*, "These proceedings are now closed."

Crab Cakes

Seattle Times, January 18, 1990

RIGHT NOW, I CAN THINK OF 3,283 REASONS why you should stop reading this column—unless you have a passion for crab cakes. Merely liking crab cakes won't get it; you have to lust after the damned things to sustain any interest in what follows.

Crab cakes are indigenous to Maryland. They are all over the place. Crab cakes in Baltimore are like beans or cod in Boston, like steak in Kansas City, like oysters in New Orleans, like fresh salmon and espresso in Seattle. For most of my life, I read about crab cakes in Maryland. But then I made the mistake once of going there, or at least the mistake of ordering them in several restaurants—always hoping for that singular taste triumph so highly trumpeted.

In recent years, crab cakes have made an appearance in Seattle. For the most part, they turned out to be better than the ones I remember on the East Coast. The other day, as it happens, I was browsing through *The Great American Seafood Cookbook*. It was written by a lady named Susan Hermann Loomis, who once lived here, but is now—I'm told—residing in New York.

Here are some things she had to say about these concoctions: "Crab cakes are to Maryland what bubbles are to soda. Everywhere you go in Maryland, from restaurants to roadside stands, you'll find crab cakes, and they range from sublime to awful."

My experience was slightly different. Everywhere I went, I found the crab cakes to range from unfortunate to inedible. Loomis said she searched "all over Maryland for the perfect crab cake to no avail." She doesn't mention any that were sublime. But she did find the perfect crab-cake recipe—in South Carolina. A friend of hers, she says, "has made crab cakes for years and she uses a traditional Maryland recipe with a little extra crab."

So the other night, to avoid being picked up as a street delinquent, I stayed home and made crab cakes. According to Loomis' "perfect" recipe, here's how it goes:

The ingredients consist of a cup of soft fresh bread crumbs; 1 large egg; 5 tablespoons of mayonnaise; 2 scallions (green onions) chopped up; 1 tablespoon chopped fresh parsley; 1 teaspoon dry mustard; salt and pepper; then 1 pound of cooked crab meat.

All this is mixed together, holding back 1 tablespoon of mayonnaise. If the mixture seems too dry, use the tablespoon you held back.

Shaped into patties, the crab cakes are fried in unsalted butter and bland vegetable oil over medium-high heat.

I won't go so far as to say these crab cakes were sublime. But they were certainly better than any I found in Maryland, or locally.

My guru in matters like this is, of course, François Kissel, of Maximilien-in-the-Market. When I showed him the above recipe, he did not flinch, possibly out of politeness, but he made a couple of suggestions.

"Crab," he said, "is boiled, then washed and frequently frozen. It loses some sweetness. So instead of dry mustard, I would use a mixture of Japanese green mustard and Dijon, to reintroduce the sweetness."

Chinese chives or regular chives, in season, could also be added to the crab-cake mixture. In this case, Kissel says, it would be wise to sauté the scallions. "Use unsalted butter and olive oil, not vegetable oil," he said. "You might even try a little finely chopped apple in the mixture."

Now you know more than you care to know about crab cakes.

▼

Love at First Slurp

Seattle Times, August 16, 1990

IT IS GIVEN TO SOME MEN TO KNOW A LOVE so profound, so pure, so all-enrapturing, that their spirits can soar to the heavens and their passions flame at the very sight of their consuming desires. I have been given such a love.

I refer, of course, to my ardor for the family *Ostreidae*. These seductive love objects can be found, as a general rule, between tidal levels or in shallow waters along the coasts of all continents. These bivalves in Europe are known as *Ostrea edulis;* on the Eastern and Gulf coasts of the U.S. as *Crassostrea virginica;* on the California coast, *O. conchophilia*; and here, in our beloved Northwest, as *O. lurida*.

You must know by now that we are talking about oysters.

Right you are: The heat of August is a lousy time to arouse one's passion for oysters. This exquisite mollusk is but a soft, flabby caricature of its real self in November—cold, firm, succulent, inviting. But a love for oysters knows no season; those of us with this passion can't help ourselves.

You will excuse a personal lapse. I fell in love with my first unsullied, unaccompanied raw oyster at the age of 13. In a misguided Depression-era venture, my dad got control of some oyster beds in Willapa Harbor. He came home with a sack of these things one day, cracked one open and called me to the kitchen. "Eat this," he said, proffering the half shell.

It looked awful—large, grayish, and slimy; utterly repellent. But I slurped it down—and wow! It was delicious. "Gimme another," I said.

Then came another and another. It was love at first slurp. It may have been the only time in my young life when my father was really proud of me.

My love affair with the oyster matured and flourished. It reached its apex of gustatory orgasm at Von's, the great old all-hours eatery just off Fourth Avenue and Pike Street. Here the night people gathered—show biz people, legitimate actors, the sports crowd and midnight-prowling insomniacs. Von's had, probably, the largest menu in the world. Chief among its items was an Olympia oyster cocktail, for $1.25. This was in the 1950s, and the late Mike Donohoe and I used to gulp these tiny delicacies down by the shovelful.

But the Olympia perished, the victim of pollution and neglect. Only lately has it made a comeback. But the Olympia cocktail we ate then would cost, probably, $20, or even more, today.

I claim at least some credit for pushing the oyster to its present eminence in the Seattle of 1990. A friend of mine, Sam Bryant, and I started a trend that eventually resulted in a local oyster craze. We opened the city's first oyster bar Feb. 18, 1979. For two years we had a monopoly. We were written up in travel magazines and by visiting food authors from dozens of cities. People came from all over the world—principally from England and Australia—to eat our raw oysters by the dozen.

Competition came two years later. First there was Shuckers. Then F. X. McRory's Steak and Chophouse. Today more than a dozen restaurants feature these lovely bivalves on their menus.

What kinds of oysters? Well, in Puget Sound we have the Minterbrook and the Shoalwater from the south Sound. There is the Hamma Hamma from Hood Canal and, lately, the Snow Creek. This latter breed is said to be firm in hot weather because some humans don't allow them to spawn.

There is no "best" oyster on Puget Sound. It is a matter of taste, of mood, degree of hunger. But to pick a personal best I would choose the Canterbury oyster from the benign waters of Quilcene Bay. Years ago, I used to fly a float plane to the Canterbury oyster headquarters and pick up jars of these delicious mollusks. The elder, late Ray Canterbury and I became friends. So when Sam Bryant and I opened our oyster bar, his son Ray agreed to let us have an allotment from his relatively small farm.

(To allay any misgivings about conflict of interest, I sold out my share of the oyster bar to Sam Bryant three years ago. He has not changed the name of the place because he can't afford to put up new signs.)

Back to the Canterburys. So far as I know, Ray sells only to Shuckers, The Other Place, Trader Vic's and Canlis. Because of my long ago friendship with Ray's father, Sam gets a regular supply of the Quilcene Canterburys.

The oysters in Seattle, circa 1990, are not cheap. The average price for a half-dozen on the half-shell is $5.95. To a real oyster lover, this is like sampling peanuts—a half-dozen is just a start. So it is that people run up tabs of $60 to $70 inhaling raw oysters. These are the true nuts, the passionate believers, the real bivalve junkies among us.

Now, there are dozens and dozens of recipes for cooking oysters—broiled, fried, in loaves, oysters Rockefeller, et cetera and et cetera. They are all good, because I've never met an oyster I didn't like. But the one true and exalted way with oysters is to eat them raw, on the half shell. Plucked right out of the water if possible. Here you will taste them at their exquisite best—firm, clean, very much alive, blended with the sea salt taste of Puget Sound.

Life cannot offer much better.

▼

Corned Beef Hash

Seattle Post-Intelligencer, August 5, 1981

PARKED OFF THE ROAD: I forget the name of this campground, but it's not a state park, so I turned Tiger loose to roam around and hunt squirrels. The trees are thick and shady. This being mid-week, the campground isn't crowded with those infernal folks from Iowa, California, Texas and Illinois, arriving in their dreadnoughts on wheels. My only worry is that Tiger might encounter a big mastiff who will make an hors d'oeuvre out of him. Big dogs, some of them guard dogs, no doubt, are in fashion these days. Thus, Tiger's puppyhood has been one of a Lilliputian living among Brobdignagians. My camper must be carrying 35 pounds of books. I have books on economic history, a collection of Hemingway, some critical essays by Malcolm Cowley, a half-dozen novels, and another tome entitled *How to Be Your Dog's Best Friend*. With Tiger, this is easy. Give him his own way and throw lots of balls for him.

Anyway, this lazy day was spent "pick reading" through all these books. About 4 p.m., I came across a collection of poems, columns, recipes and essays by Pierre Berton, a Canadian of great gifts and some renown. In this book, Berton has a recipe for corned beef hash. Suddenly, I was ravenously hungry. With a great thrashing and muttering, I checked the camper's larder: "Canned corned beef—got that. Onion, potatoes, got those. Celery salt, yep. Eggs, of course. But no MSG, no red wine, no parsley." I remembered that there was a small store "down the road a piece," as we say in the country.

"Tiger, this will blow your mind," I said as we hit the road. "Beats dog food all to hell. We have to find parsley, red wine, monosodium glutamate and dry mustard."

We landed in the small roadside store, the kind that carries half of its stock in hardware and fishing lures. I found the wine, the dry mustard, and luckily, a few sprigs of parsley in the vegetable section. "You got any MSG?" I asked the proprietor. "What kind of dog is that?" he replied. I said Tiger was a poodle. "He's a runt miniature, more like a toy," I said. The man looked skeptically at Tiger. "Used to have a small dog once myself. Let me tell you about him . . . " As I've mentioned before, Tiger seems to trigger everybody's dog stories. Finally, the man said, "You mean some of that stuff you rub on to help your arthritis?"

"I don't have arthritis," I said. "Heard it helps," he said. "You should use it to help your arthritis." "I don't have arthritis," I repeated, finally getting the drift. "I want some MSG for corned beef hash. You're thinking of DMSO." "Well, we don't have DMSO," he said, "but you can get some down the road a piece."

So I gave up on the MSG, which was no great loss. Back at the campground, I went furiously to work on Pierre Berton's hash. Now, good corned beef hash is hard to come by; most places chomp it up too coarsely and fry it into a mass that looks like a cow dropping. Charred, full of half-cooked onion, it could ruin the digestion of a healthy goat. But real corned beef hash, the genuine article, lovingly prepared, is ideal for cooking out. If you recoil at the thought of using canned corned beef, here's what Berton says: "Why corned beef hash cannot be made of fresh corned beef I cannot tell, but it is a fact that in this instance, the tinned stuff is far better."

First, says Berton, you chop up your large potato and a whole onion in tiny pieces. Chop and chop. "These pieces must be small enough to hold together in a firm mass when they are fried. Not only that, but there also must be enough outer surface so that there will be plenty of crispness when they are cooked."

Now, I was mixing the finely chopped onion and potatoes with the corned beef. Then, Berton says, "break a raw egg over the result and mix again." That's your binder. "Then add about two tablespoons of red wine— a good dry Canadian claret or a chianti." Then, you season—"gently," Berton says—with ground pepper, celery salt, chopped parsley and MSG. By now, I had a pain in my elbow that felt like arthritis. But no MSG, or DMSO, either. Next step: "Now, sift a small amount of pancake flour into the mixture, not too much, just enough to hold it together. Mix again."

Pierre Berton suggests a good iron skillet, but I tend to favor a teflon pan, even in this pan using bacon grease and/or vegetable oil. You cook it to brown on the bottom, getting it crisp. "While this is going on, cover the uncooked top with a thin coating of dry English mustard, which can be patted firmly into the meat."

Now you can turn it over; if it crumbles, so what? Work it into shape again, flatten it down, and sprinkle on some more mustard. Get it well-browned on both sides. "Then, break a raw egg over the whole steaming mass. If the pan is properly hot, the egg should cook almost instantly on top of the hash. Stick a fork into the yolk and spread it around a bit so that the whole is congealed in one bubbling unit." The final shot is this: "When the white of the egg has thickened and turned milky, take about a tablespoon of the red wine and carefully pour it into the crevices." Cook only a few moments more, then slide the hash onto a plate.

It was delicious, but much too rich for Tiger. He got straight hamburger.

Mash Note to The Potato

Seattle Times, January 23, 1992

YOU WILL THINK I HAVE BEEN UP TO NOTHING USEFUL when I tell you that I have been concentrating on the potato lately. But I regard it as my duty to think about potatoes.

As a few of you may have learned, perhaps to your sorrow, I have appointed myself a publicist—indeed, a propagandist—for the noble tuber. "Couch potato" and "potato head" are only a couple of denigrations people use to downgrade the splendid spud. Yet we do far worse than libel the potato. We freeze-dry it. We pummel it. We pulverize it. We squeeze the juice out of it. We commit terrible atrocities on it in our kitchens, both domestic and commercial.

So the potato needs all the help it can get.

But because of Christopher Columbus, things are looking up for the spud. The recent avalanche of publicity about the 500th anniversary of America's "discovery" by Columbus has given new depth to the potato's role in human history. It matters not if you think Columbus was a starry-eyed heroic, idealistic sailor who "found" the New World (actually he was looking for something else). It also matters not if you regard Columbus as a greedy, dimwitted charlatan and a cruel mercenary. Certainly Ferdinand and Isabella, who were in charge of Spain, got so outraged by his behavior toward the original American citizens that they threw Christopher into the slammer.

But the important thing here, I submit, is the spud. In addition to slaves and spices, Columbus brought the potato back to Europe. The potato had existed in South and Central America for some 13,000 years. Columbus, followed by the conquistadors, introduced the potato to the Old World. To put it mildly, the Old World went bananas over potatoes.

The tuber invaded and revolutionized the cuisines of Spain, Italy, France, Germany and even Russia. And when sailing ships began bringing it back across the ocean to North America, there were high-fives all around. Here is the impact the potato had on the world: It supported whole nations; it fueled armies; it determined the outcome of wars; it provided the nutritional firepower that made possible the Industrial Revolution.

So potato propagandists like me were not surprised when the potato was featured at the National Museum of Natural History last October. We are not surprised, either, to learn that there is a Potato Museum near Washington, D.C.

It was founded by Meredith Sayes Hughes and her husband, Tom. Mrs. Hughes authored a wonderful historic piece on the spud in the October issue of the prestigious Smithsonian magazine. Even the Smithsonian went a little bonkers when it titled her piece "Potayto, Potahto—either way you say it, they a peel."

In my own small way, I have done what I could for the "Potahto." I once journeyed to Boise, Idaho, to interview Mr. J. R. Simplot, the acknowledged spud king of the world. Mr. Simplot has made about as much spare change out of potatoes as Bill Gates has made out of computer software.

Due to an ancient superstition among aborigine editors, it was long ago determined that a column can be only about 800 words long. This primitive notion prevents me from telling you as much as you need to know about spuds. But here are a few samples:

The potato, as was once believed in the Old World, is not an aphrodisiac. That's probably just as well; we've got too many people around as it is.

But the potato is the world's sole complete nutritional vegetable. Whole populations thrive, prosper and procreate while eating nothing but spuds.

The world's No. 1 producer of potatoes is not us, but what is left of the Soviet Union. You ready for another surprise? The second leading potato-producing country is rice-loving China.

Potatoes by no means increase waistlines, being low in fat. Spuds practically explode with vitamins and minerals. Back in the 1700s, Catherine the Great warded off famine in Russia by being pro-potato and, as a side effect, the Russians got more vodka to drink than was good for them.

As a further public service, this department will close today with a potato recipe.

Get yourself a casserole with a good cover. Quarter three peeled potatoes and mix them with one chopped onion. Add two, maybe three, tablespoons of water. Bake in a 350-degree oven till potatoes are done.

Here comes the fattening part: To this exquisite mixture of potatoes and onions, cut in maybe half a cube of butter. Then cut in a small container of sour cream. For color, add a few chopped chives or green onions.

That is it. For about $2.34 you have enough to feed four people. I guess we do owe something to Columbus.

The Frugal Gourmet

Seattle Times, April 28, 1988

MY FRIEND, THE FRUG—scholar, teacher, preacher, traveler, Democrat, gentleman—is just back from a cooking safari into Greece, Hong Kong and Rome—unloading about 18 metric tons of film.

The Frug, of course, is short for Frugal Gourmet, and Smith is short for that. Jeff Smith. He's my Pike Place Market neighbor, known far and wide on PBS station outlets—the biggest thing to hit TV cooking shows since Julia Child first chattered her way into gastronomic immortality.

"Boy, have I got a recipe for you!" enthused The Frug. "Pasta. Absolutely delicious, out of this world!"

That's the way he is, The Frug. If we had a flood of Noah proportions, he would have a stateroom on the second coming of the Ark and he would be proclaiming the joy of tying up to the peak of Mount Rainier. Nothing gets this guy down.

The foregoing metaphor is valid, because The Frug is a Methodist minister by training; hence, his study of theology and theological history with a concomitant spinoff into the history of food and the cooking thereof.

"One guess," he said. "Who invented the frying pan?"

"The Chinese," I said.

"No, the Chinese invented the wok. The Greeks invented the frying pan. The frying pan predated the Christian era. It is more than 2,000 years old. The Romans got the frying pan from the Greeks and added their own designs."

"When did the Chinese invent the wok?" I asked.

"Pasta was invented in China. In southern Italy they invented pasta entirely independent of the Chinese. Isn't that amazing? All modern cooking descends from either Greece, Italy or China.

"The Greeks taught the Romans, the Romans taught the French and the English. And the Chinese were doing everything first.

"Of course, the French don't like to admit that their cuisine came from Italy. There is only a grudging mention of this in the classic French *Larousse Gastronomique*."

It seems that Italian cooking was brought to France in the 1500s by Catherine de Medici, who married King Henry II. She is much credited with establishing French cuisine, although she was otherwise unpleasant. She brought her own chefs from Italy and the French took off from there.

We are a long way from my question about Chinese woks.

That's the way The Frug is. He answers any question that occurs to him before he gets around to answering yours. My patience was rewarded when he went on to say: "The wok was invented by the Chinese when they were invaded by the Mongols in the cycladic period, which was many, many centuries before Christ. You see, the Mongols wore these big metal helmets and when supper time came they took off their helmets and cooked in them. That gave the Chinese the idea for the wok.

"And do you know about chopsticks? I learned this in Hong Kong from Willie Mark, who is a food authority and historian. Willie said that the Chinese invented forks. But they decided forks are too crude. So they invented chopsticks.

"China did everything first. You know, forks didn't come into Europe until the 1600s, and they didn't come into wide use in our country until the Civil War."

The Frug said the way a Chinese gentleman compliments his guest is by giving him ivory chopsticks. That came out of the historical fact that ivory turns black when dipped into food that is poisoned. "With ivory chopsticks, the Chinese gentleman is saying, 'Look, everything is out in the open, you have nothing to fear.' "

While he talked, The Frug was destroying some creamed chipped beef on an English muffin at the Athenian. At 49, having been through heart surgery, he clearly does not have a cholesterol problem. He has no money problems, either. His cookbooks continue to sell in the millions, and he has enough film in cans to produce 39 scheduled TV shows beginning about a year from now.

Meanwhile, his current series shows on Channel 9. When he thinks of it, he believes his life is almost too good to bear. "I make my living eating and teaching; I have the best of all possible worlds."

The Frugal Gourmet promised us a recipe. Here it is:

Drain a 2-ounce can of anchovies and soak them in milk for 15 minutes. Throw away the milk. Sauté anchovies and three cloves of diced garlic in 3/4 cup of olive oil until you can mash anchovies into a paste.

Add two sweet red bell peppers diced in 1/4-inch pieces. Sauté until tender but not soft. Add black pepper and salt, careful with the salt. Anchovies, you know. Toss with hot pasta; parsley for garnish.

▼

Ignoring the Geoduck

Seattle Post-Intelligencer, February 14, 1972

IN THE COURSE OF A RATHER SHAPELESS LIFE spent mostly in the Northwest, I have managed to survive by not thinking much about the geoduck. It is not hard not to think about a geoduck. It amazes me how easy it is, really. The last time I thought about a geoduck was many years ago, when the then city editor of Brand X, Mr. Henry MacLeod, explained, first, what a geoduck was, how you hunted or captured it, and the way you made chowder from it. As Mr. MacLeod (he's now a managing editor, or Heloise in disguise) spoke in detail about the geoduck, I found my mind wandering. Thus began my long career of not thinking about geoducks.

It was not Henry's fault. He was quite eloquent on the subject. But I was thinking about a pay raise, or something. Maybe it was a memo I'd received, for having used the word "vicious" when I really meant "savage" in describing a sports event. A scolding memo from another editor of that period. "Look up the precise meaning," said the memo. Shortly thereafter, I mistook the address on my way to work and wound up at The P-I, where, it developed, my contract did not call for thinking about geoducks.

(Where is this getting us?)

Well, the long period of not thinking, caring, or even tasting a geoduck has been brought to an end. Lately, people have been thrusting documents under my nose, demanding that I take a stand on geoducks. "You are very big on fair weather," said one critic. "You strike out fearlessly in favor of motherhood and pasteurized milk. People stand in awe of your courage in denouncing poor toilet training. But where do you stand on geoducks? You're a spineless jellyfish." (I don't think much about jellyfish, either, but that's another story.)

What touched this off was a story about the giant clam, the geoduck, in the December issue of Pacific Search. It is written by Harriet Rice, who happens to be the sister of Stimson Bullitt. You know how it is with the Bullitt family. They are always starting a lumber fortune, a TV station, a magazine or an argument. In this case Ms. Rice wrote about geoducks. Citing the American Heritage Dictionary (the Late City Edition), she lists such alternate spellings as geoduck, goeduck, gooeyduck, or gweduc.

She then quoted François Kissel, the French chef of the Brasserie Pittsbourg, on how to cook gooeyduck, or whatever. A vicious, or savage, thought occurred at this point—namely that the plans for the Boeing roto-dome are not quite as complicated as Monsieur Kissel's recipe for cooking this glorified clam. As I read on, I thought of Mr. MacLeod, who was only trying to hustle a little chowder out of the beast.

That should be the end of it, right? But no. A columnist in Portland, Doug Baker, opened an attack on Ms. Rice. According to Baker, "Ms. Rice also errs when she says, 'the neck is what you are after.' [Gweducs, or gooeyducks, or whatever, have long necks, but don't let that depress you.] The people who are currently diving for geoducks in Puget Sound in 50 feet of water, using compressed air guns to force them from the sea bed, have little regard for the neck, which, I understand, is ground up for pet food"—he obviously has never met Mr. MacLeod. "It's the steaks in the main body of clam they are after.

"I would like to invite Ms. Rice to visit Portland, where at least half a dozen restaurants serve a tasty version of geoduck (gweduc, if she prefers) without benefit of wine sauces and complicated recipes."

Now that we both have learned more than we care to know about geoducks, the end is at hand. Ms. Rice, who turns out to be a Mrs., accepted the challenge. She and her husband, Sid, visited Portland. Aside from the fact that it seems like a hell of a long way to travel for an over-size clam, things went off well enough. François Kissel and his wife, Julia, were invited, but declined because of illness—there being no truth to the rumor that they became ill from eating their own gweducs.

Up to now I have only recited the facts of the case. I prefer to come out on more controversial issues, like fresh air, although I'd be curious to know in what kind of sauce M Kissel would cook a spineless jellyfish. Someday, if you insist, we will print M Kissel's recipe, now that Ms. Rice has declassified it. For all I know, it may be cited in the Ellsberg trial.

As you can see, the whole thing is a vicious circle. Or do I mean savage?

The Thompson Turkey

Digressions of a Native Son, 1982

HOLIDAYS ARE THE DOG DAYS for anyone charged with writing daily. During holidays, people are busy making plans to get out of town or, if it's Christmas, they are running up big numbers on their Visa cards. Good columnists, or at least smart ones, make plans ahead and write holiday columns in advance so they are not stuck with the task of composing in the thick of everybody's holiday spirit. This never worked for me. On Labor Day it was obligatory to say something nice about the people who labor; no easy trick when you consider that old labor battles are long past, and the guy to whom you might be paying tribute is now heading off on his three-day weekend, driving his motorhome, towing a boat, with two motor bikes strapped on the side. He also might be a woman.

The Fourth of July is another. The obligation here is to mix a stew of patriotism, nostalgia and warnings about firecrackers, with perhaps obeisance to Mom and her famous apple pie thrown in. I always struggled with this one. For one thing, too many scoundrels in my time have used patriotism to attack the First Amendment and generally foul up the air with the kind of rhetoric which says you are disloyal if you don't believe that nerve gas is essential to the preservation of Our Way of Life. As for nostalgia, that can only take you so far, and the editorialists (also stuck for something to say) issue their own solemn warnings about the hazards of firecrackers. That leaves Mom, and it seems to me that no intelligent mother these days is going to spend her holiday baking when she can buy a perfectly good apple pie at one of a proliferation of bakeries we have spawned in the last few years.

Christmas is the worst. I am convinced that people simply give up reading newspapers the week before Christmas. I did a fair job on a couple of occasions in lathering on Christmas sentiment, but to repeat such stuff, or work variations on it for twenty years running, is more than any muse can stand. Older readers should also understand that this occupational syndrome is why newspapers used to (and still do) run that awful chestnut, "Yes, Virginia, There Is a Santa Claus."

But about twenty years ago, I stumbled on a scam that got me over Thanksgiving. Back in the late 1930s there was a columnist named Morton Thompson, who wrote a funny book called *Joe, The Wounded Tennis Player*. Thompson had a swift, breezy style, and he was a fellow who liked to cook. So in his book he printed his recipe for what became known, as years passed, as the Thompson Turkey. Being stuck for a column one Thanksgiving, I ran the Thompson Turkey recipe. This was long before Julia Child and James Beard and Craig Claiborne got their hooks into us; long before such spices as cumin, coriander and oregano became commonplace in kitchen cupboards.

Thus, to do the Thompson Turkey, those early-day readers had to chase all over town looking for poppy seeds, turmeric and mace. The response in the first few years was frequently inflammatory. One guy called and threatened me with bodily harm on sight "for ruining our Thanksgiving." People called in to complain that the preparation took so long that they didn't sit down to dinner until nine. In one episode, a man and his wife, with a living room full of guests, pulled the paste-encrusted bird out and, when they tried to pull the blackened crust away, they tore all the skin off the turkey. They ended up in a screaming kitchen fight, throwing bread at each other, while the guests presumably coughed politely into their drinks in the living room.

But a curious thing began happening. About two weeks before each Thanksgiving, calls would increase, requesting a rerun of the Thompson Turkey, "because we forgot to clip and save the recipe from last year." Some of the callers were phoning long distance. Letters arrived with similar requests, some with tips on modifying the recipe. And as Thanksgiving followed Thanksgiving, the complaints lessened. I could only surmise that it was because more people, having joined the Julia Child cult of gourmet cuisine, felt at ease with Mr. Thompson's complicated creation. Certainly there were more specialty stores and gourmet shops available, so such things as turmeric and coriander were quickly available or kept on hand. So I always looked forward to Thanksgiving with joy, since it meant merely rerunning the Thompson Turkey. This took about twenty minutes to type up, and it meant a day off without striving to re-create the old "to grandmother's house we go" type of column each year. I revere the memory of Morton Thompson. As for the recipe itself, it probably never will run in the dear old P-I again, so this is my last shot with it.

A few cautionary notes are in order. Architects of the big bird should remember that turkeys themselves have changed in the forty-plus years since the Thompson Turkey was launched. Modern birds, being more scientifically raised and fed different diets, are said to cook a bit faster than the turkeys of the 1930s. A 16-to-22-pound size, as stated in the recipe, is about right for this scrimmage. Oven temperatures do vary, so watch that.

Remember, this recipe comes to you only with the poetic instructions first created by Mr. Thompson. Done correctly, the Thompson Turkey is a joy. Over the years I have modified certain instructions in the recipe according to reader suggestions or complaints. Good luck to all:

Rub a 16-to-22-pound bird inside and out with salt and pepper. In a stew pan, put the chopped gizzard, liver, the neck and the heart, to which add one bay leaf, one teaspoon of paprika, a half teaspoon of coriander, a clove of garlic, four cups of water, and salt to taste. Let this simmer while you go ahead with the dressing.

Dice one apple and one orange in a bowl and add to this bowl a large can of crushed pineapple, the grated rind of one-half lemon, one can of drained water chestnuts and three table-spoons of chopped preserved ginger. [Editor's note: cut drastically or eliminate ginger.]

In another bowl, put two teaspoons of Colman's mustard, two teaspoons of caraway seed, three teaspoons of celery seed, two teaspoons of poppy seed, two-and-a-half teaspoons of oregano, one well crushed teaspoon of mace [Ed.'s note: Cut down or eliminate the mace.], four or five finely minced cloves of garlic, four cloves (minus heads and well-chopped), one-half teaspoon of turmeric, four large well-chopped onions, six well-chopped stalks of celery, one-half teaspoon savory and one tablespoon of poultry seasoning. Salt to taste.

In another bowl, dump three packages of bread crumbs. Add three-quarters pound of ground veal and one-quarter pound of fresh pork, a quarter-pound of butter and all the fat (first rendered) you can pry loose from the turkey.

Mix the contents of each bowl. When each bowl is well mixed, mix the three of them together. And mix well. Mix it until your forearms and wrists ache. Then mix it some more. Now toss it enough so that it isn't any longer a doughy mass.

Stuff your turkey, but not too full. Skewer the bird. Turn on your oven full force and let it get red hot. Put your bird breast down on a rack.

In a cup, make a paste consisting of the yolks of two eggs, a teaspoon of Colman's mustard, a clove of minced garlic, a tablespoon of onion juice, a half teaspoon of lemon juice and enough sifted flour to make a stiff paste. Take a pastry brush or an ordinary paint brush and stand by. [Ed.'s note: Increase the paste by half; you may need it.]

Put your bird in the red-hot oven. Let it brown all over. Remove the turkey. Turn your oven down to 325 degrees. Now, while the turkey is sizzling hot, paint it all over with the paste.

Put it back in the oven. The paste will set in a few minutes. Drag it out again. Paint every nook and cranny of it once more. Put it back in the oven. Keep doing this until you haven't any more paste left. [Ed.'s note: Be sure and have enough paste; see above.]

To the giblet-neck-liver-heart gravy that has been simmering, add one cup of cider. Don't let it cook any more. Stir it well. Keep it warm on top of the stove. This is your basting fluid.

Baste the bird every fifteen minutes. That means you will baste it from twelve to fifteen times. Turn it on its back the last half hour. It ought to cook four-and-one-half to five-and-one-half hours. When you remove it, the turkey will be dead black. You will think, "I've ruined it."

Be calm. Take a tweezer [Ed.'s note: or small tongs] and pry loose the paste coating. It will come off readily. Beneath this burnt, harmless, now worthless shell, the bird will be golden and dark brown, succulent, giddy-making with wild aroma, crisp and crackling.

The meat beneath will be wet, juice will spurt from it in tiny fountains high as the handle of the fork plunged into it. You do not have to be a carver to eat this turkey. Speak harshly to it and it will fall apart.

And that, dear friends, is the classic Thompson Turkey. Increasingly, as the years have gone by with repeats of this recipe, tributes have poured in. A few complaints, but mostly hosannahs. Many people are now veterans of the Thompson Turkey, wouldn't cook it any other way. By now, I suspect, hundreds, if not thousands, of kitchens in Seattle have this recipe clipped and filed away. If not, this is your final reading, as far as I'm concerned.

This scrumptious bird, this joy of creation, this splendid edifice is a tribute to our never-ending pursuit of elegant dining. It sounds so good that someday I may even try it myself.

Part 9
The Vertical Pronoun

As long as there are people with writing machines, the vertical pronoun "I" will never go on the endangered species list. How tempting to reach up and touch the "I" key. And why not? It is just one more example of mankind's yearning to talk about himself, for deep within all of us is this belief, almost instinctive, that we are the center of the universe. We must preserve our egos, protect our spirits and above all else emphasize the "self" in our self-esteem. It is why people boast, why they color stories to put themselves in a favorable light, why so many zillions of chance encounters begin with this sentence, or its equivalent: "I must tell you what I did today (or yesterday, last evening, a week ago)," because within us all is this desperate need to be recognized. Columnists are the worst offenders, if indeed ego satisfaction is an offense at all. Each of us, you, you, you and, yes, me, likes to talk about ourselves. We are fascinating, entertaining people—aren't we? I don't know about you, but I am. My ego told me so.

So it is that writers need that "I" key. Watch all columnists, especially the new ones just starting out. They begin at some cosmic level, detached and pleasantly opinionated. Watch them as they go—soon they write about a mechanic they know, then their spouses, then their children, then their household problems. Spontaneity flows. Then something happens. It isn't that columnists are any more ego-driven than you are. What happens is the damned dailiness of it all. It is as though, to go on existing, you had to give an interesting little talk each day. And after a few of these, what will you talk about? Why, you will talk about "me," of course.

As I think I've said elsewhere, writers cannibalize the world around them. They fasten onto a friend's wisecrack; they find adventurous material (so they think) in just going to the store. One of the best columnists I ever read was Charles McCabe, of the San Francisco Chronicle. Most of what McCabe wrote was about himself—his drinking habits, his marriages, his religious beliefs, his tastes in books; most of it entertaining but all of it about I, me, and me, myself. On the other hand, there was Red Smith, the great sportswriter. I was always tempted to ask Red why he didn't put himself into his column stories. Because Red always referred to his own part in a story as "a man said," or "an observer noted." It even got to the point where the Village Voice (I think) wrote a gentle rebuke of Red and his capacity for staying rock-solid in the third person, sometimes the second. "C'mon, Red," the writer chided. "You can do it . . . write 'I' just once, Red. It isn't hard."

From the first, I never had any trouble finding the "I" key. Part of that was because I admired so many writers like Dorothy Parker, John Lardner, Alexander Woollcott, Philip Wylie, Betty MacDonald (*The Egg and I*), Hemingway, A. J. Liebling—all of whom came down hard on that vertical pronoun key. In a sense, when you write like that, you put your butt on the line.

There is another reason, too. One of my good friends was the late Bob Ward, who was a star of the first order on the old P-I. In a way, he out-Welched the great Doug Welch; he had ideas and humor and imagination and zip

and go. But abruptly he quit journalism. He explained later, "The realization hit home that I was living vicariously. The only fun I had was listening to people who were doing interesting things." So he quit and became a crop duster, a publicist, an entrepreneur, a free spirit. He died broke, but he died having fun.

My own case was slightly different. Puddling around on the edge of middle age, I suddenly realized I didn't know how to *do* anything, except write about people who did things. So in my 40s, I tried to learn about fishing. The only fishing I had done before was being a kid with a salmon egg. Then it was skiing—God, what a torturous, punishing thing, to try skiing in your middle years. I was always drawn to people who fly airplanes. So I took up flying and became quite proficient at it—an instrument rating, no less. In my 40s, too, I learned to play golf and tennis. The best years of my life had been wasted trying to be a ballplayer, or getting what pleasure I could from writing about those who were good at baseball.

The next stage—this is the equivalent of a writer who thinks he can make an interesting story out of a trip to the store—was writing about all these newly discovered wonders. So I wrote a lot about skiing and flying and fishing and owning too many cars, and tennis instructors I came to know, like Janet Hopps Adkisson and Amy Yee. So it was natural to give the old "I" key a good workout as you revealed your successes and failures at—

well, *doing* things. I even exploited my dog, Tiger, and wrote about taking him to obedience school. I wrote so much about Tiger that a friend said, "If that dog ever gets an agent, you are out of business."

But one rambles on; or is it *I* ramble on?

The Watson Farm

Seattle Post-Intelligencer, July 29, 1981

OFF TO SOMEWHERE: TIGER AND I woke up on the Snoqualmie River, where we'd parked the camper in a stand of alder, cottonwood and a lot of brush I can't identify. Tiger was sitting on my chest. He is an early riser, so he sits on my chest and paws tentatively at my face. It's morning and he wants action. I make coffee and Tiger has his breakfast. I have a rule about what Tiger eats. We don't buy any brand of pet food that is hawked obscenely on TV. The pet food racket is all advertising and no substance. The whole process, those incessant, gooey ads, showing cats that dance and dogs that slurp, has brought me to a favorable view of euthanasia. Not for the pets. For the people who create those expensive color ads. We went down on the river bank and I tried spin casting a "hotshot" lure. I tried several lures, then some eggs, too, but no luck. For all the good it does, I should write my $12.25 fishing license off as a charitable deduction.

We packed up the camper and headed toward Carnation. "I'm going to show you where I went to school," I told Tiger. "Just because you passed novice obedience class doesn't mean you're the only scholar in the family. I won a spelling contest there in the sixth grade." The old Carnation Grade School is gone now, of course, but the new one, at the north end of town, is in the old spot. My school was a two-story, square-framed structure. The principal was Mr. Weaver and he'd line us up in two segregated lines, boys and girls, and parade us in, drill fashion, every morning. "Pow-see-shon!" he would bray. That meant "position," as in "shape up." Once in a while he would bound down the steps and turn some sixth-grade Beetle Bailey over his knee and whale away. I was scared spitless of Mr. Weaver. I don't remember the names of any of my teachers, and I'm quite sure they all made a determined effort to forget mine. The high points of my career were winning that spelling bee and being in love with Lois Dodge.

The railroad tracks passed behind the school and went past my dad's farm about a mile south. I got so good at walking a single rail that I could do the entire mile without losing balance. An old covered railroad bridge once spanned the Tolt River. The bridge had water barrels spaced beside the tracks in case of fire. I learned to smoke on an old cigarette brand called "One-11's," which I used to stash in a water barrel before I got home from school. They cost 11 cents.

We drove down to my dad's old farm. It is now the famous Remlinger Farm, the headquarters for the Remlinger U-Pick berry empire. The Remlingers built a beautiful brick home up on the hill where the old Watson place stood, built around it, and I can still look up and see what was once my bedroom window. I was an incorrigible reader. I'd lie awake in that bedroom reading *Tom Sawyer* and *Huckleberry Finn*, tons of Zane Grey, great gobs of pulp westerns (Max Brand was my favorite) and a zippy old magazine called Captain Billy's Whiz-Bang.

I was too young to dig some of Captain Billy's raunchy jokes, but the cartoons set my pubescent fantasies ablaze. Look out, Lois Dodge! They didn't have any sex education in Carnation Grade School, but who needed it when your older brother brought home Captain Billy's Whiz-Bang?

I showed Tiger the little stream where I used to catch dog salmon by the tail in spawning season. They were so big a 12-year-old could scarcely hold on. "Actually, Tiger, I hated this farm. You're a city-bred dog. I was a city-bred kid. I was raised on asphalt and pavement and playgrounds and movies every Friday night. You understand, don't you? I was lonely on this farm." We were standing down by Remlinger's classy berry and vegetable shed where people come to shop and Tiger wasn't listening because a small female dog was running loose among the cars. He had shot off like a rocket. Tiger doesn't need Captain Billy's Whiz-Bang to get the idea.

I really did hate that farm. As a "city kid" I wasn't much accepted by my peers. Because I only milked three cows, I was looked down upon by kids who milked 18 or 20. It was the bottom of the Great Depression. My old man couldn't sell anything he grew. One year it was peas. We must have raised enough peas to feed a small industrial nation. I had to hoe them and string them and pick them. The end of all this labor was that nobody would give my dad a dime for them, so we trucked the peas into Seattle and gave boxes of them away to our old neighbors.

My dad had pride. He took pride in running a self-sufficient farm. We made our own butter, slaughtered our own pigs, cured our own hams, raised potatoes for the root cellar to feed the pigs and ran the primitive farm machinery out of my dad's own blacksmith shop. He was an all-purpose man, my dad, but the Depression killed him. When he lost the farm to the bank and we moved back to Seattle, where he had to go on welfare, it killed this wonderful, tough, hard-working man. The spirit went out of him, the same as it did in so many other fine men crushed by an economic force they didn't understand. Don't tell me about your goddamned trickle-down supply-side economics.

▼

The Joy of Skiing

Seattle Magazine, December, 1964

NO MATTER HOW VIGOROUSLY I MIGHT WISH TO DENY IT, the hellish fact is that I am middle-aged. To evade this conclusion is to directly ignore the testimony of a dozen doctors, to scorn the advice of loved ones, and to stand, in a ludicrous posture of self-deception, before any available mirror. In many ways, the years have been unkind. I wear a hearing aid. A distant bout with polio left one leg noticeably weaker than the other. I smoke too much, eat too heavily and have, over the years, become acquainted with an appalling number of bartenders.

At a casual glance, which is all I'm worth, you would peg me as Mr. Mean Average—a fellow who gets most of his exercise pulling cotton from aspirin bottles. A skier? You would laugh at the suggestion, and you would not be the first. But I *am* a skier—a good, sound, recreational skier. This simple declaration surprises even me, for, indeed, skiing has lately become one of my uncontrollable passions.

From painful experience I can testify that skiing is a sport of the senses, for it demands an acquired sense of balance and timing, a developed sureness which alone can overcome the primary sense of fear. To take its pleasures, one must accept an apprenticeship filled with foreboding and exhaustion. One must encounter blisters, cuts, sprains and dark periods of despair—and endure the preposterous interludes of flailing helplessness before the amused eyes of one's fellow man.

Skiing can be dangerous. To say that this is not the case is to tell an untruth, or to lapse into the shibboleths of its mindless devotees. And it is expensive, especially when a whole family is involved. In five years I have spent enough on ski clothes and equipment (mine is a family of four) to underwrite a cruise in the Mediterranean. The outlay for airline tickets, car repairs, orthopedists, ski instructors, physical therapists, Minit-Rub and lodge bills adds up to another shameful figure—enough, say, to hire a psychiatrist to cure me of skiing.

But a psychiatrist isn't going to. In all of the 11 Western states, there are not enough wild horses, let alone psychiatrists, to keep me away from the slopes of Snoqualmie, Ski Acres, Crystal Mountain or the other four Cascade playgrounds.

The affliction defies self-analysis. My daydreams often take the form of squalid little schemes to evade responsibilities and contrive a trip to Aspen, Mammoth Mountain or Sun Valley. By early September, I begin to loiter around ski shops, running a finger along metal edges, balancing poles and slipping my hands inside the soft, fragrant linings of new boots. Barnum never knew of stretch pants, but he had me in mind.

Baldly, then, it must be proclaimed that I am one of a breed—the Northwest skier, harmlessly nuts, but fantastically devoted to the joys and hazards of his monomania. The rest of the world may ski in sunshine, in places where powder snow is almost guaranteed by the management, but those of us here will ski any time we can, anywhere and always, under all kinds of conditions.

Experts have called us the best recreational skiers in the nation—and who are we to quarrel with experts? No less an authority than Emile Allais, the celebrated French teacher, has said: "I can spot a Seattle skier anywhere, by the way he is able to make quick turns and the way he bends his knees to take the moguls."

How does it all begin? To each his own story, but mine begins in a floundering, ignominious heap on the top of the second chair lift at Sun Valley's Mt. Baldy—just below the famed Round House.

By a combination of circumstances too dreary to detail, I was acting as a sort of native bearer for a television photographer, and I had a battery of cameras hanging around my neck. In order to follow him around, it was necessary for me to put on skis. Disaster ensued.

Stepping from the lift, I flew off in several directions, tumbling in a clatter of crossed skis, flying poles and dangling cameras. The most compassionate onlooker could only laugh. The lift had to be stopped, for by no combination of pushing, tugging or grasping was I able to hoist myself to an upright posture—not, that is, without help.

This came from a short, stocky man who stepped out of the crowd, grinning broadly, and pulled me out of the way. By coincidence, he was a Seattleite—and a celebrated skier. "My name's Buzz Fiorini," he said, after helping me to put the spare parts back together. "I hope nobody thinks you were in one of *my* ski classes."

A moment later he had gone, as though by magic. Gingerly, I moved over to the edge of the slope, looked down—and shuddered. There I beheld the spectacle of this man barreling down what then seemed to be a sheer drop. The longer I looked, the more I shuddered.

That night, out of curiosity, I checked an area map, found the Round House, and located exactly where we had stood. "Canyon Run," the map said. "For advanced skiers. Vertical drop, 1,039 feet. Approximately 0.9 miles in length. This canyon is narrow, but not too steep to negotiate even for a less experienced skier."

I didn't realize it at the time, but that was the beginning. In a vague, disturbing way, the memory kept returning: of this man (*my own age!*) casually disappearing down that awful, narrow canyon, swiftly and without apparent effort.

The area map had said: " . . . even for a less experienced skier." Less experienced than what? Curiosity gnawed. How does a man feel when he lets himself go like that, looking relaxed and confident, yet somehow reckless, too, riding easily, cutting, turning, now running straight at some incredible speed? And all those bumps of snow!

How long does it take, I wondered, to ski like that?

Walter Mitty was a man of indeterminate age, and I think of him often. I remember him then as 40, and since then as old as I have happened to be. Walter Mitty is now 46. A year after the Canyon Run episode he was 41, and Walter Mitty dreamed of standing on that ledge, chatting easily with a friend, perhaps flicking his cigarette away and hurling himself down that forbidding canyon with no more ceremony than a cheery "See you later."

The next winter was agony. At 41, the little poisons of fatigue come quickly, and the Distant Early Warning System of caution is more sensitive than it was at 22, so you develop an almost unconscious tendency to stay within easy telephone distance of the Medical-Dental Building.

My apprenticeship started on the gentlest of slopes, where I literally learned to walk on skis, sweating and puffing, suffering through the ridiculous, tiring posture of the herringbone. A simple kick turn was an ordeal of contortion, and always there was that damned falling down. No matter how you practice it, the simple fact of falling is an offense against the dignity of man; and having fallen, the struggle to arise, attached to those wretched skis, makes you regret every cigarette and second helping you've ever taken.

At this age, your eyes are hypnotically riveted to boots and skis; the smallest bump triggers panic, and a true mogul—those awesome mounds of snow, so common in the crowded Cascades—can be as terrifying as Mt. Baker itself. Any slight change in snow surface, whether a ski track, a rut or a bare patch, brings on tension followed by sprawling chaos.

The simple litany of your instructor—you *have* to have an instructor—becomes as complicated as celestial navigation: "Down, up, down . . . lean over the hill, down, up, skis together . . . down, up, weight on the downhill ski . . . down, up, unwind, turn . . . " All those things to remember!

My life began to take on a furtive quality. Middle-aged vanity is a formidable force, and I avoided the slopes on crowded weekends—preferring, instead, to sneak out of the office on Wednesdays and Thursdays. My instruction was haphazard; because I refused to allow fellow skiers to witness my incompetent floundering, I began to buy private lessons from any available instructor.

My absolute low point, a sort of moral corruption, occurred one afternoon at Ski Acres. There I found Ken Syverson, an historic figure in Northwest skiing, working patiently with a group of five or six women. It was a "housewives' class," and these middle-aged females were unabashedly enjoying a beginner's flops and spills, joking together about their painful accomplishments. Like some outcast coyote, I skulked behind this happy pack, straining to catch The Leader's pearls of wisdom, and, from a discreet distance, imitating his students' work.

Worse was yet to come: the day when skiing cost me $285. A hearing aid can comfort the afflicted in a relatively quiet room, but when tucked under a skier's stocking cap, it picks up a back-lash that makes it screech like some malfunctioning p.a. system. To avoid this, I tucked the hearing aid in a pocket, but forgot to zip it closed. Later, while taking one of my innumerable egg-beater sprawls, I lost $285 worth of hearing aid in the snow. Wearily, until dark, I scrounged around on hands and knees, almost tearfully exploring every spot where I had tumbled. *Gone—forever.*

"You are a fool, you'll never learn this way. Once or twice a week—not a man of your age." The speaker was a stranger whom I had casually met in the Snoqualmie Summit Skihaus. He was speaking a brutal truth, as strangers often do—and friends seldom will. "Get out of here," he said. "Go to Sun Valley and stay a week, two weeks. Turn your body over to them. They'll put you through torture, but you'll learn to ski."

A year passed before I could afford it. But the day finally arrived, a lovely winter morning with the sunshine glowing pink on the mountain tops and the air thick with Austrian accents.

"You dere! Shkee down here, und schlide der shkees!" This was the Monday morning shape-up, at which members of beginning classes, seemingly hundreds in number and widely varied in age, are graded and then assigned to instructors according to ability. I was scared. To a certain kind of novice, the Sun Valley instructors' corps—slim, agile, tanned, trimly dressed and outwardly arrogant—looks like the Elite Guard of the SS.

An instructor stood in front of the class to which I had been assigned, a man in his 40s who was cautiously looking us over. He was tall, slim-waisted, with a rather sharp chin and prominent nose, wavy gray hair and cold blue eyes. Nervous thoughts ran through my head: "He's the mean type, probably gets sore if you can't understand his lousy English. Well, if he pulls any of that 'Schlide der shkees' on me, I'll . . . "

"My name is Bill Jones," he said, pleasantly. "I think it would be nice if we learned each other's names as soon as possible. How many are there—six? That's a good size for a class. Now then, shall we begin?"

From that instant, he was my hero. And for six straight days, Bill Jones became the all-obsessive personality in my life. His moods stayed on a level platform of pleasantness, never giving way to scornful impatience; he was firm and persuasive, and I thought of him as a cross between Jim Owens and Norman Vincent Peale.

He led us through the gentle beginning hills, on Half Dollar Mountain, then on to Dollar Mountain, a more formidable rise, tireless at repeating pointers and superb at giving demonstrations. Above all, he instilled in us a sense of friendly competitiveness that accelerated our desire to do better.

Nights were only for sleep; eight or nine hours simply didn't seem sufficient. Little bruises or cuts multiplied as the days wore on. Legs trembled with weariness. On Thursday, Bill Jones took us to the top of Mt. Baldy—to a beginner, it seemed as formidable as Everest—then he brought us back to Dollar Mountain. "See?" he said. "See the difference? Two days ago you were all scared of Dollar. Now it looks easy."

But there had to be a limit, and on the sixth day my legs gave out. No matter how hard I tried, my knees would not bend, my skis kept wavering and my falls became ever more frequent. My final tumble was definitive—a head-over-skis cartwheel that sent my cap, gloves and poles flying.

"You all right?" asked Bill Jones solicitously.

"Go away," I said. "Just leave me alone and send a dog back with some brandy."

It took a long week of rest to recuperate, but from that time on skiing became a sport, a recreation, a joy of anticipation. No longer was it a self-imposed agony, marked by a mere struggle to survive, for, though I could not ski well, or even smoothly, and certainly not with full control, I was, at least, a passable specimen of middle-aged mobility on those treacherous runners. From then on I was a member of that wonderful, adventurous army of Cascade skiers who speed to the mountain each weekend some 45,000 strong.

In this superbly endowed land of the Northwest, I am respectful of the steelheader who braves wind and rain to extract great sea-going rainbows from cold and swollen rivers; although the rudiments of trout fishing can be learned in a week, I honor the skill of its devoted practitioners. Neither do I sneer at the sodden patience of the salmon-chasers—even though each season brings its tale of a small boy who caught a 30-pounder using gumdrops for bait.

On occasion, I feel a pang of envy for skippers of boats and their ability to afford them, and I would have higher regard for hunters, as a class, if they at least took the pains to distinguish a deer from a Holstein, or from another hunter.

Golf? I can understand the golfer's psychic misery, but I regard the patois of this game's addicts as the greatest bore in all Christendom, and I have nearly suffocated in the Babbitry of their locker rooms.

In my book, none of these types of sportsmen compares with skiers. I am brought to this conclusion (having tried the others) after six years of association with this unique, hardy breed—and I am proud to be counted among the worthy.

(Make no mistake about it: Any skier who has waited till later life to master the sport's demanding techniques has earned the pleasure he finds. I know of one remarkable woman who has broken her leg three times in the past five years and who awaits, with glowing anticipation, this year's first snowfall. She is 67. The distinguished Dr. Merritt Stiles, who is president of the U.S. Ski Association, was a tottering beginner at 55, and now, in his 60s, skis gracefully and well.)

Scratch almost any skier's memory, and you will elicit a recitation of sprained ankles, twisted knees and minor contusions. I myself have strained the resources of the King County Medical Association for treatments of a separated rib cartilage, X-rays of a bruised shoulder, a damaged instep and a badly twisted knee. This latter affliction, while of no great interest to anyone else, brings on poignant memories.

Two years ago, through one of those strange, generous impulses that occasionally occur among publishers, I found myself aboard the Pacific Northwest Ski Association charter flight to Europe. Aboard were doctors, lawyers, businessmen, teachers, footloose divorcees and shop girls who had slavishly saved to make this trip. Ahead were 25 days of skiing at St. Anton, Zermatt, Innsbruck, St. Moritz—the established mecca of the world's foremost ski resorts.

On the third day, at the little Austrian resort of Kitzbühel, I cracked up. Taking a large mogul badly, I piled in a heap, and the crunch of a knee was almost audible. That's the way it happens, sometimes. With no shame at all, I confess to standing there, in that wide, wonderful snowfield, surrounded by all those goddamn Alps, with a right knee taking on the dimensions of a basketball, and, because it just seemed appropriate, I cried.

The other members of our group fared far better; indeed, they performed spectacularly well. These Northwest-bred recreational skiers ranged all over the mountainous mecca of Europe and they skied not only as well, but noticeably better than their French, Italian, German and Austrian counterparts. Even to my unpracticed eye, they proved superior in handling Europe's crankiest slopes with confidence, style and discipline.

Several reasons have been advanced to explain the superiority of this region's skiers. For one thing, the Northwest has a far richer tradition than most of us suspect. It has turned out a sizable supply of champions—such names as Jack Nagel, Don Amick, Gretchen Fraser, Jannette Burr and Paul Gilbreath come readily to mind. These and many others have come back to contribute their names and gifts to Northwest skiing.

Then, of course, there is the matter of proximity. It is difficult to name any other population center within 50 to 90 minutes' drive of seven major ski areas, and such easy access makes regular commuters of us all. (Seemingly, every organization except the Black Muslims now sponsors a ski school.) Moreover, the plentiful dumping of snow on the Cascades, from mid-November through April, gives us one of the nation's longest seasons.

But let us admit a drawback: This plentiful snow is frequently wet. Skiing in the Cascades can be as capricious as an imaginative, unforgiving

Providence can make it, and I have skied in weather that would drive a sensible penguin to cover.

True, Cascade skiing can be beautiful—the days of sunshine and powder snow are jewels. But, on many occasions, it afford the most miserable, wet, cloud-laden, fog-shrouded, unpredictable conditions extant—a veritable grab-bag of dew points and temperatures.

All this is our burden, but such grim conditions also serve us well, for no truth is more frequently uttered, from Mt. Baker to Mt. Hood, than this one: "If you can ski here, you can ski anywhere."

Once released to places less plagued by dampness and rain, the Northwest skier finds he has slipped his chains. A skiing style forged and developed in snow that sometimes resembles the consistency of wet concrete adapts easily to a wide range of conditions. It is also true—alas, the paradox—that while we annoy strangers by constantly boasting about our skiing, we will do almost anything to escape it. It is no accident, for example, that Sun Valley gets some 35 per cent of its patronage from Seattle and the Pacific Northwest.

Even now I am plotting a trip to Sun Valley in February, and, in my mind, it is a pilgrimage to a sun-bathed shrine. From now on, it always will be thus. It became so one afternoon last February while I was standing near the Round House on Mt. Baldy with Bill Jones. Leading up to this moment were three glorious weeks of skiing with this man of 360-degree vision, following him over moguls, down valleys and through trails, hearing his constant exhortations: "Weight forward, press, press . . . I hear those skis chattering . . . bend those knees, get that check, down, up, slide, check . . . "

This was my final day, and we had just completed a final run. The sun was high and warm, and the snow was absolutely right, packed solid but with a few inches of fine powder for cover. We were standing there after our long run, breathing heavily, noses running wet from the wind. "You've got it down pretty good," Bill said. "You've come along fine. Someday soon, you'll be a good skier."

Nothing in all of Sun Valley held as much joy for me as those few words—and I showed it. There is that last long journey from the Round House down Canyon Run, and so on down through River Run to the floor of the valley below. There are easier ways to do it, but I took Canyon run, vertical drop, 1,309 feet, narrow but not too steep to negotiate "for a less experienced skier." Walter Mitty didn't fall.

This is another "I" column, one in which I let everybody down. I went public with my efforts to quit smoking. By so doing, went the reasoning, I would ensure that I would really cast out the weed. It worked for four months. Then I went back to cigarettes. I did not confess my betrayal because I figured I had perhaps helped some other people to get off the weed. A poor excuse, but mine own. I am still ashamed of the whole episode.

Quitting Smoking

Seattle Post-Intelligencer, February 21, 1971

PEOPLE ARE STILL PRONE TO WONDER—prone wonderers are the best kind; they look so peaceful—how it goes with my anti-smoking campaign. Not anti-smoking, really; I don't care if the whole world prefers to live in Marlboro country. It's just that one peaceful Sunday afternoon, on Sept. 27, 1970, I decided that smoking was no longer for me. I quit that afternoon, struggled through Sunday night and Monday morning, then wrote a column, announcing that I had quit tobacco, once and for all.

There ensued possibly some of the dullest prose extant as I reported, almost daily, on the progress of my will power, my feelings, my nerves, etc. In the death throes of its final issue, Seattle Magazine beseeched me to shut up and start smoking again. The idea was not self-glorification. Writing about not smoking was the insurance against starting up again. Once you put yourself on public record as having performed a certain act of will, it becomes virtually impossible to cop out.

All this was back in late September and early October. More than four months ago. And even today, people call or write to ask, "Are you still off cigarettes?" Several phoned in to confirm the rumor that I'd "gone back to cigarettes"—and what was the truth? I do not fool myself by thinking that many people were truly concerned about my problem. It was just that I'd stumbled onto a topic that is of interest to anyone from, say, age three to creaking old age. The reason it is of interest is that the populace is made up almost exclusively of people who smoke now and wish they didn't, people who have quit (some of them several times) and people who have long ago given up trying to get off the weed. In short, misery loves company, and sometimes vice versa.

The first days, of course, were agony. I could scarcely put down a comprehensible sentence on paper. (I scarcely can now, but in those days even I couldn't understand it.) Concentration on anything was impossible. As I slogged away, letters came in, offering advice, encourage-ment and unique, if not sure-fire methods for quitting. As time went on, I learned that the pain of quitting does not subside after three or four days, only slightly after three or four weeks. Of all the letters I received, the most significant and prophetic was one from the wife of a friend, who said in part: "Most important of all—you must realize that you will never hate the thought of cigarettes. Rather, you will come to view them as you would an old girl friend. The acute physical longing will be gone—replaced by a sort of wistful, nostalgic affection and a mature, reasoned judgment."

Very well. Where are we today? Have I gone back to cigarettes? The answer is no, but the past four months add up to a crazy, perilous journey—one that I would not care to repeat. You have heard of "withdrawal symptoms"? Deny yourself something and you are sub-jected to strange physical maladies. For example, the first time I quit smoking, some 16 years ago, I was off the weed and doing fine. Except for one thing: an incessant tingling at the tip of my tongue. In no time at all, I decided I must have cancer of the tongue. Terrified, I went to the doctor, who examined, probed, and clucked. Conclusion: "There is nothing wrong with your tongue. It is all mental. Perhaps you gave up smoking."

This time I was ready for withdrawal symptoms. Perhaps a tingling of the tongue again, dizzy spells or itchy scalp. When withdrawal symptoms came, I would not panic. So the weeks of early agony passed. It came on winter, and I began to look at the rain with dread. Each day I awoke a bit more depressed than the day before; I began to look upon life as one big swamp of despair. Since there was nothing physically wrong, I went to see a psychologist. We talked for an hour or more, while I described this strange feeling of depression.

We talked about guilt feelings and possible feelings of inferiority. (As I recall, he implied that in my case they were probably well-founded.) "As for your depression," he said, "I think the answer is quite simple. It's just that you've lost a friend." "Lost a what?" I said. "You have lost a friend," he said. "He's no longer around to help you over the rough spots." "What friend???" I almost shouted. "Your friend, the cigarette," he replied. "When you quit smoking, it was like losing a trusted friend. To put it on a level even you can understand, you are going through withdrawal symptoms. That will be $25, please."

Then I remembered my friend's wife's letter. "You will come to view them as you would an old girl friend—the acute physical longing will be gone—" But the memory lingers on. Since then, the depression gradually lifted. Today I am my old, lazy, slothful self—but at least I feel better. And someday soon I've got to get around to quitting something else. Anybody got a good diet handy?

Being Sick

Seattle Post-Intelligencer, December 29, 1980

FOR THE PAST COUPLE OF WEEKS a message has appeared in this space accompanied by a picture of an obvious impostor. "Emmett Watson is ill," the message says. "His column will resume when he returns." Returns from where? The message did not say. From McRory's steakhouse? The grave? The laughing academy? Purgatory? To begin, I would like to strike down this scurrilous message. I was not ill. I was sick. Ill is a term that implies delicate health, the way your aging aunt used to have what they call the "vapors," or when someone was "off his feed." Sick. Now, there is a word that has a lip-smacking sound to it, a description to arouse the attention of friends, foes and Blue Cross alike. When you are sick you have full privileges in such endeavors as harvesting sympathy, glorying in self-pity and wallowing in "get well" cards. This you can do with impunity.

How I got into the hospital is almost beside the point. But that's where I was. "When do I get a sponge bath?" I asked the nurse. "You've only been here 10 minutes," she replied. "First things first. I must take all your money." "In *advance*? Can't they total up the bill first?" "This is for safekeeping," she said. "As for TV, you can watch anything but the Seahawks. The doctor says it might cause depression and delay your recovery."

A trim-looking man in a tweed coat came in the room. "I am your neurologist," he announced, pleasantly. "My what?" "Your neurologist. I am here to poke you and ask questions. But first we have a few little machines we'd like to try out on you." So they wheeled me out, up an elevator, down a corridor, and into a room that looked like the inside of a rotary engine. Things buzzed and hummed, and finally I was wheeled back and told to take 17 pills of varying colors. I fell asleep for a while and woke up to hear two nurses talking outside my door. "They took him in for a brain scan and came up empty," one of them said. "Now they're not sure if his head is empty or the machine doesn't work."

The next morning a brisk young woman with a clipboard came in.

"I am your nutritionist," she said. "From now on, you can no longer eat thick steaks, butter, pastries, bread, creamed soups, jelly doughnuts, spareribs, hash browned potatoes and—" "Bring back my neurologist," I said, "I liked him better."

Days passed. The Seahawks blew it big to Dallas and I bootlegged a few peeks. The medic was right—depressing. A friend came by and I wheedled shamelessly. "Get me some spareribs," I said. "Go out and buy some spareribs. Once they say I can't have something, I go crazy for it." He smuggled in some very nice spareribs and I felt much better. Next morning another doctor arrived.

"How is your circulation?" he said. I said it was about 200,00 daily and 220,000 Sundays. "That is not what I mean," he said. "I was talking about your own circulation. It was a rhetorical question. Like your newspaper, you could use a little more circulation. Also like The P-I, your delivery system could stand improvement. By the way, how long is your column?" "About 800 words," I said. "You should write shorter columns," he said. "You mean if I write shorter columns I will feel better?" "No, but your readers would. Now, about these pills. What are your favorite colors?"

Whatever my favorite colors are, he filled the need. "Take the salmon-colored ones and the white ones in the morning," he said. "Or is it the blue ones and the white ones? I forget. It will all be on your instruction sheet. And don't forget the orange-tasting drink, either. The oblong blue pills, I forget what they are for, but take them anyway. Regularly. They might be good for your character. Those are some things you should do. Now for a brief list of things you should not do. Don't stay up late, don't smoke any more, don't overeat, don't overreact, and don't over-anything. Do what I tell you and you will have a long and happy life."

"Like hell I will," I said.

So the next day they turned me loose, out of stir, so to speak. The first stop was at a discount house where I bought a small pocket calculator. "I think I have the prescription for the calculator right here," I said, fumbling in my pockets. "You don't need a prescription to buy a calculator," said the clerk. "Yes I do," I said. "It's on doctor's orders, so I can keep track of my pills." Since then, I have been back to see the doctor a couple of times.

The last time he reached out and patted my shoulder. "You are doing fine," he said, "just follow my advice and you will be back to where you were before." "But doc," I said, "maybe that's not where I want to be."

My Heart Attack

Seattle Times, June 18, 1985

AS I WAS SAYING BEFORE I WAS SO RUDELY INTERRUPTED . . .

Well, here we were tootling down I-5 into Southern California, me at the wheel of my Ford 350 XLT one-tonner. On our CB radio, in back-and-forth chatter with the big truckers, our rig became known as "Tiger One-Ton," aptly christened because of my 11-pound apricot poodle, name of Tiger, who rides shotgun on these adventures.

Tiger One-Ton was pulling a highway trailer nicknamed Westin I, a luxury suite that outdoes most Westin accommodations; it measures 40 feet in length and rides along on six wheels. This mastodon is currently tethered at the Seattle North RV Park, and I wouldn't trade it for the whole top floor of the Westin Hotel.

Tiger rides much of the time with his rear paws on the seat and his front paws propped on the open glove compartment door. This gives him a chance to second-guess the driver, namely me, and spot dogs to bark at in other cars.

There also was a lovely lady along on this trip. She is sort of red-headed and tall and willowy, with a gift of droll humor that sometimes blows the circuit-breaker on your funny bone. She is beautiful as all hell. She is skeptical of most things I say, but I wouldn't trade *her* for a studio full of Miss America candidates. Her name is Nancy, and she thinks I am—well, maybe mildly nuts with my mad schemes to take the humdrum out of life. But like most daughters, she is resigned to the kind of father she got stuck with. We've gotten quite attached over the 30-odd years we've known each other.

That's the way things were going on I-5.

Then suddenly it happened. A little way out of Bakersfield, it was unmistakable. Bam! Chest pain. Bam! Chest pain. Bam! Another one. Ye gods! Down the left arm. No doubt about this one. Heart attack. Welcome to the club, oh great adventurer.

Without boring you with details, I was very soon in a Bakersfield hospital. They wired me up like a City Light substation. Angina pectoris, the guy said. He said he would like me to stay a while in his hospital. He went out of the room, and this gave me time to think. Suddenly my thoughts turned to our 34th president of the United States.

"You will be very comfortable here in the next few days," the doctor said when he returned to the room.

"That's something we'll never know, will we?" I said.

"What do you mean?"

"I mean, I want out of here in the next 10 minutes. Have you ever heard what W. C. Fields said he wanted as the epitaph on his tombstone? When somebody asked W. C. what he wanted on his tombstone, he said, 'Offhand, I'd rather be here than in Philadelphia.' That's the way I feel about Bakersfield."

There were releases to sign, of course, because I was considered "very high risk" if allowed to walk out. This is where our 34th president comes in. You see, down in Rancho Mirage, near Palm Springs, they have this Taj Mahal of medical centers.

Palm Springs is where a lot of rich old crocks go to die. But before they die, they want to postpone it as long as they can, so they set up the Eisenhower Medical Center to stay one jump ahead of the old man with the scythe. I figured Eisenhower Medical Center would have some top-drawer heart mechanics.

So goodbye, Bakersfield, and here we are again, barreling down I-5 once more. Nancy at the wheel of Tiger One-Ton, me sucking on nitroglycerine capsules, and Tiger the dog taking a very calm view of the whole thing.

Nancy, who had never driven a big truck before, much less a truck pulling a land-rolling battleship, was a champion. She got on the CB horn, she pumped that rig over Tejon Pass, and not long after that she was the biggest celebrity on I-5. Truckers waved and grinned, because the network of CBs warned everybody that there was this girl, this mere woman, for God's sake, high-balling this huge rig down the highway. The truckers even got on the CB and warned her that "Smoky" was up ahead.

Well, I was right about one thing. Eisenhower is the place to go if you feel compelled to have a heart attack. It is a place that is swimming in money, because its donors are rich, as in real rich. The combined wealth of Eisenhower donors could rub out the national debt.

But more than that, Eisenhower Medical Center has a first-rate staff, which takes pride in its work—upbeat, cheerful, competent and helpful. EMC also has a guy named Jack Sternlieb. Sternlieb, who is only 37, heads up something called the Heart Institute of The Desert. The Heart Institute consists of a team of five top cardiologists, a battery of assistants, specially recruited and trained, and 13 special heart-care nurses who work directly for Jack Sternlieb.

Dr. Jack Sternlieb was only 31 when he founded the Heart Institute in 1978. He is the only one there who does heart surgery. In his time, Jack has performed almost 1,000 open-heart operations. His success rate is better than 98 percent, which is remarkable when you consider that the average age of his patients is 68. The national average age for such operations is 54.

So that's the guy who gave me a triple-bypass operation.

One minor scenario preceded this excavation, which left me with a beautiful racing stripe down the middle of my chest. Jack Sternlieb was counseling us on the forthcoming surgery the night before. There were Nancy and I, another patient due for surgery and the patient's wife. By now, Nancy was a bit frazzled and exhausted by all these goings-on; she was very close to tears. The other woman took her aside, put her arm around Nancy's shoulder and said:

"Here's what you are going to do with yourself. You are going to find a nice Southern California bar, one that has a nice, understanding bartender. You are going to give this nice bartender the keys to your truck. Then you are going to sit there for the next few hours, think of your dad and get pie-faced. Then you are going to take a taxicab home and sleep it off, and when you wake up, you'll know that your old man is going to be all right."

All this may explain my absence for so long. I apologize for the delay.

Learning to Fly

Seattle Post-Intelligencer, July 23, 1961

IN RECENT DAYS THE AIR ABOVE the jagged surface of Seattle has been subjected to a series of weird disturbances, namely me. Do not panic. It's only that I'm learning to fly. Again I say: do not panic.

This middle-aged flirtation with gravity and mechanics is being watched closely by the CAA, the CAB, the ABC, CBS and NBC (the latter are afraid I'll hit their TV towers on QA Hill), not to mention the John Birch Society, which is interested in seeing if I learn to fly the 100 per cent pure American Way.

Since it's your house I'm flying over, you have every right to know what kind of a guy I am. Given half a day's practice and 16 borrowed wrenches, I can fix a leaking water faucet so that it will positively leak better. My genius lies in such things as misreading schedules, speedometers, calendars, thermometers and movie time tables. At least once a week, I push the wrong button or get stuck in an automatic elevator.

Your next question is anticipated.

Why does a left-footer like me want to fly an airplane?

"Because it's there."

(Mountain climbers having been getting by on that one for years.)

My instructor is a chap named Henry Reverman, who was placidly running the Lake Union Air Service on Westlake N. before he met me. Things have livened up since then. Mr. Reverman is a wiry fellow with a pale complexion, and he is going to get more wiry and much paler before he finishes with me. Mr. Reverman has taught hundreds of people, including service personnel, to fly. But I think he regards me as his greatest challenge.

After our first lesson, he gazed off into space, as though reviewing his life's work, took a deep breath and declared: "In 14 years down here, I have sent 500 students out and everyone has come back. In your case . . . " Mr. Reverman let the sentence hang for a moment. One knuckle was poised above the wooden top of his desk. " . . . in your case, I think we can do it."

His knuckle didn't knock on the wooden desk. That was the decisive moment in our relationship.

According to Mr. Reverman, the first step in learning to fly is familiarization with the airplane.

"Take the aileron, for example," said Mr. Reverman. "It is—"

"The what?"

"The aileron," he repeated. "Those things on each wing. They are used to bank the airplane, or keep it in level flight. This is the rudder here, and those are the elevators."

He looked at me thoughtfully for a while, as though making up his mind about something. At last he spoke again. "And that," he added, pointing, "is what we call the propeller."

It's amazing how much technical knowledge a man can absorb if he listens closely.

▼

Flying a Canadian Jet

Seattle Post-Intelligencer, August 7, 1974

DON'T ASK ME HOW IT HAPPENED, but there I was, somehow, standing next to a beautiful red-white-and-blue Tutor (CT-114) Canadian jet trainer—one of nine which make up the Canadian Armed Forces' precision-flying demonstration team. In elegant letters alongside the cockpit were the words "Capt. Runner Shaw." What a beautiful name for a pilot! I commend it to Ernie Gann for his next flying novel. Three of us would go up, and I hoped I would draw Capt. John (Runner) Shaw. Two fellows from local radio, Phil Harper, of KING, and Charlie Brown, of KJR, would fly in the other planes. The three of us shared a common nervousness about this flight—with one importance difference: I was dying to get my hands on the controls of that Tutor jet.

The team leader, Major George Miller, gave us all a preflight briefing. "If you have to bail out . . . " he was saying. ". . . any emergency, we'll come back as a unit." Major Miller looked at my oxford loafers. "You should wear laced shoes," he said. We began walking toward the planes, and I asked the pilot next to me, "Why didn't he like my shoes?" "In case we have to eject," he replied, "the force would tear your loafers right off." I looked at the name on his jacket. He was Capt. Runner Shaw.

On the way to the plane, I lobbied shamelessly to get at the controls. I told a few lies about my piloting experience. "We'll see how it goes," he said, noncommittally. After an interminable period of getting strapped in (parachute, helmet, oxygen mask, emergency instructions), we began taxiing to Runway 34 at Paine Field. Ahead was the team leader, Major Miller; to the left was Capt. Mike Murphy; and to the right was Capt. Runner Shaw, a rugged, mustachioed, 29-year-old, who flies "right wing" for the Snowbirds. The microphones were inside the oxygen masks, and we talked freely.

"Check your instrument panel," he said, pointing to the bank on the copilot's side. "Turn and bank, vertical speed indicator, air speed indicator . . ." I made a quick memory scan of the panel. Captain Shaw patted a pocket on my flight suit. "The sick bag is in there if you need it," he said. And now we were hurtling down the runway, three planes no more than five feet apart; instantaneously, all three jets were climbing like scalded cats. For a while it was easy, wing-to-wing formation flying, then all hell broke loose.

Capt. Runner Shaw pulled back the stick. Cheeks sagged. Arms felt heavy. Nothing to see but blue sky above and Major Miller's lead plane. The VSI (vertical speed indicator) was reading 6,000 feet a minute. We peaked at maybe 5,000 feet, Captain Shaw pushed the stick forward, and now we were diving—straight at Puget Sound and Whidbey Island. "Jeezus!" I said. "You sick?" he asked. "No, just ecstatic," I replied. A few minutes later, Major Miller, the team leader, moved farther out ahead.

Captain Shaw reached over and tapped the stick on my side. "You got it," he said. "Go ahead, fly it. Remember, it takes a very light touch." My eyes darted to the altimeter, which abruptly showed a climb of 200 feet. Bad flying. "Easy does it," he said. Ahead, and slightly to the left, was Major Miller. "Just follow him," said Captain Shaw, "do what he does." Now we were climbing, 4,000 feet a minute. In the Cessna I fly, you climb at maybe 600 feet a minute and you're glad to get it. "Just don't shorten your turn and cut him off," warned Captain Shaw. Glorious minutes passed. Now we were going up again, 380 miles per hour, in a lovely, climbing chandelle. Now we peaked, now we dove, 6,000 feet a minute.

"God, I could do this forever," I said, to nobody in particular. Capt. Runner Shaw seemed pleased. "I know," he said. "There are times when I think there are only two things worth doing in this world—flying and making love." I can't testify to his capacity in the love department, but he can fly this mother-lovin' jet.

"I'll take it now," he said, as the planes moved together. Up to the top—nothing but the sky. Boy! Floating against the seat straps. Down, down, down—leveling out at 300 feet over water. Eyeballs fairly popping out of the sockets. Steep turns, then suddenly the earth revolved—a slow roll. Back up again, the gradual loss of speed, then over and down. There were moments there, when it was all touch and feel, sky and earth, an exhilarating stoppage of time, when you somehow felt that nothing you would ever do, after this, could be anything but a bore.

On the ground again, Capt. Runner Shaw and I went for coffee. He talked about his life as a flyer ("you have to have the desire"), explained some of the maneuvers, then added: "You see, we weren't climbing at 6,000 feet a minute. More like 10,000 feet a minute. The indicator doesn't register beyond 6,000." We talked a few minutes more, and then I had to say it:

"There's something else I like about your air force." "What's that?" he asked. "The thing I like about your air force," I said, "is that you don't go out and attack anybody with it." Capt. Runner Shaw flashed a smile. "Maybe that's why I like it, too," he said.

Bad Landing

Seattle Times, April 10, 1984

IT WAS A STUPID THING, ALL IN ALL. Just stupid. Dumb. It wasn't really a landing at all; just an arrival. When you are flying around the mountainous parts of Arizona it pays to scan your charts and read the airport guidebooks, and here is what one "pilot's guide" said about Sedona:

"Warning: Be cautious of Density Altitude affecting takeoff and landing distances . . . Airport on 400-foot mesa . . . Turbulence and downdraft in vicinity of airport . . . Wind shear off both ends of runway . . . Land uphill on runway 03 and take off downhill on runway 21— winds permitting . . . Occasional deer on runway."

You have to see Sedona to believe it. About 25 miles south of Flagstaff, it's an incredibly beautiful green, mountainous valley surrounded on all sides by high, jagged, step-like red canyon rocks; not for nothing do they call Sedona "The Lady of The Red Rocks."

The airport itself sits up on a mesa and to get the idea you have to think of this towering mesa as a narrow rectangular Parson's table in the middle of a room, placed on a green carpet. I mean, spectacular; but you also have to think of that wind shear, which I very definitely did not do.

Old Cessna 42852 does what you tell it to do. But it can't do your thinking for you. So on this lovely evening, just at dusk, I brought the old hog around on final right into a stiff breeze coming off Runway 21, the wind shearing down off the mesa into the valley below. Jeeholyhosaphat! Cessna 42852 suddenly began to sink because I made the landing too flat, too fine, instead of coming in high to avoid the wind shear. Then I ballooned the landing.

We porpoised down the runway like a silly-headed beachball—up and down, up and down—before I finally settled on the blacktop. Tiger, my dog companion, made three complete bounces on the co-pilot's seat before we negotiated an uneasy détente with the runway. If looks speak words, these were his: "Oh, great Pilot-in-Command, where did you learn to fly, in a paper-airplane contest? One more like that and you can ship me home on a bus."

Well, we taxied up to the gas pump, and I was hoping against hope the ramp attendant hadn't witnessed my humiliation. But he had.

"Came in kinda flat, didn't ya, friend?" he said. "All you have to do is come in high and take the first third of the runway and you beat the wind shear."

I didn't say anything, hoping he'd just shut up and pump gas. But he was a talker. "Get maybe four or five accidents a year on that runway. Nobody got killed yet, but comin' in low like you did, that downdraft could put you right into the wall of the mesa. Like a bug on a windshield."

But that night, and the next day, and the next, were heaven. It was brisk and cool, but the sun was bright, and we spent two days lounging in a beautiful resort called Poco Diablo. We explored the Red Rock country, paid homage to the Chapel of the Holy Cross, built high on red rock spurs, poked through the shops and art galleries, and took a lot of pictures and ate ourselves silly.

Next stop, Grand Canyon. This was something I'd always dreamed of doing, flying through and into the Grand Canyon. Some ditch. You fly along the edge at maybe 6,500 feet and you can stare right down in the middle of it—a mile down—where the much-abused Colorado River winds deep and dirty red, sucking up the silt as it has, perhaps, for the last 2 billion years.

That's just a guess, of course. Nobody knows. But what they do know is that Grand Canyon caves have yielded evidence that prehistoric man lived down there about 4,000 years ago. The river runs southward through 62 miles of the Marble Gorge and takes off westward through the Kaibab Plateau.

In all, the Grand Canyon measures some 280 miles; its greatest width is 18 miles between embankments and in some places the canyon narrows to only a tenth of a mile. Lordy, it's a sight from the air! You could fly it forever, gas permitting, but it takes a poet, not a scribbling pilot, to give it proper due.

Now I've got to tell you about a place called Bullhead City. Far to the west of the Grand Canyon the Colorado River has been domesticated. Hoover Dam, then Davis Dam and yet another dam farther down have made a lake of the Colorado River. Here in the desert, incredibly, you see boat marinas and tiny ferries that take people back and forth. I will now explain why these ferries are free.

You see, Bullhead City is located at the very southern tip of Nevada, at the confluence of borders for three states—Nevada, Arizona and California. Off to the west in the high desert country is Edwards Air Force Base, where the righteous brethren of *The Right Stuff* do the primary testing of Uncle Sam's hottest rocket ships. This is where Chuck Yeager took the X-1 through the sound barrier so many years ago, and in Bullhead City they heard and felt the world's first sonic boom.

Now here is why those ferries are free. The Bullhead City Airport runs right alongside the Colorado, now deep and wide because of all those dams. So when you land in Bullhead City you are still in Arizona, but there is no reason to stay there and be bored. Because across the river are Nevada's casino hotels, garish and bright and inviting, another little Las Vegas out here in the desert.

The casinos run those ferries. All you have to do is walk down to the water's edge, board one of those little canopied ferries, powered by outboard motors, and they'll deposit you within 50 feet of the first slot machine.

That night we stayed on the Arizona side, and maybe because I felt guilty about scaring Tiger with the bad landing at Sedona, I scrounged up a feast for him in the hotel dining room. Purely in a spirit of sharing and self-sacrifice, mind you, I ordered prime rib with the bone left in. Then I gave the waitress $2 and offered an explanation:

"Don't tell the front desk, but I have this small friend back in the room. I lost the can opener to his Alpo and this little guy hasn't eaten since early this morning, and I don't have a car to get another can opener.

"I mean, would you bag this bone for us? Then I'd like you to go out in the kitchen and talk the cook into giving you one of those third-of-a-pound hamburger patties you advertise on the menu. It isn't stealing, really, is it? And if you could see this little guy, alone and hungry in the room, looking all floppy-eared and sad, you'd know that he is very hungry and . . . "

The waitress left and came back with a bag. "Here's the hamburger," she said, "but please can all that crap about your cute little mutt."

So that night Tiger had a feast and I went for a walk along the Colorado River. By now it was dark and the lights from the casinos lit up the clear desert sky and splashed across the river, and I am a fool and it was wonderful.

The ferry trip took only four or five minutes and sure enough, as fate would have it, I was bellied up to a blackjack table for the next hour. The dealer was a woman and she had thin lips and a tight smile and a cold, laser-beam look as she shuffled and flipped the cards in that cold dispassionate way they must learn at a charm school for dealers.

I'd get a 19, and she'd get a 20. I'd get a 20, and she'd get a blackjack. I'd hit a 12 and draw a 10, she'd hit a 12 and draw a nine. All my luck had been used up on that high-mesa airport in Sedona.

Final score: Nevada, $137.00; E. Watson, $00.00.

▼

That Sinking Feeling

Seattle Post-Intelligencer, November 6, 1977

NOW AND AGAIN, PROVING THE LACK OF THINGS people have to talk about, somebody asks me, "Are you a Seattle native?" The reply has always been, yes, and I usually add that I was born not far from the Duwamish mud flats, and I was raised with wet feet and once set an interscholastic primary grade school record for consecutive colds in one winter.

"If that doesn't make me a native," I sometimes add, smugly, "I think this might cinch it—I own a boat."

Everybody in Seattle, it seems, has at one time or another owned a boat. It is sort of the seal on your citizenship papers. At least that's what I always thought. But now a slight reservation has crept in; being born here and owning a boat is not the automatic entry to native Seattleism. You have not quite passed the initiation rites. It is not enough to have owned a boat—the true test comes when you try to sell one.

Let us have a synopsis, if you are still awake. A little over two years ago I bought a small speedboat, in partnership with a couple of other guys. This was a hot number. A ski boat. Turn on a dime. We even thought of entering it on one of the limited hydro races that abound in these parts. Well, I got a grand total of two (2) turns at the wheel before it sank. The insurance company paid off, we owners went our separate ways, and I got out clean. It was like leaving the city limits of Las Vegas in a solvent condition.

No, that wasn't enough. You see, I have this friend, and he lives on Lake Washington. His name is Fred Brack, pronounced as in crock, but this has no significance. He is a reporter-journalist, sports nut, intellectual, gourmet and gourmand, who likes to wander to and fro upon the earth, examining life's delights. I have traveled halfway around the world with him, investigating the seamier sides of Southeast Asia, Scandinavia, Greece and God knows where else.

We have this much in common, but nothing more than this: When conversation lapses, or time hangs heavy, we both have a fatalistic impulse to do something foolish. "Let's buy this boat," I said one day. "I found it sitting in some guy's yard. It is a classic wood hull, planked and all, with a marvelous old mahogany deck." "Okay," he said absently, "go and buy it. Deal me in."

We bought the boat. Then we bought a 60-horse outboard for it. Then we had the keel repaired. Then we bought some more stuff for it. These were flush times. Brack was in a hot streak at poker and I had just sold a free-lance story to the Butcher's Quarterly. We docked it down at his place. I was at the wheel a total of two (2) times. Then it sank. I had a streak of two sinkings in succession, which is more than the captain of the *Lusitania* could say.

Once again, a friendly—but not very happy—insurance adjuster came to the rescue. The boat was completely re-done; engine overhauled, new electrical system. The works. Then, as usually happens with Brack and me, we got bored with the whole thing. "Let's sell it," he said, "and use the money for a trip to Peru." I held out for Spain. He said he'd compromise for the south of France. "We'll just put an ad in the paper," he said, "and next week I'll put the money in a special travel account for us."

That was a year ago. We put ads in both papers. We labored over the prose of our ads. At one point we hinted in our ad that this boat was once owned by Guy Lombardo, the early speed boat king, but got a warning letter from the Attorney General's office. Not a nibble. Not one phone call. "Put it in the next ad that we want $1,500 for it," said my friend Brack, "and if anybody calls, the price is—ah, negotiable." Still no calls.

Do you know where this boat is now? It is chained to a pole at Hadfield's Garage and Union 76 station, 3127 E. Madison. It has been there for months. Nobody will even try to steal it. The Hadfield brothers have shown remarkable patience. Drop by and see them, then you can see our boat. All this is the outgrowth of a conversation Brack and I had the other day. "You write a column about the boat," he said. "Get lots of feeling into it. I doubt if you have any more readers than the classifieds, but if anybody should call—ah, tell them the price is negotiable."

Deals On Wheels

Seattle Times, January 17, 1984

JUST TO MAKE LIFE A BIT MORE DIFFICULT FOR YOU, I will now recite an event, growing out of some inner compulsion that baffles most head shrinkers, which occurred last Saturday. It is the kind of thing I do periodically, sometimes with alarming frequency, an aberration that many people take to be an unnatural relationship with the internal-combustion engine. I bought a truck.

Taken by itself, that is no big deal. Everybody buys cars and trucks. But in my case, it is a lifelong attachment to older heaps, a sort of promiscuous desire to acquire and possess these vehicles, sometimes three or four at the same time.

Once, at lunch, I sat across from a lady of mature, but not disabling, years. After a couple of drinks she waxed philosophical about her life and began counting on her fingers the number of men she had made love to, or with, as the case might have been. When she ran out of fingers the first time around and was well into the second 10 fingers, she abruptly stopped, smiled with faint embarrassment and said, "Let's change the subject, shall we?"

I feel similarly abashed in talking about cars I have owned. Sensible people usually can count four or five cars they have owned in a lifetime. I can count to the number of 18 cars, only one of which, back in 1954, was certifiably new. The remaining 17 have been "previously owned," as the British say. To make matters worse, I have often owned several at the same time.

With each of these cars there is a story I like to tell. That is why I don't get invited to many parties. At any rate, last Saturday morning the old, compulsive, used-car-junkie feeling came on and I went out to kick some tires. It was a lovely day, and as I drove along (in my 1973 Fiat) I began counting fingers, the way the lady did at lunch that day, which is how I got up to 18 cars.

In college there was a 1931 Chev, which had a snap-down hood that opened on the sides. The buckles, or snaps, were long since rusted out. When I went over a bump the hood would fly up on each side until the car looked like a seagull flapping its wings.

After that came a couple of Model A Fords, then a 1935 Plymouth, another Model A, followed by a 1947 Cadillac, which was once owned by Radio Speaker John C. Stevenson, a legendary politician of yesteryear, who bought it from Local 174 of the International Brotherhood of Teamsters.

The only new car I ever owned in my life was a 1954 Mercury, which expired at the last minute of the last day when the final payment was made. It was then I resolved never to buy another new car. There followed, as the years passed, a 1954 MG, a Chev, a Ford, another Chev, then a 1962 Pontiac, another Chev, the 1973 Fiat, a 1960 Thunderbird, a 1964 Jeep Wagoneer, a 1971 3/4-ton GMC truck and, more recently, a 1980 Datsun, which made me feel uneasy since it was too new. I got rid of it. This may not add up to 18 cars, but I left a few out for reasons of space.

You remember that crazy guy who used to smash cars with a sledgehammer on television? The guy who had that maniacal laugh? That's right, Dick Balch. That's the guy I bought the Fiat from.

Am I drawn to people like this? Perhaps. So the other Saturday morning, where did I find a huge lineup of used trucks? You have guessed it. At Glen Grant Chevrolet. Glen Grant is the amiable screwball who gets on television and says, "Have I got a deal for you!"

Heaven only knows how many used-car dealers I know, but somehow it seems like hundreds. As for mechanics who keep these heaps running, they should throw an appreciation banquet for me.

Given my lust to add yet another truck to my fleet, it took the salesman, a pleasant fellow named Ben White, all of 15 minutes to close the deal for a 1975 Chev 1/2-ton with a 454 engine and a measly 72,489 miles on it. Ben White said, "They're asking $3,975 for this beauty, but go ahead and make an offer. They might take it. This is sort of a horse-trading business, you know."

Did I know? Little did Ben White realize that he was dealing with the most experienced used-car buyer in the semi-sovereign state of Washington. I offered $3,000, and while Ben White went off to talk to "they" about it, I spent the time examining price stickers on new cars. There they sat—$26,852 for one number, a Corvette, more money than I have paid for my last 10 cars.

Anyway, I got this little cream puff for $3,150, contingent on a compression check, and drove out of there on Cloud 9. With my usual shrewdness, I signed the deal before I showed this half-ton darling to my latest in a long list of consulting mechanics. His name is Elwood C. Avery and he ministers to sick cars at Charlie's Auto Repair down on Western Avenue.

His real name is Elwood but his nickname is Tiger, which causes some confusion since my dog is named Tiger. And because I see a lot of both Tigers, I refer to them as "Tiger, the mechanic" and "Tiger, the dog."

Tiger, the mechanic, looked over my latest acquisition. He listened to the engine with a practiced ear; he poked here and there; he smelled the transmission oil; he crawled under the frame and then he ran his hand over the tires. For years, Tiger has looked on my used-car fixation with mixed tolerance and exasperation, but finally he said, "You have surprised me—I think you got a nice truck here."

I told Tiger about the $26,852 Corvette. I told him that a new truck would cost $12,000 or more. "There is no way I am going to mortgage my life to a damned hunk of metal," I said, and that is the truth. At bottom, I really hate cars and what they do to people's sense of values. People may live in rundown houses, but they will bust their paychecks for the ego, or status, or whatever, that goes with driving some super deluxe state-of-the-art model with digital clocks and chrome steering wheels and built-in stereo players.

Elwood C. Avery, the mechanic, is a philosopher-logician who knows the fallacy in my thinking. He is fully aware that the flaw in my argument comes not in owning a used car, but in owning several at one time. "But maybe you are right," he agreed, with a wry smile. "When you buy a used car it is like knowing an adult rather than a new child whose personality is not yet formed."

There is another fatal economic fallacy in my position on previously owned cars. While I can buy like a demon, I am no good at selling. As a used-car salesman, I am a flop. That is why I sometimes end up owning three or four used heaps at once.

So if you feel the need of a used car some day, just drop around. Boy, do I have a deal for you!

▼

No Silver Lining

Seattle Post-Intelligencer, April 19, 1983

IT IS OF SOME SURPRISE TO ME THAT A FRAGMENT of my financial welfare is in the hands, more or less, of two ladies who call themselves the Aden Sisters. They should not be confused with the Brontë sisters, who wrote a different kind of literature; neither can they be compared with the two "advice sisters," Dear Ann and Dear Abby, who operate out of Chicago, dispensing succor and balm to the unhappy. I first learned about the Aden Sisters when I bought some silver at the "spot price" of $11.22 an ounce a few days ago. To be truthful, I bought 100 ounces for $1,122. Never mind where I got this spare cash; it is a private matter between me and my bookmaker. A friend of mine, Mr. Frank Bartenetti, "plays the silver market," so to speak. When I noticed Frank smoking a more expensive brand of cigars, this quickened my interest in silver. Mr. Bartenetti put me in the hands of Mr. Dee Sanders, who runs the Rare Coin Gallery on downtown Third Avenue. Mr. Sanders has been dealing in coins, gold and silver at the same address since 1963. He introduced me to the Aden Sisters, who put out a monthly newsletter out of the East on price fluctuations of gold and silver. "There are several such advisory services," said Mr. Sanders, "but I tend to like the Aden Sisters best. They do nothing but research the prices of gold and silver."

My plunge into silver speculation took place about two weeks ago, and it is a fair guess that Mr. Sanders now wishes he had never heard of me. When you have 1,122 clackers tied up in silver, you take an interest in it. I now turn on morning TV to get the "silver price." I buy a couple of papers each day to check the price further. Then I call up the Rare Coin Gallery to bend Mr. Sanders' ear—or more properly, in hopes that he will bend mine. "The price of silver," he said one day, "is now $11.87. You have made several dollars. We will not get another price on silver until tomorrow morning. You don't need to call here every 20 minutes."

Quite honestly, the possession of $1,122 worth of silver came as something of a letdown. The first thing that happened is that Mr. Bartenetti came into my office and dropped a rectangular, rounded-edged thing on my desk. "Here is your silver," he said. After he left, I sat there looking at it for a long time. Then I called up Mr. Sanders again. "How much does this thing weigh?" I asked him. "The silver you have comes to 100 ounces so therefore it weighs 6.25 pounds." I went back to staring at my silver. It had no sex appeal. There were no screaming eagles designed on it. Just a hunk of metal. I began using it as a paperweight and it got buried beneath a lot of the paper which clutters my desk.

The silver was sexless, but the price was not. I called Mr. Sanders for another routine check on the price of silver. "This thing looks very cold sitting on my desk," I said. "It has no razz-ma-tazz to it. Surely, for $1,122 I should get something nice to look at." Mr. Sanders was aghast. "You mean it's still sitting on your desk? Anybody could walk in and take your silver. Put it in a safety deposit box. Don't take it home with you. Silver is the easiest thing in the world to convert into cash." So now it is in the office safe and I can't even use it for a paperweight.

The next day I called Mr. Sanders again. "Silver," he said wearily, anticipating my question, "is now at $11.30 cents. You are still ahead of the game." I told him I had the silver tucked away in a safe. "That is good," he said. It was then that he introduced me to the Aden Sisters. "What are their first names?" I asked. He said he didn't know, but that it isn't important. "The Aden Sisters are famous because they were the ones who predicted that gold would drop in price three years ago. All they do is research the gold and silver market. I have great faith in the Aden Sisters."

He said the Aden Sisters did a study on gold in 1980. Shortly after they predicted that gold would plunge in price, it took a nosedive—down from $850 to $300. A lot of people, he said, saved money by listening to the Aden Sisters. "How do they feel about silver?" I asked. He said he wasn't sure at this point, although his own belief is that silver will go up in price quite handily in the next three or four years. "I base this guess on the economy," he explained. "You see, silver is very much an industrial metal. When times are good, they use a lot of silver in manufacturing. It looks like the economy is turning around. They also use a lot of silver in bombs and things. All our missiles use silver."

This put me in a moral quandary. Here's a guy (namely me) who is fiercely critical of President Popular's economic program. Here is also a guy who is against more missiles of any kind. In order to make money on my silver, I have to root for supply-side economics and a huge defense budget. This dratted silver was making an instant Republican out of me. Nevertheless, I decided to stick with the Aden Sisters for a while. "Can't I turn in this bar of silver and get something I can play with?" I asked Mr. Sanders. "You mean like silverware?" "No, maybe I can get it in silver dollars. Then I can run my hands through the dollars and feel rich."

The only silver dollars with any silver in them, he explained, were minted from 1878 to 1921, and from 1921 to 1935. The older silver dollar, he said, has a liberty emblem on one side and a screaming eagle on the other. The ones from 1921 to 1935 are what were called the "peace dollars." They have a peace symbol on one side and the eagle on the other. Well, it turns out that I can't get 1,122 silver dollars for $1,122. "These dollars," he explained, "have a 90 percent silver content. But they also have a numismatic value." "They have a what?" "Numismatic," he said. "It's a term used by coin collectors. It means that the numismatic value is higher than the actual silver content. A 'peace dollar' is now worth $14.75." "How many numismatic dollars can I get for my dumb-looking hunk of silver?" Mr. Sanders made some clicking noises on his calculator. "Bring your bar of silver in and I will get you 85.62 peace dollars."

He then said that if I wanted to trade my silver for Eisenhower dollars, I would have more of them to run through my fingers. "Eisenhower dollars were minted until 1970," he said. "They have a picture of Ike on one side and some kind of an Apollo space shot symbol on the other. There is no silver in an Eisenhower dollar—only copper and nickel. If I gave you 1,122 Eisenhower dollars, all you'd be doing is selling your silver. Paper money is a lot easier to carry."

Owning silver, it seems, is not as much fun as I thought it was. Mr. Sanders also seems tired of my questions. He said he would try to get me the Aden Sisters' unlisted number.

A Fool and His Money

Seattle Times, April 2, 1987

MONEY. THE REASON I AM THINKING of money right now is that my kindly bank has just informed me how little I have of it.

I get startled like this quite often. Mind you, we are not talking much in the way of savings even in the most prosperous of times. It's just that I keep a little salted away in case of emergency, like a sudden illness or an acute trip to Las Vegas.

There are people who know how to "manage" their money. I am not one of these people.

Never in all of my life have I ever managed money in any functional sense of the word. In fact, I don't even understand it. I have no conception of its permanent importance in the overall scheme of things—it's just something you carry around in your pocket. If it crackles, times are good. If it just jingles it is time to visit the cash machine. By the same token, I am unable to bargain for money, or even to bargain a price down to save some money. You know those coupons they give away in advertising inserts? A coupon will get you 20 cents off on a tube of toothpaste or maybe some disposable diapers. People who watch me handle money think I should wear the diapers, financially speaking. I am a mewing infant when it comes to any kind of finance.

All of my life I have identified with Heywood Broun, the late, great newspaper columnist, in matters of money. At the height of his eminence in the 1920s on the New York World, Mr. Broun was authorized to hire W. O. McGeehan, a gifted sportswriter of that era. Broun opened salary negotiations with McGeehan on this level: "I am empowered to offer you $50 or $55 a week. Which will you take?"

Like Mr. Broun and many other writers, I cannot seem to take money seriously. I am intellectually incapable of grasping its long-range implications as it pertains to my welfare.

I once worked for a man named Lou Tice, whose mission in life is to help people realize their full potential. Part of his curriculum is taken up explaining to people that it is OK—in fact, desirable—to make money as long as you do it honestly. But a lot of people, Tice argues, are what he calls "poverty conscious." Because they have low self-esteem, or whatever, they can't see themselves making a lot of money. "Oh, that's not like me," they say to themselves. "I wasn't meant to have money—that's too good for me." Through such poverty conscious "self-talk," they bring about their own self-fulfilling prophecy. If, as sales people, they suddenly have a big month in commissions, they can't sustain it. They flatten out the next month and make only what they think they are worth, or deserve. By the same token, if they come into some money, they'll get rid of it; they have to get back to "where they belong."

I worked three years for Mr. Tice at Pacific Institute and listened to his lectures dozens of times. Hell, I even wrote a 15-pound application guide based on his lectures. I still can't get it through my thick head that money is something to be acquired and used judiciously and wisely.

I guarantee you: If tomorrow morning, say, some dim-witted philanthropist deposited $50,000 in my bank account, no strings attached, I would go crazy. Sooner or later I would blow the whole wad. I don't know how but I'd find a way. Then one day I would happen around to my friendly bank and the bank would say, "Hey, buddy, you're just about tapped out. How did you spend it all?" "How the hell do I know?" I would say.

Money is not the root of all evil. The love of money is the root of all evil. This proposition was around many centuries before Jesus drove the money changers out of the temple. And if that is true, then I am as pure, evil-wise, as Ivory soap. Maybe I'd be better off if I loved money. So what's a little evil between friends? I just have a very platonic relationship with money: easy come, easy go. I'm not emotionally attached to it.

A close friend of mine, a successful lawyer, has this attitude toward money. "Money is good for only three things," he says. "It should get you a decent place to live, enough good food to eat and enough to travel on."

To that extent, I guess I am OK. I have only one dependent, a runt miniature poodle named Tiger. He has had a good education. We reside in comfort, we eat well and we have traveled to and fro to many places upon this earth.

Dear bank: You should be so lucky.

▼

Not Tied Down

Seattle Post-Intelligencer, November 12, 1980

TODAY I WOULD LIKE TO DISCUSS TIES with you since I had the poor judgment to wear one the other day. You see, I rarely wear ties—to work, to dinner, to theater, to movies. The exceptions are weddings, funerals, the infrequent occasions when I deliberately enter a church, or when invited to lunch at a private club. It was on this latter occasion that I wore a tie the other day. Judge Solie Ringold, of the State Court of Appeals, invited me to lunch at the Harbor Club, a noted hotbed of proper neckware. It was strictly a social lunch, and out of respect for Judge Ringold I decided not to crash the place without a tie. So that morning I showed up at this Hearstian aviary wearing a tie. "Hey, getta load o' him!" was the first remark. "Whatcha dressin' up for?" "Dig this, man, Watson is wearing a tie!" That sort of thing. Man and boy, my wardrobe has been the bane of publishers and editors since the first Eisenhower administration.

It's not that I don't own ties, just that I regard them as unnecessary nuisances, something you have to study and match, something that always drops in the gravy. "Don't you even *own* a tie?" somebody once asked. The fact is, tucked away in various closets, I probably own more ties than the Salvation Army. People are forever giving me ties—a hint, no doubt. Each Christmas, the redoubtable Larry Fry, of Littler's, sends me a tie, just as Bob Littler did before him. I have never had the nerve to try and trade it in as a down payment on a shirt. Ties arrive, mysteriously, in the mail. I have Sounders ties with little soccer balls on them; I have Mariner trident ties and basketball ties from the Sonics. I have Countess Mara ties, Christian Dior ties, and a ton of ties bearing such labels as Albert's, Brooks Brothers and ties with the Brittania label, dispensed by the estimable Walter Schoenfeld.

I have narrow ties and wide ties. I have gone through several fashion generations in ties—wide to narrow, narrow to wide—but I just don't like to wear ties. Bill Veeck, famous for his tieless attire, is my hero. Because he is famous, Bill Veeck can enter almost any hoity-toity establishment in the land without a tie. I get coldly rebuked, and since I have the resolution of a jellyfish in these matters, I meekly wear a tie when necessary. Usually it turns out badly.

The last time I wore a tie before my luncheon with Judge Ringold was early in the Carter administration. John L. Scott, the convivial realtor, invited me to lunch at the Rainier Club. This was during the Bert Lance affair. Mr. Scott herded me into the bar, which was absolutely stuffed with bankers. They all eyed me coldly. "I guess they don't like my tie," I concluded, until somebody, a non-banker, chortled, "Hey, did you read what Watson said about bankers this morning?" It was a horrible moment. That morning, it seemed, I had written a column defending President Carter for making Bert Lance his budget director. "Don't blame the President," I wrote, "Lance was probably the most honest banker he could find." Mr. Scott seemed vastly amused by all this.

There was another interlude of sartorial trauma in my life. This occurred during the publishing reign at The P-I of Robert E. Thompson, a man of elegance, style and taste. Bob Thompson threw several black tie dinners for local dignitaries and visiting Hearst Co. executives, and these were held, variously, at the Broadmoor Golf Club and the Mirabeau's private dining room. Black tie was not "optional," as they say. Before long, I totaled up the damage and found I was in $120.85 for tuxedo rentals. (With tuxedos, you also rent the tie.) Since this was becoming economically destructive, I called for sealed bids on a new tuxedo. The lowest bidder came in at $285, not including cuff links or tie. "Ye gods," I gasped, "what if I buy this thing and don't get invited to any more parties?" The solution lay elsewhere.

I went up to the Wise Penny, a classy secondhand store, which was then on Broadway. They had a back room full of castoff tuxedos. I found one that fit (the tie went with it) for $15. I took it home and hung it in the closet. There it sits, unused to this day, complete with tie. I often wonder whose it was. Ned Skinner's? Herman Sarkowsky's? Lloyd Cooney's? No matter. You want the tie, you can have it. It will make somebody a nice dog collar.

Garage Sale Junkie

Seattle Post-Intelligencer, June 14, 1981

WE ARE INTO THE HIGH SEASON OF GARAGE SALES, that peculiar institution that brings out the best (thrift, adventure, fun) and the worst (sheer greed, the neurotic wish to possess) in us. Check the ads under "Miscellaneous." All papers, from the large dailies to the smallest neighborhood weeklies, are crammed with garage sale ads. Some are called "estate sales," others "yard sales," but mostly garage sales. I confess an incurable weakness for such miscellaneous marts. Over the years, I have haunted garage sales in many districts, neighborhoods and suburbs of various West Coast towns. Somebody once had a bumper sticker made: "Caution, I brake for all garage sales." They must have had me in mind. It can take me up to three or four hours, on Saturdays and Sundays, to get from one point to another. Garage sale signs act on me like a magnet. I still have stuff I have picked up in Phoenix, Los Angeles, Chelan, Bellingham, Eugene, Yakima and any other place I have been on weekends.

My kitchen is crammed with peelers, cutters, canisters, spoons and spatulas. I may hold the record in Seattle for the owner of five canister sets, eight slotted spoons and six spatulas. I am also rich in toaster ovens, deep fat fryers and electric percolators. Bargains abound. Only three weeks ago I hit the brakes for a yard sale in a little town in the Skagit Valley. As sales go, it was depressing; the usual junk, flagrantly overpriced. But in one box, tucked under a table and unnoticed, was a complete 12-volume cooking encyclopedia. It was 13 years old, but in mint condition. Clearly, it had been used sparingly, if at all. I got the whole 12 volumes, crammed with knowledgeable essays and some 1,200 recipes, for seven bucks.

One of my frequent companions on garage safaris is Ann Faber, a writer of flawless prose and a woman of exquisite taste. Ann has always contended that greed motivates us sale junkies. "I have thought a lot about this," she once explained, "and I can't come up with a better word than greed. An insatiable desire to possess things. For just a few dollars, you can buy almost anything on earth at garage sales."

You see, the joy of garage sales—to me, at least—is stumbling on something you never knew you wanted. You don't know you need it until you see it. Admittedly, that is a somewhat elitist view. Many people, especially young people, find garage sales more functionally serviceable. Setting up housekeeping, they can save hundreds of dollars in equipping a small apartment.

Poking around garage, yard and "estate" sales, I have encountered some phenomenal bargains. I once bought three distinguished library lamps, each retailing for about $250 apiece, for $5 each. It was the end of a sale at a huge home in a rich district; they just wanted to get rid of the stuff. Another time I bought an expensive I. Magnin suit, which I still wear, for $5. Of course, you must wade through a lot of junk to find these treasures. Of much of this junk Ann Faber says, "They were made to sell for $3, look like they cost $5, and were given to somebody by a friend with lousy taste."

To maximize your pleasure in garage sales requires, first of all, some knowledge of city neighborhoods. A city map saves gas. A schedule of stops is then laid out and a gas-saving route is formed. Better neighborhoods can yield treasures but working-class neighborhoods should not be overlooked. Here you can find fantastic bargains in tools; why pay $8 for a hammer when you might find one for $1?

Surprising things can happen at garage sales. Once, while touring to find something I just couldn't live without, I took my dog along. He was then a puppy of poodle persuasion. The proprietor of the garage fell in love with him on sight. "Look," he said, "I'll make a deal with you. Give me the dog and you can have anything here, the whole works. I'll send everybody else away." I said no, I'd rather keep the dog (not without a quick assessment of the yield, I might add) and he said, "Okay, go in my house. If you see something in there you like, maybe we can make a deal."

Nothing came of it, but I still take the dog along on junk-sale expeditions. Nobody has made a similar offer.

Garage sales, it seems to me, have become ever more popular. Inflation may have driven more people into the hunt. Nowadays, if the ad is particularly enticing ("loads of valuables, 12-family sale!") a line of searchers has formed before the sale opens. And I have found, for the most part, that people holding garage sales are honest. They tell you if an appliance is defective and needs repair. What you see is usually what you get, although I am sure some people have been stung. "Buyer beware" is still the best policy.

Milton Katims, the symphony conductor, told me that he and Leonard Bernstein once found themselves (I forget how) locked in Frederick & Nelson after closing hours. Bernstein, he said, yelled with joy and danced in the aisles, fingering clothes, trinkets and other goods. "I always dreamed of being alone in a department store," he explained. I suspect there is an element of this in being addicted to garage sales.

Tuning Out the Guv

Seattle Times, June 19, 1990

A COUPLE OF WEEKS AGO IT WAS DISCOVERED that our governor, Booth Gardner, is hard of hearing in his left ear. An audiologist confirmed this. The audiologist said that Gov. Gardner shows "significant hearing loss in the higher frequencies," especially in his left ear. The audiologist suggested that his eminence be fitted for a hearing aid. Gardner did not think much of the idea. Gardner shrugged off his hearing impairment by saying, in effect, that this is no handicap. Indeed, he said, it gives him unbounded relief, if not joy, when he is seated at the right side of a crashing bore.

Word of the governor's hearing handicap clears up a great mystery for me. Stand by for an explanation.

Some months ago, as it happened, I was seated next to Gardner at a dinner. This was the annual banquet of the American Society of Something or Other, a group that by definition was subdued and self-pitying. This gave the governor and me ample time to talk. Most important, it gave me ample room to expound. At each of my utterances, the governor would smile knowingly. He seemed to be hanging on my every word, nodding in agreement.

"What an intelligent fellow," I thought. "A leader who listens to people. What a statesman!"

To break the ice, I gave the governor one of my famous explanations of baseball's infield-fly rule. He seemed enchanted. Thus encouraged, I moved from there to the field of tax reform. "Get rid of the sales tax," I told him. "A regressive yoke on the people. We need a stiff, graduated income tax. You can never go very far wrong by soaking the rich." He rocked back and forth, delightedly. He beamed as though he had discovered a great truth. "Get rid of the state lottery," I went on. "A morally indefensible device to play upon our baser instincts. What we've got now is a legalized numbers racket. Impose a luxury tax on yachts, BMWs, big property transfers." The look on Gov. Gardner's face was one of rapt attention, an eagerness to understand, to conceptualize, to think and govern in broad, bold strokes.

"Furthermore," I told the governor, "knock off this namby-pamby, wishy-washy style and get down to the nitty-gritty. Be like Harry Truman. Give 'em hell." As the governor beamed his approval of what I was saying, the time passed quickly. Soon the Something or Other group ended its dismal dinner and we went home. Clearly, it seemed, I had made a profound impression on the governor's thinking.

Days passed. Weeks went by. Nothing happened. Where was this new tiger I had unleashed on local politics? Where was the born-again populist, the Fighting Guv, the man of the people, the Great Commoner, who would lead our state with renewed vigor? Not a peep out of him. I was mystified. Then it all came out with the audiologist's report. Governor Gardner can't hear anything with his left ear. He hadn't heard a word I was telling him; instead, he was just humoring me. I was just another bore, to be tolerated with kind looks, with nods of approval and benign smiles. It is really depressing when you think of it. Here is a guy who passed up a golden opportunity to partake of my wisdom—all because he is disabled in his left ear.

Am I sore about this? Of course not. The issue is greater than mere petulance. Actually, the governor and I have much in common. His left ear hearing is impaired. Both of my ears are impaired, giving me a 2-1 margin over the governor. Did I say "impaired?" Hell, I am deafer than an antique fire plug. I wear a hearing aid that is so powerful it can pick up talk shows in Taiwan. Because of modern technology in the field of sound amplification, I am a walking public address system.

To prove that I am not sulking over his brushoff, I am ready to give the governor some more advice. This advice does not go into his impaired left ear, but can easily be read to him by an aide, speaking into his right ear. The advice is this: Get yourself a hearing aid, pronto and right now. You will be a better governor because of it.

As a veteran hearing-aid user, I can assure you that suffering fools and bores, seated on your left, is as nothing compared to the advantages. Who knows who might be seated on your left in times to come? The list of great minds is endless—philosophers, physicists, political scientists, educators. Granted, you will encounter more bores than great minds, but there is a solution to this as well.

You see, every hearing aid is equipped with a shut-off switch. You simply reach up, pretend to pull an ear lobe and tune the dull ones out. Here I speak from experience, and a confession is in order. On the night you could not comprehend all my brilliant advice, I had you tuned out, too.

Hair Today, Hair Tomorrow

Seattle Times, December 20, 1990

THIS BEING THE SEASON OF CHRISTMAS and a New Year approaching fast, I am reflecting upon some advice friends are giving me with increasing frequency. They are saying, "Learn to grow older gracefully."

Now, that is a crock of uncolored margarine. As I grow older, I intend to do so kicking and screaming; I intend to be a lousy, insufferable loser when it comes to counting up the years. It is this department's platform that age is overrated. Catherine Drinker Bowen once wrote an eloquent essay on the magnificence, the grandeur, of age. She was not convincing.

My dog, Tiger, and I are both getting up there. Neither one of us is finding that life is better now than it was, say, 30 years ago—in Tiger's case, 10 years ago; he is 11.

I know of only one thing I can do as well now as I could do 30 years ago.

Otherwise, I have slipped with age.

Not necessarily in order of importance, the slow-down list includes running; it includes eating; it includes endurance; it includes resiliency; it includes hearing, eyesight, hand-eye coordination; it includes almost anything physical.

But not everything. The one thing I can do as well now as before is to grow hair.

I even get letters about this ability to grow hair. People write in and call me "an ignorant hairy ape," or a "tousle-headed misanthrope." For that matter, even Tiger gets hate mail. One guy called him "a scruffy, no-good cur."

This business of growing hair should not be taken lightly. I glory in it. Ponder hair, if you will. In these United States, there are more unscrupulous operators in the field of hair-growing than you can count.

These people live on hope—bald people's hope. Bald men are willing to try anything some quack will sell them, all kinds of nostrums, devices, therapies and what-not are offered to hopeful, yearning bald people who would give anything to grow a full head of hair.

Now and then, I compare myself to great writers. The list includes Mark Twain, William Faulkner, F. Scott Fitzgerald, Robert Frost, Mr. Hemingway, Edgar Allan Poe and Walt Whitman. These were all full-thatched geniuses who maintained their magnificent swatches of hair until the day they died. In putting myself in the company of these, I am only talking about hair, not talent.

Right away, I expect a batch of letters listing all the great bald writers we've had. Even William Shakespeare was somewhat bald. The point is granted. But there was not one of the baldies, I would guess, who didn't envy a fellow scribbler with a full head of hair. It is the burden of being a skinhead.

The growth of beards is sure to get into this. Many bald men have the ability to grow beards, and that is all to their credit, I suppose, but they are not complete. All but one or two, I venture, would trade in their beards for a full crop of hair on the tops of their heads. One is reminded of an old Burma Shave sign we used to see on the highways, before highways became freeways: "Within this vale of toil and sin, Your head grows bald but not your chin."

"The best is yet to come," people tell me, as I grow older. That is industrial strength sheep-dip. The best is right now, Dec. 20, 1990, and I am enjoying the hell out of it, not waiting for some grab-bag nirvana the spiritualists are always telling you lies ahead. If you behave.

Meanwhile, there are the barbers' bills. If anything, Tiger can grow hair faster than I can, which is a drain on the budget. A competent shearing of Tiger comes to a $20 bill. In my own case, I've used everything from barber schools to the ultimate in "hair styling." It doesn't matter. No matter how lousy the haircut, it always grows out very fast.

Come to think of it, it's time for another shearing.

▼

Nothing to Hide

Seattle Post-Intelligencer, June 14, 1978

EDITORIALISTS HAVE BEEN IN FINE, hand-wringing form over the recent Supreme Court decision which gives policemen a license to search newspaper offices. The score was Cops 5, Newsies 3. Some editorialists have called the Court's decision "a license to browse" among news folks' notes for evidence. While I have not heard the inspiring crackle of paper shredders at work, there is a noticeable nervousness about the idea of cops poking their heads in file drawers, riffling through notebooks and generally making themselves nosy. Another fear, expressed by editorialists, is that sources will "dry up," as the saying goes. I have no fear on this latter score since all three of my sources have joined AA, so the phone rarely rings at 3 a.m.

Still, I have been taking inventory of this office. It is a congenital mess, frankly, piled high and stuffed full of a bewildering potpourri of unexplainable things. For example, there are 72 partly used matchbooks, picked up God knows where. For all I know, a match from one of these books touched off the Ozark Hotel fire, so the cops are welcome to these for evidence. They can also have the 14 styrofoam cups filled—to varying degrees—with stale coffee, some of it flecked with green mold. The police crime lab may find something in these, but I doubt it.

In fact, Chief "Bud" Vander What's-his-name can send his boys right over. They'd better bring a Bekins truck along to collect the debris. They'd better send somebody who can read, too, since this place is packed with books. This office is heavy on cookbooks, Raymond Chandler mysteries, and road maps of Southeast Asia, where I once visited. There is a receipt from a Bangkok massage parlor, an American League press-radio-TV guide for the season of 1969, plus "A Report on the Art & Technology Program of the Los Angeles County Museum, 1967–71." There is a copy of Jane Adams' book *Sex and the Single Parent* plus a copy of Prof. Ron Pion's splendid instructional guide *The Last Sex Manual,* in case any of the cops can't get with it.

Stacks of notebooks, old newspapers, obscene fan letters and bumper stickers ("Let's Go, Pilots" and "Say goodbye, Dick") clutter the place. The notebooks will baffle the cops' handwriting experts; they baffle me, and I wrote them. "D. B. Cooper" is a single entry in one. The Missing Persons bureau can forget that one, because I remember clearly that a lady in Magnolia named her cat after the skyjacker. She thought it would make a cute item. She was wrong.

This office is big on containers. We have four vases, one filled with dead flowers; a thermos, contents unknown; one coffee pot; two half-gallon bottles of vitamin pills and a jar of dried peas. I do not attempt to bribe Chief Whats-his-name's lawmen, but they are welcome to a 15-year-old unopened six-pack of Olympia, in the lower file drawer. In plain sight, too, are a couple of bottles of dehydrated Seattle rainwater.

There is nothing subversive in this office, unless you count the two Indian totem poles carved by an Italian immigrant grocer from Anacortes. *The Sayings of Chairman Mao*, which I picked up in a communist bookstore in Dublin, of all places, is neatly balanced off with *None Dare Call It Treason*, by John Stormer. I haven't read either one. This office also contains six cans of dog food, in case they send the K-9 unit.

In summation, before I hear the sirens wailing, I have two full boxes of paper clips (for straightening), one stapler (without staples), a half-eaten box of limp Triscuits, an airplane mobile that looks like it lost an aerial dogfight, a hairbrush, one slide rule, seven phone books, two boxes of addressed (but unmailed) Christmas cards, one jigsaw puzzle from the British Museum, two strings of Christmas tree lights, a scrub brush, and two half-used tubes of Crest toothpaste. I have just thrown out a short biography of Byron "Whizzer" White, and if they don't understand the significance of that gesture, then Chief Vander What's-his-name is sending the wrong cops.

I also have several autographed pictures, mostly from people in the media. Such as this one: "For my friend, Emmett, anything I can do for you, just holler. (signed) Charles Royer, Ch. 5."

Easy Does It

Seattle Times, February 13, 1986

MILDLY OFFENDED BY RECENT REPORTS that he writes his column in 20 minutes, William F. Buckley, the conservative panjandrum, fired back with some rapidly written words. He took some 1,500 words (writing time, one hour) in the New York Times Book Review to make his case.

His case, as I got it, is that yes, he writes fast. Yes, he thinks fast. Yes, he types fast. But what's wrong with being fast? He does not deny, and more or less confirms, that he writes his columns in 20 minutes—some take a little longer, but he doesn't say how much.

To presumed critics who say Mr. Buckley cannot possibly put enough thought into his work, writing as fast as he does, he argues "against the suggestion that to think longer (endlessly?) about a subject is necessarily to probe it more fruitfully."

This whole business of speed-writing fascinates me. Mr. Buckley points to such authors as Anthony Trollope, who imposed a daily quota on himself of 3,500 words—i.e., a shorter goal of 250 words every 15 minutes. He indicates that if Trollope had had a word processor, instead of writing in longhand, he would have produced some 16,800 words daily. Presto. A book every week.

Another book-a-week man is Georges Simenon, the great French writer. Murray Morgan tells me that the late novelist John O'Hara claimed great speed in writing, but as Murray adds, "Some of his stuff sounds like it."

Murray himself is quite a slow writer, estimating that his output, when applied to completing a book, averages between 800 and 1,000 words a day. Leroy Ostransky, the great Tacoma musical authority, who has written several fine books and many columns, was very fast when he was writing at the top of his game.

In fact, Leroy upset the whole UW Press establishment one time by turning in a book manuscript four months ahead of the agreed-upon deadline. "They were used to writers who were a year or two overdue with finished manuscripts," Murray recalls. "And suddenly here's Leroy dropping a manuscript at their doorstep like a premature foundling child."

Jack Olsen, the Bainbridge Island fireball, wastes no time getting his stuff on paper. Jack is a superb researcher, so in his case speed has no adverse effect on quality once he gets out of the starting blocks. Olsen once told me that he wrote a 10,000-word introduction to a Time-Life book in one day, which ain't exactly dawdling.

If anyone is at all interested, I have made a careful study of my own output, which works out to four hours and five minutes per column. Here is the way it is broken down, all times approximate.

Get coffee, instant, heated in microwave oven (three minutes) . . . clean off desk, sort of (18 minutes) . . . pause to read something that surfaced on desk (16 minutes) . . . crank up word processor (two minutes) . . . answer bill collector's phone call: "Of course I'll pay you!" (six minutes) . . . start typing, rub out first sentence (three minutes) . . . Go to bathroom (three minutes) . . . try new lead (18 minutes) . . . rewrite new lead (14 minutes) . . . get despondent over new lead (19 minutes) . . . plug away at column (13 minutes) . . . throw ball for Tiger, my dog (eight minutes) . . . plug away some more at word processor (22 minutes) . . . straighten paper clips (15 minutes) . . . find lost ball for Tiger (six minutes) . . . plug away again (12 minutes) . . . go to bathroom again (four minutes) . . .

. . . rewrite middle third of column (17 minutes) . . . pace room to feign thinking (eight minutes) . . . plug away (14 minutes) . . . drink rest of cold coffee (one minute) . . . finish column in a blaze of typing (23 minutes) . . . take Tiger out for much-needed walk.

And there you have it. One hour and 49 minutes of necessary pauses, two hours and 16 minutes actual writing. Where did the day go?

Returning once more to Mr. Buckley and his 20-minute columns, Rosa Morgan, Murray's wife, recalls the Buckley-Costigan debate during the Vietnam War. When UW Prof. Giovanni Costigan accused Buckley of writing a certain column, the great speedster denied ever writing it.

Costigan then pulled out the clipping and read it to him aloud. "You shouldn't write so much," Costigan politely suggested. "You should think more."

That goes for all of us, I guess.

A Columnist Defines Himself
Seattle Post-Intelligencer, October 14, 1980

EVERY FEW YEARS IT BECOMES APPARENT that nobody has asked me what a columnist is, what a column consists of and why anybody would want to read one in the first place. But since when do people have to ask an opinion in order to get one? Certainly, that is one of the rare privileges of columndom. Being known as "a columnist" can make one feel insecure. If you are known as "a plumber," the vision of you is solid—honest overalls, a ton of tools, occult skills with pipes and drains, plus a splendid marketing leverage when somebody's basement starts flooding. If you are known as "an engineer" there is even an aura of mystery about you—you might be the genius who executed the fliptop beer can, or whose skills launched the first ape into outer space. But being known as "a columnist" is to be thought of as something nebulous, a non-doer, a scribbler of low rank, probably untrustworthy. "Oh?" they say politely. "And what do you write about?" Plumbers and engineers are above such questions.

The other day a lady began being a columnist on a community

newspaper. "If you have any advice for a budding columnist," she wrote, sending along a clipping of her work, "please feel free to write." Thus our first lesson. When a hack columnist, like me, whose legs are going bad on him, feels free to write, he doesn't do it in letters. He tries to fashion a column out of it. Like squirrels, we columnists hoard every kernel we can; nothing is given away free.

What is a columnist? A few weeks ago, one of the better practitioners in this strange business, Charles McCabe of the San Francisco Chronicle, had a go at that question. "I can only speak for myself," he wrote, "but I think one of the species is pretty much the same as the rest. A columnist is a kind of strip-teaser. He is a person, or a personality, whichever word you prefer. He sells that person or personality with whatever prose he is capable of . . .

" . . . That is really what it is all about. It is the crotchets and eccentricities of the columnist that make him sufficiently interesting to be read by a sufficient number of people for the management to pay him a decent screw."

To switch gears for a moment, the sports world seems to have moved out in front in efforts to teach writers how to write. At a recent luncheon for scribes and broadcasters, hosted by the Seattle SuperSonics, the boys and girls were given a lecture in journalism. The basketball coach, Lenny Wilkens, told the media how best to cover his team and himself. The Sounders also have expressed views on how they think writers should write about their game, which is soccer. Maury Wills, the new Mariner manager, has given some lectures to local writers on how to write about Maury's team, his strategy and other of his more important thoughts.

Now, these are all distinguished teachers of journalism, I grant you; it is easy to know that they are unbiased, because they tell you so. The same situation obtains in politics, war, theatre reviewing and other public activities. I have listened to many such lectures, and I'm still learning.

Getting back to what a columnist is—and what he produces—it's still pretty nebulous. "It is this marketing of a personality, day in and day out, that gives the columnist his hold over people and such power as a minor newspaper functionary may possess." That is Charles McCabe talking again. "In due time if you are successful you become so hateful to some people and so lovable to others, that you become a part of their life. Then you have, as they say, made it."

I cannot define it, but I can tell you what it is like. Once in a while, being a columnist helps you get a good table in a restaurant. But I've noticed that it usually happens when the restaurant isn't very crowded anyway. It is dangerous, at best, to go around flashing anything that smacks of "press." You won't impress anybody, and you just might inflame somebody who hates you enough already. It is to be regarded, vaguely, as a pretender. "If the guy is supposed to be a writer, why doesn't he do books?" is a question that defies a clear answer. Most columnists I know make less money than most engineers and certainly not as much as a plumber. "I read your column every day," is a nice thing to hear, but should not be taken seriously. Nobody reads anything every day. What they are saying is, "Well, I've heard of you."

I said that being known as "a columnist" can make one insecure. The other day I dropped off some cleaning, and the guy recognized the name. "Oh, yes," he said, looking up brightly, "how long have you been retired now?"

Index